NINE MEN IN GRAY

Charles L. Dufour

NINE MEN
IN GRAY

Introduction to the Bison Book Edition
by Gary W. Gallagher

University of Nebraska Press
Lincoln and London

First Bison Book printing: 1993
Most recent printing indicated by the last digit below:
10   9   8   7   6   5   4   3   2   1

Library of Congress Cataloging-in-Publication Data
Dufour, Charles L.
Nine men in gray / Charles L. Dufour; introduction to the Bison Book edition
by Gary W. Gallagher.
p.   cm.
"Bison."
Originally published: Garden City: Doubleday, 1963.
Includes bibliographical references.
ISBN 0-8032-6596-4
1. United States—History—Civil War, 1861–1865—Biography. 2. Confederate
States of America—Biography. I. Title. II. Title: 9 men in gray.
E467.D88   1993
973.7′42—dc20
93-9529
CIP

Originally published in 1963 by Doubleday & Company, Inc., Garden City, N.Y.

∞

For
MARIE JEANNE DUFOUR
who *really* didn't lose her father
in the Civil War.

Introduction

By Gary W. Gallagher

Biographical studies of Confederate leaders account for a significant portion of the imposing literature on the Civil War. Military officers have been especially popular with both professional historians and other writers, and virtually every prominent Confederate commander has been the subject of at least one book. The lives of some, including R. E. Lee, Nathan Bedford Forrest, and "Stonewall" Jackson, have inspired what amounts to a series of sub-literatures. Beginning with John Esten Cooke's *The Life of Stonewall Jackson* (first published in 1863), these books frequently have reached a broad audience. Jefferson Davis and other politicians also have received a good deal of attention—though American readers usually evince less interest in them than in their military counterparts.[1] Several late-nineteenth and early-twentieth-century authors presented series of shorter biographies in single volumes, the most famous collection being Gamaliel Bradford's *Confederate Portraits*. Bradford's book differed from earlier works of this type, such as Edward A. Pollard's *Lee and His Lieutenants* and William P. Snow's *Lee and His Generals*, because it allocated a substantial number of pages to nonmilitary figures. These last three titles, as well as *Frock Coats and Epaulets* by Alf J. Mapp, Jr., shared a focus on persons in the upper echelons of power in the Confederacy.[2]

Charles L. Dufour adopted a model similar to Bradford's for *Nine Men in Gray* but selected less famous individuals.[3] Recognizing the popularity of biography as a genre, Dufour sought to introduce readers to a group of Confederates who played secondary yet still significant roles. As he remarked in his preface, most students of the war are familiar with all nine men; indeed, Edward Porter Alexander, Patrick Ronayne Cleburne, and Richard Taylor would strike many as major figures. Although less renowned, Lucius B. Northrop, Turner Ashby, Henry Hotze, and William Mahone also occupied positions of considerable influence. Only William Ransom Johnson Pegram and Charles W. "Savez"

Read really fit into the category of little-known figures. Dufour's subjects represent a nice cross section of Confederates from a number of perspectives: seven served in the army, among them three infantry officers, two artillerists, one cavalryman, and the head of the southern commissariat; one fought in the navy; and one served in a civilian capacity. Three men spent their wartime careers primarily in Lee's Army of Northern Virginia, one in the Army of Tennessee, another in the trans-Mississippi theater, and a sixth in the Shenandoah Valley. The nine included two West Pointers and a graduate of the United States Naval Academy, two born in foreign countries, and one son of a United States president. The youngest was nineteen years old when war erupted, three were in their twenties, four in their thirties, and the oldest not quite fifty.

Although not a historian by training, Dufour brought skills as a writer and researcher to his project. Born in New Orleans in 1903, he attended Tulane University for three years before departing in 1924 to pursue a career as a journalist with the *New Orleans Item*. He left the *Item* in 1940 to work for WDSU radio in New Orleans, joined the U.S. Army during World War II, and returned to his native city in 1946. Nicknamed "Pie" from an early age, Dufour began writing a column called "A La Mode" for the *New Orleans States* in November 1946; over the next thirty years, nearly ten thousand columns addressing such topics as travel and history appeared in the weekday *States-Item* and the Sunday *Times Picayune*. Dufour returned to Tulane to complete his degree in 1953 and subsequently taught at Tulane's University College. A course titled "New Orleans Up to Now" proved one of the most popular of Tulane's non-credit seminars, and in 1979 Dufour received an honorary doctor of humane letters degree from the university. "You have offered an outstanding example of what it means to be truly educated," remarked President Sheldon Hackney of Tulane in conferring the honorary degree, "by continuing to investigate, to read, to learn throughout your life."[4]

The Civil War constituted one of the principal areas of Dufour's "continuing" investigation.[5] Reared on stories told by a grandmother who lived in New Orleans during the war—he described her "as a little girl ordering occupation [Federal] troops out of the yard"—Dufour helped found the Civil War Round Table of New Orleans, held the presidency of the Louisiana Historical Association, and served on the Advisory Committee of the Civil War Centennial Commission. He published his first book on the Civil War in 1957, a biography of a colorful Confederate officer who led the famous Louisiana Tigers titled *Gentle Tiger: The Gallant Life of Roberdeau Wheat;* three years later Dufour's account of the Union capture of New Orleans appeared as *The Night the War Was Lost*. Both books combined research in printed materials and manuscripts with a strong narrative style and elicited generally positive comment from reviewers.[6]

Nine Men in Gray, Dufour's third and final title on the Civil War, exhibited many characteristics common to the earlier pair. Relying chiefly on printed materials, including numerous primary accounts, he also consulted a range of manuscripts (the sketches of artillerists Alexander and Pegram drew most heavily on unpublished materials). His book endeavored to convey in a lively text the story of these "'forgotten'—or at least little-remembered—Confederates whose adventures were among the most vital and exciting of the conflict."[7] Although Dufour spends most of his time on the battlefield, readers will gain insights into activities central to the war effort that occurred far from the military front. For example, the treatment of Commissary General Northrop, whom Dufour aptly labels "one of the three most detested of President Davis's appointees," sheds light on the Confederacy's difficulties in delivering food to its soldiers.[8] Similarly, the essay on Henry Hotze and *The Index* effectively introduces a range of foreign-related topics, among them cotton and Confederate policy, the uses of propaganda in Europe, and efforts to slow Irish immigration to the North.

Dufour generally adopts a positive tone and sometimes betrays an overly romantic admiration for his principals. The latter phenomenon seems most apparent in the essay on "Savez" Read, who, on the merits of his record, might impress some readers as among the least admirable of the nine characters. Most students familiar with Turner Ashby's chronic inability to control his troopers also might quibble with Dufour's suggestion that "the Beau Sabreur" of Jackson's army simply faced so many tasks "he had little time for drill and discipline" (Dufour cites Henry Kyd Douglas, whose writings abound with untrustworthy observations and conclusions, to support this notion about Ashby). Dufour's clear favorite is Porter Alexander, whom he considers "one of the South's most brilliant soldiers" and "not only a great Confederate but a great American as well."[9]

Despite occasional lapses, Dufour usually avoids any special pleading. At his analytical and dispassionate best with the much-hated Northrop, he demonstrates that problems in supplying food cannot be attributed entirely to that unhappy man. Nor does Dufour shrink from describing the less attractive behavior of his subjects. The blunt description of William Mahone's conduct during the Battle of the Crater features quotations from B. F. Phillips, an Alabama trooper who "remembered General Mahone walking in front of the line and telling the men that the negroes in the Crater had yelled: 'Remember Fort Pillow! No quarter.' Mahone said it was a life and death struggle 'and go among them and give them hell.'" Phillips recalled that "We tried to obey orders. Just before the job was completed, General Mahone sent orders to us not to kill quite all of them." Dufour handles Dick Taylor's petulant exchanges with Edmund Kirby Smith equally well, concluding that "Regardless of the merits of Taylor's complaints and charges, there is no question but that he was guilty of insubordination."[10]

Reviewers characterized *Nine Men in Gray* as a work aimed primarily at beginning students of the war from which more experienced readers might also benefit. "Combining a broad knowledge of the period with a skillful pen, Mr. Dufour has written a lively, reliable, enjoyable narrative," wrote one professional historian. "The scholar will find *Nine Men in Gray* acceptable; the general reader will find it delightful." Another review echoed this judgment: "Author Dufour has done a neat job of condensing into an average of fewer than forty pages each the stories of these men. The Civil War neophyte will profit by all of them, and we suspect that old pros will learn a thing or two, particularly from the chapters on Read, Northrop, and Hotze."[11] These evaluations capture the essential qualities of Dufour's book. For example, many veteran readers probably believe that Davis named Northrop commissary general at least partly because they had been friends and classmates at West Point—a notion Dufour effectively refutes. Others might be surprised to learn that several of these Confederates had been antebellum Whigs. Readers new to the subject will learn not only basic details about Dufour's nine men, but also that the war raged in places far from Virginia (a fact still left lamentably murky in many writings) and that politics, diplomacy, and military events intersected in myriad ways.

When Dufour wrote *Nine Men in Gray*, Turner Ashby, Patrick Cleburne, and William Mahone had been the subject of books and Porter Alexander and Richard Taylor had published famous memoirs.[12] Since 1963, biographies of Alexander, Ashby, Cleburne, and Taylor have appeared, as has a second major set of reminiscences by Porter Alexander and a useful collection of Pegram's letters.[13] *Nine Men in Gray* manifestly does not offer the last word on its cast of nine Confederates. But it contains the best available biographical sketches of Hotze, Northrop, and Read and remains an engaging introduction to the other six men's lives and Confederate careers—ample virtues that give it continuing value as part of the biographical literature on the South during its quest for nationhood.

NOTES

1. C. B. Richardson of New York published Cooke's book. A recent spate of titles on Jackson underscores the continuing popularity of leading Confederate military figures as biographical subjects. See Bevin Alexander, *Lost Victories: The*

Military Genius of Stonewall Jackson (New York: Henry Holt & Company, 1992); Paul D. Casdorph, *Lee and Jackson: Confederate Chieftains* (New York: Paragon House, 1992); Byron Farwell, *Stonewall: A Biography of General Thomas J. Jackson* (New York: W. W. Norton & Company, 1992); and A. Wilson Greene, *Whatever You Resolve to Be: Essays on Stonewall Jackson* (Baltimore: Butternut and Blue, 1992).

2. Bradford's book (New York: Houghton Mifflin, 1914) offered essays on Joseph E. Johnston, J. E. B. Stuart, James Longstreet, P. G. T. Beauregard, Judah P. Benjamin, Alexander H. Stephens, Robert Toombs, and Raphael Semmes; Pollard's (New York: E. B. Treat & Company, 1867) had chapters on forty-eight officers, many of whom served in theaters far beyond Lee's arena of command; Snow's (New York: C. B. Richardson, 1865) covered eighteen generals, several of whom, as in Pollard's book, technically were not Lee's lieutenants; and Mapp's (New York: Thomas Yoseloff, 1963), which resembled Bradford's and appeared the same year as *Nine Men in Gray*, contained essays on Jefferson Davis, Lee, Jackson, Benjamin, Johnston, and Stuart.

3. The first edition was published by Doubleday & Company of Garden City, New York, in 1963.

4. "Charles L. 'Pie' Dufour," *New Orleans Times-Picayune*, June 3, 1966; "Pie Dufour's a la Mode," *New Orleans States-Item*, November 9, 1978; Pat Butters, "Expert Shares a Wealth of Information on the War," *New Orleans Times-Picayune*, January 15, 1987; "Dufour Given Honorary Doctorate by Tulane," *New Orleans Times-Picayune*, November 11, 1978 (quotation). Dufour retired as a journalist in 1979 but remained active as an author and lecturer through the 1980s.

5. Dufour also published eight books and several pamphlets on Louisiana, New Orleans, and the Mexican War, among them *Ten Flags in the Wind: The Story of Louisiana* (New York: Harper & Row, 1967); *New Orleans*, with photography and design by Bernard M. Hermann (New Orleans: Louisiana State University/ Louisiana Press, 1980); *If I Ever Cease to Love: One Hundred Years of Rex, 1872–1971*, with Leonard V. Huber (New Orleans: School of Design, 1970), and *The Mexican War: A Compact History, 1846–1848* (New York: Hawthorn Books, 1968).

6. *Gentle Tiger: The Gallant Life of Roberdeau Wheat* (Baton Rouge, La.: Louisiana State University Press, 1957); *The Night the War Was Lost* (Garden City, N.Y.: Doubleday & Company, 1960).

7. This quotation graced a flyer announcing the publication of *Nine Men in Gray* and inviting interested readers to an autographing session at the Basement Book Shop in New Orleans on April 21, 1963. Copy of the flyer in the Howard-Tilton Memorial Library, Tulane University, New Orleans, Louisiana.

8. The quotation is on page 197 below.

9. The quotations are on pages 63 and 339 below.

10. The quotations are on pages 259 and 33 below.

11. The two reviewers were F. N. Boney in *Civil War History* 10 (June 1964): 210–11, and Robert D. Hoffsommer in *Civil War Times Illustrated* 2 (October 1963): 50.

12. The biographies are Thomas A. Ashby's hagiographic *Life of Turner Ashby* (New York: Neale Publishing Company, 1914) and Frank Cunningham's thin *Knight of the Confederacy: Gen. Turner Ashby* (San Antonio, Texas: Naylor Com-

pany, 1960); Charles E. Nash's *Biographical Sketches of Gen. Pat Cleburne and Gen. T. C. Hindman, Together with Humorous Anecdotes and Reminiscences of the Late Civil War* (Little Rock, Ark.: Tunnah & Pittard Printers, 1898); Irving A. Buck's *Cleburne and His Command* (New York and Washington: Neale Publishing Company, 1908), both written by men who knew Cleburne well; and Nelson M. Blake's *William Mahone of Virginia: Soldier and Political Insurgent* (Richmond, Va.: Garrett & Massie, 1935), which devotes fewer than a hundred pages to Mahone's wartime career. Edward Porter Alexander's *Military Memoirs of a Confederate: A Critical Narrative* (New York: Charles Scribner's Sons, 1907) and Richard Taylor's *Destruction and Reconstruction: Personal Experiences of the Late War* (New York: D. Appleton and Company, 1879) are among the most famous and often-quoted books by participants in the conflict. See also Jackson Beauregard Davis's "The Life of Richard Taylor," a master's thesis published in the *Louisiana Historical Quarterly* 24 (January 1941): 49–126, and Willard E. Wight, ed., "Some Letters of Lucius Bellinger Northrop, 1860–1865, in *Virginia Magazine of History and Biography* 68 (October 1960): 456–77.

13. See Maury Klein's solid *Edward Porter Alexander* (Athens, Ga.: University of Georgia Press, 1971); Millard K. Bushong's laudatory *General Turner Ashby and Stonewall's Valley Campaign* (Verona, Va.: McClure Printing Company, 1980); Howell and Elizabeth Purdue's plodding *Pat Cleburne Confederate General: A Definitive Biography* (Hillsboro, Texas: Hill Junior College Press, 1973); T. Michael Parrish's impressively researched and gracefully written *Richard Taylor: Soldier Prince of Dixie* (Chapel Hill, N.C.: University of North Carolina Press, 1992); Edward Porter Alexander's *Fighting for the Confederacy: The Personal Recollections of General Edward Porter Alexander,* ed. Gary W. Gallagher (Chapel Hill, N.C. University of North Carolina Press, 1989); and James I. Robertson, Jr., ed., "'The Boy Artillerist': Letters of Colonel William Pegram, C.S.A.," in *Virginia Magazine of History and Biography* 98 (April 1990): 221–60.

Preface

THE nine men who are the subject of this book will not be unfamiliar to Civil War enthusiasts but, to the average American, they are "little remembered" if not, indeed, "forgotten." Yet each in his way played a dramatic role in the Confederate service.

Three of these Confederates—Turner Ashby, Pat Cleburne, and Billy Mahone—have had books written about them, but none has been widely circulated.

Two others, Dick Taylor and E. Porter Alexander, wrote about the war in which they served so brilliantly. But whereas many know Taylor's *Destruction and Reconstruction* and Alexander's *Military Memoirs of a Confederate*, how many know these two remarkable soldiers themselves, or their exploits throughout four years of bitter fighting?

Parts of the astonishing saga of Charles W. "Savez" Read of the Confederate Navy have been told in various places, but the entire career of this fantastic young Mississippian has never before been extensively treated.

The same is true of the careers of the much-despised Lucius B. Northrop, Commissary General of the Confederacy, and the much-loved Willie Pegram, a dazzling cannoneer.

The remaining member of the *Nine Men in Gray* did not, after the first three months of the war, wear a Confederate uniform for he was sent to England as the Confederate propaganda agent. In that capacity, young Henry Hotze distinguished himself to such a degree as to emerge as one of the ablest of all persons in the Confederate service.

Six of the nine came into the Confederacy from civilian life—Taylor, Ashby, Cleburne, Pegram, Mahone, and Hotze. Northrop and Alexander, West Point graduates, resigned from the United States Army, while Read, a graduate of Annapolis, resigned from the United States Navy, to cast their lot with the South. Six of the nine survived the war, Ashby, Cleburne, and Pegram being killed in action.

In the sketches of those who lived through the war, a brief summary of their postwar careers has been given; in all pieces the prewar lives have been outlined. But the emphasis throughout has been on their Confederate careers.

The author is under great obligations to many persons and institutions for assistance during the researching of this book. Robert Talmadge, librarian of Tulane University and his staff, specifically, Mrs. Connie Griffith, Miss Betty Mailhes, Mrs. Dorothy Whittemore, Mrs. Patricia Segleau, and Bill Nañez, have put the author deeply in their debt by their cheerful cooperation and innumerable services.

So, too, have Mrs. Carolyn A. Wallace of the Southern Historical Collection, University of North Carolina; Miss Mattie Russell, Curator of Manuscripts, Duke University, and her assistant, Mrs. Virginia Gray; and Howson W. Cole, Curator of Manuscripts, Virginia Historical Society, Richmond, and his staff.

Ray D. Smith of Chicago, who has undertaken the monumental task of indexing *The Confederate Veteran*, graciously furnished the author with many references to each of the nine Confederates in that publication.

Valuable help is acknowledged from the following:

Vergil Bedsole, director of the Department of Archives and Manuscripts, Louisiana State University, and his staff; Arthur Ben Chitty, University of the South, Sewanee, Tennessee; Don Dosch, National Park Service historian at Shiloh, Tennessee; Gilbert E. Govan of Chattanooga; Tom Harrison, National Park Service historian at Petersburg, Virginia; Congressman F. Edward Hébert of Louisiana; Robert W. Hill, Curator of Manuscripts, New York Public Library; Stanley F. Horn of Nashville; William Kay, National Park Service historian at Richmond, Virginia; Dr. Grady McWhinney of Northwestern University; E. B. "Pete" Long, Oak Park, Illinois; Mallory J. Read of Arlington, Virginia; John R. Peacock, High Point, North Carolina; Ray Samuel of New Orleans; Frank B. Sarles, Jr. of Omaha, Nebraska; Miss India Thomas, regent, the Confederate Museum, Richmond, and her assistant, Miss Eleanor Brockenbrough; Mrs. E. M. Trigg of Savannah, Georgia; Lee Wallace, National Park historian, Washington, D.C.; and Dr. T. Harry Williams of Louisiana.

As always, the Library of Congress Manuscripts Division and the National Archives provided matchless service. The usual fine cooperation came from the New Orleans Public Library, Jerome Cushman, librarian.

Kenneth T. Urquhart, director of Memorial Hall of the Louisiana Historical Association, New Orleans, was generous in the loan of valuable source material.

To my colleagues on the New Orleans *States-Item*, Hermann B.

Deutsch, Crozet Duplantier, and Dan Galouye, go thanks for reading the galley proofs. Previously, Mr. Galouye read the manuscript and made valuable suggestions.

Also lending a vigilant eye to the proofs were Mrs. Tess Crager, Leonard V. Huber, René LeGardeur, Jr., and Donald Schultz, all of New Orleans.

Edison B. Allen of Tulane University, a keen student of the Civil War, accompanied the author on field trips to many of the battlefields, and he read the manuscript, detecting errors and making valuable suggestions. He also read the proofs.

To Ezra Warner of La Jolla, California, the author is indebted for the loan of pictures from his valuable Civil War collection. A similar debt is acknowledged to Miss Regina Rapier of Atlanta, Georgia, who supplied a photograph of Henry Hotz.

Special thanks are due Polly LeBeuf for her patience in typing the manuscript and also for reading proofs.

For whatever errors remain after the careful assistance of these gracious friends, the author assumes full responsibility.

CHARLES L. DUFOUR

Author's Note

In many cases, Civil War battles bear two names. Usually, the Confederates named them after man-made objects or places, while the Union employed natural features, e.g.:

Shiloh (Confederate) and Pittsburg Landing (Union)

Murfreesboro (Confederate) and Stone's River (Union)

Sharpsburg (Confederate) and Antietam (Union)

Mansfield (Confederate) and Sabine Cross Roads (Union)

In all cases, except that of Antietam, the Confederate names for battles have been used.

Contents

Photographs

I

The President's Brother-in-Law:

GENERAL DICK TAYLOR

I

Down the Valley Pike, stepping jauntily as if on parade, the Louisiana Brigade marched, 3000 strong in new uniforms and white gaiters. Regimental bands played at the head of their units and not a straggler broke the smooth, precise movement of the columns, the polished bayonets of which caught the declining rays of the sun. Along the pike, the battle-tested men of Stonewall Jackson stood and gaped as the trim, disciplined Louisianians passed by and wheeled from the road into their bivouac area.

Brigadier General Dick Taylor pridefully noted the impression his men made on the Shenandoah Valley soldiers and years later he expressed in print what he felt at the time: "Indeed, it was a martial sight, and no man with a spark of sacred fire in his heart but would have striven hard to prove worthy of such a command."

After attending to necessary camp details, General Taylor sought out Stonewall Jackson, whom he had never met. A figure sitting on the top rail of a fence by the side of the road was pointed out to him. As he came up, Taylor first noticed "a pair of cavalry boots covering feet of gigantic size, a mangy cap with visor drawn low, a heavy, dark beard, and weary eyes."[1]

Had Jackson regarded the handsome, well-groomed young general striding toward him with attention, he would have noted a slightly built man, about five feet eight inches tall, with high forehead, deep-set hazel eyes, and a dark brown beard and hair.[2]

Taylor saluted and gave his name and rank, noticing as he did so that Jackson had in his hand a lemon on which he was sucking.

The lemon-sucker acknowledged the salute, asking in a low gentle voice the distance Taylor had marched and the route he had taken.

"Keazletown Road, six and twenty miles," replied Taylor.

"You seem to have no stragglers," commented Jackson.

"Never allow straggling," answered the Louisianian confidently.

"You must teach my people," said Stonewall Jackson. "They straggle badly."

Taylor bowed in acknowledgement of Jackson's compliment. At that moment the regimental band of the 8th Louisiana struck up a gay waltz and Taylor's "Cajuns," as was their frequent custom in camp, paired off and danced "in couples with as much zest as if their arms encircled the supple waists of the Célestines and Mélazies of their native [Bayou] Teche."

Jackson tugged at the lemon contemplatively for a moment and then said: "Thoughtless fellows for serious work."

Taylor expressed the hope that the work would not be less well done because of the gay nature of his troops and when Jackson returned to his lemon without reply, Taylor saluted and retired.[3]

Before many days passed, General Jackson would see that the "thoughtless fellows" could attend to "serious work" as well as any troops in his little army in the Shenandoah Valley. In less than three weeks, they and their brilliant civilian commander would win the admiration of the Mighty Stonewall for their marching, discipline, and fighting.

Dick Taylor, the son of a President of the United States and the brother-in-law of the President of the Confederate States of America, was one of the bright young men of his day. Highly educated, and well read and traveled, Dick Taylor's only military experience was in the Mexican War, when he served his father, General Zachary Taylor, as military secretary. By his wide reading of history, Taylor learned much from the great captains of the past. And he self-educated himself by two practices to which he adhered throughout the Civil War:

"The first was to examine at every halt the adjacent roads and paths, their direction and condition; distances of nearest towns and cross-roads; the country, its capacity to furnish supplies, as well as general topography, etc., all of which was embodied in a rude sketch, with notes to impress it on memory. The second was to imagine while on the march an enemy before me to be attacked, or to be received in my position, and make the necessary dispositions for either contingency. My imaginary manoeuvres were sad blunders, but I corrected them by experience drawn from actual battles, and can safely affirm that such slight success as I had in command was due to these customs."[4]

How well this wealthy Louisiana sugar planter and politician succeeded in mastering the techniques of war is evidenced by the fact that among the 17 officers who gained the rank of lieutenant general in the Confederacy, Dick Taylor was one of three who did not attend West Point, the other two being Nathan Bedford Forrest and Wade Hampton.

That his promotion from colonel to brigadier general stemmed from his close relationship with Jefferson Davis is unquestioned. Davis's first wife was Taylor's older sister, Sarah Knox Taylor. Had Taylor proved a failure, the same sort of criticism leveled at the President for his stubborn support of General Braxton Bragg, Secretary Judah P. Benjamin, and Commissary General Lucius B. Northrop would have surely resulted. But Taylor did not prove a failure and his future recommendations for promotion came from those under whom he served.

Actually, Taylor possessed marked attributes for leadership—an active and incisive mind, a broad liberal education, courage, confidence and determination. Although only thirty-five years old when the Civil War broke out, he had been active for many years in the civil affairs of Louisiana. "His absolute self-reliance," wrote a close friend, "amounted to a total irreverence for any man's opinion . . . He was marked in the expression of his friendships and of his antipathies—these regard the conduct of men rather than the men themselves . . . ."[5]

Shortly before he died in 1879, General Taylor published his war memoirs, *Destruction and Reconstruction*. The noted historian, Douglas Southall Freeman, called Taylor "the one Confederate general who possessed literary art that approached first rank," and hailed his book as "written with the unmistakable touch of cultured scholarship."[6]

II

The youngest of Zachary Taylor's four children, and his only son, Richard Taylor was born in New Orleans on January 27, 1826.

Some accounts of his early life assert that he was born at Louisville, but Taylor himself referred to Louisiana as "the state of my birth." It has also been said that he was educated in Edinburgh and in France, but one of his oldest intimate friends, D. H. Maury, wrote at his death that Taylor's "scholastic experience was confined to America."[7]

He entered Harvard, transferred to Yale, from which institution he was graduated in 1845. Although he was what later generations would call an "Army brat," Dick Taylor showed no inclination for the Army. However, his three sisters had all married Army officers. One of them, Sarah Knox Taylor, died just a few months after marrying a dashing young lieutenant, Jefferson Davis.

When the Mexican War broke out in 1846, young Taylor, despite bad health, insisted on joining his father, General Taylor, in Texas. But as the climate did not suit his condition, General Taylor sent him back to New Orleans. Two years later, Dick was assigned to manage his father's cotton plantation in Jefferson County, Mississippi.

In 1851, Dick Taylor married Myrthé Bringier and he bought a plantation of his own, having inherited a substantial fortune from his father's estate. This plantation, "Fashion," was situated in St. Charles Parish, about thirty-five miles above New Orleans, on the west bank of the Mississippi River. During the Civil War it would be devastated by Federal troops and confiscated.

Taylor settled down to the life of a well-to-do planter. He built up a large library, acquired an extensive knowledge of English, French, and Spanish literature, established a racing stable, and dabbled in politics, first as a Whig, then in the American party, and finally as a Democrat. He was elected to the Louisiana Legislature in 1855 and was still a member of the Senate when the secession crisis developed in 1860.[8]

At the National Democratic Convention in Charleston, South Carolina, in April 1860, Taylor was a delegate from Louisiana. When the split over the platform seemed imminent, Taylor pleaded in vain for peace and harmony. But the unity of the Democratic party was shattered when Alabama led the Southern States out of the Charleston Convention. The election of Lincoln in November as President of the United States was inevitable.

Taylor also participated in the rump convention which, meeting successively in Richmond and Baltimore, finally nominated John C. Breckinridge as the Democratic South's presidential standard bearer.

Shortly after the election of Lincoln, Governor Thomas O. Moore called a special session of the Louisiana Legislature to determine the relations of the state to the Federal Union. On the opening day, December 10, 1860, Senator Dick Taylor introduced a bill calling for a state convention and setting January 7 as the date for an election of delegates. Elected a representative delegate from St. Charles Parish, Taylor, among several assignments, was made chairman of the Military and Naval Affairs Committee.

When the ordinance of secession was adopted on January 26, 1861, by a vote of 113 to 17, Taylor voted with the majority. Although he was not nominated as one of the commissioners to the convention in Montgomery of the seceded states, when the balloting came he received a complimentary vote from Alexandre Mouton, president of the convention.

Taylor reported to the convention that "the State was found to be utterly defenceless," and presented an ordinance creating a standing army of between 1700 and 1800 men for Louisiana, consisting of a regiment of artillery, a regiment of infantry and the necessary general and staff officers. The bill passed easily.

Convinced that war was inevitable, Taylor urged that Louisiana make immediate preparations, but to no avail. In *Destruction and Reconstruction*, he recalled his efforts: "As soon as the Convention adjourned, finding myself out of harmony with prevailing opinion as to the certainty of war and the necessity for preparation, I retired to my estate, determined to accept such responsibility only as came to me unsought."

An invitation from his friend, General Braxton Bragg, to visit the Confederate forces at Pensacola drew Taylor from his retreat at "Fashion." While in Florida, he received a telegram from Governor Moore which removed him from the ranks of civilians and cast him in a military role in which he would become one of the Confederacy's most successful generals.[9]

III

As soon as Dick Taylor received news that he had been appointed colonel of the 9th Louisiana Infantry Regiment, he returned to New Orleans and received his commission on July 2, 1861. He hastened to Camp Moore, 80 miles from New Orleans, to inspect his regiment, which was mustered into the Confederate service on July 6, and ordered immediately to Virginia.[10]

Instructing Lieutenant Colonel E. G. Randolph to move the regiment to Richmond by the first available transportation, Taylor returned to New Orleans to procure equipment for his troops and to put his business affairs in order. Realizing that the heavy concentration of troops in Virginia would create a scarcity of small-arms ammunition there, Taylor obtained 100,000 rounds for his regiment from Louisiana authorities.

Reaching Richmond on July 20, Colonel Taylor found that the 9th Louisiana, about 1000 strong, had just arrived and gone into camp. Everywhere he went, Taylor heard rumors of an impending battle at Manassas, where his fellow Louisianian, P. G. T. Beauregard was in command.

"A multitude of wild reports, all equally inflamed, reached my ears," he narrated. ". . . Reaching camp, I paraded the regiment, and stated the necessity for prompt action, and my purpose to make application to be sent to the front immediately. Officers and men were delighted with the prospect of active service, and largely supplied want of experience by zeal. Ammunition was served out, three days' rations were ordered for haversacks, and all camp equipage not absolutely essential was stored."

Having prepared the regiment for an immediate move to the front, Colonel Taylor then called on Secretary of War Leroy Pope Walker to inform him of its readiness. The latter was happily surprised to find that the 9th Louisiana Regiment needed nothing except transportation. So many of the troops assembled in Richmond were unable to move forward because of lack of ammunition and other shortages. But Colonel Taylor's regiment was ready and eager and the Secretary of War did everything he could to speed its departure. He "thought" that a train would be ready by 9 P.M.

Doubtless the Greeks before Troy had a word for the now well-established military maxim: "Hurry up and wait." If GI Joe of 1861–65 did not employ it, it was not for a lack of reason or occasion. Taylor marched the regiment to the railroad station well before 9 P.M., and then began a long and exasperating wait. It was not until well beyond midnight that the train put in an appearance. When it finally huffed and puffed its way out of the station, Taylor was hopeful that his men would reach Manassas fairly early in the morning, as the run normally required only six hours. ". . . But this expectation, our engine brought to grief," he wrote. "It proved a machine of the most wheezy and helpless character, creeping snail-like on levels, and requiring the men to leave the carriages to help it up grades."

What made the tortuous trip even more exasperating to Taylor and his men was the realization that they were missing the big battle that everyone in Richmond had talked about the previous day. "At every halt of the wretched engine," said Taylor, "the noise of battle grew more and more intense, as did our impatience." At dusk on July 21 the weary engine wheezed into Manassas Junction. The 9th Louisiana Regiment had missed the Battle of Manassas.

Bivouacking his men by the railroad, Taylor went off in the dark in search of General Beauregard's headquarters to report his arrival and receive orders. These came the next day, instructing Taylor to select a suitable camp, a clear indication that no follow-up of the Confederate rout of the Federals was contemplated.

All about Manassas, Colonel Taylor discovered that the Confederates were tremendously disorganized by their victory. With a fine eye for description, he noted:

"The confusion that reigned about our camps for the next few days was extreme. Regiments seemed to have lost their colonels, colonels their regiments. Men of all arms and all commands were mixed in the wildest way. A constant fusillade of small arms and singing of bullets were kept up, indicative of a superfluity of disorder, if not of ammunition. One of my men was severely wounded in camp by a 'stray,' and derived no consolation from my suggestion that it was a delicate attention of our comrades to mitigate the disappointment of missing the battle."

Taylor heard fine things about Louisiana troops in the battle, troops with which he would soon be closely associated. Roberdeau Wheat, famed soldier of fortune and filibuster, whom Taylor had known in the Mexican War as a mere boy, and his madcap Louisiana Tigers had fought valiantly at Stone Bridge and Wheat was critically wounded. Colonel Harry Hays's 7th Louisiana arrived on the field in midafternoon to help swing the tide of battle. Colonel Henry B. Kelly's 8th Louisiana was under heavy fire along Bull Run in the center of the Confederate line. On the Confederate right, Colonel Isaac G. Seymour's 6th Louisiana marched and countermarched without getting into action. The crack

Washington Artillery Battalion from New Orleans was busy and brave all day long.[11]

Just four days after the rout of the Federals at Manassas, the Confederate Army was reorganized and Taylor's 9th Louisiana was brigaded with the 6th, 7th, and 8th Louisiana and Wheat's Battalion, the Louisiana Tigers. Officially, this became the 8th Brigade in Beauregard's 1st Corps, but it wasn't long before it was generally known as the Louisiana Brigade. Temporarily in command was the gallant old Isaac G. Seymour, editor of the *Commercial Bulletin* in New Orleans and one-time Indian fighter.

However, the command of the Louisiana Brigade soon devolved upon Brigadier General William H. T. Walker, a Georgian who had graduated from West Point, served gallantly in the Mexican War, and later acted as commandant of cadets at the Military Academy. A distinguished-looking figure, Walker was an excellent instructor and his new brigade was quickly impressed with the way he prepared them for action.

During the fall of 1861 disease swept through the camps like a forest fire. Measles, mumps, whooping cough, chicken pox—all children's diseases—vied with typhoid fever, dysentery, and other virulent maladies in laying the troops low. Taylor's regiment was particularly hard hit and he spent many hours in the hospitals helping to nurse the sick and comfort some dying lad, far from home. The ordeal was more than he could take. He fell ill, a low fever sapping his strength and impairing the use of his limbs. When General Joe Johnston heard of his condition, he ordered Taylor to Fauquier Springs, near Warrenton, to recuperate.[12]

On October 21, 1861, Taylor was promoted to brigadier general and the next day general orders shifted General Walker to command Georgia troops and assigned Taylor to command of the Louisiana Brigade.

Walker was furious and rightly so. He had in two short months turned the Louisiana Brigade into one of the best in the Army and the officers and men were devoted to "Fighting Billy" as they called him. In an indignant letter of resignation Walker denounced President Davis and Secretary of War Benjamin for promoting over him men whom he had ranked in the Old Army and his transfer from the Louisiana Brigade he considered "to cap the climax" of "insults and indignities."

To Taylor, his promotion to brigadier general was gratifying but terribly embarrassing. Of it, he wrote:

"Of the four colonels whose regiments constituted the brigade, I was junior in commission, and the other three had been present and 'won their spurs' at the recent battle . . . Besides my known friendship for President Davis, with whom I was connected by his first marriage with my older sister, would justify the opinion that my promotion was due to favoritism."

He had rejoined his regiment on October 30, but immediately asked permission to visit Richmond to confer with President Davis. Taylor had truly sensed, and quickly, the resentment in the brigade over the shift of commanders. The hold on the imagination of the Louisiana soldiers that "Fighting Billy" Walker had was amply shown before he bade them farewell. Taylor learned of the delegations of officers from the 6th and 7th Louisiana Regiments who had called on Walker and expressed their confidence in him and their sorrow on his departure. And he heard, too, how the band of the 8th Louisiana had serenaded the general.

As soon as he was ushered into President Davis's office Taylor explained the situation, told of his feelings and those of the brigade and requested Davis to rescind the promotion. It was a fact, which Taylor knew, that Davis had planned for some time to organize regiments from the same state into brigades and to place in command a general from the state. Accordingly, Walker, a Georgian, had been assigned to a Georgia brigade. This created the opening for a brigadier general in the Louisiana Brigade. And Davis had picked his brother-in-law. But what about the three other colonels, all of whom ranked him, all of whom had fought at Manassas?

The President listened patiently and said that he would take a day to reflect before deciding on the matter. The next day Taylor returned to the Army, and shortly thereafter President Davis's reply came. Taylor wrote:

"The President had employed the delay in writing a letter to the senior officers of the brigade, in which he began by stating that promotions to the grade of general officer were by law intrusted to him, and were made for consideration of public good, of which he alone was the judge. He then, out of abundant kindness for me, went on to soothe the feelings of these officers with a tenderness and delicacy of touch worthy of a woman's hand, and so effectually as to secure me their hearty support."

Taylor was gratified to learn that General Walker bore him no ill will. In keeping with the rest of the brigade, he held Walker in high regard and cordial relations had existed between them. That they still existed, Taylor had ample evidence when General Walker left his own tent and field equipment for Taylor's use.

Walker went home to Georgia, returned later to the Army and was killed in the Atlanta Campaign in 1864. In his book, Dick Taylor wrote affectionately of "Fighting Billy":

"No enterprise was too rash to awaken his ardor, if it necessitated daring courage and self-devotion. Truly, he might have come forth from the pages of old Froissart. It is with unaffected feeling that I recall his memory and hang before it my humble wreath of immortelles."[13]

IV

On November 4, 1861, Brigadier General Richard Taylor assumed command of the Louisiana Brigade. All of his units, except his former regiment, had already been under fire. Not having as yet demonstrated his ability to command a regiment, it was now up to Taylor to prove up as a brigade commander.[14]

These were the do-nothing days as far as the war was concerned, for outside of picket duty and a skirmish here or there, neither the Federals nor Confederates made a move in the winter of 1861–62. One Southern soldier summed up the situation this way: "The only reason we did not fight was that the enemy was afraid of us and we of them and that was all that kept us apart."

But General Dick Taylor was busy, continuing the work with the brigade which General Walker had started. Picking up where Walker left off, Taylor spent many hours in the instruction of the men in the use of their weapons and in marching, "the only military quality," he remarked, "for which Southern troops had no aptitude."

Taylor had a double incentive to make good. His own innate qualities of leadership dictated one; the circumstance of his promotion the other. He was conscious that people were saying, as Mary Boykin Chesnut wrote in her diary: "The President is accused of making a place for his brother-in-law, Dick Taylor." He knew that Davis's enemies were watching him for a slip.[15]

During the time that the Army lay around Centreville, close to Washington, Taylor not only trained his regiments but with the instinct of an expert psychologist, he studied the men and officers of each unit, instilling confidence in all and deriving from the experiment pride and confidence in his brigade. The 6th Louisiana, commanded by the much-loved Colonel Isaac Seymour, was composed mainly of New Orleans Irishmen, "stout, hardy fellows, turbulent in camp and requiring a strong hand, but responding to kindness and justice, and ready to follow their officers to the death." The 7th Louisiana, commanded by a New Orleans lawyer, Colonel Harry Hays, was, in Taylor's eyes, "a crack regiment." Taylor derived much amusement from the 8th Louisiana, commanded by Colonel Henry B. Kelly. It was composed partially of Acadians—Cajuns, in popular parlance—from the Bayou Teche country, southwest of New Orleans. From long experience in Louisiana, Taylor knew them as simple, home-loving folks, who spoke French and little English, and who "had all the light gayety of the Gaul." Taylor's old regiment, now commanded by Colonel Leroy A. Stafford, was made up of planters and planters' sons from northern Louisiana, the Anglo-Saxon part of the state. Many of them were wealthy and to all "soldiering was a hard task to which they only became reconciled by reflecting that it was 'niddering' in gentlemen to assume voluntarily the discharge of duties and then shirk."[16]

The remaining unit of Dick Taylor's Louisiana Brigade was the Louisiana Tigers, a battalion commanded by a giant of a man, Roberdeau Wheat, clergyman's son turned soldier of fortune, who had soldiered in Mexico, Cuba, Nicaragua, and Italy, whenever, as Taylor expressed it, "the pleasant business of killing was going on." Wheat's Tigers were wild and unruly, and, as one observer wrote of them, "made not a pious crew, but they fought." Indeed, when Yankees weren't available, they'd compromise by brawling with another Confederate unit, and that failing, they'd fall back upon rioting among themselves.

One Virginia soldier noted in his diary that "they neither fear God, man or the Devil," while a youngster from South Carolina called them "the worst men I ever saw . . . mostly wharf rats from New Orleans, and Major Wheat was the only man who could do anything with them."

"So villainous was the reputation of this battalion that every commander desired to be rid of it," wrote General Taylor, "and General Johnston assigned it to me, despite my efforts to decline the honor of such society." With delicate sarcasm, Taylor called them his "gentle Tigers," and the day was not long off when he would be happy to have them in his brigade whenever there was fighting to be done.[17]

The Tigers were the cause of the first disciplinary problem that Taylor had to handle. Late in November, some of these obstreperous fellows created disorder after tattoo and several Tigers were arrested and confined in the brigade guardhouse. Another group of Tigers, hearing of the confinement of their mates, desired to free them. Two reckless young Irishmen, Dennis Cochrane and Mike O'Brien, led the assault on the guardhouse and, in the ensuing fracas, the officer of the guard was rudely handled and struck.

The attempt failed and the ringleaders, Cochrane and O'Brien, were subdued and put into irons for the night. The next day, November 29, a speedily called court-martial found them guilty of violating the Articles of War and sentenced them to be shot.

Immediately, the Tigers' commander, Major Wheat, besought clemency for the two condemned men. He begged that some other punishment be given them, however severe. In vain did he plead that one of the men had saved his life at the Battle of Manassas. Taylor was adamant. A grievous offense against discipline had been committed, the guard had been manhandled and its officer assaulted. He felt the discipline of the brigade, even that of the Army, called for the extreme penalty. Taylor ordered the firing party to come from the Tiger Rifles, the company to which the two men belonged.

Wheat and the other battalion officers begged Taylor not to impose such a hard task upon them, and even suggested that perhaps the firing squad would refuse to fire on their comrades. "I insisted for the sake of the example," wrote Taylor, "and pointed out the serious consequences of the disobedience by their men."

The execution took place on December 9, before Taylor's and other brigades under arms and thousands of other troops, many in trees or on the roofs of nearby houses. One of the soldiers who witnessed it returned heavyhearted to his tent and wrote in his diary of the "effecting sight and heart rendering affair." He sensed the moral in the seemingly harsh sentence:

"These two men I think are the first that have been shot and I hope the last. My idea of this decision is that the men are now going into winter quarters and to prevent them slipping off home for they thought they would have to make an example of some one and they concluded this the best time and it fell to these poor Tigers to share such an unfortunate lot."

The shooting of the two hapless Tigers was, indeed, the first military execution in the Army. ". . . Punishment, so closely following offense, produced a marked effect," said General Taylor.[18]

About this time, General Joe Johnston sent Taylor to Richmond to make known his view to President Davis on the question of reorganization of the Army. Taylor failed to win Davis to Johnston's ideas and he discerned for the first time the growing estrangement between the President and the commander of the Army. Both Davis and Johnston listened patiently to his appeals and he felt justified in hoping that the cloud, then "no greater than a man's hand," would evaporate. But Taylor was thinking wishfully. "Destiny willed that Davis and Johnston should be brought into collision, and the breach, once made, was never repaired," declared Taylor. "Each misjudged the other to the end."[19]

The bitter Virginia winter of 1861–62 found Taylor, habitually subject to rheumatism and nervous headache, suffering considerably. But he did not neglect his brigade's training. When he was under the weather, he became impatient and irritable, but when he was in good health his spirits were high. Frequently, Taylor joined the men at their campfires, and, in "rich melodious voice," would discuss historical events or witty passages from literature. One of his listeners later recalled that General Taylor seemed "the most brilliant and fascinating talker . . . in the Southern army."

During the winter, the Louisiana Brigade was shifted from one division to another, but in the snowbound inactivity this really made little difference. Early in November 1861, the brigade was in General E. Kirby Smith's division. On November 16, it was shifted to General Earl Van Dorn's command. On January 14, 1862, it was back in Kirby Smith's division. When General Smith was ordered west, the newly promoted Major General Richard Stoddert Ewell took command of the division on February 21.

The next day, the Confederate Army at Centreville and along Bull Run, began preparations to withdraw to the Rappahannock. Johnston and the Richmond authorities agreed this was defensively sound to meet any threat to Richmond by General George B. McClellan in the spring. Taylor's brigade which was on lower Bull Run, not far from Manassas Junction, got its marching orders and on March 9, the Louisianians were in motion. The road assigned Taylor for his march was "rough and tough" and there were many small streams to cross, all of which, he said, "drew heavily on the marching capacity—or rather incapacity—of the men."

Straggling, Taylor noted for the first, but not the last time, was "the vice of Southern armies." So he bent every effort to prevent straggling in his brigade during the withdrawal from the Bull Run line. Frequent halts were made to allow the slow of foot to close up. And Taylor set an example for his officers by riding to the rear of the column to relieve weary men of their muskets or to hoist a footsore soldier upon his horse behind him. Morale had to be high in a unit whose commanding officer and subordinates showed such real concern for the welfare of the troops.

But Taylor's solicitude didn't stop there. He gave his men advice on fitting their shoes and urged cold foot baths to relieve fatigue. He instructed them in caring for abrasions, and generally taught them how to march. "The men appreciated this care and attention . . . and soon held it a disgrace to fall out of ranks," wrote Taylor. "Before a month had passed the brigade learned how to march, and, in the Valley with Jackson, covered long distances without leaving a straggler behind."[20]

No wonder, two months later, as his straggler-free brigade marched past a bearded lemon-sucker on a rail fence, Dick Taylor's heart was filled with pride as he brought his hand up in salute to Stonewall Jackson.

v

If General Taylor had left nothing to readers of the future other than his magnificent character sketches of Dick Ewell and Stonewall Jackson, his contribution to Civil War literature, for all its brevity, would have been invaluable. These sketches provide some of the most entertaining reading in *Destruction and Reconstruction*, itself one of the two or three finest Civil War narratives written by participants. Douglas Southall

Freeman said that Taylor presented pictures of Ewell "that Thackeray would not have disowned" and that "no firmer, more accurate pictures are to be found in Confederate literature than those Taylor penned of Stonewall."

Taylor and Ewell had been friends for years, but now that they were brought into almost daily contact their friendship ripened. This close and constant association with Ewell afforded Taylor abundant opportunities to study one of the most original characters among the generals in gray. His description of Ewell is delightful:

"Bright, prominent eyes, a bomb-shaped, bald head, and a nose like that of Francis of Valois, gave him a striking resemblance to a woodcock; and this was increased by a bird-like habit of putting his head on one side to utter his quaint speeches."

Because he fancied he had a mysterious internal malady, Ewell would eat only frumenty, a wheat preparation, and nervousness prevented him from regular sleeping habits. Taylor often saw him pass nights "curled around a camp stool, in positions to dislocate an ordinary person's joints." After long silences, he'd suddenly look at Taylor and with a "sharp accent that ended in a gentle lisp" ask some faraway question, such as: "General Taylor! What do you suppose President Davis made me a major general for?"

Ewell, Taylor said, was a superb horseman. Although he had a fine tactical eye in battle, "he was never content with his own plan until he had secured the approval of another's judgement." Ewell loved to get into the fight and he chafed under the responsibilities of command which kept him from rushing forward with the skirmish line. Wrote Taylor of this:

"On two occasions in the Valley, during the temporary absence of Jackson from the front, Ewell summoned me to his side, and immediately rushed forward among the skirmishers, where some sharp work was going on. Having refreshed himself, he returned with the hope that 'old Jackson would not catch him at it.' He always spoke of Jackson, several years his junior, as 'old,' and told me in confidence that he admired his genius, but was certain of his lunacy, and that he never saw one of Jackson's couriers approach without expecting an order to assault the north pole."

Once, when Ewell ordered a bridge burned, Taylor's countenance clearly recorded his disapproval. It was the only bridge for some miles up and down the stream which was fordable in many places.

"You don't like it," exclaimed Ewell.

"At the close of the Napoleonic wars," answered Taylor, "Bugeaud, a young colonel, commanded a French regiment on the Swiss frontier. A stream spanned by a bridge, but fordable above and below, separated him from an Austrian force four times his strength. He first determined to destroy the bridge, but reflected that if left it might tempt the enemy, whenever he moved, to neglect the fords. Accordingly, he masked his regiment as near his end of the bridge as the topography of the ground permitted and waited. The Austrians moved by the bridge, and Bugeaud, seizing the moment, fell upon them in the act of crossing and destroyed the entire force. Moral: 'Tis easier to watch and defend one bridge than many miles of fordable water."

"Why did you keep the story until the bridge was burnt?" exploded Ewell.[21]

Whereas Dick Taylor had known Ewell for a long time prior to serving under him, Thomas Jonathan Jackson, called Stonewall after Manassas, was a total stranger. The legends had not yet grown up about him in May of 1862, when Taylor's brigade joined Jackson in the Shenandoah Valley for the writing of one of the most brilliant chapters of the Civil War.

Taylor quickly learned the foibles of his new chief. If silence be golden, then Stonewall Jackson was a bonanza. "He sucked lemons, ate hard tack, and drank water, and praying and fighting appeared to be his idea of the 'whole duty of man.'" Whereas Dick Ewell sat his saddle as if born in it, Jackson was "an ungraceful horseman" who rode a "sorry chestnut with a shambling gait." As he rode along in silence, his huge feet with outturned toes thrust into his stirrups, Stonewall's countenance, such as the low visor of his moth-eaten cap permitted to be seen, was wooden. Taylor was compelled to admit that his new commander "was not prepossessing."

Once, when Taylor appealed to Jackson on behalf of General Winder, a splendid brigade commander, who had resigned in a huff over some interference in his command, he caught "a glimpse," Taylor stated, "of the man's inner nature," for a brief instant. "It was but a glimpse. The curtain closed, and he was absorbed in prayer. Yet in that moment I saw an ambition boundless as Cromwell's, and as merciless." Continuing, Taylor summed up this complex man admirably:

"I have written that he was ambitious; and his ambition was vast, all-absorbing. Like the unhappy wretch from whose shoulders sprang the foul serpent, he loathed it, perhaps feared it; but he could not escape it—it was himself—nor rend it—it was his own flesh. He fought it with prayer, constant and earnest—Apollyon and Christian in ceaseless combat. What limit to set to his ability I know not, for he was ever superior to occasion. Under ordinary circumstances it was difficult to estimate him because of his peculiarities—peculiarities that would have made a lesser man absurd, but that served to enhance his martial fame, as those of Samuel Johnson did his literary eminence."[22]

VI

After reporting to Stonewall Jackson, General Taylor didn't have to wait long for an opportunity to study his new commander at informal close range. Late that night, Jackson came to Taylor's campfire. He said that the army would move at dawn and then he asked a few questions about the marching of the Louisiana Brigade, with which he apparently had been much impressed. These answered, Stonewall lapsed into silence, broken only when he arose to leave after several hours of staring into the fire.[23]

Jackson's Valley Campaign, in itself, was a masterful tactical operation, but it had far reaching strategic purposes. By demonstrating in the Valley, Jackson could strike the forces of Generals John C. Frémont and Nathaniel Banks in detail, before they could combine against him, and threaten to swoop down on Washington from the north. This would compel General Irvin McDowell's 40,000 troops to remain in the defense of the Federal capital instead of marching toward Richmond to take the Confederates in flank while McClellan attacked frontally.

With the arrival of Taylor's and Ewell's other brigades, Jackson had a total of less than 18,000 troops. With these, by rapid marches and bold strokes, he was able to immobilize 70,000 Federals and throw official Washington into a panic.

Before sunrise on May 21, 1862, Jackson's army was in motion with Dick Taylor's brigade leading. The silent Stonewall rode at Taylor's side as the devious march brought the army to Luray, where it camped for the night. After three long marches the Louisiana Brigade was but a short distance from where it had left to join Jackson several days before. "I began to think that Jackson was an unconscious poet," Taylor wrote whimsically, "and as an ardent lover of nature desired to give strangers an opportunity to admire the beauties of his Valley." But Taylor soon discovered that it was method not madness that motivated Jackson. He wanted to strike the Federals at Front Royal by surprise and capture the town so quickly that the small garrison could not escape or send a call for reinforcements.

On May 23, as they approached Front Royal shortly past noon, Taylor was riding alone at the head of the column, Jackson having been called to the rear. Out of the woods ahead, a pretty girl emerged, running breathlessly toward the advancing troops. She was Belle Boyd, the Confederate spy. She told Taylor, "with much volubility . . . with the precision of a staff officer making a report," that the town was just beyond the woods, that it was filled with Yankees, that Banks was at Winchester, 20 miles away, and that the Federals had no idea where Jackson was,

believing him miles off near Harrisonburg. She also said that the wagon
bridge over the Shenandoah was covered by Yankee guns on the heights
on the far side of the stream but that the nearby railroad bridge was
not.

Convinced of the correctness of Belle Boyd's information, Taylor ordered his command forward on the double. He hoped to "surprise the
enemy's idlers in the town, or swarm over the wagon bridge with them
and secure it." At this time, Stonewall Jackson galloped up and ordered
Taylor to deploy his men as skirmishers on both sides of the road, while
Rob Wheat's Tigers and the 1st Maryland Regiment, which was attached to Taylor's command temporarily, were sent on a wide loop
to sweep into the town from the east. Little time was consumed in
getting into Front Royal and clearing it of Federals, who scurried across
the wagon bridge to their camp.[24]

Taylor drew up his brigade for action and then rode down to the
river's edge to survey the Yankee position through his field glass. His
horse, heated by the march, walked into the river and began drinking.
Instantly the Yankees opened up with a brisk fire directed at horse and
rider, the bullets striking all around them in the water. This was the
first time Dick Taylor had been under fire. He wrote of the experience:

"I had not yet led my command into action, and, remembering that
one must 'strut' one's little part to the best advantage, sat my horse with
all the composure I could muster. A provident camel, on the eve of a
desert journey, would not have laid in a greater supply of water than did
my thoughtless beast. At last he raised his head, looked placidly around,
turned and walked up the bank."

A cheer went up from Taylor's men as he galloped back to them amid
renewed enemy fire. Jackson, sitting his horse, motionless, was lost in
deep thought. Taylor suggested that the troops could use the railroad
bridge to attack, carefully stepping on the cross ties. Jackson only nodded
and Taylor ordered his 8th Louisiana across. Taylor now thought an effort should be made to secure the wagon bridge, but at that moment the
Yankees set fire to combustibles, previously placed in the center of the
bridge. Taylor looked at Jackson again, and once more he got an affirm-
ative nod. With Taylor at their head the rest of the brigade rushed forward.

The heavy smoke concealed the sudden charge of the Louisiana Brigade and saved Taylor from heavy losses. ". . . It was rather a near
thing," he wrote. "My horse and clothing were scorched and many men
burned their hands severely while throwing brands into the river." Soon
the brigade was across and the Yankees in full flight for Winchester,
leaving behind men, guns, and supplies. As Taylor emerged from the
smoke and flames of the burning bridge, he was startled to find Stonewall
Jackson at his side. "How he got there was a mystery," wrote Taylor,

"as the bridge was thronged with my men going at full speed; but smoke and fire had decidedly freshed up his costume."[25]

Late that night, Jackson seated himself by Taylor's campfire. He mentioned that Taylor would move with him in the morning and then he just sat there through the night, silent and motionless, staring into the fire. Taylor interpreted Stonewall's presence as approval of the behavior of the Louisiana Brigade that day.

The next day, Jackson took off early. With him at the head of the column was a small body of horse, a section of artillery, and Major Wheat's Tigers, who were instructed to keep close to the guns. Taylor remained with the rest of his brigade, which, after several hours of marching, had fallen some distance behind Jackson and the advance group.

Sounds of guns and cheers in front caused Taylor to put his brigade on the double and when it reached the Valley Pike at Middletown, he discovered that Jackson had attacked a large Federal cavalry group and a wagon train, hurrying north, had taken many prisoners and captured the wagons. "The gentle Tigers were looting right merrily, diving in and out of wagons with the activity of rabbits in a warren," wrote Taylor, "but this occupation was abandoned on my approach, and in a moment they were in line, looking solemn and virtuous as deacons at a funeral."[26]

That night, Taylor rode at Jackson's side through the darkness. A hard-riding officer, who proved to be Jackson's chief quartermaster, overtook them, reporting to Jackson that his wagon trains were far in the rear, a bad road in Luray Valley impeding their progress.

"The ammunition trains?" snapped Jackson sternly.

"All right, sir," replied the quartermaster. "They were in advance, and I doubled teams on them and brought them through."

"Ah," uttered Jackson, in a relieved tone.

"Never mind the wagons," put in Taylor jokingly. "There are quantities of stores in Winchester, and the General has invited me to breakfast there tomorrow."

The humorless Jackson, taking Taylor seriously, reached out to touch him on the arm, as if in reproof. Jackson, having few physical needs himself, forgot about others and paid little attention to the commissary. "But woe to the man who failed to bring up ammunition!" declared Taylor. "In advance, his trains were left far behind. In retreat, he would fight for a wheelbarrow."

At midnight, Taylor noted other troops coming on to the Valley Pike from other roads from Front Royal and so he halted his jaded command for a much-needed rest. With sunrise, Taylor was in motion and, as he approached to within a few miles of Winchester, he heard ahead sustained artillery and small-arms fire. One of Jackson's staff officers rode up at full speed to tell Taylor that Jackson wanted him and his brigade at once.[27]

When Taylor reached Jackson, the attack on Winchester had begun. On Jackson's right, Dick Ewell was pressing the enemy center. From a strong position on high ground overlooking Jackson's approach Yankee gunners, laying down a frightful fire, blasted the Confederate artillery. Supporting the Federal battery, some infantry behind a stone wall delivered hot volleys into Jackson's ranks.

"General, can your brigade charge a battery?" asked Jackson, pointing to the ridge.

"It can try," was Taylor's rejoinder.

"Very good. It must do it then. Move it forward."[28]

Taylor saluted, gave orders for the brigade to move up and then rode to his left to study the terrain. Before him a small stream, Abraham's Creek, flowed at the base of the ridge. He perceived that "the ascent . . . was steep, though nowhere abrupt." At one point he discerned "a broad, shallow, trough-like depression," which had to be crossed in the charge.

Sending Wheat's Battalion to the extreme left, Taylor dressed his regiments on the Tigers in a long line to the south, and then gave the command to advance. To his surprise, Taylor found Jackson at his side. "This is not the place for the commander of the army," Taylor exclaimed, but Stonewall ignored the comment. When the men reached the depression, the enemy's fire was scorching. Some men fell, many began to duck as shot and shell whistled by.

"What the hell are you dodging for?" bellowed Taylor. "If there is any more of it, you will be halted under fire for an hour."

Jackson, still at Taylor's side, cast a surprised and reproachful glance at him. He placed his hand on Taylor's shoulder and said quietly: "I am afraid you are a wicked fellow." Then Stonewall wheeled his horse and rode back to the pike.[29]

It was about 7:30 A.M. when Taylor moved up the ridge and it was a thrilling sight to the Valley Army. One of Stonewall's troopers described it:

"The enemy poured grape and musketry into Taylor's line as soon as it came into sight. Gen. Taylor rode in front of his brigade, drawn sword in hand, occasionally turning his horse, at other times merely turning in the saddle to see that his line was up. They marched up the hill in perfect order, not firing a shot! About half way . . . he gave in a loud and commanding voice . . . the order to charge!"[30]

While he was leading the charge, Taylor related, his attention was caught by a bluebird, a worm in its mouth, which flew across the brigade front. Pride in his gallant brigade is reflected in Taylor's brilliant description of the charge:

"Progress was not stayed . . . closing the many gaps made by the fierce fire, steadied the rather by it, and preserving an alignment that would have been creditable on parade, the brigade, with cadenced step and eyes on the foe, swept grandly over copse and ledge and fence, to crown the heights from which the enemy had melted away."

Once on the heights, Taylor's men sent up a cheer, which was picked up by the other troops. To the astonishment of all, Jackson let out a yell or two himself and waved his cap excitedly in the air. He issued a quick command: "Order forward the whole line, the battle's won!" And then he exclaimed: "Very good! Now let's holler."[31]

On the edge of Winchester, Taylor encountered Jackson, who paused for a moment to grasp Taylor's hand, a gesture, the latter remarked, "worth a thousand words from another."

Taylor looked in vain for Confederate cavalry pursuit of the fleeing Yankees, racing toward the Potomac River over the Harpers Ferry and Martinsburg roads, but no cavalry came forward. Joining Jackson again, Taylor asked: "Where is the cavalry?" Stonewall glowered and held his tongue. He was furious and later expressed himself with vehemence: "Never was there such a chance for cavalry! Oh, that my cavalry were in place!"

As Taylor's men marched through Winchester, in futile pursuit of the fleeing Yankees who did not stop until they had crossed the Potomac, Taylor remarked an amusing incident, an incident which would have perhaps scandalized the strait-laced Jackson. A buxom and bright-eyed woman in the crowd that cheered the troops exclaimed:

"Oh! you are too late—too late!"

One of Taylor's Cajuns from the Teche leaped from the ranks of the 8th Louisiana, took her in his arms and kissed her soundly on the lips, calling back as he returned to the ranks: *"Madame! Je n'arrive jamais trop tard!"* ("Madam! I never arrive too late!")

After several days in the Winchester area, collecting the vast supply of captured guns, wagons, supplies, and ordnance and medical stores, Jackson started back up the Shenandoah Valley. On the night of May 31, he came to Taylor's campfire at Strasburg in the most communicative mood the latter ever saw him. Frémont, he told Taylor, was only three miles off to the west, with a large force. General James Shields was moving up from Luray Valley and would undoubtedly strike at Stonewall's trains at Harrisonburg. Jackson said that saving the immense trains, filled with captured goods, was of prime importance to which he would devote his attention. Ewell, in command of the army, would deal with Frémont. Jackson's concern over the wagons prompted Taylor's men to say that Old Jack's "anxiety about the wagons was because of the lemons among the stores."[32]

Jackson's remarkable feat of eluding Shields, brushing by Frémont and bewildering McDowell by the rapidity of his march, was one of the amazing incidents of the war. British Colonel G. F. R. Henderson, first important biographer of Jackson, points out that within fourteen days, "the

Army of the Valley had marched one hundred and seventy miles, had routed a force of 12,500, had threatened the North with invasion, had drawn off McDowell from Fredericksburg, had seized the hospitals and supply depots at Front Royal, Winchester and Martinsburg, and finally, though surrounded on three sides by 60,000 men had brought off a huge convoy without losing a single wagon."[33]

By June 6, Jackson's main force was at Port Republic, where the North and South rivers join to form the South Fork of the Shenandoah. The Valley Army controlled the only bridge there and thus Jackson lay between Frémont and Shields, who now had no ready means of joining forces to overwhelm the adversary who had humiliated them. Jackson's course was clear. He would dispose of Frémont, northwest of the river. Then crossing to the east side, he would engage Shields. After whipping both, he would give them the slip and speed to keep a rendezvous with Robert E. Lee on the Chickahominy before Richmond.

Jackson fought Frémont at Cross Keys on June 8, but Taylor's brigade, in reserve, was not employed as the inept Frémont lost heavily in men and material and withdrew with alacrity. To get his men across South River, Jackson ordered a wagon bridge built by laying planks on the under structure of the wagons. So uncertain was it, however, the troops had to cross in single file. Early on June 9, a Sunday, Taylor's brigade crossed the rickety bridge, one by one, the 8th Louisiana leading the way, followed by the 9th Louisiana, Wheat's Battalion, and the 6th and 7th Louisiana.

Firing broke out up ahead, first the rattle of small arms and then the roar of artillery. The bottleneck at the improvised bridge of necessity forced the troops to be committed piecemeal, battalion by battalion. Taylor spurred his horse forward for about a mile to see what the shooting was about. He saw that on a ledge to his right six Yankee guns were "sweeping every inch of the plain to the south," a thousand yards of clear and open country between the mountain and the river and over which Winder's brigade, heavily outnumbered, was being hard-pressed by the enemy.

As Taylor watched the havoc that the battery on the ledge was producing, Jackson rode up.

"Delightful excitement," observed Stonewall.

"It's pleasant to know you're enjoying yourself," said Taylor, "but I think you'll have an indigestion of such fun if the six-gun battery is not silenced."

Jackson promptly assigned Taylor the job of silencing it. Colonel Kelly's 8th Regiment, in the van of Taylor's brigade, was by now joined by the 9th Regiment and Wheat's Tigers. With a scout showing Taylor a roundabout path, the three elements of the Louisiana Brigade disappeared into the thickly wooded hills. Still blazing away from the ledge, on which was an abandoned charcoal kiln, the Federal battery continued to do great damage. A Rebel artilleryman, exposed to the blistering barrage, recalled: "The fire of that battery was terrible for a while. . . . The thunder of the artillery shook the ground . . . and the air was full of screaming fragments of exploding shells . . ."

A little later, this gunner, from a vantage spot, saw and heard what Stonewall Jackson was waiting to see and hear. "After we had been under this dreadful fire about thirty minutes, I heard a mighty shout on the mountain side in close proximity to the coaling," he related, "and in a few minutes after I saw General Dick Taylor's Louisianians debouching from the undergrowth, and like a wave crested with shining steel rush towards the fatal coaling and deadly battery with fixed bayonets, giving the Rebel yell like mad demons."[34]

In close support up came the 6th Regiment, and Taylor, who was with them, took command of the brigade in the furious fight for the Federal guns. Colonel Kelly of the 8th Louisiana vividly described the fight:

"At the word of command . . . the line moved forward, soon coming into plain view of the batteries and of the infantry of the enemy beyond the ravine, which at once opened fire on the advancing brigade. With one volley in reply, and a Confederate yell heard far over the field, the Louisianians rushed down the rough declivity and across the ravine, and carried the batteries like a flash . . . By the impetus of the charge over the rough ground all formation was lost, and officers and men were thrown in one unorganized mass around the captured guns."

Surprise had aided the brigade, but the Federal infantry rallied and drove out the Louisianians. A second charge by Taylor's men repossessed the Yankee battery after furious close-range fighting with knives and stones and fists. A second time the Yankees rallied and drove off Taylor's men. Before they did, Major Rob Wheat had whipped out a knife and slashed the throats of the artillery horses to prevent the Yankees from drawing off their guns. "It was a sickening sight," recalled a Confederate in the fight, "men in gray and blue piled up in front of and around the guns and with the horses dying and the blood of men and beasts flowing almost in a stream. Major Wheat was as bloody as a butcher . . ."[35]

A third time Taylor called for a charge and even the drummer boys got into the thick of the fight. This time the Federals, who had fought valiantly, broke and withdrew, not in a rout, but in orderly fashion, even when Taylor's men turned the Yankee guns upon them. The Federals were, said Dick Taylor, "formidable to the last."

Jackson rode up "with intense light in his eyes," and warmly grasped Taylor's hand and awarded the captured battery to the brigade. The Louisianians went wild. One Irishman, his face and whiskers seared with powder burns, called out to Taylor from his perch on one of the captured guns: "We told you to bet on your boys."

The Battle of Port Republic ended Jackson's remarkable campaign and it established Dick Taylor as one of the Confederacy's best fighting generals. Taylor, himself, gave the credit to his brigade. He wrote with pride:

"The Louisiana brigade . . . in twenty days . . . marched over two hundred miles, fought in five actions, of which three were severe, and several skirmishes, and, though it had suffered heavy losses in officers and men, was yet strong, hard as nails, and full of confidence. I have felt it a duty to set forth the achievements of the brigade, than which no man ever led braver into action, in their proper light, because such reputation as I gained in this campaign is to be ascribed to its excellence."

But this wasn't the opinion of Stonewall Jackson, who immediately after the Battle of Port Republic dispatched a message to Adjutant General Samuel Cooper in Richmond. It read:

"I respectfully recommend that Brig General Richard Taylor be promoted to a Major General. The success with which he managed his brigade in Camp, on the March, and when engaged with the enemy at Front Royal, Middletown, Winchester, and yesterday near Port Republic makes it my duty as well as pleasure to recommend his promotion."[36]

Jefferson Davis's brother-in-law had outfought all charges that presidential favoritism had made him a general.

VII

In the calm that followed the Valley Campaign, a weariness and depression settled over General Taylor. For one thing, his health bothered him and he feared a return of his illness of the previous autumn. And for many weeks he had not heard from his wife and family in New Orleans, which, meanwhile, had fallen to Farragut and his fleet. Accordingly, Taylor secured a few days' leave to go to Richmond to see what he could learn. To his relief there were letters from his wife, who had escaped the city with the children on a steamer that left just as Farragut's vessels began to arrive.

While in the War Office, Taylor received a pointed hint that if he knew what was under way, he'd get back in a hurry to his command. The brief change of scenery and the news of the safety of his family relieved Taylor's concern and he felt much better when he detrained at Charlottesville, where he found Jackson and his Valley Army marching to the southeast.

Lee and Jackson had played a neat little game of deception. Reinforcements, ostentatiously announced, had been sent to the Valley and when the word reached Washington, Federal authorities feared that Jackson's recent foray would be followed up by a genuine attack on the northern capital.

But Jackson, on instructions from Lee, no sooner got his "reinforcements" than he and they started to join the Confederate Army before Richmond. And so it was that on June 25, Jackson's army camped near Ashland, 16 miles north of Richmond on the railroad to Fredericksburg. All that day, as the Louisiana Brigade marched, Taylor had been seized with severe pains in the head and loins. There was no improvement during the night and the next morning, Taylor found it impossible to mount his horse. Remaining behind in a small ambulance, Taylor sent his brigade forward under the command of Colonel Isaac Seymour of the 6th Louisiana. At nightfall, Taylor received a message that the brigade had gone into camp at Pole Green Church. The general was in great agony, with pains in his head and back and having lost the power to move his limbs. He lay on the floor of a vacant house, seeking sleep to dull his pain. But this was denied him until nearly daylight when exhaustion prevailed.

Several hours later, the constant rumble of distant artillery awakened him. Taylor's slave, Tom Strother, who had been his playmate and then his bodyservant, and who had followed his master to war, raised Taylor to a sitting position and gave him strong coffee to drink. As the firing continued, Taylor's inactivity was unendurable. Ordering Tom to place him in the ambulance, he ordered the driver to head for the sound of the guns, instructing Tom to follow with his horses. Taylor wrote vividly of his ride to the front, where the bitter battle of Gaines' Mill was being fought:

"We took the route by which the troops had marched, the din of conflict increasing with every mile, the rattle of small arms mingling with the thud of guns. After weary hours of rough road, every jolt on which threatened to destroy my remaining vitality, we . . . met numbers of wounded. Among these was General Elzey, with a dreadful wound in his head and face. His aide . . . stopped a moment to tell of the fight. Ewell's Division . . . had just been engaged with heavy loss. This was too much for any illness, and I managed somehow to struggle on to my horse and get into action."

Taylor rode into a wild scene, for the battle was raging close at hand. Overhead shot and shell whistled by and all about him lay the dead and wounded. The losses in his own command were distressing to Taylor. Big, generous, gallant Roberdeau Wheat had fallen at the head of the Louisiana Tigers and the brave old Seymour, Indian fighter, editor, and fine soldier, was cut down while leading the brigade. Many others in the Louisiana Brigade, officers and men, had fought their last battle. "I had a wretched feeling of guilt, especially about Seymour, who had led the brigade and died in my place," said Taylor.

Throughout the rest of the Seven Days' Battles before Richmond, as

Lee maneuvered McClellan away from the city, Taylor sought frequent rests in his ambulance. He recalled that Senator Louis T. Wigfall of Texas and General Wade Hampton visited him there. Hampton had just been promoted to brigadier general but had not yet been assigned a command. Wigfall told Taylor, jokingly it is presumed, that he hoped some brigadier would be killed to make a place for Hampton, to whom he intended to attach himself as volunteer aide and enjoy the fun. "Finding me extended in my ambulance, he doubtless thought he had met his opportunity," said Taylor, "and felt aggrieved that I was not *in extremis.*"

The Seven Days, Taylor later stated, were "a series of blunders, one after another, and all huge." Years later, Taylor was still amazed and even then could scarcely realize "our ignorance in a military sense of the ground over which we were called to fight." President Davis was a West Pointer and had served for seven years. Robert E. Lee, and his predecessor, Joe Johnston, had both been engineering officers in the old Army. And yet, said Taylor, "the Confederate commanders knew no more about the topography of the country than they did about Central Africa. Here was a limited district, the whole of it within a day's march of the city of Richmond . . . and yet we were profoundly ignorant of the country, were without maps, sketches or proper guides . . . McClellan . . . was superior to us in knowledge of our own land."

With the end of the Seven Days' Battles, Taylor's illness reached a crisis and a paralysis of the lower limbs set in. He was taken to Richmond for treatment. While recuperating he learned of his promotion to major general on Stonewall Jackson's recommendation and his assignment to his native Louisiana.[37]

On July 26, President Davis issued the promotion. Two days later, Taylor was named commander of the District of Western Louisiana.

Happy to be able to see his wife and children again and serve in defense of his own state, Dick Taylor nonetheless left Virginia with a heavy heart. It was hard to bid farewell to Stonewall Jackson, Dick Ewell, his regimental commanders and his men. A testimonial to their love and devotion to Taylor was embodied in a letter from the officers and men of the 9th Louisiana, his old regiment. The meat of the message was this: ". . . Our desire to still be a portion of your command has grown and ripened into an attachment which we trust may never be interrupted . . . We wish to be and remain with you. Whenever you go, we desire to go, and let your destiny be our destiny."[38]

VIII

The far-reaching consequences of the fall of New Orleans to the Federal fleet in April 1862 affected the destinies of the Confederacy. But, more immediately, at home it was crippling to Louisiana.

Federal occupation of the South's greatest city and Baton Rouge, the state capital, and control of the lower Mississippi River up to Port Hudson put about half of Louisiana's population and three-quarters of its resources inside the Federally occupied territory.

The Confederacy had no troops, no arms, no munitions, and no money in Louisiana, General Taylor discovered when he arrived at Opelousas on August 20, 1862, to take charge of the District of Western Louisiana.

Some weeks before Taylor's arrival in Louisiana the Trans-Mississippi Department had been created with Major General Theophilus H. Holmes in command. It comprised the District of Texas (Texas and Arizona Territory); the District of Arkansas (Arkansas, Missouri, and Indian Territory); and the District of Western Louisiana.

When Taylor surveyed his district and saw what little resources he had at his command, he must have smiled in spite of himself at his instructions from the War Department. All he had to do, with nothing, was keep the Yankees from using the rivers and bayous or from getting supplies from the interior; raise troops not only for himself but for the Louisiana brigades in Virginia; establish communication lines in his district; organize and equip light batteries which could run into position to embarrass Federal navigation on the Mississippi and then withdraw to safety; destroy all wood prepared for steamers on the river bank; carefully inspect and control his partisan troops; and, finally, "confine the enemy within the narrowest limits, and recover from his possession, as opportunity may serve, any and all positions in the State of Louisiana which by the fortunes of war have fallen into his hands."

Taylor immediately sought help from his friend, Governor Thomas O. Moore of Louisiana, but Moore had no means at his disposal. On August 25, Taylor directed a plea to Governor J. L. Pettus of Mississippi, asking for arms. "We are so destitute of material on this side of the river . . ." he said.[39]

As for troops, Taylor had just a handful, including a couple of Louisiana companies of mounted men, armed with fowling pieces, whom Governor Moore had organized and transferred to Confederate service. Also in his "army" was Colonel Edward Waller's battalion of mounted riflemen recently arrived from Texas. Requesting Confederate authorities to send him reinforcements, Taylor took measures of his own to increase his ranks. He applied a rigid enforcement of the Conscription Act of April 16, 1862, which applied to all men between the ages of eighteen and thirty-five. As a result, by October 1, Taylor's force had grown to 5840 officers and men, of whom 4697 were present for duty. These included 1746 infantry, 1402 cavalry, and 199 artillery.[40]

A year earlier, General Taylor had to demonstrate that he was something more than Jefferson Davis's brother-in-law, and, accordingly, one of the President's "pets." He had to prove himself all over again to the people of Louisiana, whose spirit was crushed and whose energies were be-

numbed by the fall of New Orleans. His rigid application of conscription,
the enormity of the task he had tackled and the apathy of the people
which had to be shaken out of them all combined to bring unmerited
criticism and abuse upon him. Blinded by their own frustration and despondent over the turn of events, the people struck out at the man who
embodied the Confederacy in their midst.

A year later, however, before 1863 had run out, Taylor had scored
another popularity victory. His trials and the way he met them during
his first year in Louisiana were admirably described by Governor Thomas
O. Moore in a letter to President Davis:

"I confess I was not prepared for the exhibition of the high qualities of
a Commander which his services here have developed. We owe it to him,
that the State is not now entirely overrun and occupied by the enemy,
and it is the greatest merit, in that at no time have forces under his command been adequate to accomplishment of such results.

"His bearing, under unmerited obloquy, should also be brought to
your notice. Shortly, after he assumed command, a shower of calumnies
fell with fierce rapidity upon him . . . General Taylor found literally
nothing here. He had to develop resources, and to awaken the public
from their apathy. They moved upon him with the fury of wild beasts.
Designing and factious men invented unscrupulous stories of misconduct,
which imposed upon public credulity. Now that it has all passed, it is
ludicrous to remember the baseless fictions that were accepted as truths
beyond question. General Taylor did what few men have the moral courage to do under like circumstances. He steadily advanced in the performance of duty, never attempting to defend his conduct—turning neither
to the right nor to the left to repel calumny. He was untiring in labor,
denying himself every Social enjoyment . . .

"This noble contempt of defamation produced its legitimate and inevitable results. His adherence to the plain path of duty soon excited admiration. The idle tales which had been passed into the popular ear were
found to be utterly without foundation, and the General has become
the object of the people's admiration, to the same extent that he had been
the object of their execration . . ."[41]

What had Dick Taylor done to effect this change in public opinion and
merit the governor's unstinted praise?

In September 1862 he had scored a trifling victory by capturing the
Yankee garrison at the village of Des Allemands, about 30 miles from New
Orleans, but this was the first Confederate victory in Louisiana since the
fall of New Orleans and it did provide something to cheer about, as insignificant as it was.

By skirmishes here, attacks there, and withdrawals and advances in
the face of greatly superior troops; by captures of stores, guns, and am-
munitions, and even the Federal gunboats *Diana* and *Indianola;* by feints

at New Orleans, and efforts to relieve pressure on Vicksburg and Port Hudson from the west bank of the Mississippi; and by establishment of fortified works on the Red and Ouachita, General Dick Taylor had, by March 1864, worked wonders in his district.

Since his assumption of command in August 1862, Taylor had recovered large portions of Louisiana from Federal control and, above all, had restored the confidence of the people in their ability to maintain their reacquired authority. Every objective that Taylor had believed possible to achieve with the limited means at his disposal had been attained. Moreover, in the smashing victory at Berwick Bay, when the town of Brashear City (now Morgan City) was captured, on June 23, 1863, Taylor secured enough materials to serve his little army the rest of the year and in the Red River Campaign of 1864. More than 5000 rifles, a large amount of ammunition, a dozen guns and military stores worth two to three million dollars were taken. It was with confidence, therefore, that Dick Taylor awaited the next Federal move in Louisiana.[42]

IX

On March 7, 1863, Lieutenant General Edmund Kirby Smith assumed command of the Trans-Mississippi Department and Dick Taylor was once more under him. Briefly, in Virginia, Taylor's Louisiana Brigade had been a part of Smith's division.

Less than three months after General Smith's arrival in the area, rumors began to spread of dissension between him and General Taylor, although the department commander had, in forwarding Taylor's reports to Richmond, noted "the ability and energy displayed by that gallant officer in the discharge of his duties as district commander."

On June 3, Smith complained to Taylor that rumors from his headquarters were "calculated to injure me." Taylor had been opposed to the Vicksburg relief operation and had vigorously criticized General Smith's plan, but beyond that he had not contributed to the reported strained relations between them.

That these were, indeed, or were about to become, strained is evidenced by events in the fall. An Alexandria newspaper had published several attacks on General Smith and the latter wrote to Taylor asking for an explanation of them.[43]

In January 1864, Taylor and Smith disagreed over the constructions of the fortifications of Fort De Russy, on the Red River near Alexandria. Smith entrusted these to Major Henry T. Douglas, his engineering officer. Taylor resented the order of Smith that the "chief engineer will be held responsible for the character of the works erected," declaring that "when I applied for an engineer officer, I did not for a moment suppose that I surrendered my volition and all control of my district."

Kirby Smith recognized, even as the estrangement grew, Taylor's worth. "Taylor is the only district commander in whom I can rely; he is a good soldier and a man of ability, and could he only forget his habits and training as a politician, would be all that could be asked," he wrote in mid-January 1864.

A few days after this, Taylor complained to Smith that an inconsistency existed in the handling of deserters, because authority had been given a surbordinate without letting Taylor know about it. "I might then have avoided the spectacle of inconsistency recently presented to the army of deserters caught, tried, and shot by my orders while in the adjoining or perhaps same parish General Allen was granting amnesties and pardons."[44]

Relations between Dick Taylor and Kirby Smith worsened, it appears, during the next month, for on February 28, 1864, Taylor wrote Adjutant General Samuel Cooper, asking to be relieved from duty in the Trans-Mississippi Department. "As this is the first request of a personal character I have made to the Government," he wrote, "I indulge the hope that it may be favorably considered." A footnote in the Official Records states that no record of this letter was on the books of the War Department or Adjutant and Inspector General's Office. In any event, it was not acted upon, for Taylor continued as commander of the Louisiana District.[45]

Another note of discord appeared in correspondence between Taylor and Smith in late March 1864. On March 23, Taylor informed Smith that his "want of cavalry is lamentable" and "want for artillery horses is very great," but that "as soon as Green joins me I shall assume the offensive." Smith showed the letter to Duncan F. Kenner, Louisiana Congressman, who wrote to Taylor about the situation. On March 28, Taylor wrote to Smith again, stating that Kenner had said his letter of the twenty-third had been interpreted to mean that Taylor did not desire reinforcements. He continued:

"I can scarcely conceive how this could be interpreted into a declaration that I did not want re-inforcements . . . It is most unfortunate that my desire to relieve the lieutenant-general commanding from embarrassment should involve a delay in sending reinforcements to this army . . . If to obtain reinforcements it is necessary to set up a clamor . . . I cannot do it. I have given the lieutenant-general commanding the most hearty and cordial support in all cases. I have never uttered a complaint. I have been willing to shoulder all the responsibilities for the good of the cause, and feel deeply grieved that so little anxiety should be manifested to strengthen my forces. When Green joins me, I repeat, I shall fight a battle for Louisiana, be the forces of enemy what they may."

Smith replied sharply on March 31 that he accepted no responsibility for any interpretation of the letter, and continued:

"While I know you do not call for reinforcements unless compelled by necessity, that you appreciate the inadequate means at my disposal, and have always given me a hearty and cordial support, I object to the tone of your letter, which is an unjust complaint, founded on a private letter of a civilian. Mr. Kenner was given access to your letter . . . to relieve his anxiety in regard your position . . . certainly not expecting that he would write anything to impair or interrupt the harmony and good understanding that has always hitherto characterized our official relations."

On April 3, Taylor replied to General Smith, first quoting from Kenner's letter to him. "Although Mr. Kenner is a civilian, I considered his statements reliable," he stated, "and felt hurt that such a construction should have been placed on my language." He added:

"I certainly would have been the first commander possessing ordinary sense who voluntarily declined reinforcements while retreating before a superior foe . . . In reviewing my communication of the 28th ultimo I can find nothing disrespectful or improper, and I am fully impressed with what is due from a subordinate to his military superior."[46]

Meanwhile Union General Nathaniel P. Banks had launched his Red River Campaign and Taylor's heavily outnumbered army had fallen back to Mansfield, about 20 miles south of Shreveport. A modern biographer of General Kirby Smith has aptly said that "both generals could have spent their time more profitably in preparing to meet the advancing enemy rather than arguing whether or not Taylor had originally desired re-inforcements."[47]

The Federal advance was formidable, supported on the Red River by Admiral David Dixon Porter's fleet of gunboats, which had been able to pass the rapids, just above Alexandria. With Banks headed for Shreveport and General Frederick Steele in Arkansas marching to meet him, a stretch of 200 miles separated the two Union forces. On April 5, Kirby Smith wrote Taylor: "The battle must be decisive, whether with Steele or Banks . . . When we fight it must be for victory."

Believing that Taylor was in the greater danger, Kirby Smith sent several divisions to his support and when the Battle of Mansfield opened on April 8, Taylor had 8800 men in the field. Despite Banks's over-all superiority, the disposition of his troops was such that Taylor "invariably outnumbered the enemy at the fighting point." Having fought Banks in the Shenandoah with Stonewall Jackson, Taylor didn't have a very high regard for his adversary, despite the Federals' numerical superiority. "I will fight Banks if he has a million men," Taylor said to Prince de Polignac, one of his brigade commanders.[48]

At about 9 P.M. on April 7, Taylor sent a message to Kirby Smith, asking "if it accords with the views of the lieutenant-general commanding that I should hazard a general engagement at this point, and request an immediate answer, that I may receive it before day-light tomorrow morning." At 9:40 o'clock on April 8, Taylor sent another message to General Smith stating the enemy was advancing and that he had moved three divisions to the front. "I am not aware whether the enemy's whole force is in my front," he said. "If he means to move on Shreveport, I consider this as favorable a point to engage him as any other."

All morning, Taylor made his troop dispositions on ground which he had picked the previous day. This was along the edge of a wood, fronting a clearing about 800 yards wide by 1200 in length, through which passed the road to Pleasant Hill on which the Federals were advancing. On the far side of the field, opposite Taylor's position was a fence and beyond it a pine forest on rolling ground. Taylor's line, three miles from Mansfield, also covered a cross road leading to the Sabine, hence the Federal name, Sabine Cross Roads, for the battle.

Shortly before midday the Federals appeared at the edge of the pine forest, across the clearing. For several hours the enemy did nothing. Actually, General A. L. Lee was spending much of the time arguing with Banks on the danger of pushing forward, as Banks had ordered, until more troops had come up. Having ordered Lee to move on to Mansfield, Banks now reversed himself, and decided to wait.

Taylor grew impatient waiting for the enemy to develop his attack and so he decided, about 4 P.M., to take matters into his own hands. He ordered General Mouton, to open the attack on the Confederate left. "The charge by Mouton across the open was magnificent," Taylor wrote in his report. "With his little division, consisting of his own and Polignac's brigades, the field was crossed under murderous fire of the artillery and musketry, the woods was reached, and our little line sprang with a yell upon the foe." Mouton fell in this brave charge and many of his officers and men with him.

Sitting his horse, one leg hooked around the pommel, General Taylor calmly smoked a cigar, biding his time before committing his troops south of the road. As Mouton closed with the Federals, he gave the signal and Walker's Texas division moved forward to turn the Federal left, while the cavalry rode hard to strike the Union troops in their rear. The fighting was furious but Taylor's troop prevailed. The Federals broke, re-formed, retired, and re-formed again. "The enemy in vain formed new lines of battle on the wooded ridges, which are a feature of the country," reported Taylor. "Every line was swept away as soon as formed, and every gun taken as soon as put into position."

Soon the Federals were seized with panic, and outflanked on right and left, they were utterly routed. Their last stand was a ridge overlooking a small stream. Water, particularly after such a fight, was important to both sides and Taylor sent his men in again to drive the Federals off.

Once more, the fighting was severe, but the tired, weary Confederates gained possession of the creek and camped there for the night as the battered Federals retired another quarter of a mile.[49]

At 10:30 P.M. Taylor announced the victory to Kirby Smith—he had sent hopeful progress reports at 6 P.M. and 7:30 P.M.—reporting the capture of 2000 prisoners, 20 pieces of artillery, 200 wagons, and thousands of small arms. He added with confidence: "I shall continue to push the enemy with the utmost vigor."

Taylor won a smashing victory at Mansfield, and he actually had fought without instructions from Kirby Smith. In fact, during the battle, after Mouton's charge was launched, a courier rode up with a message from General Smith, which cautioned Taylor against a general engagement.

"Too late, sir," said Taylor after reading the message. "The battle is won."

Taylor then did something that few Confederate generals ever did. He provided, as General Dabney H. Maury put it, "the most conspicuous instance in which a Confederate commander having won a victory followed it up." Early on April 9, Taylor pursued Banks's retreating army 23 miles to Pleasant Hill and attacked him again. Despite heavy casualties at Mansfield, the morale of Taylor's command was superb. "There was no straggling, no plundering. The vast captured property was . . . turned over untouched to the proper officers," Taylor wrote.

His force increased by reinforcements to 12,000, Taylor threw his little army against Banks's 20,000 at Pleasant Hill, planning to roll up the Federal left with General Thomas J. Churchill's division. The plan did not work because of a miscalculation by Churchill, who did not form his line far enough to the right to outflank the Union left and he himself was outflanked. Taylor and Churchill later tried to outdo each other in shouldering the blame for not crushing Banks. In his report, Churchill states "that had my line extended half a mile more to the right, a brilliant success would have been achieved." Taylor, in *Destruction and Reconstruction*, commented: "A worthy, gallant gentleman, General Churchill, but not fortunate in war." Taylor blamed the Federal escape at Pleasant Hill on "my blunder," declaring that "instead of intrusting the important attack by my right to a subordinate, I should have conducted it myself . . . Herein lies the vast difference between genius and commonplace: one anticipates errors, the other discovers them too late."[50]

Tactically, Taylor lost the battle of Pleasant Hill. But strategically it was another smashing Confederate victory, for Banks began his retreat, forsaking his conquest of the Red River.

The twin battles of Mansfield and Pleasant Hill were hardly over before Taylor and Smith were feuding again. It started when Smith issued a general order, on April 19, 1864, paying "a well-merited tribute

to the endurance and valor" of the troops engaged in the "signal victories at Mansfield and Pleasant Hill." Taylor, replying on April 27, commented caustically on Smith's general order:

"This is the only instance within my recollection in which the officer
commanding an army was entirely ignored in an order of the kind. I note
this because it is singular in itself and in keeping with the treatment I
have lately experienced from the general commanding this department.
Whatever place my name is destined to occupy in the golden book of
the Republic I expect to engrave it there with the point of my sword.
I regret to report that my health is not good. A low fever has much
prostrated me, but I have been able to keep the saddle. The general
commanding the department may rest assured that I will persevere to
the end. No injustice, no unkindness, even from a quarter when I had
some reason to expect the reverse, will turn me from the great work
before me. The cause for which I have sacrificed fortune is paramount,
and shall have my life if need be."[51]

Smith, on a later occasion, praised the army and its commander, but in
including Taylor he did not mention his name: "No need of praise is too
great for that gallant little army and its skillful and energetic chief."

On April 28, in a long letter to Kirby Smith, Taylor berated his commander for stripping his army of troops when it had a real chance to
destroy Banks's army. "For more than a year," he wrote, "I have supported you, even when your policy was fatally wrong . . . The events
of the past few weeks have so filled me with discouragement that I much
fear I cannot do my whole duty under your command, and I ask that you
take steps to relieve me as soon as it can be done without injury to the
service." Smith returned the letter to Taylor with this indorsement:
"This communication is not only improper but unjust. I cannot believe
but that it was written in a moment of irritation or sickness."

Taylor again charged, on May 18, that the withdrawal of Walker's
division from him "prevented the capture of Banks's army and destruction of Porter's fleet." He added: "I feel bitterly about this, because my
army has been robbed of the just measure of its glory and the country of
the most brilliant and complete success of the war." Five days later, Taylor complained that for a year he had asked for artillery horses but that
since his arrival in Louisiana, "I have not received a horse for my batteries from department headquarters . . . not withstanding my constant
appeals and the urgent wants of my artillery."

On May 24, Taylor delivered another blast at General Smith, denouncing the existing "system of bureaucracy" in the Trans-Mississippi Department. "The rage for what is termed organization has proceeded so
far that we are like a disproportioned garment—all ruffles and no shirt.
The number of bureaus now existing in this department, and the army of
employes attached to them, would do honor to St. Petersburg or Paris . . .

Requisitions for the most important articles upon which depend the fate of a campaign are lost in a mingled maze of red tape and circumlocution."

Smith replied, on May 26, to Taylor's letters of May 18 and May 24, calling the complaint in the former "unjust . . . attributed to your ill-health and that irritability of disposition which at Mansfield, on April 10, you regretted and begged me to bear with." The second letter from Taylor, Kirby Smith found, "was written in the same tone and spirit" and was "objectionable and improper."

On June 5, Kirby Smith wrote Taylor at length, itemizing the latter's "inaccurate and unjust statements" and denying, answering or ignoring them, one by one. The same day, Taylor answered Kirby Smith's letter of May 26, assuring him that he had not dealt in complaints but in facts. He criticized Smith's operations in Arkansas as "a hideous failure" which turned the fruits of Mansfield "to dust and ashes." In conclusion, Taylor declared:

"The roads to Saint Louis and New Orleans should now be open to us. Your strategy has riveted the fetters on both . . . the same regard for duty which led me to throw myself between you and popular indignation and quietly take the blame of your errors compels me to tell you the truth, however objectionable to you. The grave errors you have committed in the recent campaign may be repeated if the unhappy circumstances are not kept before you. After the desire to serve my country, I have none more ardent than to be relieved from longer serving under your command."

This was the last straw. Regardless of the merits of Taylor's complaints and charges, there is no question but that he was guilty of insubordination. Reluctantly Kirby Smith put Taylor under arrest on June 10, relieving him of his command and ordering him to Natchitoches to "await the pleasure of the President of the Confederate States." Oddly, on the same date, a joint resolution of the Confederate Congress thanked Taylor, his officers and men "for the brilliant successes . . . over the enemy in Louisiana during the past year and particularly for the victories at Mansfield and Pleasant Hill."

On June 11, 1864, Kirby Smith gathered all the controversial correspondence and sent it to President Jefferson Davis with a covering letter:

"I would have arrested General Taylor on the receipt of his first letter, but acknowledging his merits as soldier and feeling kindly towards him, I passed it by. I have since borne and forborne with him with a self control that has been sustained only by love of country and a desire of promoting her best interests. General Taylor's letters are improper and disrespectful . . . They are untrue throughout . . ."[52]

If Taylor had thought about it, he would have realized that his feud with Kirby Smith was very like the Davis-Joe Johnston quarrel, which he had tried to patch by appeals to both men. What Taylor said about them applied admirably to himself and Kirby Smith: "Each misjudged the other to the end."[53]

x

Dick Taylor was inclined to forget, in after years, that he had been arrested by Kirby Smith. In *Destruction and Reconstruction,* in which his criticism of General Smith is much more temperate than were his letters, he states: ". . . I applied for relief from duty. After several applications this was granted, and with my wife and two surviving children I retired to . . . Natchitoches."

Friends rallied to Taylor's support as soon as the word got around that Kirby Smith had shelved him. "Our people are greatly chagrined at the loss of General Taylor's services," Judge Barthes Egan wrote former Governor Moore. ". . . We cannot get a general who loves Louisiana more ardently or who could better use for her defense all the resources at his command." A gentleman of Alexandria, M. C. Manning, wrote General Braxton Bragg in Richmond that "the people of this state cling to Taylor as the very sheet anchor of their salvation."

Taylor himself wrote Bragg on July 4, 1864, begging him to come to the Trans-Mississippi and take over from Kirby Smith. "Should the war continue another season this country will inevitably be lost under present management." Taylor added that after two years' hard service his career west of the Mississippi was over. "If no suitable place can be found for me on the other side I shall most cheerfully retire into the ranks."

By this time, President Davis, his Cabinet and advisers were familiar with the Taylor-Smith feud. It wasn't until later in July that it became a topic of gossip. On July 26, 1864, Mary Boykin Chesnut wrote in her diary: ". . . Dick Taylor and Kirby Smith have quarrelled. One would think we had a big enough quarrel on hand for one while." That the feuding generals made conversation for the Richmond salons and tea tables for quite a while is evident from Mrs. Chesnut's diary entry a month later, on August 23: ". . . At Mrs. Izard's, met there a clever Mrs. Calhoun. She is a violent partisan of Dick Taylor; says Dick Taylor does the work and Kirby Smith gets the credit for it."[54]

Meanwhile, on June 14 at Pine Mountain near Atlanta, General Leonidas Polk was killed, creating a vacancy for a lieutenant general east of the Mississippi. Taylor's promotion to that rank had been urged as far back as December 26, 1863, when Governor Moore sent President Davis a glowing account of the general's efforts in Louisiana. On February 4, 1864, Congressman Lucius J. Dupré wrote the President "cheerfully" endorsing everything the governor had said about Taylor. Davis sent

Governor Moore's letter to the Secretary of War "for consideration & advice." Secretary James A. Seddon returned the document to the President with this notation: "I fully recognized the merits of Genl Taylor whose Generalship has been continually displayed in his operations in La. but unless he command a Corps or is placed in charge of a Department I have no authority of how to recommend his promotion." This endorsement was dated April 15, 1864, the day before Governor (former General) Henry Watkins Allen of Louisiana added his voice in Dick Taylor's behalf, without, as he said, "the knowledge of Maj. Genl. Taylor."

On this same day, April 16, 1864, Kirby Smith demonstrated in a letter to President Davis that whatever his personal differences with Taylor he did not allow them to blind him to his surbordinate's worth. He stated that anticipating any contingency in the department, he had issued an order appointing Taylor a lieutenant general. "Of the three District Commanders Majors General Magruder, Price & Taylor, the latter is the junior & the only one of the three I consider suited to take charge of . . . the Department. He is also for his past services & eminent qualifications, justly entitled to the promotion. Should the contingency arise to which I referred, the good of our country & the cause demand that he should succeed to the command."[55]

On July 18, Taylor was assigned to command General Polk's Department of Alabama, Mississippi, and East Louisiana, with the rank of lieutenant general to date from April 8, 1864. Orders came six days later for Taylor to cross the Mississippi with the infantry of his command. Taylor felt that crossing troops at that time was impractical and asked for authority to leave the troop movement for a later date. This Kirby Smith refused and so Taylor made an effort in mid-August to cross his two divisions, but gave up when his ranks were thinned by desertion and Yankee movements on the opposite bank indicated his intentions had been detected. Finally he got authority to cross by himself and on September 6, 1864, Lieutenant General Dick Taylor assumed control of his Department at Meridian, Mississippi.[56]

Taylor knew then, as he later wrote, that Southern hopes of victory had evaporated. "Upon what foundations the civil authorities of the Confederacy rested their hopes of success, after the campaign of 1864 fully opened, I am unable to say," wrote Taylor. "But their commanders in the field, whose rank and position enabled them to estimate the situation, fought simply to afford statesmanship an opportunity to mitigate the sorrows of inevitable defeat."

Two of the three Confederate lieutenant generals who had not attended West Point came face to face in Meridian when Nathan Bedford Forrest called upon the new district commander. They made a profound impression on each other. "He's the biggest man in the lot," Forrest said of Taylor. "If we'd had more like him, we would have licked the Yankees long ago." Taylor predicted rightly of Forrest that "to generations yet unborn, his name will be a 'household word.' "[57]

Taylor made frequent trips around his department—to Mobile, Selma, Talladega—and he went to Montgomery to confer with President Davis, where he urged that Beauregard be put in command of all the Confederate forces in the west. As he traveled, usually with only one staff officer, if not alone, and unknown to the people, he could clearly evaluate the morale in his district. The citizens, he discovered, "were universally depressed and disheartened." Accordingly, he couldn't disguise from Davis his conviction that the best the South could do was prolong the fight until the spring. Davis was distressed at hearing such gloomy sentiments from his brother-in-law.

In November, when Sherman began his March to the Sea, Taylor was ordered into Georgia with all the troops available in his department to assume command of the Confederate forces opposing Sherman. Inasmuch as he had no troops to spare, Taylor went to Georgia alone. He spent two weeks there and then returned to his own Department.[58]

General John Bell Hood had launched his ill-fated Tennessee campaign and his army, reeling back from the blood bath at Franklin and the crushing defeat at Nashville, reached Tupelo, Mississippi. On January 17, 1865, Taylor was ordered to assume command of Hood's shattered army, the latter having been relieved by his own request. "This was my first view of a beaten army," wrote Taylor, ". . . and a painful sight it was."

The days of the Confederacy were running out. Soon Mobile fell, soon the swarming Federals were everywhere and the Confederates to oppose them were inadequate in numbers, material, and supplies. First came Appomattox, with Lee surrendering to Grant on April 9. Joe Johnston next surrendered to Sherman in North Carolina on April 26. Only one Confederate army, skeleton though it was, remained in being east of the Mississippi River and that was Dick Taylor's command.

As early as April 17, Union General Edward R. S. Canby had offered the same terms of surrender to Taylor as Grant had offered to Lee. Taylor asked, instead, for a truce. During the first week of May negotiations were completed and Dick Taylor surrendered. "On the 8th of May, 1865, at Citronelle, forty miles north of Mobile, I delivered the epilogue of the great drama in which I had played a humble part," wrote Taylor. "The terms of surrender demanded and granted were consistent with the honor of our arms; and it is due to the memory of General Canby to add that he was ready with suggestions to soothe our military pride." On May 26, in New Orleans, Generals Simon B. Buckner and Sterling Price, and Colonel J. L. Brent, surrendered the Trans-Mississippi to Canby. At this surrender, at the Confederates' request, and with Canby's cheerful assent, was Dick Taylor. He could rightfully say:

"So, from the Charleston Convention to this point, I shared the fortunes of the Confederacy, and can say, as Grattan did of Irish freedom, that I 'sat by its cradle and followed its hearse.' "[59]

XI

Dick Taylor returned to New Orleans penniless after the war. He had his two horses, and that was all. One of the horses he gave to the livery-man to pay his bill and the other he sold to pay the passage of his wife and children from the Red River to the city.

His plantation, "Fashion," had been despoiled and confiscated and he, as other returning Confederates, had to rely upon friends for food, shelter, and financial assistance.

Not long after the surrender, Taylor went to Washington where many of his father's old Whig supporters, having long since turned Republican, were in high place. He sought their help to get Jefferson Davis released from prison and to aid other civilian friends who had fallen into Federal hands. "Lee, Johnston, and I, with our officers and men, were at large, protected by the terms of our surrender—terms which General Grant had honorably prevented the civil authorities from violating," wrote Taylor. "If Mr. Davis had sinned, we all were guilty, and I could not rest without making an attempt for his relief."[60]

Taylor, as a parolee, got the necessary permission to travel and a friend in Washington got him to the White House to see President Andrew Johnson. In his book Taylor gives some splendid capsule comments on the powerful Washington figures, on many of whom he called in Jefferson Davis's behalf. What Taylor wanted at first was permission to visit Davis at Fortress Monroe.

President Johnson was "a saturnine man" who had "breathed fire and hemp against the South," but now appeared to have "somewhat abated his wolfish desire for vengeance." Taylor answered his questions about the South and the temper of the people and spoke for some of his friends. He left the matter of Mr. Davis for a later occasion and asked permission to return.

Secretary of State William H. Seward, an old friend of Zachary Taylor, greeted the ex-Confederate general as "the returned prodigal" while Grant, whom Taylor had known in the Mexican War as "a modest, amiable but by no means promising lieutenant," was a frequent caller, "full of kindness."

Taylor's calls at the White House were frequent and fruitless. President Johnson spoke about Southern affairs, but avoided Taylor's request. The latter soon discovered that Johnson "always postponed action, and was of an obstinate, suspicious temper." Finally Johnson told Taylor it would spare him embarrassment if he could induce Thaddeus Stevens and Henry Winter Davis of the House and Charles Sumner of the Senate to recommend the permission to visit Jefferson Davis.

"I immediately addressed myself to this unpleasant task," said Taylor. He called on Stevens first and was received "with as much civility as he was capable of." After denouncing the Constitution, the white people of the South and the President, Thaddeus Stevens told Taylor "it was silly to refuse . . . permission to visit Jefferson Davis, but he would not say so publicly, as he had no desire to relieve Johnson of responsibility." Stevens, who later led the fight to impeach the President, had already charted his course.

Taylor found Henry Winter Davis "even more inaccessible to sentiment than Thaddeus Stevens" and others "too numerous and too insignificant to particularize" were sought out. Hopeless of assistance from members of the House, Taylor then called on Senator Sumner. Taylor wrote of his visit:

"A rebel, a slave-driver, and, without the culture of Boston, ignorant, I was an admirable vessel into which he could pour the inexhaustible stream of his acquired eloquence . . . He seemed over-educated—had retained, not digested, his learning; and beautiful flowers of literature were attached to him by filaments of memory, as lovely orchids to sapless sticks . . . He . . . became the victim of his own metaphors, mistaking them for facts. He had the irritable vanity and weak nerves of a woman, and was bold to rashness in speculation, destitute as he was of the ordinary masculine sense of responsibility. Yet I hold him to have been the purest and most sincere man of his party . . . Without vindictiveness, he forgave his enemies as soon as they were overthrown . . ."

The only thing Dick Taylor got from his visit to Sumner, however, was a single brilliant page in *Destruction and Reconstruction*. Congressional assistance denied him, Taylor devoted himself to importuning President Johnson, until at last he was granted permission to visit Jefferson Davis.

The brothers-in-law "met in silence, with grasp of hands." Finally, Davis spoke: "This is kind, but no more than I expected of you." Taylor found the Confederate President "pallid, worn, gray, bent, feeble, suffering from inflammation of the eyes . . . a painful sight to a friend." He told of his efforts to see Davis and Davis told him of his cell life and they discussed many things about the South, Taylor "passing over things that would have grieved him."[61] Despite Taylor's efforts, Davis was not released until 1867.

Having discharged his duties to his imprisoned friends, Taylor returned to Louisiana. He saw, without approval, the bloody race riot in New Orleans in the summer of 1866, when many Negroes were killed.

Frequently, he was in Washington on behalf of Southern rights in the bitter days of Reconstruction. He actively canvassed for Samuel J. Tilden in the election of 1876, having previously swung Southern support to the New Yorker in the Democratic Convention.

By this time, however, he had spent several years in Europe to conduct business for some capitalists. He was lionized in England as a friend of the Prince of Wales, and established abroad an enormous reputation as a skilled whist player and a brilliant conversationalist. Marshal Mac-Mahon in France and Bismarck and Von Moltke in Germany were his hosts. Upon the death of his wife in 1875, Taylor and his family joined his sister in Winchester, Va., where thirteen years earlier the Louisiana Brigade had had one of its finest hours. There he wrote *Destruction and Reconstruction*, published shortly before his death in New York on April 12, 1879.

"He was only 53 years old when he died—young enough for a great career," wrote his friend, General D. H. Maury. "It seems probable that had he lived he would have been placed where his wonderful acquirements and endowments might have greatly served his people."[62]

2

Beau Sabreur of the Valley:

GENERAL TURNER ASHBY

I

STONEWALL JACKSON sat in his quarters at Port Republic, Virginia, entertaining a distinguished prisoner of war, Sir Percy Wyndham, British officer and soldier of fortune.

Sir Percy, who had served with Garibaldi in Italy, had cast his lot with the Union and commanded the 1st New Jersey Cavalry in the Shenandoah Valley operations. He had frequently boasted that he would bag the audacious rebel, Turner Ashby, and he had set out on June 6, 1862, to do it. But instead of bagging Turner Ashby, Colonel Wyndham himself was bagged by Ashby in a neat ambuscade at Harrisonburg, a few miles from Port Republic.

Wyndham had been furious with "impotent rage, disappointed hopes and wounded pride," as he marched to the rear under guard, but by the time young Major Kyd Douglas escorted him to Stonewall Jackson's headquarters he had cooled off considerably. On the way to the rear he had encountered an old comrade in arms in Italy, Major Roberdeau Wheat of the Louisiana Tigers, and the warm welcome he received restored to him the accustomed "nonchalant air of one who had wooed Dame Fortune too long to be cast down by her frowns."

The American Civil War, be it remembered, was "a gentlemen's war," and it was sometimes the most logical thing in the world for officers taken prisoner to receive from their captors the same courtesies due them in normal social intercourse. Accordingly, Jackson had received the captured British officer with civility and had engaged Sir Percy in conversation. They had been speaking some time when a knock on the door called the general outside. There Stonewall Jackson received staggering, bitter news: Turner Ashby was dead.

Just a few hours after he had captured Sir Percy Wyndham, General Ashby had directed another daring operation against the Federals. His horse was shot from under him and as he led his men on foot he was killed, pierced through the heart.

Jackson called an aide and instructed him to dismiss Sir Percy. "I cannot see him further tonight," said Stonewall as he went in grief to his private quarters. Later, Jackson scribbled in pencil on the margin of a newspaper a short note to Colonel John D. Imboden: "Poor Ashby is dead. He fell gloriously . . . I know you will join me in mourning the loss of our friend, one of the noblest of men and soldiers in the Confederate Army."[1]

When Stonewall Jackson learned that Ashby's body had been borne to Port Republic and lay in state with an honor guard, he went to pay silent tribute to his friend and brave surbordinate. Admitted alone into the room, Jackson remained for some time and then left "with a solemn and elevated countenance."

All night the soldiers of the Valley Army trooped in and out of the house, paying their last respects to Turner Ashby. Deep was the sorrow of all, but to the men of his command, Ashby's death was a personal tragedy. "Each felt that he had lost one who had honored him with his friendship," said Chaplain James B. Avirett, "and affection paid its tribute in scalding tears." Some of the men passed in silence, some suppressed sobs, and now and then one murmured: "Noble Ashby! Gone! Gone!" Private Black, one of Ashby's best scouts, gazed silently at his dead chief for a moment and then, in a broken voice, he said: "We shall miss you mightily, General—we shall miss you in the camp!—we shall miss you as we go out on the scout! But we shall miss you most, General, when we go out to . . ." He never finished the sentence. Sobbing convulsively, Private Black hurried from the house.

Even the Federals held Turner Ashby's "name and fame . . . in reverence," and one of Frémont's officers declared: "When we found the brave Ashby was slain, there was no rejoicing in our camps, though by it we had gained a great advantage, and I have not yet heard an unkind or injurious word by either the officers or soldiers of our forces . . ."

In the skirmish in which Ashby fell, Union Lieutenant Colonel Thomas Kane of the Pennsylvania Bucktails was captured. In chatting with some Confederate officers before the news of Ashby's death came in, he said:

"I have today saved the life of one of the most gallant officers in either army, Gen. Ashby; for I admire him as much as you can possibly do. His figure is familiar to me, inasmuch as I have seen it often on the skirmish line. He was today within fifty yards of my skirmishers, sitting on his horse as if unconscious of his danger. I saw three of them raise their rifles to fire, but I succeeded in stopping two of them, and struck up the gun of the third as it went off. Ashby is too brave to die in that way."[2]

When Ashby's funeral cortege, escorted by officers and men of his command, moved the next day toward Charlottesville, Union prisoners along the road stood with uncovered heads in silent respect.

Young Major Douglas voiced the sentiment of the Valley Army when he wrote a young lady of Ashby's loss: "Thus died one of the finest, most attractive men I ever knew & I got to know him very intimately & one of the bravest, most chivalrous, dashing & successful Cavalry Officers the country has ever seen."

It remained for Stonewall Jackson to sum up best the considerable talents of Turner Ashby:

"An official report is not an appropriate place for more than a passing notice of the distinguished dead, but the close relation which General Ashby bore to my command for most of the previous twelve month, will justify me in saying that as a partisan officer I never knew his superior; his daring was proverbial; his powers of endurance almost incredible; his tone of character heroic, and his sagacity almost intuitive in divining the purposes and movements of the enemy."[3]

II

The family of Turner Ashby, which traced its English origins to the Norman Conquest, was established in Virginia in 1635.

Four generations of Ashby's ancestors held military commissions in Virginia and fought in the Colonial wars, the Revolution and the War of 1812. The third of six children, and the second of three sons, Turner was born to Colonel Turner and Dorothy Green Ashby at "Rose Bank," his father's home in Fauquier County, on October 23, 1828.

Turner Ashby's formal schooling was slight. First tutored at home, he later attended a private school operated by a neighbor, Major Ambler. A biographer and kinsman said that Turner Ashby's education was the usual one received by boys of the locality who did not go to college. He learned to read, write, spell, do arithmetic, and was taught the fundamental branches of knowledge. His scholarship was negligible, but he learned the more practical things that a boy in the country has to learn, especially how to ride and shoot. One who knew him during the war said: "His intellect, outside his profession, was rather mediocre than otherwise, and he wrote so badly that few of his productions are worth preserving."[4]

As a small boy, Turner became an expert horseman, and the reputation that he later gained as a superb rider was well established in his youth. One of his schoolmates at Major Ambler's recalled that "whenever a colt was found too wild and vicious to be ridden by any one else in the neighborhood, it was his pleasure to mount and tame him." As he grew to maturity Turner Ashby rode in the hunts and participated in the tournaments which were popular in his section of Virginia. In the latter, he was recognized as "the most distinguished of his associates . . . with a dash and fire few young men have ever possessed . . . for it was seldom that he failed to carry off the first honors . . . His superb management of his horse, his daring feats, and his grace were the marvel of his day."

Financial reverses in 1853, when Turner Ashby was twenty-five, caused his mother to sell "Rose Bank" and go to live with one of her married daughters. Her youngest son Richard, an inseparable companion of Turner, went with her, but then set out for the Western frontier, where he remained until the Civil War broke out. Turner, who had done well in the mercantile business, bought a place high up in the hills not far from his old home.

When the Manassas Gap Railroad was being built in the middle 1850s, the large number of imported laborers laying the road bed frequently got out of hand and made trouble for the people of the vicinity. To act as a vigilante group, a small company of cavalry was organized by Ashby and the young men of the neighborhood flocked to join. When the road was completed and the laborers were gone, the cavalry company did not disband. Indeed, new additions increased the roster. And Turner Ashby took great pride in it. As for his men they took pride in serving under so brilliant a horseman as Ashby.

Ashby got into local politics and, running as a Whig in a predominantly Democratic district, was unsuccessful in his bid for a seat in the Virginia Legislature. Although a stout defender of States' Rights, he was opposed to the idea of secession and up to the time of John Brown's raid, he had no stomach for a war between the North and the South.

When John Brown and his twenty-one followers seized the Federal Arsenal at Harpers Ferry on the night of October 16, 1859, the alarm spread rapidly throughout the Virginia countryside. Fears of a rebellion of the slaves under the impetus of Brown's action sent the Virginia militia and the United States Marines rushing to Harpers Ferry. Turner Ashby's mounted company from Fauquier County, hastily called together the next day, rode over the mountains to join the assembled forces.

Mounted on his handsome white stallion, Turner Ashby made an impressive figure, one which in less than two years would be familiar to all the people along the upper Potomac and the great Valley of Virginia. There wasn't much that Ashby and his men did at Harpers Ferry. They performed picket and patrol duty and Captain Ashby (captain without commission) met for the first time Robert E. Lee, Thomas Jonathan Jackson, and James Ewell Brown Stuart, soon to be universally known as Jeb.

John Brown was captured on October 18 and taken to Charlestown for trial. Ashby continued to patrol the Potomac but on December 2, when Brown was hanged, he and his company were on hand. In a few weeks, the scare of a servile uprising blew over and, by January 1860, Ashby and his men returned to the pursuits of peace—at least for a while.[5]

In keeping with the custom of the day, Turner Ashby frequently entertained at his home, "Wolf's Crag." One incident, after the John Brown affair, but before the coming of the war, indicates the spirit and temper of the young man. He gave a reception on the occasion of a tournament and invited a neighboring family and their guest, a young man from the North, who was paying court to the daughter of the house.

A rejected suitor of the girl took occasion to approach this gentleman, while he was talking to the young lady, and directed toward her a question:

"Isn't it a sublime piece of impudence for a Yankee and a Black Republican to come down here now and accept the hospitality of a Virginia gentleman after all that has happened?"

The young lady was equal to the insult. "You should be the last person to criticize the catholicity of my father's hospitality. You have profited by his indisposition to draw social lines too sharply. You have been received by him as a guest on several occasions."

Stung by the rebuke the young man turned on his heels. The Northerner, fearing that the young man might be reflecting popular opinion, decided to leave Ashby's home. In the cloak room, he was accosted by the man: "What I have just said had reference to you and was meant to be insulting."

The Northerner, in his first encounter of this kind, had no inclination for an affair of honor. But he knew that his proposal to the young lady would be scornfully rejected by her family should he fail to show qualities of manhood. Whereupon, he struck the other across the cheek with his glove. Other gentlemen stepped in to prevent a fist fight, but in moments a challenge had been given and accepted and arrangements made for an immediate settlement by the light of torches in a grove not far from the house.

Just as the party was preparing to leave, Turner Ashby entered the cloak room in a rage. He had heard that trouble was brewing and burst into the room, determined that no guest of his should be insulted. Addressing himself to the young man, he said in a low, but deliberate voice:

"What is the time set for our meeting?"

"I am to fight Mr. C.D. immediately."

"I beg your pardon," snapped Ashby, "but Mr. C.D. has nothing to do with this affair. He came to my house tonight as my guest. When I invited him to come the invitation was Turner Ashby's word of honor that he should be treated here as a gentleman . . . I am sorry to have to explain these points of good breeding to you . . . but you have shown your ignorance of them by insult to my guest. The insult is mine, not his, to resent . . . If you are not prepared to make a proper and satisfactory apology at once, both to my guest and me, you must fight Turner Ashby, and the time and place agreed upon will answer as well as any other. What do you say, sir?"

This was more than the young man bargained for. He stammered the excuse that he had been drinking too freely and agreed to sign the two apologies that Ashby had written out.[6]

III

The election of Abraham Lincoln on November 6, 1860, took the secession movement out of the talking and agitating stage and brought the people of the United States face to face with reality.

South Carolina began the parade of Southern states out of the Union on December 20, 1860, and by February 4, 1861, six other slave states had joined her to form the Confederate States of America.

A fact that is frequently overlooked is that when the Confederacy came into being at Montgomery, Alabama, and Jefferson Davis was elected provisional president, there were actually more slave states in the Union than out of it. Still unwilling to break their ties with the nation were Delaware, Maryland, North Carolina, Tennessee, Kentucky, Missouri, Arkansas, and Virginia.

Turner Ashby, a strong Union man and fundamentally opposed to the concept of secession, voted for John Bell, the Constitutional Union Party candidate, who carried Virginia by a margin of 358 votes over the out-and-out secessionist, John C. Breckinridge. That the majority—almost 58 per cent, in fact—of the people of Virginia opposed secession and desired a peaceful solution of the crisis within the framework of the Constitution and the Union, is evident from the combined votes for Bell, Stephen A. Douglas, and Lincoln, which totaled 92,900 to Breckinridge's 74,323.[7]

However, after the firing on Fort Sumter on April 12, 1861, and President Lincoln's call upon the states for 75,000 volunteers to suppress the rebellion, sentiment in Virginia changed. Among those now supporting secession rather than be party to the coercion of Virginia's sister Southern states, was Turner Ashby. When Virginia passed its ordinance of secession on April 17, 1861, Ashby had already called his company together. Orders came quickly, directing him and his men to Harpers Ferry, where Federal authorities had destroyed or burned government property before evacuating the town.

Harpers Ferry is situated at the junction of the Shenandoah and Potomac Rivers and because of the mountains on all sides, it was not an easy place to defend. Its chief importance lay in the facts that the Baltimore & Ohio Railroad ran through the town and that across the Potomac from it, on the Maryland side, was the Chesapeake and Ohio Canal. Possession of the town by the Confederates cut the rail communications between Washington and the West.

At the head of his company, Captain Ashby rode into Harpers Ferry on April 19 and reported to Colonel Kenton Harper, who was in charge of the Virginia militia assembling there. So impressive was Turner Ashby astride his horse—he had two spirited, beautifully trained stallions, one milk white, the other coal black—that many who served with him saw more of the horseman and less of the man. Everyone agreed that he had no superior in the saddle. Ashby was dark, almost like an Arab, and he had a long flowing beard—some said jet black, others dark brown—that reached to his chest. His eyes which lighted up with excitement were also dark. He was not a big man, being of medium height with a lithe frame. He had boundless energy and tremendous endurance.

Ashby was assigned to picket and guard duty along the Potomac from Harpers Ferry to Point of Rocks, twelve miles down stream, where a railroad bridge crossed the river. To his command were added several companies of infantry and a battery of six guns under John Imboden. Ashby was constantly in the saddle. "He would come and go like a dream," a contemporary recorded, ". . . deaf to every caution."[8]

Once, to get information of the enemy across the river, Ashby borrowed a homespun suit from a farmer, hired a plow horse and he entered the enemy's lines as a horse doctor, his saddlebag full of rustic remedies for spavin or ringbone. During the night he returned to his command with much valuable information.

On April 28, Colonel Thomas J. Jackson, a professor from Virginia Military Institute, was assigned to command all the troops at and around Harpers Ferry, with instructions to train the men and organize them into battalions and regiments. On May 24, Brigadier General Joseph E. Johnston assumed command at Harpers Ferry, relieving Jackson. Several days prior to this, Lieutenant Colonel George Deas, Inspector General of the Confederate Army, inspected the troops at Harpers Ferry. His report was high in praise of what he saw in Turner Ashby's command:

". . . I visited the position opposite the Point of Rocks, distant twelve miles from this point, where Captain Ashby, of the Virginia cavalry, an excellent officer, is stationed, with two companies of cavalry, six pieces of light artillery, and a company of riflemen, together with some men from Maryland, only a part of whom are armed. His cavalry is employed in active reconnaissance of the surrounding country, and his artillery has complete command of the bridge crossing the Potomac, the piers of which are mined, and can be instantly destroyed, in case of necessity;

in addition, he holds possession of the road at the Point of Rocks in such a manner as to prevent the passage of a train."

Colonel Jackson had given Ashby instructions to break the railroad whenever he considered it necessary for his defense and General Johnston had repeated the order immediately on taking command. On May 26, Ashby reported to Johnston that, on the basis of information received that morning, he was about "to throw a mass of rock upon it by blasting."[9]

Not long after this, Ashby became involved in correspondence with General Johnston over the status of his command. Upon his arrival at Harpers Ferry, he had been assigned to a cavalry regiment put together from volunteer companies by Colonel Angus McDonald, a West Point graduate of the class of 1817. And though Ashby later went on detached duty, he considered himself a part of McDonald's regiment, which would soon enter the Confederate service as the 7th Virginia Cavalry.

General Johnston ordered Ashby to report to Colonel J. E. B. Stuart, who commanded Johnston's cavalry at Harpers Ferry, but prior to this Ashby had been ordered by Colonel McDonald to join his own regiment.

On May 27, Ashby wrote Johnston that he had just received orders from Stuart to report to him and also Johnston's order confirming it. He reminded Johnston that he belonged to a different regiment from Stuart and was on duty "only twelve miles from the Colonel of my own regiment, who has already issued orders for me to report to him as soon as I am relieved from duty on detached service." He reminded Johnston that he had been taking direct orders from Colonel Jackson and had been led to believe in a conversation with Johnston on the day he took command "that I was to receive all orders from you direct, and was to make reports to you direct."

On June 5, Colonel McDonald and his command moved from state service into that of the Confederacy and he was ordered to report to General Johnston to secure "such troops of horse as he can spare from his command" and proceed to the Cheat River Bridge and "if practicable destroy the same, and as much of the road, bridges, and tunnels as you can accomplish."

Colonel McDonald presented his order to Joe Johnston on June 7, but the latter told him "he could not spare a single man."

On June 10, Ashby made application verbally to Johnston to be permitted to join McDonald's regiment and followed it up the next day with a short note. Johnston replied the same day:

"With every desire to oblige and gratify you, my views of the public interest compel me to adhere to the opinion I expressed yesterday, that I cannot, without injury to the body of troops under my command, relieve you from duty in this district . . . But permit me to ask you to consider, how few of us are serving in our own sections of the State;

and how small the body of cavalry under my command is, compared with the service required of it."

Ashby replied on June 12 with a long letter, expressing resentment that Johnston should assume that his devotion and that of his men to "the great cause in which we have staked and are still willing to stake our lives . . . is cribbed within the *section which contains our homes!*" Nothing he had said or written justified such an interpretation. He and his men came into the service as volunteers. "No press-gang captured and compelled us to bear arms in defense of our State." He and his men desired to serve as volunteers in the form and manner in which they entered service. "We protest against being captured by military technicalities, and bound in bonds which must cramp, if not crush the spirit which voluntarily sprang forward to serve our State." He could emancipate himself, Ashby avowed, by resigning, but duty compelled him to protect, as their captain, the rights of his officers and men. He could not expect to secure Johnston's confidence and respect "if, as a soldier and an officer, I should show myself so dull as not to prize, or so craven as not to assert and vindicate the rights of my command as well as my own." He reminded Johnston that the Governor of Virginia had turned over to the Confederacy state troops "expressly by regiments."

On receiving an order to destroy the bridge and abandon his position at Point of Rocks, Ashby said the order did not instruct him to report to Johnston, and, perhaps, that would have been the proper time to have reported for orders to his regimental commander. "But, desiring to manifest all respect to your authority, I felt called upon to report that I had executed your order—not dreaming that I should thereby so sever myself and my company from my regiment and the military district within which it is bound to do duty."

On June 15, Johnston gave Ashby permission to join McDonald and in a cordial note the next day, terminated the discussion:

". . . I assure you that the knowledge that you were between us and the enemy made me sleep very soundly last night; and that your presence among the troops, under my command, would always have such an effect.

"Wherever I may be serving under circumstances agreeable to you, be assured that it would be a matter both of professional and personal gratification, to be associated with you."[10]

Shortly after Ashby joined McDonald, the latter urged Secretary of War Leroy Pope Walker on June 25 to promote him to lieutenant colonel. "As to Captain Ashby, I need not speak of his qualities," he wrote, "for already he is known as one of the best partisan leaders in the service. Himself a thorough soldier, he is eminently qualified to command."

But someone else had already spoken for Turner Ashby's promotion, perhaps Joe Johnston himself. For on June 23—two days before Mc-

Donald's request—Ashby received his promotion to lieutenant colonel with orders to report to General Johnston. "The General directs me to say, that he will leave it optional with yourself, either to remain with Colonel McDonald, or report to himself," wrote Johnston's adjutant.[11]

Colonel McDonald established his headquarters at Romney, in what is now West Virginia. About forty-five miles west of Winchester, Romney was on the Baltimore & Ohio Railroad and McDonald's mission was to destroy as much of the tracks and its bridges as he was able, especially the heavy structure over Cheat River. Dividing his command, McDonald sent Turner Ashby to patrol the south branch of the Potomac River, six miles north of Romney.

Ashby made his camp on the farm of Colonel George Washington, and began at once the active outpost duty for which he was fast becoming famous. For one thing, Colonel McDonald, at sixty-two, was not in the best of health and his activities were of necessity limited. The tireless Ashby, in the saddle almost from sunup to nightfall, checked his pickets and patrols and tracked down Union sympathizers in the area, who were serving as spies for the Federal forces at nearby Cumberland, Maryland.

Ordered by Colonel McDonald to arrest a particularly conspicuous Union man, Ashby on June 26 sent out a party of a dozen men to round him up. The group was commanded by his brother Richard, who had joined Ashby on the outbreak of war and who had succeeded to command of the company when Turner was promoted. Larger and handsomer than his brother, Richard Ashby at twenty-nine had dash, daring, and fire and he too was an impressive horseman. The devotion of the Ashby brothers to each other was noted by their comrades.

Captain Dick Ashby was chagrined, on calling at the Union man's home, to discover that the man had taken refuge inside the Federal lines. Determined to get something out of the expedition, Captain Ashby decided to scout close to the enemy. Upon striking the railroad, he and his band rode down the bed of the road into a Federal cavalry ambush. He saw at a glance that he was heavily outnumbered, so Captain Ashby ordered a retreat. Drawing up the rear, he turned in his saddle to discharge his pistol at the leading Yankee pursuer, and at that moment his horse, attempting to leap a cattle guard, fell and threw his rider. Captain Ashby jumped to his feet and entered into an unequal fight, refusing to surrender. Riddled by half a dozen bullets, he fell on the tracks. One of the Federals ran a bayonet through his abdomen and the group departed leaving the young Confederate for dead.

Close at hand on a patrol was Turner Ashby with some of his cavalry and when he heard the firing, he rode rapidly in the direction of it. Soon the patrol encountering the Federal cavalry and Ashby promptly attacked and routed them. His brother's riderless horse, however, chilled the pleasure of driving off the enemy. Convinced that Dick was dead, Turner searched for his brother's body. He discovered Dick, barely alive, under a tree to which he had crawled.

A week later, on July 3, 1861, Richard Ashby died, after apparently rallying. "We all believed for a part of the time that he would recover," Turner wrote his sister. "At one time he thought so, too." Turner buried his brother, a bachelor like himself, at Romney, saying, "Should I live through the war, I will have him removed to Fauquier."

The Reverend James B. Avirett, chaplain of the 7th Virginia and the first biographer of Turner Ashby, denies that there were any heroics at the grave, as a romantic story of the day had it. Turner's grief was not "excessive or demonstrative," Avirett declared. "He did not break his brother's sabre and cast the pieces into the grave; nor did he kneel to register a vow of vengeance. His grief, too deep for words, was too holy to be tinctured with the earthborn passion of revenge."[12]

IV

As July reached its mid-mark in 1861, it was evident that the war would soon begin in earnest. There had been small fighting in western Virginia, where Union sentiment was strong enough to organize the section to secede from Virginia. There had been a hot skirmish at Big Bethel, near Hampton, and some mild shooting in the vicinity of Alexandria. Out west, in Missouri, pro-Southern elements had taken up arms against the Union, and several small engagements had been fought.

General Joe Johnston had evacuated Harpers Ferry and had disposed his army of about 11,000 around Winchester to protect the Shenandoah Valley from General Robert Patterson's force of about 18,000, poised at Martinsburg. At Manassas Junction, the "hero of Sumter," General P. G. T. Beauregard, held the line of Bull Run with about 22,000 men, just 25 miles from the Federal capital where General Irvin McDowell, with about 50,000 troops, was being badgered into premature action by the press, politicians, and the public.

McDowell had a sound plan. With 35,000 men, he would attack Beauregard at Manassas while the aged Patterson, enjoying a three to two advantage over Joe Johnston, would engage the latter in the Valley so that he could not reinforce Beauregard.

On July 16 Beauregard learned from spies that McDowell was ready to march. He pulled in his pickets as the Federal general, reluctant to move until his troops were better trained, finally yielded to the Northern clamor, "On to Richmond!" Beauregard, on July 17, telegraphed President Davis for reinforcements. Adjutant General Samuel Cooper telegraphed Joe Johnston at Winchester: BEAUREGARD IS ATTACKED. TO

STRIKE THE ENEMY A DECISIVE BLOW A JUNCTION OF ALL YOUR EFFECTIVE
FORCE WILL BE NEEDED.

That same day, General Johnston sent orders to Colonel McDonald
to quit Romney with the 7th Virginia Cavalry and to join him at once
at Winchester. It was not until July 19 that Turner Ashby rode into
town to find that the bulk of Johnston's army had left for Manassas to
join Beauregard. The next day, July 20, Ashby led a scouting party
that demonstrated on Patterson's front effectively. Jeb Stuart's cavalry
had been doing the same thing for several days and poor old Patterson
was completely befuddled by their combined efforts. He still thought
Johnston's army was before him in full force. To an urgent telegram
from Washington inquiring if Johnston had stolen a march and reinforced Beauregard, he telegraphed: . . . THE ENEMY HAS STOLEN NO
MARCH UPON ME. I HAVE KEPT HIM ACTIVELY EMPLOYED, AND BY THREATS
AND RECONNAISSANCES IN FORCE CAUSED HIM TO BE REINFORCED . . .[13]

On July 21, Ashby's regiment passed over the Blue Ridge at Ashby's
Gap, and as the troops rode on, they heard the distant rumble of guns.
The Battle of Manassas, first great battle of the war, was under way.
The next day as they continued the march to Manassas word of the great
victory reached them long before they bivouacked in the vicinity of the
battlefield.

Orders came on July 24, directing the 7th Virginia Cavalry back to
the Shenandoah Valley. The column headed for Staunton from where
new orders sent the regiment marching down the Valley to protect the
crops in the field and to organize a border patrol. When the 7th Virginia
reached Winchester, it split up. Colonel McDonald took eight companies
into the vicinity of Romney to protect the farms from Yankee raids.
Lieutenant Colonel Ashby, with the rest of the regiment, was ordered to
Kearneysville, on the Baltimore & Ohio Railroad about midway between
Harpers Ferry and Martinsburg, to protect the crews collecting materials
from the wreckage of the railroad destroyed by General Joe Johnston.
Ashby had secured about 300 militia infantry from General James H.
Carson at Winchester and a couple of militia cavalry companies had
also attached themselves to his command. Because of the distance be-
tween him and Colonel McDonald, Ashby now had virtually an independent force. But from where would his orders and instructions come?

In an undated letter, in September 1862, Ashby wrote Adjutant General
Samuel Cooper asking for instructions on what to do with goods seized
from a store operated by a Union sympathizer who had fled within the
Union lines. He told the Adjutant General that two Federal infantry
regiments were across the river, guarding the Baltimore and Ohio Canal,
but that he was confident, "if not inconsistent with the present policy
of the Government, that I can move over at some convenient point and
break the canal, securing a large amount of salt said to be now in depots

opposite this place." He reported that he had had several skirmishes with the enemy who had crossed the river twice, but had driven them back easily. But they were troublesome, for "they fire at every man, woman, child, or horse that passes the river upon this side," and he had occasionally permitted his men to return the fire with long-range small arms.

Ashby then pointed out to General Cooper his "peculiar position, acting by order of Colonel McDonald, who is . . . in a different locality, too far to give his attention to the minutiae of my movements." Moreover, with other troops than McDonald's regiment under his command, he had "no defined instructions as to policy to be pursued towards the enemy in this locality. Will you give them to me?"

On September 19, the Adjutant General, through an assistant, replied to Ashby that "it has been our object, with the President, for some time past, to destroy the canal at any point where it could not be repaired . . . A disappointment at the failure of all past attempts to effect them has been proportionate to the importance attached to their achievement." But the Adjutant General urged that attempts be made with "The greatest caution," to assure the safety of the command.[14]

With 300 militia armed with flintlock muskets and four companies of cavalry and supported by two guns, Turner Ashby attacked the Federals on Bolivar Heights at Harpers Ferry on October 16. Both sides claimed the victory. Ashby reported that his men "drove the enemy from their breastworks" and held the position for four hours, when they withdrew in order in face of heavy Federal reinforcements. His losses, said Ashby, were one killed and nine wounded. Colonel John W. Geary of the 28th Pennsylvania reported, on the other hand, that "the victory was complete" and that the enemy's killed and wounded exceeded 150. Ashby's report estimated the Federal dead at 25, with others wounded. Geary reported his loss as four killed and seven wounded.

For several weeks, Ashby had been trying to put into effect plans to cut the Chesapeake and Ohio Canal, as instructed "with the greatest caution" by the Adjutant General. On November 7, he wrote General Cooper again:

"The instruction in regard to breaking the Canal has been pursued with all the means in my power, but owing to the overpowering force of the Enemy I have had to move rapidly from point to point to keep them in check without being able to carry out a plan which I had to break it. I am however pleased to inform you that the Elements have accomplished what my great desire was to perform. The Apron protecting the wall of Dam No. 4 has been carried away, washing over the Bank for several hundred feet . . . Owing to the high water I am unable to make an accurate report, but it is believed the Damage done cannot be repaired for several months."

In this same letter, Ashby noted that Major General T. J. Jackson had arrived in Winchester to command the Valley Department, but as yet he had received no orders to report to him. "I write to know if I shall do so, and receive my orders from him in the future. You will remember that I have received orders only from your Department thus far."[15]

Stonewall Jackson was appointed on October 22 to command the newly created Valley District and on the night of November 5 he assumed his new command. "In the small body of cavalry which he found at Winchester, a conspicuous officer was Lieutenant Colonel Turner Ashby," wrote Mary Anna Jackson, Stonewall's wife. ". . . He was as brave and chivalrous a gentleman as ever drew a sword . . . He was an invaluable auxiliary to General Jackson in guarding the outposts of his army—his coolness, discretion, and untiring vigilance being as remarkable as his daring and bravery."[16] Jackson remembered Ashby from John Brown's raid, for the younger man had made a profound impression upon him.

On November 13, 1861, having received authority from the War Department, Turner Ashby organized the first horse artillery in the Confederate Army, mounted artillery which would accompany the cavalry into action. In command was a remarkable youngster of eighteen, Captain R. Preston Chew, who before the war ended would command, at twenty-two, all the horse artillery in Robert E. Lee's army. Chew's battery started out with 35 men and three guns and where Ashby was, Chew and his smoking cannons usually were, too. Chew served with Ashby until the latter's death and despite the disparity of a dozen years in their ages, they were warm friends.

Ashby, Chew said, "was very fond of the roar of artillery and was with us constantly on the battlefield, and when we were shelling the enemy." Chew declared that he had seen Ashby "under fire in full a hundred battles and skirmishes" and he always was "without consciousness of danger, cool and self-possessed and ever alert and quick as lightning to take advantage of any mistake of the enemy."

Many times Chew and others cautioned Ashby about his reckless exposure to the enemy. Ashby had a standard reply: "An officer should always go to the front and take risks in order to keep his men up to the mark."[17]

Another brilliant young artillerist, Lieutenant William Thomas Poague, who had joined Stonewall Jackson in the Valley, was sent in early December to report to Ashby at Charlestown. He whimsically told how he found Ashby in his room at the hotel, "sitting up in bed with nothing but a red flannel shirt on." The next day, young Poague witnessed Turner Ashby in action for the first time, or as he put it "witnessed one of those daring exploits so frequent in his brilliant career."

Ashby had got wind of a Yankee scheme to capture him on his rounds along the Potomac. Leaving his guns and the bulk of his command hidden behind the crest of a ridge, he took about twenty men with him and "swooped down on a house about half a mile from the river. In a short while, he rode leisurely back with a bunch of blue coats as prisoners." Across the river, a Yankee force looked on helplessly as their comrades were captured. Ashby ordered Poague to toss a few shells into the camp and this caused "a general stampede much to the amusement of Ashby's men."

In the middle of December, Stonewall Jackson determined to destroy one of the dams on the Chesapeake and Ohio Canal. He sent infantry to join Ashby's cavalry to cover the work party and he went along to watch the job. Volunteer workers went waist-deep into the icy waters of the Potomac but their efforts, directed at Dam No. 5, were seriously hampered by enemy sharpshooters. The work started on December 17, and by the morning of the twenty-first, the dam was finally breached.

During this operation, Lieutenant Poague saw Ashby under heavy fire for the first time and he, as everyone else, marvelled at his audacity and complete contempt for danger. Poague wrote amusingly of the incident:

"We soon found ourselves under fire, for the enemy seemed to be searching the whole region with his fire. Jackson was afoot and right in front and now and then would duck his head as shells came near. As we neared the top of the ridge we found every man and officer behind a big tree and all dodging first one side and then the other . . . Jackson did not take to a tree, but occasionally bowed to those infernal shells.

"Did I dodge? Yes: just as low as my saddle pommel would allow. But who was that man out there walking slowly back and forth . . . in the open field, with arms folded apparently enjoying a quiet promenade, totally indifferent to the hellish fire raining all about him. That was Turner Ashby—a man of the coolest courage and finest nerve I ever knew or saw in the Army."[18]

v

Before Stonewall Jackson came to Winchester to command the Valley District, friends of Turner Ashby had already begun pushing the Richmond authorities to promote him to colonel and permit him to raise a regiment of cavalry of his own.

A leader in this matter was A. R. Boteler, a member of the Confederate Congress from the region where Ashby roamed and in whose home, "Fountain Rock," Ashby frequently stopped on his patrols. On September 6, 1861, Boteler had informed an unidentified correspondent whom he addressed only as "Dear Phil," that there would be no difficulty in organizing an efficient cavalry regiment for Ashby as soon as he was promoted. He urged "Dear Phil" to talk to Secretary of State R. M. T. Hunter and enlist his aid in speeding Ashby's commission. He added:

"Mr. [Secretary of War] Benjamin told me that Ashby's merits are well known to the Govt & that he sh. be promoted in accordance with our plans for the defence of this border with such a Regt as Ashby will organize including the artillery company which Avirett is raising so we'll be enable to guard the right bank of the Potomac from Harper's Ferry to Hancock & be in a condition to cooperate officially with the main army of Manassas when it will be ready to cross into Maryland . . . Please attend to this matter . . . as soon as possible and oblige all the loyal people of this border . . ."

A month later, in Richmond, Boteler presented verbally to Benjamin sentiments which a citizen of the area had written on October 5 to the Secretary of War: "The management of military affairs in this quarter is in utterly incompetent hands." Another citizen addressed himself to the Secretary of War on October 6: "The gallant Ashby will do to lead cavalry, but we want a man to lead infantry and artillery."

Upon his return to Charlestown, Boteler received a letter from Secretary of State Hunter which indicated that there was a misconception in the War Department over the promotion of Lieutenant Colonel Ashby. On October 24, 1861, Boteler replied to Hunter:

"Our main object in asking that he be advanced to a full colonelcy is that we may thereby be enable to organize under him an additional force of several hundred young men who are anxious to be attached to his command, but will not volunteer under another colonel. If they organize under Lieutenant Colonel Ashby now they will constitute a portion of Colonel McDonald's command, and although Lieutenant Colonel Ashby is at present detached from McDonald's regiment he is under his order, and the young men I speak of wish to be assured that Ashby alone shall command their regiment.

"The condition of our border is becoming more alarming every day. No night passes without some infamous outrage upon our loyal citizens. Ashby's force is too small to prevent these things, but if he be made a colonel, and those he has with him now be re-inforced by the volunteers ready to rally to his regiment, I promise you that a better state of things will exist up here . . .

"I . . . hope you will favor us with your good offices in securing the full colonelcy for Ashby."[19]

Such was the situation when Stonewall Jackson took command of all the Valley forces. He soon had occasion to evaluate the worth of the intrepid and tireless cavalryman, for Ashby quickly became, as Jackson's adjutant, Dr. Dabney, said, the General's "eyes and ears." Ashby became a legend and "his activity, daring and seeming immunity from wounds, filled the Federal soldiers with a species of superstitious dread." Dabney said that Ashby went into action with a yell on his lips and his men chorused "Ashby!" as they followed into the fight. "Ever guarding the outposts of his [Jackson's] army with rare discretion, and sleepless vigilance, he detected the incipient movements of the enemy," recorded Dabney, "and his sobriety of mind, which was equal to his daring, secured implicit confidence for his reports."

In the operations in January and February 1862, to Romney, Bath, and Hancock, Ashby rendered valuable service. Jackson commended his energy at Bloomery Pass, barely 20 miles from Winchester, where Ashby, responding to Jackson's orders "with his accustomed promptness," dispersed an enemy force which had seized the position. In his first report from the Valley, dated February 21, 1862, Jackson said of Ashby: "I am under many obligations to this valuable officer for his untiring zeal and successful efforts in defending this district."[20]

In the last week in February, the efforts of Congressman Boteler, first exercised the previous September, bore fruit. On February 21 and 22, Secretary of War Benjamin sent Lieutenant Colonel Ashby authority to raise cavalry, infantry, and heavy artillery troops. Supplementing the previously sent general terms of Ashby's authority, on the latter date Benjamin instructed him to raise ten companies of cavalry, "either by re-enlistment, and recruiting existing companies, or by enlisting new companies." As soon as the ten companies were raised and mustered into the Confederate service, Ashby was to organize them into a regiment.

Three weeks later, the second goal of Congressman Boteler's campaign for Turner Ashby was achieved when Secretary Benjamin issued his commission as colonel. Dated March 12, 1862, the commission was forwarded to Ashby on March 14 by General Jackson with a brief note, hurriedly scribbled in Stonewall's horrible hand: "*My Dear Colonel, It gives me great pleasure to forward your well earned appointment as colonel of Cavalry. Very truly your friend, T. J. Jackson.*" Jackson had added his voice to Boteler's after seeing Turner Ashby in action.[21] Whatever may have been the War Department's inclination to yield to what might have appeared to be political pressure in the matter, it could hardly ignore the recommendation of the commanding general of the Valley District.

On March 17, just three days after receipt of his promotion, Colonel Ashby reported to Secretary Benjamin that he had mustered into the Confederate service eighteen companies, one of artillery and the rest cavalry. Some were new companies, some had been already under his command. Four or five more cavalry companies and several infantry were about ready to organize, he said.

"I have not raised many companys [sic] as I could have done," he told Benjamin, "as I have not wished to interfere with companys and Regiments which have been in the Service belonging to other commands but have devoted myself to enlisting from those who have not been in the service before."

Ashby asked the Secretary of War for arms for his troops and also for the necessary equipment. "We have hitherto Battled our way through by individual enterprise, procuring such arms as we could procure in this way," he said. "In a charge made by me a few days ago, one of them was riden bare backen [sic] and Armed with a club."

In the meantime, while Colonel Ashby was getting a new command and a promotion, events had conspired almost to lose Stonewall Jackson to the Confederacy. Late in January, Secretary Benjamin had instructed Jackson to pull General W. W. Loring out of Romney. This Jackson considered as an unjust intrusion into his command. With alacrity he executed the order, but then, on January 31, furious at Benjamin, he wrote out his resignation. Under the persuasion of General Joe Johnston and Governor John Letcher of Virginia, Jackson withdrew the resignation on February 4, and remained as commander of the Confederate Army in the Valley District.[22]

When, on March 9, 1862, General Johnston had withdrawn from the line of Bull Run to the line of the Rappahannock, it became necessary for Jackson to fall back in the Shenandoah Valley. Otherwise he was vulnerable to flank attack by the numerically superior Federals on his front. Union General Banks, with 38,000 troops, had crossed the Potomac at Harpers Ferry late in February and had taken up a line between Charlestown and Martinsburg. But he was reluctant to advance on Jackson, until General McClellan launched his attack on Johnston at Manassas. Inasmuch as Johnston had left Manassas on March 9, McClellan, instead of pursuing him, decided to launch his drive against Richmond by way of the peninsula between the York and James Rivers. Now more or less on his own, Banks's advance was tentative, for he had ideas that Stonewall Jackson's army was much larger than it actually was.

Although occupied with enlisting troops, Colonel Ashby was in the saddle more than not, scouting for information, patrolling or riding the picket line. On March 7, he skirmished with a Federal column at Bunker Hill, just four miles away from Winchester, and Jackson began to plan a reluctant withdrawal. On March 11, when Banks pushed his left to Berryville, Jackson realized he had to get his little force of about 5300 effectives on the march or else they would be enveloped by the overwhelmingly superior Federal army. Jackson dropped back up the Valley to Strasburg, 18 miles from Winchester, with Turner Ashby's cavalry covering the withdrawal. The last Confederate to quit the town was Colonel Ashby, a striking figure on his white stallion. John Esten Cooke, a Confederate who wrote so glowingly of the wearers of the gray, gives a glamorous account of Ashby's departure from Winchester:

"He waited until the Federal column was nearly upon him, and had opened a hot fire—then he turned his horse, waved his hat around on his head, and uttering a cheer of defiance, galloped off. All at once, as he galloped down the street, he saw before him the two cavalrymen sent to cut off and capture him. To a man like Ashby, inwardly chafing at being compelled to retreat, no sight could be more agreeable. Here was an opportunity to vent his spleen; and charging the two mounted men, he was soon upon them. One fell with a bullet through his breast; and, coming opposite the other, Ashby seized him by the throat, dragged him from his saddle, and putting spur to horse, bore him off. This scene, which some readers may set down for romance, was witnessed by hundreds both of the Confederate and the Federal army."

Unfortunately, none of the "hundreds" of witnesses ever substantiated John Esten Cooke's story, which does, however, serve to demonstrate how legends grew up around Turner Ashby. Since Cooke wasn't on hand to see this feat for himself, the evidence of one who was there is more valuable. Ashby's chaplain and first biographer, the Reverend James B. Avirett, described the evacuation of Winchester in this manner:

"Fighting and falling slowly back, Ashby retarded the advance of the enemy until Jackson effected the evacuation of Winchester, which was completed on the night of the 11th of March. On the morning of the 12th, as the enemy continued to advance, the Confederate infantry retired by the turnpike leading up the Valley to Staunton. Skirmishing almost to the limits of the town, Ashby, as quiet as if on dress parade, followed his men down the street, and though followed closely by the enemy, coolly stopped to take a biscuit offered him by a noble-hearted lady."[23]

When Banks dispatched General James Shields up the Valley in pursuit of Jackson, the latter fell back from Strasburg, on March 15. The timid Shields didn't reach there until the nineteenth. Jackson halted at Woodstock and then moved part of his force on to Mount Jackson, 24 miles from Strasburg. Under instructions from General Joe Johnston to prevent Federal troops from leaving to reinforce McClellan, Jackson hopefully expected his withdrawal would lure Banks farther up the Valley.

VI

Riding the outposts of Jackson's little army and keeping a sharp eye on the movement of Federal troops, Colonel Ashby on March 21 made the startling discovery that the Federals were pulling out of Strasburg. When his dispatch with this information reached Jackson late in the day, Stonewall reacted immediately. He gave orders for the army to move at dawn. "Apprehensive that the Federals would leave this military district," Jackson reported, "I determined to follow with all my available force."

Jackson reached Strasburg on the night of March 22, some of his troops having marched 24 miles, others 14 miles, in blustery weather.

Meanwhile, Ashby, reconnoitering and skirmishing with the Yankees from Strasburg almost to Winchester, received word from within the town that all Federal troops except four regiments and some artillery and cavalry had left for Harpers Ferry. This information reached Jackson on the march as he approached Kernstown, and he had also learned that a large Federal force was then leaving the Valley via Castleman's Ferry on the Shenandoah.

By 2 P.M. March 23, most of Jackson's army had reached the outskirts of Kernstown. Jackson's first intention was to attack the next morning, but when he noted that his troops "were in good spirits at the prospect of meeting the enemy," he decided to strike at once.

Ashby's information had been only partly correct and when Jackson attacked Shields at Kernstown with less than 3100 men—2742 infantry and 290 cavalry—instead of meeting a comparable force, he found himself opposing 7000 Federals. A hurried call to the troops at Castlemans Ferry had brought them countermarching in time to give the Yankees about a three to one edge over Jackson before the fight at Kernstown ended.[24]

Jackson ordered his cavalry split and 140 men under Major O. R. Funsten were sent to the Confederate left, while Ashby with 150 men and Chew's guns remained at the Valley Pike on the right of Jackson's line. The fighting was furious and though Jackson's outnumbered army broke several Federal charges, fresh troops renewed the pressure and the Confederate left eventually began to crumble. Meanwhile Ashby, whose orders were to threaten the Yankee front and left, placed his guns accordingly, two bearing on the front and one on the Federal left. Ordering a charge on the Yankee's extreme left, he drove the advance back upon the main line.

About this time, Jackson's hard-pressed left gave way, its ammunition having been exhausted. General R. B. Garnett, to Jackson's chagrin, ordered a withdrawal on the Confederate left, which made it necessary for the troops on Garnett's right also to drop back, or be rolled up by the advancing Federals. Jackson, who would later have General Garnett before a court-martial, contended that the latter's order of withdrawal prevented Jackson's reserves from coming up to get into the action. Jackson was now compelled to fall back, which he did in good order. Colonel Ashby covered his front effectively until all the infantry had disengaged and Stonewall Jackson later noted his contribution to the safety of the outnumbered little Valley Army: "Colonel Ashby fully sustained his deservedly high reputation by the able manner in which he discharged the important trust confided to him."

Years later, Ashby's brilliant young artillerist, Captain Preston Chew, wrote: "I have always believed his audacity saved Jackson's army *from total destruction* at the Battle of Kernstown." Chew said Ashby's boldness deceived the Federals as to the size of his cavalry.

Jackson had taken a tactical beating at Kernstown, but he had served the established strategic purpose of preventing Union reinforcements from leaving the Valley for the Peninsula Campaign. Also, his defeated little army had inflicted considerable loss in killed and wounded on the enemy. "Under the circumstances," Jackson reported, "I feel justified in saying that, though the field is in possession of the enemy, yet the most essential fruits of the battle are ours."[25]

Retreating up the Valley while Ashby disputed virtually every foot of ground with the cautious Federals, Stonewall Jackson established his headquarters near Mount Jackson and set himself to the task of reorganizing his little army and increasing its number by recruiting. Ashby's activities as Jackson's rear guard proved a great impetus to attracting recruits to the cavalry and his twelve companies soon increased to twenty-six companies.

During the "hill to hill" fighting with the slowly advancing Federals, Ashby spent much time with Chew and his guns. "Aren't we a little lavish in the expenditure of ammunition?" Chew once said to him. Ashby replied: "I believe in firing at the enemy whenever they show their heads." Ashby's delaying tactics were brilliantly conceived and executed with boldness. "He would form a skirmish line," said Chew, "and open on them with artillery, compel them to halt and form line of battle and when their superior forces drew dangerously near to his men, he would skillfully withdraw and form on the next hill."

Ashby and his proud white horse were the admiration of his men and, it seems, grudgingly of the Federals. "I think our men had a kind of admiration for him as he sat upon his horse and let them pepper away at him as if he enjoyed it," said a Union officer. One morning during the retreat, as Ashby sat his horse watching the skirmishers, Captain John Henderson rode up at a time when the enemy fire was particularly hot, with minie balls whistling all around.

"Good morning, Colonel," said Captain Henderson. "I have brought you some breakfast, but this is rather a warm place to enjoy it."

"Never mind that," replied Ashby. "Your kindness is well timed, for I'm very hungry."

Accepting the proffered hard-boiled eggs, Ashby shared them with Captain Randolph, who was with him. Then tossing a leg over the pommel of his saddle he enjoyed his breakfast, oblivious to the enemy fire.[26]

Not long after this, when attempting to burn the bridge over the North Fork of the Shenandoah, near Rude's Hill, Colonel Ashby had a narrow scrape with death or capture. Falling back slowly, he had ordered Chew's battery to take a position on Rude's Hill to cover the bridge and part of the turnpike. This done, he got his troops across while he remained some distance behind. Recognizing the lone horseman on the handsome white charger the Federal cavalry galloped up with spirit, intent on capturing the fabulous Turner Ashby.

The bridge had been prepared for firing, but the guard assigned to it, took off in all directions when the Yankee horsemen bore down upon them. Ashby tried to light the fire himself, but four Federal cavalrymen headed for him, calling for his surrender. This demand, of course, Ashby ignored and they fired their pistols, missing him but striking his horse. Some of Ashby's men now came up, firing. Three of the Federals fell from their saddles and the fourth took off. They led Ashby's magnificent horse to the rear, its left side red with blood. As the proud animal stepped well and tossed its head, everyone hoped that the wound was trifling. "When we had presently taken up the march and gone a very short distance we saw the noble animal near the west side of the road," said a Confederate officer, "and cavalrymen were cutting off hair from its long white mane and tail for souvenirs."[27]

VII

The two bearded figures in gray faced each other in a tent near Conrad's store, where the road across the Blue Ridge passes through Swift Run Gap. To the "foot-cavalry" of the Valley Army, Conrad's store was a familiar landmark, for when the troops weren't camped there, they were usually marching to or from or by it.

To Stonewall Jackson's tent at Conrad's, there came Colonel Turner Ashby, his swarthy countenance clouded with anger, his dark eyes flashing with determination.

They made an odd couple: the lithe, medium-sized Ashby, with his cascading raven-black beard, and the gangling Jackson, with enormous hands and feet, whose short but thick dark beard surrounded a tight-lipped, ascetic mouth, dedicated to reticence. His eyes, which lighted up in battle, were tired-looking in repose.

Colonel Ashby had angrily resigned his commission on April 24, when Jackson had virtually deprived him of his command, but he had accepted Stonewall's invitation to come to his tent for a talk.

It all began when Jackson, annoyed at the lack of discipline of Ashby's men, determined that the cavalry be "organized, drilled and disciplined."

It was common knowledge in the Valley Army that Turner Ashby was no disciplinarian. One Confederate officer, noting that the cavalry was neither well drilled nor disciplined, said the men were held by Ashby in "little restraint." The perceptive General Dick Taylor, who saw him for only the last weeks of Ashby's life, admired his daring, his courage, and his superb horsemanship, but concluded "he was without capacity or disposition to enforce discipline on his men." John Esten Cooke said that "want of discipline" was Ashby's only fault as a soldier. Jackson's adjutant, Dr. Dabney, who undoubtedly reflected Stonewall's feelings, declared that "Colonel Ashby had little genius for organization and discipline."[28]

In Turner Ashby's defense, it may be said that with his command scattered over many miles on picket or patrol duty and with almost constant action with the enemy—he had at one time in the Valley 30 brushes with the Yankees in 28 days—he had little time for drill and discipline.

Major Kyd Douglas, Ashby's friend and admirer, voiced this thought:

"His idea of the superior patriotism of the volunteer and that he should not be subjected to very much starch and drill, made him a poor disciplinarian and caused the only failures he ever made . . . His service to the army was invaluable, but had he been as full of discipline as he was of leadership his success would have been more fruitful and his reputation still greater. Yet it should be remembered that he had little time for instruction of any kind. From the beginning his only drill ground was the field of battle . . . He was compelled to organize his troops while on the gallop."[29]

While Jackson had probably been planning for some time to correct the indiscipline of Turner Ashby's men, two incidents that occurred shortly after mid-April 1862 hastened his action. On the first occasion, an entire company of cavalry, numbering 50 men, was captured because of neglecting to mount a guard. And on the second, one of Ashby's companies on a bridge-burning expedition miserably failed in its mission because most of the men were drunk. Jackson's topographical engineer, Jed Hotchkiss, who was on the assignment, wrote his wife on April 20, 1862: "I never saw a more disgraceful affair—all owing to the state of intoxication of some of the men and to the want of discipline . . . When Ashby's men are with him, they behave gallantly, but when they are away they lack the inspiration of his presence, and being undisciplined they often fail to do any good . . ."

In an undated order, probably written on April 23, Jackson took the step he had contemplated. When Colonel Ashby rode into his camp after patrolling the picket lines, his adjutant handed him a paper. His anger mounted as he read:

Headquarters, Army of the Valley

The General Commanding:

Hereby orders companies A, B, C, D, E, F, G, H, I, K, of Ashby's cavalry to report to Brigadier-General Taliaferro, and to be attached to his command; the other companies of the same command will report to Brigadier-General Winder, to be attached to his command.

Col. Turner Ashby will command the advance guard of the Army of the Valley, when on an advance, and the rear guard when in retreat, applying to Generals Taliaferro and Winder for troops whenever they may be needed.

By order of
MAJOR-GEN. T. J. JACKSON

This amounted to stripping Ashby of his command. Under the order he had no troops of his own, but could "borrow" cavalrymen as required on advance or retreat. Ashby was indignant. He declared that Jackson was overstepping his authority and that he was empowered by the War Department to organize his own command and that he would not submit to such treatment. He vehemently declared, that if they were of equal rank, he would send Jackson a challenge, despite his high regard for him as a soldier and his appreciation of his value to the Confederacy. "Before I will tamely submit I will tender my resignation, and it will be necessary to forward it through General Jackson as my chief," he declared.

Writing out his resignation, Ashby gave it to Dr. Thomas L. Settle, a surgeon on his staff, to deliver. Settle later told the story:

"On reaching General Jackson's quarters, I met . . . H. Kyd Douglas, a member of his staff, delivered the document and said I expected to return in about an hour and would call for a reply. When I got back Major Douglas informed me there was no answer. Next day Generals Winder and Taliaferro came down to Ashby's quarters, spent the greater part of the day . . ."

McHenry Howard, a staff officer of Jackson's, tells a slightly different version, asserting that Ashby forwarded his resignation to Stonewall through General Winder. He recalled in later years that he had ridden out with Winder to the cavalry outpost, where the latter engaged Ashby in long conversation. Winder then went to General Jackson and had several conversations with him and again with Ashby. "To General Winder's offices was largely due the settlement," said Howard, "or smoothing over of what at the time threatened serious trouble."[30]

Winder, indeed, had kept the door open for Ashby, but the matter wasn't settled until the two great fighting men came face to face in Stonewall Jackson's tent. The morning after he had received Ashby's resignation Jackson wrote him a note, asking him to come to headquarters for a talk.

As soon as Ashby entered the tent Jackson asked him to withdraw his resignation. He told Ashby how he had resigned when the Secretary of War had meddled with his command at Romney, but had withdrawn his resignation when asked to do so by General Johnston and Governor Letcher.

Ashby replied that he had acted in earnest and wanted the resignation forwarded to the War Department. He told Jackson what he had told his officers: that but for the fact "he had the highest respect for Jackson's ability as a soldier, and believed him essential to the cause of the South, he would hold him to a personal account for the indignity he had put upon him."

With that, Ashby left Jackson's tent and joined young Captain Chew and several other officers on the porch of Conrad's store. He told them about the interview and was, or so the Reverend Mr. Avirett thought, "in fine spirits." Chew recalled that Ashby said he would "organize an independent command and operate in the lower Valley and the Piedmont country. All the officers present declared their intention to go with him." Within an hour, Jackson had revoked his order and restored Ashby to his command and the latter immediately "rode his usual long wearisome rounds on outpost duty."

General Jackson, in a letter to General R. E. Lee's adjutant on May 5, 1862, gave all the details of his controversy with Colonel Ashby and also the reasons for restoring his command to him:

"I so felt the importance of having the cavalry more thoroughly organized, drilled and disciplined as to induce me to take action in the matter; but Colonel Ashby claimed that I could not interfere with his organization, as he was acting under the instructions of the late Secretary of War, Mr. Benjamin. These instructions or authority are contained in letters written on the 21st and 22nd of February last, and authorize Colonel Ashby to raise cavalry, infantry, and heavy artillery . . . Colonel Ashby and Major Funsten are the only field officers belonging to the cavalry . . . Colonel Ashby reports that there has never been any regimental organization of any part of his command. When I took steps for organizing, drilling, and disciplining the cavalry, both of its field officers sent in their resignations, and such is Colonel Ashby's influence over his command that I became well satisfied that if I persisted in my attempt to increase the efficiency of the cavalry it would produce the contrary effect, as Colonel Ashby's influence, who is very popular with his men, would be thrown against me."

Jackson said that he had taken no further action, pending War Department disposition of the matter. He stated that the cavalry was at the moment, May 5, without a field officer, both Colonel Ashby and Major Funsten being ill. "It is important," Jackson concluded, "that the cavalry should be organized into regiments at the earliest practicable moment."

General Lee endorsed Jackson's letter to the War Department asking for "explicit instruction" concerning Ashby and his command. "I did not know that Colonel Ashby's command embraced more than cavalry which I have been endeavoring to get organized and instructed," Lee added.

The day after Jackson sent this letter to Lee, he wrote Congressman Boteler, who was now pushing for a brigadier generalship for Turner

Ashby. "With regard to Colonel Ashby's promotion I would gladly favor it, if he were a good disciplinarian," wrote Stonewall, "but he has such bad discipline and attaches so little importance to drill, that I would regard it as a calamity to see him promoted. I desire so soon as he gives proper attention to these matters (which are so essential to success in operations with large masses of troops) to see him promoted. I recommended him for a colonelcy, and will always take pleasure in doing all I can for his advancement consistent with the interest of the Public Service . . ."[31]

VIII

Early in May, Stonewall Jackson took off on one of his mysterious moves which kept the Federals—and frequently his own surbordinates—in a state of befuddlement. Rightly assuming that the unenterprising Banks, who had encamped between Harrisonburg and New Market late in April, would not strike at him, Jackson left the picturesque General Dick Ewell to watch the enemy. Then he rapidly moved to the west of Staunton to attack a force under General Robert H. Milroy, who was moving to a junction with Banks.

During Jackson's absence, Colonel Ashby had an important mission. He was to annoy Banks by frequent demonstrations, and generally create, by the swift movements of his cavalry, the impression that Jackson was preparing an attack. Under the combined efforts of Banks's own lethargic caution and the skillful masking operations of Ashby, the Federals didn't have the slightest idea where Jackson was.

Meanwhile, about to fight the Battle of McDowell, Jackson sent to Ashby for ten companies of cavalry, while the remainder continued to keep Banks in the dark as to Jackson's whereabouts. In fact, concerned that Jackson might be trying to get to his rear, Banks evacuated Harrisonburg and withdrew to New Market, 19 miles away. Ashby rode on the fringe of the retiring Federals, doubtless maintaining in Banks's mind the idea that Jackson intended to attack at a favorable moment.

Ashby, who did not take a day's leave from the army during his whole career, was compelled at this time to remain inactive for several days when he became severely ill with fever and dysentery.[32] But by the time Jackson got back from whipping Milroy and sending him off in retreat, Ashby was in the saddle again.

In mid-May 1862, Banks having moved farther down the Valley to Strasburg, Ashby was in camp at New Market. There he awaited the return of his troops who had accompanied Jackson to McDowell. He maintained constant pressure on Banks, without committing himself to a fight, so as to cause the enemy, he informed Jackson, "to believe you were behind them upon this road."

Banks's intentions were very much on the minds of Confederate authorities in Richmond as well as on Jackson's. If Banks left the Shenandoah Valley to join in the attack on Richmond, that would be decidedly unadvantageous to General Joe Johnston. However, if Banks could be driven from the Valley, that was another thing, for that would not only keep him from joining McClellan, but it could open the road for Jackson to threaten Baltimore and Washington. On May 16, Robert E. Lee wrote Jackson that "whatever Banks' intention, it is very desirable to prevent him from going either to Fredericksburg or the Peninsula . . . A successful blow struck at him would delay, if it does not prevent, his moving to either place . . . Whatever move you make against Banks do it speedily, and if successful drive him back to the Potomac, and create the impression, as far as practicable, that you design threatening that line."

That was all Jackson needed. While Ashby continued to demonstrate before Banks, Jackson pushed on to Harrisonburg, despite delays by high water. The same day he wrote General Dick Ewell that Ashby had reported Banks had not left the Valley "and it may be that a kind Providence will enable us to unite and strike a successful blow." Unfortunately, Ewell on May 17 got orders from General Johnston to join him at Richmond. When Ewell transmitted this information to Jackson, Stonewall promptly instructed him not to act until he could communicate with Richmond himself. He pointed out to Lee that while an attempt to defeat Banks should be made, he didn't feel "at liberty to make an attack, in the light of Johnston's order to Ewell."

Lee agreed. Ewell, instead of moving from Swift Run Gap for Richmond, crossed the Blue Ridge to join Jackson in the vicinity of New Market. On May 20, 1862, Jackson was in camp near that place and Ewell was marching to join him. Before Strasburg, which Banks had fortified, Ashby with part of his command kept watch while others of his troops did picket duty from Franklin on the west to beyond the Blue Ridge on the east.[33]

On May 23, Jackson pounced down upon the Federals at Front Royal, taking them by surprise, routing them and capturing the town. Ashby, during the operation had made a wide swing to the northwest to reach Buckton Station on the Manassas Gap Railroad, midway between Strasburg and Front Royal. Two companies of Federal infantry held Buckton, and when Ashby attacked, they put up stout resistance from the railroad station. It took two charges by Ashby to dislodge them. Telegraph wires to Strasburg were cut and the stores and baggage in the railroad station were burned. Then Ashby lined up for the third charge at the Yankees, who were now strongly positioned behind the railroad embankment, from which they held the railroad bridge across Passage Creek.

"It would have been well if he had retired instead," wrote the Reverend James B. Avirett, Ashby's chaplain. "But in his desire to cover the railroad connection by burning the bridge, he did not pause to weigh consequences." Adulation for Ashby characterizes almost every page of Avirett's book, but he felt "compelled to condemn the manner of this attack." He said that Ashby should have dismounted his men for "to charge a fortified or covered position under any circumstances is sufficiently dangerous, but doubly so with mounted men."

It was a bold, if rash, charge, and his men responded to his command: "Forward, boys! we will get every mother's son of them!" Over rough ground and over fences they rode, but the hot fire of the Federals behind the embankment checked the attack. Falling back, Ashby rallied his men and ordered a second charge in a desperate effort to rout the Yankees and destroy the bridge. But again the Federal position proved too strong. Ashby bemoaned the fact that Captain Chew and his ever-active Blakely and other guns were not with him. "If my little Blakely were here," he said, "these people should not escape."

The next day, Jackson moved toward the Valley Pike, with Ashby's cavalry, the batteries of Chew and Poague, and Major Rob Wheat's wild Louisiana Tigers of Dick Taylor's brigade in the van. When the head of the column reached Middletown, the turnpike was crowded with retreating Federal cavalry. For Turner Ashby this was too good to be true and without a moment's hesitation he charged with the guns and the cavalry all rushing together. The Tigers followed on the double. Captain Chew, who was in the fight, says the guns were unlimbered within a few hundred feet of the Yankees, into whom rapid fire was poured. "This was done with perfect success," wrote Jackson's preacher-adjutant, Dr. Dabney, "which was a novel instance of a charge effected by field artillery." Chew declared that "this manoeuvre of charging with the horse-artillery was often employed afterward, but was first inaugurated by Ashby."[34]

Stonewall Jackson, himself, in his report gave the most graphic picture of the confusion this charge produced:

". . . In a few moments the turnpike, which had just teemed with life, presented a most appalling spectacle of carnage and destruction. The road was literally obstructed with the mingled and confused mass of struggling and dying horses and riders. The Federal column was pierced, but what proportion of its strength had passed north toward Winchester, I had then no means of knowing. Among the surviving cavalry the wildest confusion ensued, and they scattered in disorder in various directions, leaving, however, some 200 prisoners, with their equipments, in our hands. A train of wagons was seen disappearing in the distance towards

Winchester, and Ashby, with his cavalry, some artillery, and a supporting infantry force from Taylor's brigade, was sent in pursuit."

But the pursuit was short-lived, because the Yankee wagon train and cavalry horses were too much of a temptation to Ashby's men who, recorded Dr. Dabney, "Disgracefully turned aside to pillage." This charge, in after years, would be denied by some of Ashby's men, but the evidence is strong that it was true. Wrote Dr. Dabney:

"Indeed, the firing had not ceased, in the first onset upon the Federal cavalry at Middletown, before some of Ashby's men might have been seen, with a quickness more suitable to horse-thieves than to soldiers, breaking from their ranks, seizing each two or three of the captured horses, and making off across the fields. Nor did these men pause until they had carried their illegal booty to their homes, which were in some instances, at the distance of one or two days' journey . . ."

Young Captain Poague, who was in the fight with Ashby, said "his cavalry were looting wagons and capturing horses, utterly undisciplined. This was Ashby's weak point. Not a man of our guns was out of place. They only peeped into the wagons and picked up a few oil cloths and blankets of the hundreds scattered along the road."[35]

But the best evidence comes from Stonewall Jackson, himself, who declared in his report:

". . . There was reason to believe, if Banks reached Winchester, it would be without a train, if not without an army; but in the midst of these hopes I was pained to see, as I am now to record the fact, that so many of Ashby's command, both cavalry and infantry, forgetful of their high trust as the advance of a pursuing army, deserted their colors, and abandoned themselves to pillage to such an extent as to make it necessary for that gallant officer to discontinue further pursuit. The artillery, which had pushed on with energy to the vicinity of Newton, found itself, from this discreditable conduct, without proper support from either infantry or cavalry . . ."

On May 27, Jackson issued General Orders No. 54, stating that any soldier possessing captured goods for which he could give no satisfactory explanation would be assigned to duty that "will exclude him from those posts of honor where distinction is to be won, and which requires exhibition of the highest qualities of the patriot soldier." The General Orders deplored "the shameless pillaging" which forced "the gallant Ashby . . . to discontinue the pursuit." Until the guilty troops demonstrate "that their disgraceful conduct will not be repeated," they will not be placed again in the van of the army. It was emphasized that the appropriation of captured goods by individuals was nothing less than theft. "It is hoped that this army will discountenance acts which tend to tarnish its well-earned reputation."

After the Middletown fight, Jackson faced some stout resistance by

Federal artillery which came up to cover the disastrous retreat. Skirmishing continued practically all night as the Federals withdrew to Winchester, but Jackson pushed on, with an occasional brief rest for his weary men. The next morning, May 25, Jackson launched his attack on Winchester from two sides, and General Dick Taylor's Louisiana brigade, sweeping up the hill on Jackson's left broke the Yankee resistance and precipitated a hurried withdrawal, as the whole Confederate line rushed forward. "The Federal forces, upon falling back into the town, preserved their organization remarkably well," noted Jackson in his report. "In passing through its streets they were thrown into confusion, and shortly after, debouching into the plain and turnpike to Martinsburg and after being fired upon by our artillery, they presented the aspect of a mass of disordered fugitives."

Jackson looked in vain for his cavalry. Colonel Ashby was nowhere to be seen and General George H. Steuart of Ewell's command stood on ceremony when Jackson sent him an order to pursue the Federals, because it had not come to him through his commander.

No wonder, when General Taylor inquired of Jackson: "Where is the cavalry?" Stonewall held his tongue as he fumed inwardly.[36]

Where, indeed, was Ashby? After the war, Dr. Dabney wrote that on the morning of the battle Ashby's command was so scattered that he could gather but a handful of men and with these "he had undertaken an independent enterprise to cut off a detachment . . . on their left; and passing around the scene of action he joined in the pursuit many hours after, at Bunker Hill."

This, like the charges of looting at Middletown, was vehemently denied by Ashby's men. "I was never aware of any *independent enterprise* of Gen. Ashby's," declared Preston Chew in 1867, "nor do I believe he was anywhere but at the front of the army with a small force of his cavalry." Chew says that Ashby was with Jackson on the morning of the Battle of Winchester, while Stonewall was posting his batteries.

Once again the evidence of Jackson's report is incontrovertible:

"I had seen but some 50 of Ashby's cavalry since prior to the pillaging scenes of the previous evening and none since an early hour of the past night . . . Upon inquiring of . . . Ashby why he was not where I desired him at the close of the engagement, he stated that he had moved to the enemy's left, for the purpose of cutting off a portion of his force."

Jackson must have felt that Ashby had done all he could do with the limited means at his command for there is no suggestion in the report that Ashby's reply was unsatisfactory to him. There can, however, be no doubt that Dr. Dabney's characterization of it as an "independent enterprise" was an accurate description of Ashby's participation at Winchester.[37]

Meanwhile, Congressman Boteler had been pushing the War Department for Turner Ashby's promotion to brigadier general and his efforts were finally successful. On May 27, Ashby with a small escort rode into Winchester from Martinsburg to answer a summons from Jackson. When he entered the general's headquarters, Jackson's brilliant young staff officer, Captain Sandie Pendleton, handed him a paper, saying: "I do this with great pleasure, General Ashby, hoping that as you are soon to command a brigade, the country may expect less exposure of your life."[38]

Several days later, Jackson got word that Shields was moving from Fredericksburg on his right and Frémont on his left, aiming at a junction that would concentrate a heavy force on the Confederate rear and cut Jackson's escape route up the Valley.

Having frightened the Lincoln government almost out of its wits, and kept reinforcements from going to McClellan, and taken 2300 prisoners, and captured huge quantities of commissary, medical, and ordnance supplies, including 9354 small arms, Jackson decided it was now time to leave. Stonewall moved out of Winchester on May 31, and his famous retreat up the Shenandoah Valley began.

By June 2, Jackson was being pursued by Federals as well as being threatened on both flanks, but he eluded all attempts to bag him. On that day, the enemy's advance got within artillery range and shelled the rear guard heavily. Most of the cavalry under General Steuart and that part of the artillery nearest the enemy retreated in disorder.

"This led General Ashby to one of those acts of personal heroism and prompt resources which strikingly marked his character," reported Stonewall Jackson. Leaping from his horse, Ashby collected roadside stragglers and placed them quickly in a woods bordering the turnpike to await the Federal cavalry, following up the panic produced by the shelling. "As they approached within easy range," said Jackson, "he poured such an effective fire into their ranks as to empty a number of saddles and check their farther pursuit for that day." Jackson immediately transferred the 2nd and 6th Virginia Cavalry from General Steuart to General Ashby and he placed the latter in command of the rear guard.[39]

It was a fight all the way and General Ashby and his men had few moments of respite from action as they battled from hill to hill to protect Jackson's army and his heavily laden wagon train.

On June 5, 1862, the head of Jackson's column reached Harrisonburg early in the morning and turned eastward in the direction of Port Republic.

IX

The heavy rains that dogged Jackson's retreat had ended and June 6 was a day bathed in bright sunshine.

On the preceding night the rear guard under General Turner Ashby had bivouacked two miles from Harrisonburg on the Valley Pike, but with the dawn it followed Jackson's main body down the road to Port Republic.

Ashby was up with the sun, and to his staff he seemed "all energy and life" as he rode up and down the east flank of the army and then to the rear, conscious that Jackson still needed time to get his precious wagon trains over the miserable muddy road to the safety of Port Republic.

These were Ashby's two missions, to keep Shields, advancing up the valley of the South Fork of the Shenandoah, from striking Jackson by surprise and to protect the Valley Army from an attack on its rear by cavalry operating with Frémont.

Considerable skirmishing, but none of it of a serious nature, occupied much of the morning. In the early afternoon, several miles south of Harrisonburg, General Ashby had dismounted his men and the horses were allowed to graze in fields on each side of the road. Suddenly Ashby discerned in the distance, coming from Harrisonburg, some Union cavalry, advancing at a spirited pace. "Mount and form!" he shouted and his men sprang into the saddle.

Quickly, Ashby made up his mind what he would do. He dispatched some of his men into the woods on either side of the road to pounce down upon the Federals after they had passed, while he, himself, prepared to lead a charge against the coming enemy.

"Now is our time boys," he called out. ". . . Follow me, we'll drive them back or die."[40]

Ashby's sharp command aroused Private James Baumgardner, Jr., of Company A of the 52nd Virginia Infantry, which was part of the cavalry support. "Immediately afterwards I saw General Ashby gallop up to the high . . . fence between the field and the road," Baumgardner later recalled. "The splendid stallion on which Ashby was mounted leaped over the fence and landed in the road a few feet in front of me, then leaped over the fence into the field on the north of the road. General Ashby galloped to the center and front of the cavalry there and gave the command to move forward."

A characteristic of Ashby was to meet a charge with a countercharge and this he did. Private Baumgardner saw Ashby's men start forward on the road, first at a walk, then at a trot and finally into a gallop which soon took them out of his sight.

The Yankee cavalry, led by British Sir Percy Wyndham, who had made it known about the countryside that he intended to capture the Rebel Ashby, rode on oblivious of the ambush into which they were about to fall. The two cavalry groups met head-on but Ashby's onslaught, followed quickly by the attack by his two flanking forces, proved too much for the 1st New Jersey Cavalry. Private Baumgardner and his comrades heard "wild yells and shouts, the cracking of pistols, and the clanking of sabers, and then all was quiet." The New Jersey Cavalry which had set out to bag Ashby broke and retreated, leaving Colonel Sir Percy Wynd-ham and 63 Yankees in Turner Ashby's hands.

When the first prisoner, a private, was brought to the rear, he was asked what happened. The Yankee replied: "Percy Wyndham met the man he had so long sought, and I didn't think he'd care about seeing him soon again, for we've been smashed all to flinders." The Confederate infantrymen had a ball when the elegantly attired Englishman passed down the line. One Reb yelled to his mates: "Look yonder boys; there's a Yankee Colonel!" Sir Percy, swearing like a trooper as he came up, stopped and with a contemptuous look at the soldier, exclaimed: "I'm not a Yankee, you —— Rebel fool!"[41]

General Ashby did not rest on his laurels, but schemed to ambush more of the advancing enemy and asked General Ewell for some supporting infantry. Ashby had seen Frémont's infantry moving in his direction after the capture of Wyndham and the rout of his cavalry.

"General, you've done a handsome thing already," said Colonel Tom Munford. "Do you think they will be as easily fooled again?"

"They have had it all their way long enough," Ashby answered. "I am tired of *being crowded* and will make them stop it after today."[42]

General Ashby put Munford in charge of the cavalry, and ordered him to place two of Captain Preston Chew's guns in the woods by the roadside, shielded by a squad of cavalry, the main body of which would be in support. Ashby placed the 1st Maryland Infantry in the woods to strike the Federals in flank, while he himself led the 58th Virginia.

Ashby sent back orders to Munford to let the enemy advance as far as they would until near enough to make sure of fight. When he, Ashby, struck on the flank, Munford was to open fire and charge with the entire cavalry. "The distribution was made," said Munford, "and ere long heavy firing was heard in the woods—it was soon evident that Ashby had himself been ambuscaded."[43]

Soon the 58th Virginia was hotly engaged and the enemy, the celebrated Bucktail Rifles from Pennsylvania, from behind a fence, delivered a withering fire into Ashby's ranks. Ashby rode all over his front, urging and encouraging his men who were recoiling from the blistering barrage. His horse was shot from under him and together they went down. General Ashby, disengaging himself from his dying mount, jumped to his feet, shouting: "Charge men! For God's sake, charge!"[44] He waved his sword in the direction of the foe and took a couple of steps.

And then a bullet pierced the heart of Turner Ashby and the Beau Sabreur of Stonewall Jackson's little Army of the Valley fell dead.

3

Stonewall of the West:

GENERAL PAT CLEBURNE

H E WENT to war in 1861 as a private, but when he died on the bloody field of Franklin in 1864, Pat Cleburne was a Confederate major general and known universally in the Army of Tennessee as the "Stonewall of the West."

Of him, it was admirably said by a comrade in arms: "Cleburne rose to be a military authority in our army. He knew the very rudiments of fighting and had the genius to use his knowledge. Always ready and watchful, never depressed, beloved by his good men, feared by his bad men, trusted by all, indomitable in courage, skillfully headlong in attack, coolly strategic in retreat, thorough master of detail, yet with large Generalship, obedient to the letter, capable in any crisis, modest as a woman, a resolute disciplinarian, Cleburne was a gem of a warrior."[1]

When the war was over, the men of his command cherished the memory of "Old Pat," as they affectionately called their thirty-six-year-old leader. A county in Arkansas bears his name as do two towns, one in Texas and the other in Kansas.

And in the pantheon of the Confederacy his name and fame are secure, placed there shortly after the war by his commanding officer and warm friend, Lieutenant General William J. Hardee: "When his division defended, no odds broke its lines; where it attacked, no numbers resisted its onslaught, save only once, and there is the grave of Cleburne."[2]

Patrick Ronayne Cleburne was born in Desertmore, County Cork, Ireland, on St. Patrick's Day, March 17, 1828. Through a common seventeenth-century ancestor, he was related to the American Claibornes, descendants of the famous "King" Claiborne who settled in Virginia in Colonial days.

His father, a doctor, had hopes that his son would follow in his footsteps. Young Cleburne went to Trinity College in Dublin to study pharmacy as a preliminary, but his inability to handle Latin, Greek, and

French resulted in his failure to pass his examinations. Feeling a sense of shame, Cleburne, without telling his friends or family, enlisted on February 27, 1846, in Her Majesty's 41st Regiment of Foot, stating that by trade he was a laborer. Cleburne must have been a good soldier, for on July 1, 1849, he was promoted to corporal. Years later, when Lieutenant Colonel Arthur J. L. Fremantle visited Cleburne's camp during that British officer's three months in the Confederacy, Cleburne told him that he "ascribed his advancement mainly to the useful lessons which he learned in the ranks of the British Army."

Cleburne did not enjoy his corporal's grade very long because on September 22, 1849, he purchased his discharge from the British army. On November 11, 1849, accompanied by a brother and sister he sailed in steerage aboard the bark *Bridgetown* from Queenstown, bound for the United States. After 44 days at sea, Cleburne reached New Orleans on Christmas Day. He did not tarry in New Orleans, but went upriver to Cincinnati, where he secured employment in a drugstore. In April 1850, Cleburne settled in Helena, Arkansas, becoming associated in the drugstore of Dr. C. E. Nash.

The people of Helena looked the twenty-two-year-old Irishman over and decided that he was a young man worthy of acceptance into the community. He was not handsome—a long and prominent nose and high cheekbones precluded this—but he made a striking appearance. His six-foot frame he always carried erect, and his broad shoulders helped to make him an impressive figure. A heavy shock of dark brown hair surmounted a moderately high forehead on a head which was long and narrow and perched on a long neck. Cleburne's gray-blue eyes, not far apart, were active, quick to sparkle in humor or grow dark and stern.

Cleburne interested himself in many things. He joined a debating society, espoused Whig politics, became a vestryman in St. John's Episcopal Church, entered the Masonic order, studied law and was admitted to the bar in 1856. He became an expert with the pistol, quick on the draw and deadly in aim, a talent which saved his life one day when one of the "bad men" of the neighborhood, furious that Cleburne had supported a friend in a controversy, shot him in the back from a doorway. Cleburne was dangerously wounded, the ball passing through his body, but as he fell, he drew his pistol and killed his assailant.

His first employer and later business partner, Dr. Nash, said that Cleburne was "one of the most fastidious young men I ever knew." He never used "a vulgar expression, nor could he bear to hear anyone else use bad language."

Normally temperate, Pat Cleburne once got drunk on cognac after a chess match. By nature he was modest and shy, and Cleburne's friends noted his awkwardness in society. Dr. Nash thought him "a very bashful young man." Another friend, later his law partner, and still later a member of his staff, Judge L. H. Mangum, recalled Cleburne's lack of grace and embarrassment in all company, except that of his close friends. He summed up Cleburne of his Helena days, thusly:

"He was a man of great activity and of great powers of endurance . . . He was not a good conversationalist except when in the company of congenial friends whose intimacy freed him from all shackles of embarrassment . . . The most pronounced characteristic of the man, to those who knew him best and saw him in all the aspects of his life, was his courage. He had indeed the lion's heart . . . He never grew noisy or furious, never exhibited the slightest form of bravado, and he never quailed before odds or difficulties . . . In all the relations of private life he was what he afterwards showed himself to be in tent and field."[3]

Although Arkansas did not formally join in the first phase of the secession movement which swept the lower South after Lincoln's election, Governor Henry M. Rector seized the Federal arsenal in Little Rock in February, 1861. Present at the seizure as a private in a volunteer company, the Yell Rifles, was the thirty-two-year-old lawyer and now a leading citizen of Helena, Patrick Ronayne Cleburne.

Cleburne had become a Democrat when the Know-Nothing Party absorbed the defunct Whigs and, although he himself owned no slaves, he sympathized with the Southern position in the sectional "cold war" in the decade before secession.

After the surrender of Fort Sumter and Lincoln's calls for volunteers, secession moved into its second phase, during which time Arkansas cast its lot with the Confederacy. In May 1861 the Yell Rifles entered the service of the state of Arkansas, and Cleburne was elected captain. When the company was combined with others to become the 15th Arkansas Regiment, the young Irishman was elected colonel. In July, Cleburne's regiment joined the command of General William J. Hardee at Pitmans Ferry in northern Arkansas on the Missouri line.

General Hardee, who had written the standard text on infantry tactics in the Old Army, quickly recognized qualities of leadership, character, and military ability in the young Irish colonel from Arkansas. He watched approvingly Cleburne's devotion to details; the painstaking way in which he drilled and instructed the men in his command, his persistence and industry in mastering everything connected with tactics. From morning until night, day after day, Cleburne busied himself superintending squad, company, and battalion drills, mounting guard, and inspection. Hardee was much impressed with Cleburne's "qualifications as a disciplinarian and commander" together with his "unremitting study and labor" and he not only marked him early for promotion but made of him a warm personal friend.

A fellow officer, Basil W. Duke, recalled seeing Cleburne "during the hottest hours of the hottest days of August instruct squad after squad in the bayonet exercise until I wondered how any human frame could endure the fatigue that his exertions must have induced."

Although generally circumspect in his language, Cleburne, when angry or surprised, sometimes swore briefly, but energetically. His slow, clear precise speech normally had little of the Irish accent, but when Cleburne was excited, he lapsed naturally into a thick brogue.

An incident occurred during the early days of the war which clouded Cleburne's spirit until the day he died. At Greenville, Missouri, which Hardee had invaded in July, a number of Federal prisoners were brought in. One of the guards, housed in the same building in which Cleburne was quartered, was a sleepwalker, and one night while in this state, he noisily entered Cleburne's room. The latter, jumping to the conclusion that a raid was underway or an attempted breakout by the prisoners, saw the man advancing on him. Quickly he drew his pistol and fired, mortally wounding the innocent intruder. Although fully exonerated, Cleburne never forgave himself for killing the man, and he brooded the rest of his life over the slaying.[4]

Pat Cleburne's high ethical sense was revealed shortly after this when Hardee was ordered into Kentucky. He sent Cleburne in mid-November on a probing movement to Tompkinsville, during which time, to Pat's chagrin, some of the teamsters in the rear guard and also malingering stragglers, who drifted to the rear under pretense of illness, stole poultry and other things along the road. Out of his own pocket, Cleburne paid for the articles stolen by his men. Throughout the war, Cleburne never lost his sense of justice.

On the strong recommendation of General Hardee, Cleburne was made a brigadier general on March 4, 1862, after having led a brigade as a colonel for some while. By this time, General Albert Sidney Johnston had withdrawn from Kentucky, following the fall of Forts Henry and Donelson and, having abandoned West and Middle Tennessee, had concentrated his forces at Corinth, Mississippi.[5]

Cleburne was soon to get his baptism of fire, as were the bulk of the Confederate forces in the West, then known as the Army of the Mississippi and later as the Army of Tennessee.

II

General William T. Sherman, encamped near Shiloh Church, not far from Pittsburg Landing on the Tennessee River, wrote General Ulysses S. Grant on the afternoon of April 5: "I do not apprehend anything like an attack upon our position." And Grant, the same day wired General Henry W. Halleck in St. Louis: "I have scarcely the faintest idea of an attack (general one) being made upon us."[6]

At this very time, the Confederate Army of 40,000 men was poised less than two miles from Grant's line, ready to strike at dawn on April 6. But both Grant and Sherman insisted later that they were not surprised by Albert Sidney Johnston's attack at Shiloh.

The Confederate plan was to attack Grant at Pittsburg Landing, on the Tennessee River, roll up the Union left and drive Grant away from his base and into the swamps of Owl Creek and Snake Creek into which it flows. The latter empties into the Tennessee, north of the Landing. The attack would be in three waves along a corps front, with Hardee's corps leading, followed by that of General Braxton Bragg, a thousand yards in Hardee's rear, and that to be followed by the corps of General Leonidas Polk and General John C. Breckinridge.

Hardee, in advance, reached Mickey's, about eight miles from Pittsburg Landing, on the morning of April 4, and that afternoon elements of Cleburne's brigade had a brush with some Union cavalry, taking a few prisoners.

Torrential rains delayed the advance so that it was not until about 10 A.M. on April 5 that Hardee's Corps reached the outposts and developed the lines of the enemy. Hardee immediately deployed his three brigades, and Gladden's brigade from Bragg's Corps, about a mile and a half from the small log Shiloh Church. He extended his right toward Lick Creek which generally parallels Owl Creek and flows into the Tennessee south of Pittsburg Landing, while his left rested almost on Owl Creek, about three miles away.

Cleburne's brigade was on the left of Hardee's command and soon after daylight on April 6, he began the advance, moving through woods for some time without opposition until his skirmishers made contact with Union skirmishers, driving them back on to their lines. As Cleburne's brigade emerged from the wooded area, he saw the Union encampment behind which a line of battle had formed. Cleburne immediately realized that the enemy was advantageously placed, overlapping his left flank by at least half a brigade, while on his right, the Union troops were firing from a breastwork of logs and bales of hay.

From close range, Union musketry and artillery "swept the open space . . . with an iron storm that threatened destruction to every living thing that would dare to cross them," as Cleburne later reported. Jutting out from the foot of the high ground on which the Federals were posted was an almost impassable morass which impeded the progress of Cleburne's center, and soon caused a wide gap in his brigade between the regiments on his left and on his right.

In an effort to restore the integrity of his line, Cleburne rode into the morass, but his horse soon became bogged down and finally threw its rider. The Irishman must have drawn upon his seldom used but eloquent expletives as he picked himself up with difficulty from the muck and remounted to lead the assault upon the Federal line. Brigade artillery, which had supported Cleburne's advance, was now caught in a cross fire of Union batteries and it withdrew to a less torrid position and for the rest of the battle Cleburne had no artillery under his command.

Two of Cleburne's regiments on the right, the 6th Mississippi and 23rd Tennessee, charged into the encampment but the tents, of necessity, broke the line, and a blistering fire added to the confusion in their ranks. A quick and bloody repulse resulted. The two regiments fell back about a hundred yards and the Mississippians regrouped to attack again and again, but the Tennessee regiment was rallied only with great difficulty. Cleburne was among them, exhorting and inspiring them, but the main burden of attack on Cleburne's right was borne by the 6th Mississippi. This regiment fought with courage and devotion, until 300 of its officers and men out of an aggregate of 425 were killed or wounded. Only then did the Mississippians retreat in disorder.

Meanwhile, while his right was regrouping, Cleburne galloped around the bog to see how his left was faring. There he discovered that after a desperate fight with heavy losses, the enemy's encampment had been carried by the 24th Tennessee, the 2nd Tennessee and the 15th Arkansas, Cleburne's former regiment.

Assured that his left was secure, Cleburne rode back to his hard-pressed right where about half the 23rd Tennessee and about 60 men of the 6th Mississippi had re-formed. Ordering them forward, Cleburne led the way into the enemy encampment, from which the Federals had retreated when his regiments on the left had gained the tents.

The present usefulness, however, of the two battered regiments on his right was over and the remnants of the 6th Mississippi and 23rd Tennessee were marched to the rear. Cleburne now had no command on this part of the field and he so reported to General Hardee, who ordered him to collect and bring into action a large body of stragglers who were in the rear. Despite great exertion, Cleburne only partly succeeded in gathering a force in which he reposed no confidence should the enemy let loose with heavy fire. Cleburne decided it was better to rejoin his regiments on the left, which he did at about 2 P.M.

He found the badly cut up 2nd Tennessee retiring to regroup, but the 5th Tennessee, 24th Tennessee, and 15th Arkansas were halted under the brow of a hill. Cleburne ordered an advance, but had to suspend it until Confederate artillery fire across the line of attack could be stopped. Cleburne pushed forward a half mile before his skirmishers were driven in, and soon he was heavily engaged. After half an hour of sharp fighting, the Federals hurriedly withdrew, fortunately for Cleburne, whose men had exhausted their ammunition. The terrain made it impossible for ammunition wagons to follow Cleburne's advance and so he sent a fatigue party back a mile to carry the ammunition boxes on their shoulders.

Meanwhile, bloody fighting had been going on for hours all over the battlefield. At 2:30 P.M. General Albert Sidney Johnston was killed and General P. G. T. Beauregard assumed command. The Confederate right, instead of rolling Grant's left away from Pittsburg Landing, had been held up by General Benjamin M. Prentiss's valiant defense of an area later to be known as the "Hornets' Nest." Only when General Ruggles massed 62 pieces of artillery to concentrate their fire on Prentiss's position were the Confederates able to carry the "Hornets' Nest."

When his troops were again supplied with ammunition, Cleburne ordered an advance, but progress was checked by heavy fire from Union field guns and gunboats in the river. When this firing died down, Cleburne advanced again, until word came from General Beauregard, as darkness descended over the bloody field, for Cleburne to approach no nearer the river.

A heavy rain during the night made things miserable for the Confederates and Cleburne's remnants were made doubly uncomfortable by periodic shelling by the Federal gunboats at Pittsburg Landing. "Every fifteen minutes the enemy threw two shells from his gunboats," Cleburne reported, "some of which burst close around my men, banishing sleep from the eyes of a few, but falling chiefly among their own wounded, who were strewn thickly between my camp and the river. History records few instances of more reckless inhumanity than this."

Daylight on April 7 had barely come before activity by the Federals was noted, the Confederate cavalry pickets being driven in. It was evident to Pat Cleburne, as it was to other Confederate officers on the field, that "Buell had arrived and we had a fresh army to fight." Cleburne contemplated his command with sadness as he re-formed to advance, in compliance with an order from General Hardee. He later reported:

"My brigade was sadly reduced. From near 2700, I now numbered about 800. Two regiments, the 2nd Tennessee and 6th Mississippi, were absent altogether. Hundreds of my best men were dead or in the hospitals, and, I blush to add, hundreds of others had run off early in the fight of the day before—some through cowardice, and some loaded with the plunder from the Yankee encampments."

With the gallant fraction of his brigade, Cleburne moved up about a mile, where he found a part of Breckinridge's command and he formed on its left and ordered his men to lie down. "I could see plainly the enemy's line in my front," reported Cleburne, "and that it stretched beyond my left as far as the eye could see."

Soon a message came to Cleburne from General Breckinridge, ordering him to attack the Federals on his front. Cleburne was dumfounded by the order.

"I am completely without support and outflanked on the left and will be destroyed if I advance," he replied.

Back came another message stating that the order was positive, and from General Bragg, and that Cleburne must advance at once. Never a man to disobey an order, Cleburne made his move, but his troops had gone but a little distance before a Confederate battery began firing across the line of march. Cleburne was compelled to halt. Then the Union guns opened up and more Confederate guns took up the fire. Cleburne's troops and the entire infantry line to his right were only spectators in the fierce artillery duel that was waged for fully a half hour before it became apparent that the Confederate batteries were overmatched and they withdrew.

Then, reported Cleburne, "the whole line of infantry charged the enemy. There was a very thick undergrowth here of young trees, which prevented my men from seeing any distance, yet offered them no protection from the storm of bullets and grape shot that swept through it. I could not see what was going on to my right or left, but my men were dropping all around before the fire of the unseen foe . . . My brigade was repulsed and almost completely routed in this unfortunate attack."

Cleburne valiantly tried to rally his men, but only what remained of the 15th Arkansas responded to his call. Under heavy fire, the regiment regrouped and, joined by reinforcements, it charged the enemy with Cleburne at its head. The Federals broke and ran and the 15th Arkansas continued the pursuit until ammunition was exhausted and then, all that was left of the regiment—58 men—fell back.

By now, Cleburne's brigade had lost its identity, completely scattered and disorganized. Many of the officers and men continued the fight in the ranks of other commands or on their own and Cleburne found himself with no organization which he could control.

Cleburne tried to rally stragglers and form them in lines, to help cover the Confederate general retirement which was now under way. Fortunately, the Yankees had their fill of fighting, too, and only feeble efforts at pursuit were made. Cleburne remained on the battlefield destroying property which could not be carried off and giving whatever aid to the wounded that he could. He stayed until after sunset when, upon orders from General Hardee, he left for Corinth.

When the stragglers were rounded up and a tabulation of casualties was made, Cleburne discovered that he had suffered the loss of 1043 men— 188 killed, 790 wounded, and 65 missing—for the heaviest casualties of any brigade in the attacking Confederate Army. It was not without pride that Cleburne reported:

"This was the first battle my men ever engaged in. They led the advance of our army on Shiloh and engaged and repulsed the enemy's cavalry the Friday before the battle. They fought in the foremost line both days and were never rested or relieved for a moment. They captured many stands of colors and assisted in the capture of General Prentiss' brigade . . ."

This was Cleburne's first battle, too, and he ably demonstrated that his recent promotion to brigadier general was a wise decision. General Hardee, whose personal admiration for Pat Cleburne increased with matching pace to his profound respect for his military leadership, took pride in his protégé. In his official report, Hardee said:

"During the action, Brigadier-General Cleburne conducted his command with persevering valor. No repulse discouraged him; but after many bloody struggles he assembled the remnant of his brigade and was conspicuous for his gallantry to the end of the battle."[7]

III

When General Braxton Bragg, now in command of the Army of the Mississippi—soon to be known as the Army of Tennessee—launched his invasion of Kentucky in the summer of 1862, he enlisted the cooperation of General Kirby Smith, who commanded Confederate forces in East Tennessee.

To strengthen Kirby Smith, Bragg sent Pat Cleburne in command of two brigades, his own, led by Colonel B. J. Hill, and the brigade of Colonel Preston Smith.

Kirby Smith crossed the Cumberland Mountains at Big Creek Gap and moved into the vicinity of Richmond, Kentucky, where contact with the enemy was made on the evening of August 29. General Smith decided to attack immediately and Cleburne's command moved out at daybreak on the thirtieth, as the infantry advance. Deploying his troops skillfully, Cleburne organized and directed the attack, but he was not on the field when the victory which he had prepared was gained. As he rode about the field giving orders, he paused to say a word to Colonel Lucius E. Polk, who had been wounded and was being carried from the field. As he spoke, a rifle ball entered Cleburne's left cheek, shattered his lower teeth without touching the bone and passed out through his open mouth. (General Hardee's version of the wounding of Cleburne is that the ball went through Pat's open mouth and then out the cheek.)

Thus deprived of ability to speak, the disabled Cleburne turned the command over to Colonel Preston Smith and left the field. Cleburne's brilliant handling of his first independent command did not go unnoticed. General Hardee said that Cleburne "was mainly instrumental in winning a victory, which in number of prisoners and amount of stores captured, and in the utter dispersion and destruction of the opposing force, was one of the most complete of the war."

And General Kirby Smith, who was now free to march without opposition to Lexington and to establish an outpost at Covington, across the Ohio from Cincinnati, lauded Cleburne in his official report: "General Cleburne was badly wounded in the face, and thus at a critical moment I was deprived of the services of one of the most gallant, zealous, and intelligent officers of my army."

The Confederate Congress passed a vote of thanks to Cleburne "for gallant and meritorious service" in the Battle of Richmond.[8]

It was not until October that Pat Cleburne was able to rejoin his brigade which had been returned by Kirby Smith to its proper command, Buckner's division in Hardee's corps. He was just in time to participate with conspicuous bravery in the Battle of Perryville on October 7, when Bragg attacked Buell. While riding hard in leading a charge on a stone wall from behind which the Federals were pouring a deadly fire, Cleburne's horse was shot from under him by a cannon ball, which also wounded him in the leg. Horse and rider went down and the soldiers around him thought Cleburne was dead. But he scrambled to his feet, spitting dirt out of his mouth, and waving his sword, he urged on his men, shouting: "Give 'em hell, boys!" With a yell, Cleburne's men swept forward.[9]

Bragg's Kentucky campaign, despite Federal casualties of more than 26,000 and the loss of 35 cannon, 16,000 small arms, millions of rounds of ammunition, 3700 horses and mules and a large wagon train, came to naught, for, after the Battle of Perryville, Bragg decided to retire into Tennessee. Many of Bragg's generals, Pat Cleburne among them, felt that he had let one opportunity after another slip through his grasp, opportunities for decisive victories the fruits of which might have been an invasion across the Ohio.

Bragg's own losses were far from light, but the capture of so enormous a quantity of military supplies would be useful to the Confederates, if they could be got to safety. Of this, however, there was considerable doubt for the wagons totaled nearly 4000 and progress was slow over miserable roads choked with troops and stragglers. Averaging barely five miles a day, Bragg's and Kirby Smith's wagon trains were under constant threat from the Federals, who applied considerable pressure on Colonel Joe Wheeler's cavalry, and Colonel John H. Morgan's infantry serving as the rear guard.

Despite their superb job of holding off the enemy, it seemed certain on October 15 that Bragg would be compelled to abandon his wagons to the Federals. Near a difficult spot on the retreat route, Big Hill, the train was at a virtual standstill. Kirby Smith scribbled a hurried note to Bragg: "*I have little hope of saving any of the trains, and fear much of the artillery will be lost.*" Shortly thereafter, Kirby Smith gave orders to destroy the trains.

Cleburne, who was off duty as a result of his leg wound, heard about the order and asked for the authority to try to extricate the wagon train from its impasse, employing such means as he deemed necessary. When the permission was granted, Cleburne went right to work with, as General Hardee put it, "indomitable will and energy." Hardee's description of the incident reveals admirably Pat Cleburne's characteristic determination to get a job done:

"He at once stationed guards on the road, arrested every straggler and passing officer and soldier, collected a large force, organized fatigue parties, and literally lifted the trains over the hills. The trains thus preserved contained munitions and subsistence of the utmost value and necessity to the Confederates."[10]

General Bragg, by now, was thoroughly aware of the young Irishman from Arkansas and of his worth as a military leader. He recommended to the War Department that Cleburne be promoted to major general, declaring: "Cleburne is young, ardent, exceedingly gallant, sufficiently prudent. Is a fine drill officer, and the admiration of his command, as a soldier and a gentleman." Cleburne's promotion came on December 12, 1862, and he was moved up to command the division lately headed by General Simon Bolivar Buckner, under whom Cleburne and his brigade served.[11]

Before the month was out, Cleburne would have his chance to demonstrate that he could lead a division as skillfully and energetically as he could a brigade.

After the retreat from Kentucky, Bragg had set up headquarters at Murfreesboro, Tennessee, 30 miles southeast of Nashville. General William S. Rosecrans, who had succeeded Buell in command of the Union forces in Tennessee, moved out on December 26 to attack Bragg. The latter had disposed his army to the west and north of Murfreesboro. Hardee's corps, composed of Breckinridge's and Cleburne's divisions, was in position north of the town and separated from the rest of Bragg's army by Stone's River, which, discounting bends, runs generally north.

It was Bragg's intention to apply strong pressure by his left against Rosecrans' right, roll it back and then drive the Federal army into Stone's River. On the night of December 30, Cleburne received orders to cross the river and take up a position on the extreme left of Bragg's army. Fording the river presented some difficulties and it was not until midnight that Cleburne's brigades were in line. Although his men had little or no rest, Cleburne on orders from Hardee moved to the attack before daylight the next morning.

Cleburne's leadership in the battle of Murfreesboro justified the confidence that General Hardee and General Bragg had reposed in him. His division drove the Federals according to plan, sweeping them back, in bitter all-day fighting, toward Stone's River. By 3 P.M., Cleburne had gained more than three miles of ground and had taken many prisoners, cannon, and small arms. But his troops were getting weary. "My men had had little or no rest the night before," Cleburne reported. "They had been fighting since dawn, without relief, food, or water; they were comparatively without the support of artillery, for the advance had been too rapid to enable my single battery to get in position and answer the enemy; their ammunition was again nearly exhausted, and our ordnance trains could not follow."

At this critical point the Federals, having rushed reinforcements from their left and center, where they had been heavily engaged, presented a fresh line of battle to Cleburne's tired brigades. The new Yankee battle line brought to bear a blistering artillery fire at close range and succeeded in flanking Cleburne's right.

"This was more than our men could stand," reported Cleburne. ". . . As our broken ranks went back over the fields before the fire of this fresh line, the enemy opened fire on our right flank from several batteries which they had concentrated on an eminence . . . The division was rallied on the edge of the opposite woods, about 400 yards in the rear of the disaster."

By now fresh supplies of ammunition were at hand and Cleburne prepared to meet an enemy charge that never came. He hesitated to charge again, without specific orders from Hardee, for he felt that another repulse by the fresh Federals on his front might demoralize his division and bring about its destruction. Soon came word from his superior to hold the ground he had won, rest his men, reorganize the division and wait further orders.

Hardee had nothing but praise for his protégé. "Cleburne's Division," he wrote, "in single line of battle, without reinforcements, rest or refreshments, encountered and drove before it five successive lines of battle . . . The general results of the day were not decisive in favor of the Southern arms; but this heightens the achievement of that portion of the army which was successful, and the merits of the officer whose skillful handling of his division contributed materially to that success."

Although the Battle of Murfreesboro did not end until January 2, 1863, there was not much fighting on New Year's Day. Cleburne was ordered to feel out the enemy to see if his front was still held in force. He was soon sharply engaged but, under orders not to bring on a general engagement, he retired. On January 2, Bragg attacked with his right wing north of Murfreesboro and east of Stone's River and initially a great victory was in the making. But the Federals massed 58 pieces of artillery on high ground and swept the field of the Confederate attack with a fire of 100 rounds per minute. The Confederate charge, begun so auspiciously and apparently close to a smashing victory, now turned into a disastrous retreat and rout.

Cleburne's front was quiet during the fighting on January 2, but that night an enemy reconnaissance was driven back by his skirmishers. Immediately thereafter Cleburne was ordered to recross Stone's River and take up his original position occupied before the battle began. Twenty-four bitter hours of cold and rain, but no fighting, followed. Then orders came for Cleburne to move out. Braxton Bragg had begun his retreat.

Cleburne went into action at Murfreesboro with 6045 men and lost 2081 in killed, wounded, and missing, or more than 34 per cent of his command. He played an important part in the first day's victory of the Confederates and Bragg in his official report commended the Irishman "for the valor, skill, and ability displayed . . . throughout the engagement."[12]

IV

"The Army of Tennessee . . . labored under the crippling disadvantage of shifting and inexpert leadership," wrote Stanley F. Horn, biographer of that gallant Confederate army. ". . . Its history is one long, tragic story of changing commanders and wrangling among its leaders, of victories whose fruits were not gathered, of defeats which by a slight turn of fortune's wheel might have been signal victories—a discouraging succession of disappointments and might-have-beens."

As they slogged through the mud in cold, driving rain and sleet, weary and depressed, the men of Bragg's army asked themselves the question that people all over the South were asking: What is the matter with Bragg? He fights battles, wins them and then retreats. First it was Perryville, then Murfreesboro. "What was the use of winning a battle if Bragg didn't know what to do with it?"[13]

Bragg fell back to Tullahoma and Shelbyville, southeast of Murfreesboro, and Pat Cleburne's division established itself at Wartrace, about 15 miles north of Bragg's headquarters. The commanding general became conscious of the mounting criticism of his leadership, for Southern newspapers were full of abuse of Bragg and his astonishing military formula of fight, win, fall back. Bragg would have had to possess a mighty thick skin not to feel keenly the now generally low esteem with which he was held throughout the Confederacy after the retreat from Murfreesboro.

On January 11, 1863, he dispatched a circular letter to his corps and division commanders, requesting written refutation from them of the published charge that he had insisted on retreat against the advice of his officers. "It becomes necessary for me to save my fair name," he wrote, "if I can not stop the deluge of abuse which will destroy my usefulness and demoralize this army . . . I desire that you will consult my subordinate commanders and be candid with me . . . General [Kirby]

Smith has been called to Richmond—it is supposed with a view to supersede me. I shall retire without regret if I find I have lost the good opinion of my generals, upon whom I have ever relied as upon a foundation of rock."

Bragg asked for candor and he got it. Pat Cleburne, along with Hardee and Breckinridge, didn't hesitate to speak his mind on such an invitation. "I have consulted with all my brigade commanders," Cleburne wrote, ". . . and they unite with me in personal regard for yourself, in high appreciation of your patriotism and gallantry, and in a conviction of your great capacity for organization; but at the same time they see, with regret, and it has also met my observation, that you do not possess the confidence of the army in other respects in the degree to secure success."

Hardee replied to Bragg that his generals were "unanimous in their opinion that a change in the command of this army is necessary. In this opinion, I concur." Breckinridge was no less frank. He expressed concurrence in his subordinates' opinion "that you do not possess the confidence of the army to an extent which will enable you to be useful as its commander."

President Davis, informed of the turn of events, had General Joseph E. Johnston investigate with the result that Bragg was kept in command.[14]

The Army of Tennessee remained inactive for six months in its positions around Tullahoma and Shelbyville, but Pat Cleburne devoted almost all of his time to drilling, inspecting, and generally improving his command. The efficiency of the sharpshooters which he had first organized at Corinth was improved by target practice and range-judging exercises and the best shots in all his brigades were brought together to form what later became, when the Whitworth rifles with telescopic sights arrived from England, his famous "Whitworth Sharpshooters."

A rigid disciplinarian, Cleburne was nonetheless just as rigidly committed to justice. Long ago, his troops had discovered that whereas any breach of military rule would be met by quick and certain retribution, Cleburne wouldn't tolerate any punishment that humiliated, degraded, or disgraced the guilty parties. "He rightly contended that such lessened or destroyed self-respect, without which no man could be a good soldier," wrote Cleburne's adjutant, Captain Irving A. Buck. "His method was for minor offenses, military work—extra guard duty, cleaning guns and accouterments, or withdrawing for a time any privileges enjoyed in the way of short leaves of absence from camp. For graver matters the case went before a court martial."

Once Cleburne came out of his quarters to find a soldier in front, marking time. Inquiry brought out that the man was being punished for some trivial breach of discipline. Cleburne ordered the man to return to his company and immediately raked the officer over the coals, informing him that his headquarters was not the guardhouse and that he thoroughly disapproved of such punishment. On another occasion, when Cleburne learned that one of his obstreperous soldiers, locked up for drunkenness, had been whipped with the buckle end of a belt by an officer of the guard, he didn't rest until the offending officer was broken of his commission.[15]

It was no wonder that Cleburne's men idolized him. One old veteran of his command, years later, recalled with pride "the great honor to have served under such a soldier." Cleburne, for all his strictness, said the old Confederate, "always looked to the comfort of his men, and was dearly beloved of them . . . His quiet kindly humor was so blended with reproof to both officers and men as to take the sting away." He described an inspection in which General Cleburne passed down the line, looking into the guns. He stopped before a man, critically inspected his gun and handed it back. Looking the man squarely in the eye, he said: "I hope I do no injustice, my man, but I don't think you have washed your face for several days." Thereafter, recalled the veteran, the man's gun and face were "always ready for action."

Another veteran declared: "Cleburne's division, always distinguished, was famous after the battle of Murfreesboro." It was said at the time that Cleburne's division would have made the reputation of any general. But Captain Buck, who knew the division and Cleburne at first hand contended that while "better material never existed . . . it was Cleburne's master hand that forged, tempered, and welded them into the superb fighting weapon they became."

And there were many, then and now, who agreed with still another old Rebel's sweeping boast: ". . . Taken singly or as a whole, there was never a better or braver division than Cleburne's in either army during the stormy days between 1861 and 1865."[16]

Cleburne's old regiment, the 15th Arkansas, still a part of his command, showed its affection for their former colonel by presenting him with a sword, paid for by a subscription of every officer and man. So highly did Cleburne prize it, he never took it into battle, but sent it to the rear for safety.

It was during the long inactivity at Wartrace that the army was visited by Lieutenant Colonel Arthur Lyon Fremantle of the Coldstream Guard. The young British officer and the ex-corporal in the 41st Regiment hit it off well, and Fremantle was much impressed with Cleburne, "now thirty-five years of age; but, his hair having turned gray, he looked older." The British officer wrote: "Generals Bragg and Hardee both spoke of him in terms of the highest praise, and said that he had risen entirely by his own personal merit."[17]

New flags were issued to the Army of Tennessee at Wartrace and division battle flags were ordered to be replaced by the Confederate

battle flag. Cleburne's division protested vehemently. They had fought
under a blue flag with a silver full moon at Fort Donelson. It had been
General Hardee's flag, and General S. B. Buckoner's before him, and Cleburne inherited it. The men of Cleburne's division had come to love their
banner and they importuned the authorities to let them retain it. Hardee,
himself, is authority for the statement that Cleburne's division was the only
one permitted to carry its own battle flag in action thereafter, "and
friends and foes soon learned to watch the course of the blue flag that
marked where Cleburne was in the battle."

"This was a high compliment," wrote Cleburne's adjutant, Captain
Buck, "but like all luxuries it was costly and carried with it penalties, for
the enemy had learned to whom the flag belonged, and where it appeared
there was concentrated their heaviest fire."[18]

V

Almost without firing a shot, Union General Rosecrans maneuvered
Bragg out of Middle Tennessee in the early summer of 1863, when operations were finally resumed in that theater.

July 4, 1863, was a dark day for the Confederacy, for on the Mississippi, Vicksburg surrendered; in Pennsylvania, Lee was in retreat from
Gettysburg; and in Tennessee, Bragg was virtually giving up the state
without a struggle. Bragg encamped around Chattanooga, last vestige of
Tennessee under Confederate control, and awaited the coming of Rosecrans.

In the middle of August, Rosecrans launched a movement to get
behind Bragg and bottle him up in Chattanooga. To circumvent this
wide flanking operation, Bragg evacuated Chattanooga on September
8 and concentrated his army at LaFayette, about 22 miles to the south
in Georgia.

General Hardee having been assigned to duty in Mississippi, Lieutenant General D. H. Hill now commanded Hardee's old corps. He
soon learned at first hand what sort of a soldier Pat Cleburne was. Bragg
had urged him: "Consult Cleburne. He is cool, full of resources and
ever alive to a success."[19] But Hill saw for himself on the bloody field
of Chickamauga.

Whether from his own indecision or the failure of subordinates to
follow orders, Bragg missed a brilliant chance to fall on Rosecrans' divided
army, marching from the Tennessee River toward the Confederate rear
in three widely separated columns. The opportunity was bright for Bragg
to have defeated at least two of the Union corps in detail, before a
junction of the Union army could be made. But Rosecrans escaped.
General Hill summed up the reasons for Bragg's failure as lack of knowl-

edge of the situation and lack of personal supervision of the execution of his orders.[20]

On the night of September 18 Bragg crossed his army over Chickamauga creek and early the following morning "the great battle of the West" began. All day, the bitter fight continued, first one side and then the other being the attacker, as new brigades came onto the field and were committed to action.

Cleburne's division, with Hill on the Confederate left, was ordered about 3 P.M. to cross the Chickamauga at Thedford's Ford and report to Lieutenant General Leonidas Polk, in command of the Confederate right. Cleburne had to march six miles over a road clogged with troops, wagons, and artillery. When the ford was reached his men plunged in up to the armpits and without halting marched to their rendezvous.

Polk ordered Cleburne to form a second line in the rear of the right of a line of battle already established. Just about sunset, Cleburne was in position 300 yards to the rear of the first line. His right was in front of Jay's Mill and his line extended due south about a mile in length. Lucius Polk's brigade was on his right, S. A. M. Wood's brigade in the center and James Deshler's brigade on the left, all supported by batteries of artillery.

The sun had already sunk when Hill ordered Cleburne forward, to pass through a repulsed line and strike hard at the enemy's left. Soon Cleburne's right and center brigades were heavily engaged. The enemy, behind breastworks, delivered a blistering fire of small arms and artillery. "For half an hour the firing was the heaviest I had ever heard," Cleburne later reported.

Before long the battle became one confused roar of guns, as darkness enveloped both armies. It was impossible for the soldiers to see their targets. Each side fired at the gun flashes of the other. "Few of these shots from either side took effect," observed Cleburne.

Cleburne's artillery—the batteries of Key and Semple—rushed forward under the armor of night and took position within sixty yards of the enemy and maintained a rapid fire, which soon took effect, for, said Cleburne, the "enemy quickly disappeared from my front." Because of the confused fighting, over so long a period, Cleburne halted his division, readjusted his lines, threw out skirmishers a quarter of a mile and bivouacked. In the struggle, the Union troops in front of Cleburne had been driven back about a mile and a half, with a loss of more than 200 prisoners, some artillery and colors.

At about 10 A.M., on September 20, Cleburne was ordered to advance and dress his division on Breckinridge's which had been placed to Cleburne's right. Cleburne moved forward to "the heaviest artillery fire I have ever experienced," from the Federal breastworks opposite his right and right center. These elements were exposed to direct fire from the

Union guns. The deadly artillery checked Cleburne within 175 yards of the breastworks, and to it now was added heavy small arms fire. In the space of a few moments 500 men of Wood's brigade were killed or wounded.

Cleburne ordered the brigade to fall back to re-form and moved Deshler's brigade to the right to connect up with Polk's brigade to fill the gap left in the center by Wood's withdrawal. But by now Lucius Polk's left had been driven back. Cleburne realized that it was "a useless sacrifice of life for Polk to retain his position" and he ordered him to fall back. Regrouping the battered brigades, Cleburne placed them in a strong defensive position three or four hundred yards in rear of the point from which they had been repulsed. He then sent orders to Deshler to take cover behind a ridge to which he had advanced and hold his position as long as possible. In making this move, Deshler was killed, in the very first battle in which he commanded as a general officer. Cleburne thought highly of him and in his report he characterized Deshler as "brave and efficient" and lauded the "warm zeal and . . . high conscientiousness" with which he discharged his duty.

At 3:30 P.M. Lieutenant General Leonidas Polk ordered Cleburne to advance his two re-formed brigades and move forward on a line with Deshler's brigade, which had doggedly held its ground. Meanwhile, Bragg's left wing, led by Longstreet, had been driving the Federals before them, having made a powerful break through. Now the orders came for the right wing to attack. Cleburne's batteries, at a range of 200 yards softened up the Federals with a rapid and effective fire and a Union battery which had been playing on Cleburne's lines was silenced. Then Brigadier General Lucius Polk's brigade swept forward, carrying in rapid succession three rows of Federal breastworks which the enemy precipitately abandoned.[21]

At this point the attack was called off. Up and down the Confederate line, eager troops, scenting the kill, wanted to pursue Rosecrans' shattered army. But Braxton Bragg did not pursue the retreating Federals. Nor did he do so on the twenty-first, despite the fact General Nathan Bedford Forrest, in the saddle at dawn, sent back word that the retreat to Chattanooga had become a rout. "Every hour was worth a thousand men," Forrest's message said. "But the commander-in-chief did not know of the victory until the morning of the 21st, and then he did not order a pursuit," wrote General Hill.

The gravity of the situation of the Union army at the end of the Battle of Chickamauga can no better be demonstrated than by quoting from Assistant Secretary of War Charles A. Dana's telegram to Secretary of War Edwin M. Stanton, filed from Chattanooga at 4 P.M. on September 20: CHICKAMAUGA IS AS FATAL A NAME IN OUR HISTORY AS BULL RUN.[22]

After Bragg's failure to reap the harvest of victory at Chickamauga, his generals, on October 4, 1863, petitioned Jefferson Davis to remove him from command. Davis hastened from Richmond to study the problem at first hand, and at Bragg's headquarters, on October 10, with Bragg present, he called upon the generals for a free expression of opinion.

Cleburne's adjutant, Captain Buck, of course, was not there, but he recorded what took place as he remembered the "hearsay at the time." Since no minutes were kept, the specific words uttered were lost, except by "inference drawn from communications afterwards exchanged between some of those present." The unanimous opinion, according to Captain Buck, was that a change of commander was absolutely essential. "The recollection as to Cleburne's reply is distinct—that, while he esteemed General Bragg a good organizer, disciplinarian, and a skillful soldier, the non-success attending the Kentucky, Tennessee, and Chickamauga campaigns had totally lost him the confidence of the army, and that no matter what his real ability as a general might be, this fact alone destroyed his usefulness, and his conviction was that a change was absolutely necessary."[23]

But Bragg was not removed. Davis seemed determined to give him one more chance despite his record and the "revolt" of his generals. It would be Bragg's last.

Meanwhile, Bragg had occupied Lookout Mountain, south of the sharp bend in the Tennessee River and southwest of Chattanooga, and Missionary Ridge, which extended approximately five miles, about three miles east of the town. And from the high ground, he planned to starve Rosecrans out. But while Bragg waited, week after week, Rosecrans got both reinforcements and supplies over routes which Bragg's artillery could not interdict. The only aggressive action that Bragg ordered was a raid by General Joe Wheeler's cavalry against Rosecrans' supply lines. Wheeler made a successful raid, but wore out his cavalry doing it and it was some time before it was an effective force again.

General Grant, now in command of all Union armies in the West, arrived at Chattanooga on October 23. General George Thomas, the Union "Rock of Chickamauga," had replaced Rosecrans in command at Chattanooga. Union reinforcements continued to arrive, and as the days ticked by, the opportunity for Bragg to seize the initiative lessened and lessened.

In face of the Federal buildup, General Bragg committed the cardinal military sin of dividing his forces. Early in November he dispatched Longstreet to attack Knoxville. To add folly to this wild-goose chase he ordered Pat Cleburne, with his division and Buckner's, to reinforce Longstreet. Cleburne's troops began their rail movement on the morning of November 23, the very day Grant opened the fighting around Chattanooga. In frantic haste, Bragg wired Cleburne at Chickamauga

Station to halt his movement. Shortly thereafter a second telegram reached Cleburne: . . . MOVE UP RAPIDLY WITH YOUR WHOLE FORCE. And then, a few minutes later, a third: WE ARE HEAVILY ENGAGED. MOVE UP RAPIDLY TO THESE HEADQUARTERS. BRAXTON BRAGG.

Instructing General Lucius Polk to bring up the division, Cleburne galloped ahead to Bragg's headquarters for instruction. That night Cleburne's division bivouacked behind Missionary Ridge. All of Buckner's brigades, except one, had been dispatched when Cleburne was recalled and this brigade he turned over to Bragg, relinquishing control of it.

The next morning Bragg informed Cleburne that Union troops had crossed the Tennessee both above and below the mouth of Chickamauga Creek. Instructed to send a brigade to defend the railroad bridge over the creek, just east of Missionary Ridge, Cleburne dispatched Polk with a battery of artillery. With his three other brigades he took a position on the extreme right of the ridge.

At daylight on November 25, Sherman moved to the attack against Cleburne and it became evident that Grant was going to try to turn the Confederate right, in an effort to get behind Bragg and roll up his whole front. Sherman had six divisions under his command and throughout a bitter day of fighting, each of these divisions drove against Cleburne's line on the ridge and each was repulsed. The first serious fighting of the day came at 11 A.M. when a persistent Federal charge carried to within fifty steps of Swett's battery on Tunnel Hill. Gallantly did the gunners man their weapons despite a heavy cross fire, and with canister at short range punished the enemy severely. But it took a vigorous charge by General James A. Smith's infantry to halt the progress of the enemy and send him reeling back down the hillside.

Half an hour later, another desperate charge by the enemy was met with heavy small arms and artillery fire in the front and by enfiladed artillery fire and a long-range rifle volley on his flank. Once again, the Union assault was dispersed and driven back in confusion.

A few minutes after 1 P.M. still another grand attack was made on Cleburne's position. This time Sherman sent his troops up the slope in a heavy column, aimed at Cleburne's batteries. Heavy fire stopped the head of the column just below the crest and the Union soldiers sought shelter behind trees, logs, and jutting rocks, their first line not 25 yards from Cleburne's guns, from where they opened a steady fire. "Tier after tier of the enemy, to the foot of the hill and in the valley beyond, supplied this fire," reported Cleburne, "and concentrated the whole on a space of not more than 40 yards, till it seemed like one continuous sheet of hissing, flying lead." This terrific fire pinned down Cleburne's infantry so that it could not move sufficiently forward to fire effectively down the hill, otherwise it just swept harmlessly over the heads of Old Pat's fighters.

Unceasingly, for an hour and a half, the Federal attack was pushed. When the infantry saw that it couldn't reach the Yankees with direct fire, the men began to roll heavy boulders and throw jagged rocks down the hill at the enemy. Artillerymen took the cue and, lighting the fuses of their shells and cannon balls, bowled them down the hill with good effect.

During the struggle, on a number of occasions, sorties were made against the more advanced elements of the enemy and Cleburne several times either led or accompanied the countercharges. On one occasion, Cleburne put himself at the head of the Texas brigade and rushed forward to meet and repulse the charge of a heavy column, returning shortly with prisoners and captured colors.

When dusk fell Sherman's nose had been well bloodied by Pat Cleburne. The Confederate right, badly outnumbered, and forced to defend its position virtually all day against fresh assault troops, was still intact. But as the Rebel yell of victory sounded over the northern end of Missionary Ridge, Cleburne got the astounding news that the Federal attack on Bragg's center had made a breakthrough and the Confederates, almost without the semblance of a fight, had taken off in all directions. In his report, Bragg described the debacle: "A panic which I had never before witnessed seemed to have seized upon officers and men, and each appeared to be struggling for his personal safety, regardless of his duty and his character . . ."

General Hardee ordered Cleburne to assume command of Walker's and Stevenson's divisions and form a line across the ridge to meet an attack on his flank. Meanwhile, Bragg was in full retreat across the Chickamauga and Cleburne's troops, who had borne the brunt of the fighting all day, were left to cover the precipitous withdrawal.

"By 9 P.M. everything was across except the dead and a few stragglers lingering here and there under the shadow of the trees for the purpose of being captured, faint-hearted patriots succumbing to the hardships of war and imagined hopelessness of the hour." Cleburne then ordered Smith's brigade, his last on the ridge, to move. "Sadly, but not fearfully, this band of heroes left the hill they had held so well," reported Cleburne, "and followed the army across the Chickamauga."[24]

It was not until 10 P.M. on November 26 that Cleburne reached the west bank of the East Fork of the Chickamauga, but as the night was freezing cold and the waist-deep icy stream had to be forded, Cleburne deferred the crossing to give his weary men a chance to rest in dry clothing. At 2 A.M., a member of Bragg's staff brought Cleburne verbal orders to take position in Ringgold Gap, a narrow pass in the hills to the east of the town of Ringgold, Georgia, and to hold it at all costs.

"I have less than 4200 men against vastly superior forces," stated Cleburne, "and I'll have no support whatever. It could mean the destruction of my division. However, I am accustomed to follow orders, but please, as protection for myself in case of disaster, commit General Bragg's orders to writing."

Whereupon Colonel George W. Brent sat down and wrote:

"Major-General Cleburne: . . . The General desires that you will take strong position in the gorge of the mountain and attempt to check pursuit of the enemy. He must be punished until our trains and the rear of our troops get well advanced. The reports from the rear are meager and the general is not thoroughly advised of the state of things there. Will you be good enough to report fully."

Cleburne ordered his troops forward and himself rode ahead to survey the terrain he would have to defend and to decide upon the best disposition of his forces. Directly to the east of Ringgold, he saw Taylor's Ridge, which ran north and south. Facing the town, a narrow gap, 100 yards wide at its mouth but much narrower for most of its half-mile length, cut through Taylor's Ridge. Through the gap skirting a tributary creek to the Chickamauga, ran the Western & Atlantic Railroad, and by its side a road.

Having quickly taken in the lay of the land Cleburne sent his adjutant, Captain Buck, to inform Bragg that his division and Breckinridge's Orphans Brigade, then attached to Cleburne, were in motion, and to ask for further orders.

"Tell General Cleburne to hold his position at all hazards," ordered Bragg, "and keep back the enemy, until the artillery and transportation of the army is secure, the salvation of which depends upon him."[25]

As his troops came up, Cleburne hurried them into position. He placed two regiments in a thick wood at the base of the hill north of the gap and a third regiment on its crest. On the hill south of the gap, he disposed his forces, some at the base, some on the face, fronting Ringgold and some on the crest of the hill. Still other units he placed in four lines, each about 40 paces apart, across the pass between the foot of the northern hill and the railroad embankment. At the rear end of the gap, in reserve, and to prevent a wide flanking movement of his right, Cleburne placed three regiments of Polk's Brigade.

"I had scarcely half an hour to make these dispositions," Cleburne reported, "when I was informed that the enemy's skirmishers were crossing the Chickamauga, driving our cavalry before them. Immediately after the cavalry retreated through the gap at a trot, and the valley in front was clear of our troops, but close in the rear of the ridge our immense train was still in full view, struggling through the fords of the creek and the deeply cut-up roads leading to Dalton, and my division, silent, but cool and ready, was the only barrier between it and the flushed and eager advance of the pursuing Federal army."

Shortly after 8 A.M., the attack on Cleburne began, with the Federal line moving against the ridge to the right of the gap. Cleburne's artillery, in the mouth of the gap, firing canister from close range, raked the Union right flank, which broke ranks and scurried to cover of the railroad embankment. But the left of the Federal line made a determined attack on the ridge, aimed at turning Cleburne's right. It was met first by a blistering fire and then by a bold charge by several regiments of Texans which routed the enemy. Meanwhile, Cleburne learned that other Union troops to his far right were climbing the ridge and he sent orders for Polk to move up the hill and meet the threat. After an obstinate fight near the crest, Polk repelled the thrust and the Federals were driven back down the hill.

Meanwhile, more and more Federal troops, having crossed the East Fork of the Chickamauga, were being committed to the fight and ever increasing pressure was being applied to Cleburne's right. But fighting furiously, "Old Pat's" men hurled back every attempt to gain the ridge or turn Cleburne's right. Unable to secure a foothold, the Federals now attacked Cleburne's left with no more success, heavy artillery fire blunting their charge.

Picturesque accounts of the fighting have come from soldiers in Cleburne's ranks. W. W. Gibson of the 6th Arkansas was observing the effective firing of Confederate artillery on an exposed Federal flank just as General Cleburne and General Breckinridge came along the line:

"Every man fell to the ground, and, from the way their hats, caps, guns, and accouterments went flying in the air, I had not a doubt that the entire line was annihilated, and exclaimed: 'By Jove, boys, it killed them all.' Gen. Breckinridge and 'Old Pat' smiled at my boyish incredulity, while the latter said to me good naturedly: 'If you don't lie down, young man, you are liable to find that there are enough left for you to get the top of your head shot off.'" Later in the fight, Gibson saw 'Old Pat' again.

"General, the battery didn't kill quite all of them this morning," he said, "but what was left have been taught a lesson in good manners."

"You are quite right young man," Cleburne answered, "I'm proud of what you boys have done today, and I don't think they will bother us any more this evening."

Sam Watkins of Company 'Aytch' of the 1st Tennessee, during a lull on his front, took a nap and when he woke up a short time later he had the fright of his life.

"I saw a long line of bluecoats marching down the railroad track," he wrote. "The first thought I had was, well, I'm gone up now, sure; but on second sight, I discovered that they were prisoners. Cleburne had had the doggonest fight of the war. The ground was piled high with dead Yankees; they were piled in heaps. The scene looked unlike any battlefield I ever saw. From the foot to the top of the hill was covered with their slain, all lying on their faces. It had the appearance of the roof of a house, shingled with dead Yankees."

About noon, Cleburne received word from General Hardee that the Confederate train was now well advanced and that he could withdraw at will. At 2 P.M., Cleburne retired from Taylor's Ridge and took up a new position on some wooded hills about a mile to the rear, beyond the eastern entrance to the gap. About half an hour later, the Yankees appeared in force in the gap, only to find that Cleburne had pulled out.[26]

The timidity of the Federals for more contact with "Old Pat" and his fighting men is reflected in the recollections of P. D. Stephenson, a soldier in Cleburne's command:

"We held the field until evening, then retired about a mile, to a more commanding position, and after waiting for them to come, leisurely sauntered off under cover of smoke of our camp fires, which we had ostentatiously built, and which we fed anew before retiring. The enemy barely made an appearance before this new position and that was all. The extreme, gingerly way in which solitary individuals, one by one, tiptoed towards us and at last showed themselves, was absurdly conclusive of the fact that their rashness was cured. We had fought ourselves into a good humor again, and satisfied that the worst was over, trudged along after the rest of the army."

Cleburne reached Tunnel Hill, Georgia, shortly before 1 A.M. on November 28, having lost only 221 men—20 killed, 190 wounded, and 11 missing—of his 4157 in six hours of fighting, in which a vastly superior enemy was held at bay with heavy losses. "The conduct of the officers and men in this fight needs no comments," Cleburne said, "every man as far as I know did his whole duty."[27]

VI

In mid-December 1863 officers around General Pat Cleburne's headquarters at Tunnel Hill noticed his preoccupation and the many hours that he sat at his desk writing.

One day about Christmastime Cleburne handed a manuscript to his young adjutant, Captain Buck. The latter read the document which advocated the freeing of the slaves and enlisting them in the Confederate Army to meet the growing manpower shortage in Southern arms.

"Well, what do you think of it, Captain?" asked Cleburne.

"I fully agree with your opinion as to the absolute necessity of some such step to recruit the army," replied Buck. "But, while recognizing the force of your arguments, I doubt the expediency at present for formulating your views."

Pressed by Cleburne to expand his thoughts, Captain Buck went on:

"First of all, the slave holders are sensitive as regards their property and they're totally unprepared to consider such a radical measure. Those who are not in the service cannot properly appreciate that it has become a matter of self-preservation that our ranks should be filled to reduce the enemy's heavy numerical superiority. Consequently, General Cleburne, I think it would raise a storm of indignation against you."

Cleburne did not reply and Captain Buck continued:

"Secondly, one of the corps of this army is without a lieutenant general, and, after your signal success at Ringgold Gap, and your standing among all the major generals, you might justly expect to be advanced to the vacancy. But publication of this paper will be used to your detriment and your chances for promotion will be destroyed."

"A crisis is upon the South, Captain Buck," replied General Cleburne, "and the quickest way to avert it is the way I've outlined. Accordingly, I feel it my duty to bring it before the authorities, irrespective of any results to myself."

"Do you think the negroes would make good soldiers?" queried the young adjutant.

"With reasonable, and careful drilling, yes," answered Cleburne. "Of this, I have no doubt. As deep as my attachment is for my present command, I would cheerfully undertake command of a negro division in this emergency."[28]

Cleburne turned the draft over to Buck for copying and then submitted it to members of his staff for free criticism of its contents. But he didn't stop there. One of Cleburne's favorites among the junior officers was Captain Thomas F. Key of the artillery, a fellow Arkansan, who was a frequent visitor at Cleburne's headquarters. Key kept one of the most interesting diaries of the war and his entry for December 28, 1863, indicates to what degree Cleburne exchanged confidences with him:

"I called upon General Cleburne and I had scarcely seated myself when he introduced a conversation upon the propriety of bringing into the military service, and at once beginning to drill, 300,000 negroes . . . He told me his views *in extenso* and said that in a few days he would publish them over his signature and that he and others would memorialize Congress upon the subject. This is one of the weightiest questions that has been brought forth since the beginning of this revolution. It would make or ruin the South. It will conclude the war speedily or cause blood to flow more freely than heretofore."[29]

On the night of January 2, 1864, at General Joe Johnston's headquarters in Dalton, Georgia, Pat Cleburne read his paper before practically all the generals and regimental commanders of the Army of Tennessee.

"Moved by the exigency in which our country is now placed," he began, "we take the liberty of laying before you, unofficially, our views of the present state of affairs."

He touched on the gravity of the moment, the newness of his views and the duty of submitting them to others before going further with them. Cleburne then skillfully painted a picture of the state of the Confederacy, with which his listeners could hardly disagree:

"We have now been fighting for nearly three years, have spilled much of our best blood, and lost, consumed or thrown to the flames an amount of property equal in value to the specie currency of the world. Through some lack in our system the fruits of our struggles and sacrifices have invariably slipped away from us and left us nothing but long lists of dead and mangled. Instead of standing defiantly on the borders of our territory or harassing those of the enemy, we are hemmed in today in less than two-thirds of it; and still the enemy menacingly confronts us at every point with superior forces. Our soldiers can see no end to this state of affairs except in our own exhaustion; hence, instead of rising to the occasion, they are sinking into a fatal apathy, growing weary of hardships and slaughter which promises no results."

Cleburne warned that "there is a growing belief that some black catastrophe is not far ahead of us" and said the crisis called for "some extraordinary change . . . in our condition." Every day, he declared, the evidence is mounting: "restlessness of morals spreading everywhere, manifesting itself in the army in a growing disregard of private rights; desertion spreading to a class of soldiers it never dared to tamper with before; military commissions sinking in the estimation of the soldier; our supplies failing; our firesides in ruins."

Cleburne asserted that a continuation of this state could only lead to subjugation, and subjugation meant the loss of "slaves and all other personal property, lands, homesteads, liberty, justice, safety, pride, manhood." He dwelled on the horror of the history of their heroic struggle being written by the enemy, with their children being taught "by Northern school teachers . . . from Northern school books . . . to regard our gallant dead as traitors, our maimed veterans as fit objects for derision."

Three great causes, Cleburne declared, were operating for the destruction of the Confederacy. One was the numerical inferiority of Southern armies, another was the great shortage of supplies. And the third was "the fact that slavery, from being one of our chief sources of strength at the commencement of the war, has now become in a military point of view, one of our chief sources of weakness."

On and on, Cleburne read for about twenty minutes, his inevitable conclusion being that the only possible source of manpower that could swing the Confederate tide away from disaster was the slaves:

"Adequately to meet the causes which are now threatening to ruin our country, we propose . . . that we retain in service for the war all troops now in service, and that we immediately commence training a large reserve of the most courageous of our slaves, and further, that we guarantee freedom within a reasonable time to every slave in the South who shall remain true to the Confederacy in this war. As between the loss of independence and the loss of slavery, we assume that every patriot will freely give up the latter—give up the negro slaves rather than be a slave himself."

Assuming that his assumption was correct, Cleburne, then went on to show how "this great national sacrifice" would "strip the enemy of foreign sympathy and assistance and transfer them to the South" and at the same time dry up important sources of Northern recruits, the Southern slaves and foreigners.

But what of the immediate effects of emancipation and enrollment of negroes in Southern military strength? It would, Cleburne urged, enable the Confederacy to have armies numerically superior to the North, and a reserve of any necessary size; it would enable the South to take the offensive and carry the war to the enemy; it would remove from every Southern household potential spies, "awaiting the enemy with open arms." He went on:

"It would remove forever all selfish taint from our cause and place independence above every question of property. The very magnitude of the sacrifice itself, such as no nation has ever voluntarily made before, would appall our enemies, destroy his spirit and his finances . . . Apart from all other aspects of the question, the necessity for more fighting men is upon us. We can only get a sufficiency by making the negro share the danger and hardships of the war. If we arm him and train him and make him fight for the country in her hour of dire distress, every consideration of principle and policy demand that we should set him and his whole race who side with us free."

Cleburne asked, "Will the slaves fight?" and cited in answer to his question evidence from history. Moreover, if the slaves can be made to fight bravely against their former masters, how much more willing would they not be to fight under those masters with freedom as their reward?

It was a strong, reasoned, if revolutionary, document and Cleburne ended it on a forceful note:

"We have now briefly proposed a plan which we believe will save our country. It may be imperfect, but in all human probability it would give us our independence. No objection ought to outweigh it which is not weightier than independence. If it is worthy of being put in practice it ought to be mooted quickly before the people and urged earnestly by every man who believes in its efficiency. Negroes will require much training; training will require time, and there is danger that this concession to common sense may come too late "[30]

The effect of Cleburne's paper, which was also signed by three briga- dier generals and fourteen other officers from colonel to captain, was mixed, being viewed with alarm and indignation by some and favorably considered by others. Major Calhoun Benham of Cleburne's staff, who had read the memorial when it was being prepared, strongly dissented and read a letter of protest. Others held, if not expressed at the time, similar ideas. General Patton Anderson considered it "a monstrous proposition . . . revolting to Southern sentiment, Southern pride and Southern honor." He added: "And not the least painful of the emotions awakened by it was the conciousness which forced itself upon us that it met with favor by others, besides the author, in high station then present."

Cleburne's adjutant, Captain Buck, was not present but he later wrote that "my impression is that General Hardee and Johnston were favorably disposed." However, Joe Johnston declined to forward Cleburne's paper to the War Department for transmittal to President Davis on the ground that it was a political and not a military matter.

Although bitterly disappointed at missing the chance to get his arguments into the President's hands, Cleburne was too good a soldier to think of going over Johnston's head. But, fortunately for Cleburne's hopes, one of the more indignant opponents of his proposal, Major General W. H. T. Walker, asked him for a copy of the "incendiary" paper as he felt it his duty to report it to Mr. Davis. Cleburne was delighted to do so, because that was exactly what he wanted—Davis to get the paper. General Walker sought Johnston's permission to forward Cleburne's paper, with comments from some of the officers present at the reading, through War Department channels. When Johnston again refused, Walker simply wrote to President Davis directly, excusing his military breach on the grounds of "the gravity of the subject, the magnitude of the issues involved, my strong convictions that the further agitation of such sentiments and propositions would ruin the efficiency of our army, and involve our cause in ruin and disgrace . . ."

As the weeks went by with no word from Richmond, Cleburne began to feel a little concern, but no regrets for the step he had taken. In discussing it with his staff, Cleburne said that the worst thing that could happen to him would be a court-martial and dismissal. In which event, he said, he would immediately enlist as a private in his old regiment, the 15th Arkansas.

Finally the paper was returned, endorsed by Davis (according to Buck, substantially, if not verbatim) as follows: "*While recognizing the patriotic motives of its distinguished author, I deem it inexpedient at this time, to give publicity to this paper and ask that it be suppressed—J.D.*"

Cleburne, on receipt of the paper, instructed Captain Buck to destroy all existing copies except the one returned from Richmond. And in the Atlanta Campaign, soon to open, this was destroyed when the Yankees captured Buck's desk and burned it and its contents.

Although the existence of Cleburne's memorial was known to a few its contents were known to an even less number, until the copy obtained by Major Calhoun Benham came to light after his death and was first published in the Official Records in 1898.

Many have speculated that Cleburne's proposal to free the slaves and enlist them in the army prevented his promotion to lieutenant general. The correspondence of Braxton Bragg, then serving as Davis's chief of staff in Richmond, suggests that it had plenty to do with it. On February 5, 1864, Bragg wrote a military friend: ". . . Great sensation is being produced . . . by the Emancipation project of Hardee, Cheatham, Cleburne & Co. It will kill them." And a letter from General S. R. Gist, dated March 9, 1864, replies to a letter from Bragg: ". . . I read a portion of it to our friend Genl Walker who will give you the full and secret History of the 'Abolition Document'—It is really a rich affair, and I am delighted beyond expression to know that the Traitors will meet with their just deserts at the hands of the 'powers that be'—Of course, this will be done in a quiet manner."[31]

The fact is that within eight months after Cleburne presented his memorial, three vacancies of lieutenant general occurred in the Army of Tennessee. The first resulted from Leonidas Polk's death on June 14, 1864; the second came when John B. Hood was named successor to Joe Johnston as commander of the Army of Tennessee on July 18, 1864; and the third vacancy was created when Hardee, at his request, was relieved as corps commander on September 23, 1864. The first two vacancies went to Major Generals A. P. Stewart and S. D. Lee, both of whom Cleburne ranked; the third was never filled, Major General B. F. Cheatham being assigned, without promotion, to command Hardee's corps, which he and Cleburne had both done on previous occasions.

On the other hand, a veteran of the Army of Tennessee, and an authority on its history, Judge J. P. Young of Memphis, wrote many years ago: "I am sure that the memorial incident had nothing to do with the failure by the military authorities to promote General Cleburne to the rank of lieutenant general."[32]

Barely a year after Cleburne's proposal was suppressed, the Confederate Congress passed a law on March 13, 1865, authorizing the enrollment of the slaves into the Southern army. But by this time it was too late. Appomattox was less than a month away.

General John B. Hood, in his posthumous book, *Advance and Retreat*, published in 1880, wrote of Cleburne's proposal: "He possessed the boldness and the wisdom to earnestly advocate . . . the freedom of the negro and the enrollment of the young and able-bodied of that race. This stroke of policy and additional source of strength to our Armies, would, in my own opinion, have given us our independence."[33]

About the time of his memorial, Pat Cleburne found himself involved in a romantic interlude. His friend, General Hardee, announced that he was getting married again and he invited Cleburne to be his best man. Cleburne readily accepted, drawing upon both himself and Hardee the scorn of General W. H. T. Walker, still bitter over the memorial. In a letter to Bragg, Walker wrote: "[Hardee] *introduced* the Gentle*man* [Cleburne] to the meeting and took him after *knowing* his sentiments and hearing his paper read to perform a very confidential and intimate office no less than playing Brides Man at his wedding, an office which is only intrusted to a *particular Friend*."

The forty-eight-year-old Hardee was married to twenty-six-year-old Mary Foreman Lewis at "Bleak House," the Lewis plantation in Marengo County, Alabama, on January 13, 1864. The maid of honor to Miss Lewis was Sue Tarleton of Mobile, a cotton factor's daughter, described as "a young maiden of rare accomplishments and intelligence."

Cleburne fell in love with Miss Tarleton at first sight. And when the wedding party went to Mobile after the ceremony, Cleburne assiduously paid court to the young lady, who did not outrightly reject the general's importunities. Perhaps she saw in him what the Mobile *Daily Advertiser and Register* of January 22, 1864, did, when, noting Cleburne's presence in Mobile, it commented that he was "as modest and unassuming as a girl, he had shunned the crowd of parasites and puffers, unfortunately found around headquarters. Hence, while columns are devoted to the exploits of tenth rate men, but little has been said about this extraordinary man."

Upon his return to his division, Cleburne continued his courting by correspondence and he also enlisted the aid of Sallie Lightfoot, a friend of Sue's, who was engaged to her brother, Robert Tarleton. On March 11, 1864, Cleburne wrote Miss Lightfoot that Sue, after keeping him "in cruel suspense at length consented to be mine and we are engaged." Whether the two ever met again is not certain, although Cleburne may have visited Mobile before the fighting broke out again, or Miss Tarleton may have visited the army at Dalton.[34]

Cleburne's visit to Mobile also provided encouragement for his proposal to induct the slaves into the Confederate Army. He conversed with many men of wealth on the subject and many supported his plan believing it would redound to the advantage of the South. But this was short-lived, for General Joe Johnston, on January 31, 1864, circularized instructions from the War Department, as coming from President Davis, to suppress not only the memorial, but "all discussion and controversy respecting or growing out of it."

Cleburne knew how to take orders as well as to give them. And, as a strict, but fair, disciplinarian, he knew how to discipline himself. "After such an opinion from the Commander-in-Chief of the Army and the highest officer of our Government," he wrote, "I feel it my duty to suppress the Memorial and to cease to advocate the measures mentioned."[35]

The memorial affair and his whirlwind, if long-distance, courtship of Sue Tarleton, did not keep Cleburne from his favorite military pastime when he wasn't fighting—training, drilling, inspecting his troops. While the army was in winter quarters Cleburne had a log cabin built and set up a school for all levels of his command. Every day Cleburne met with his brigade commanders and reviewed the art of war. These in turn instructed the regimental commanders who, on their part, held classes for company commanders.

At Dalton, Cleburne brought his own little *élite* unit to its finest state of efficiency, his band of sharpshooters. Blockade runners had brought in from England, at the beginning of 1864, a shipment of Whitworth and Kerr rifles, both excellent, but the former superior because of their telescopic sight and an effective range of 2000 yards. In February of that year Cleburne's division was assigned twenty Whitworths and ten Kerrs, the arrival of which gave a name to the group, the Whitworth Sharpshooters. Service in the unit was hazardous but exciting, and its members were exempt from the monotony of camp routine. The demand for a place in the Whitworth Sharpshooters was constant and vacancies were filled from a waiting list of the best marksmen in the various brigades.

During the stay at Dalton, many of the three-year enlistments in the Army of Tennessee expired, and were the men to go home when their time was up, the army would have been hard pressed for manpower. General Hardee noted the persuasive methods that Cleburne employed to talk the men into staying on:

". . . A man of warm sympathies . . . he felt profoundly the extent of the sacrifice his men were called upon to make; but, with human virtue, he set high above all earthly considerations the achievement of Southern independence. He adapted himself to the peculiar conditions of a volunteer soldiery, and laying aside the commander, he appealed to his men as a comrade to give up everything else and stand by the cause and the country. He succeeded in inspiring them with his own high purpose and exalted patriotism, and the result was the early and unanimous re-enlistment of his division."[36]

To relieve the boredom of winter inactivity, there were several sham battles staged in the snow at Dalton. At one of these, Cleburne was captured by some of his own men who were delighted to see "Old Pat" a prisoner. One soldier caused a volley of laughter when he called out in mock severity: "Arrest that soldier, and make him carry a fence rail."[37]

About this time Cleburne received a copy of the joint resolution of the Confederate Congress, passed February 9, 1864, thanking him and his command "for the victory obtained by them over superior forces of the enemy at Ringgold Gap . . . by which the advance of the enemy was impeded, our wagon train and most of our artillery saved, a large number of the enemy killed and wounded."[38]

VIII

With the passing of winter, the Army of Tennessee braced itself for General William Tecumseh Sherman's long-awaited campaign against Atlanta. Cleburne's division, which had remained at Tunnel Hill until the last days of February, was in camp near Dalton when Sherman made his move on May 4, 1864, to Ringgold. Having driven in Confederate cavalry at Tunnel Hill, Sherman, on May 7, appeared before Dalton.

Sherman opened the campaign with 98,797 men while Joe Johnston mustered around Dalton only 42,856. By the time both armies were able to concentrate all their available forces later in the campaign, Sherman had a numerical superiority over Johnston of 110,000 to 61,000.

The Federal campaign against Atlanta began on May 4, 1864, and three days later, Sherman was before Dalton. The Union commander's plan was a simple one. With such numerical superiority as he had over his adversary, he could apply pressure on Johnston's front with an equal force and still have a large number of troops to send on a flanking operation around Johnston's left.

And so with no pitched battles, but frequent skirmishes, Sherman slowly but steadily flanked Johnston southward. Every sweep of Sherman to get to Johnston's rear was met by a skillful withdrawal which interposed the Army of Tennessee between the advancing Federals and Atlanta. And thus the two armies "see-sawed" down the Western & Atlanta Railroad.

On May 9, Cleburne's brigade was in a sharp engagement near Dug Gap; on May 14, at Resaca, Old Pat's boys repulsed an assault, in which one of the Federal officers exhorted in vain: "You are the men who scaled Missionary Ridge, and you can carry this!"

As each army took up a new position, the men dug in. The Yankees soon were saying: "The Rebels must carry their breastworks with them." And for their part, the Confederates declared: "Sherman's men march with a rifle in one hand and a spade in the other."[39] Daily skirmishes occurred as Johnston bided his time for a counterattack, should Sherman make a mistake or elements of his army become widely separated. Finally, on May 27, at Pickett's Mill, near New Hope Church, "the fighting rose above the grade of skirmishing," as General Johnston put it, and Pat Cleburne and his division were actively engaged.

About 4 P.M. the Federals drove in Cleburne's skirmishers and advanced on his position "in numerous and constantly reinforced lines." The Federals pressed on courageously to within a few paces of his men and Cleburne heard some of them exclaim: "Ah! damn you, we have caught you without your logs now!" With deliberate aim, Cleburne's rifles cracked volley upon volley and the Union advanced, halted, faltered, and then fell back, leaving hundreds of dead before the Confederate lines. General Johnston wrote that the Federal dead was 700; Pat Cleburne reported the lowest estimate of enemy dead at 500. "The piles of his dead on this front," wrote Cleburne "[are] pronounced by the officers of this army who have seen most service to be greater than they had ever seen before."

Fighting kept up until dark all along Cleburne's front and then dropped off but for several vehement bursts of musketry. Sherman had tried to smash through Cleburne and had failed. At 10 P.M. Cleburne ordered skirmishers to push forward and discover what the Federals were up to. Granbury's brigade, before it could put out skirmishers had to clear its front of the enemy lying close to the Confederate lines. "The Texans, their bayonets fixed, plunged into the darkness with a terrific yell," reported Cleburne, "and with one bound were upon the enemy; but they met with no resistance. Surprised and panic-stricken, many fled, escaping in the darkness; others surrendered and were brought into our lines." Cleburne's colorful battle report of the affair at Pickett's Mill was his last.[40] He was too occupied by the continuing action thereafter to write another report.

Early in June, Joe Johnston established his line in the vicinity of Kennesaw Mountain and two lesser hills, Lost Mountain and Pine Mountain. On June 13, Cleburne and a staff officer went to the top of Pine Mountain to observe Sherman's dispositions and movements. Hardly had Old Pat shown himself than Federal shells whistled by. His curiosity satisfied, Cleburne turned to his aide: "Let's get out of this. I have seldom known one to go where he had no business but that he got hurt." The next day, at the same spot, Lieutenant General Leonidas Polk, a bishop of the Protestant Episcopal Church and founder of the University of the South, was killed by a shell when he exposed himself on the crest.

Two days later, Cleburne and the Army of Tennessee lost one of the most valued combat officers in the Confederacy, Brigadier General Lucius E. Polk, thirty-one-year-old nephew of the bishop. Severely wounded on June 16, General Polk served no longer in the field thereafter. Able, intelligent, energetic, Polk had served brilliantly in every engagement of Cleburne's division.

On June 19, Cleburne was strongly entrenched in the center of Hardee's corps on the Confederate left south of Kennesaw Mountain.

Sherman, for an unaccountable reason, switched his tactics and instead of flanking Johnston off Kennesaw Mountain, as he actually did several days later, decided to smash the Confederates with powerful frontal attacks. Probing Johnston's line, Sherman engaged Hardee's skirmishers on June 24, but was repulsed. Three days later, after a tremendous cannonade, Sherman ordered a general advance in heavy columns.

Seven lines deep, the Federals pushed forward against Cleburne and Cheatham of Hardee's corps and two divisions of Polk's corps, now commanded by General W. W. Loring. From their well-protected rifle pits, Cleburne's men poured a withering, murderous fire upon the Federals and the losses the attackers suffered were frightful, and far out of proportion. General Hardee later reported that Cleburne lost only eleven men while the enemy in his front lost a thousand.

Once again the Federals charged and once more the blistering fire from the rifle pits cut many down and sent the Union columns reeling back to their lines. To the intense heat of battle and the blazing heat of the day, a third heat was added. The dry leaves and undergrowth in front of Cleburne's position caught fire and helpless Federal wounded lay under the frightful dual threat of the burning woods and the cross fire of both armies.

Suddenly, one of Cleburne's regimental commanders, Colonel W. W. Martin of the 1st Arkansas, tied his handkerchief to a ramrod and leaped to the parapet, yelling to the Federals behind the rocks and trees within sound of his voice: "We won't fire a gun until you get them away, but be quick."

The Federals put down their guns and went to the task of rescuing their wounded comrades from a horrible death. Cleburne's men immediately joined in. An eyewitness recorded:

"Nor will [Posterity] disregard Pat Cleburne's gallant men at Kennesaw, who, at the bidding of their leader, threw down their smoking guns and, leaping the breastworks, went out under the blazing sun and the fiercer heat of the burning woods to rescue from the hissing flames, the maimed and helpless boys in blue."[41]

Sherman learned his lesson at Kennesaw Mountain and returned to flanking operations to continue his advance on Atlanta. Johnston methodically retreated to keep himself between Sherman and that important rail point, until finally in mid-July the Federals crossed the Chattahoochee at a point where it was lightly held by the Confederate troops. This was too much for Richmond, and, on July 17, Johnston was relieved of command of the Army of Tennessee and Lieutenant General John B. Hood was named his successor. Johnston's heavily outnumbered army had engaged Sherman for 74 days, limiting him to barely a hundred-mile advance in that time. The Army of Tennessee was still unbeaten; it had been outflanked, but not whipped.

What Pat Cleburne's feelings were on Joe Johnston's removal was not recorded, but it is logical to surmise that they were reflected in the action of his friend and superior, General Hardee, and in the writings of his adjutant, Captain Irving Buck. The latter wrote: "The order was received with depression by the Confederate troops . . . Hood's accession to command was the beginning of an Iliad of woes." Hardee, considering Hood incompetent to command, had at once applied to be relieved from duty. He was persuaded to stay on.

Hood immediately discarded Johnston's policy of defense and, throwing caution to the wind, set out at once to do what Richmond apparently wanted—the Army of Tennessee to take the offensive against a vastly superior foe.

Sherman was crossing Peachtree Creek with his army in three separated columns and Hood decided to strike them in detail. He chose to assault Thomas's army, reportedly in the act of crossing the creek, and smash him before the rest of the Union "army group" could come up. The attack was set for 1 P.M. on July 20, but when word came that McPherson was applying heavy pressure on Hood's right, adjustments were made to meet the threat and, as a consequence, Hardee's attack wasn't launched until about 4 P.M. In the three intervening hours, Thomas had completed his crossing of Peachtree Creek.[42]

Hood blamed Hardee for the failure to inflict a heavy defeat on Thomas and in his book, *Advance and Retreat*, he attributes to Pat Cleburne the statement that General Hardee rode along the line, and in the presence of those around him, told Cleburne to be on the lookout for breastworks.

Hood's statement would lead one to believe that Cleburne had censured Hardee. "I can recall no reply on my part at the time, save perhaps, some expression of astonishment," wrote Hood. "I could say nothing to even so worthy a subordinate. He left me to infer, however, from subsequent remarks, that his Division would have taken quite a different action on the 20th, had it not been for the forewarning of his corps commander . . . It is but reasonable to deduce from this unfortunate observation to Cleburne that General Hardee gave a similar warning to other officers. At all events, those who were able to realize the baneful effect of such a remark from the commander of a *corps d'armée*, upon the eve of conflict, know that his words were almost equivalent to an order to take no active part in the battle."[43]

This comment by Hood, full of hatred for Hardee, whom he thoroughly detested, is also full of injustice to Cleburne. Both Cleburne and Hardee were dead when Hood published it. It is incredible to believe that Cleburne, who was Hardee's friend, would have made disparaging remarks about him to his commander, especially as Hood and Hardee shared a mutual contempt.

Cleburne's division fought brilliantly in the Battle of Atlanta. Not heavily engaged in the fighting on July 20, Cleburne made up for it the next day when he defended Leggett's hill against attack in fighting which he called "the bitterest" of his life. The division was active in Hardee's flanking movement against the Union left on July 22, and Cleburne's men fought with characteristic dash and bravery. Although Hardee dealt the enemy a severe blow, Hood was not satisfied with the results. Two thousand prisoners, eight guns, and thirteen stands of colors, taken by Hardee, do not suggest that he was addicted to a "timid defensive" attitude as Hood later charged.

During the fight, Union General James B. McPherson was killed by one of Cleburne's skirmishers. This brilliant and much-loved officer, only thirty-five, had close friends in the Confederate Army, among them Hood, his boyhood chum and fellow West Pointer. McPherson had left his lines to confer briefly with Sherman, but galloped back when he heard the guns that signaled Hardee's attack. When he returned to the woods where his line had been, he found Cleburne's skirmishers. Called upon to surrender, he "lifted his hat in graceful salute, turned his horse and attempted to escape, but was instantly shot dead." Some of McPherson's troops rushed forward to rescue his body, but not before the skirmishers had searched it. Later, under a flag of truce, Cleburne had McPherson's gold watch returned to the Federal lines.

This, of course, was in character for Pat Cleburne. He was a hard fighter, but a fair one. His ardor for the Southern cause did not blind him to Northern valor. And his sense of justice impelled him to compensate, personally, for misdeeds of his men. In Kentucky, he had paid civilians for articles stolen by a few of his soldiers. During the Atlanta battles, a captured Union officer had been relieved of his blankets and hat by a threadbare member of Cleburne's command. As soon as Cleburne heard of it, he tried to find the culprit and make him return them. When his search failed, Cleburne sent the prisoner a hat of his own and his only pair of blankets.[44]

The battle for Atlanta continued through July and into August, with Sherman now determined to get to the railroad south of the city to cut Hood's supply line and thus force the evacuation of Atlanta. Cleburne's division, which had been held east of Atlanta, was moved early in August, first to the center of Hood's line, north of the city, and then to the left, each movement in answer to one by the enemy. By August 16, Cleburne's command was at East Point, where the railroad branches off, one line going south, the other southwest. For nearly a fortnight, only picket duty engaged Cleburne's troops.

Meanwhile, Sherman had worked troops as far south as Jonesboro, on the railroad, and on August 30, Hood ordered Hardee to take his corps and Stephen D. Lee's to that point, 25 miles away, to dislodge the enemy.

With Hardee commanding the full operation, Cleburne assumed command of Hardee's corps and turned command of his division over to Brigadier General Mark P. Lowrey.

An all-night march was expected to bring Hardee to Jonesboro by daylight, but Cleburne's division encountered enemy troops on its route and a time-consuming detour was necessary. It was not until 9 A.M. that the head of the column reached Jonesboro and Lee's corps did not get into position before 11 o'clock. The troops were fatigued by their forced march, but the battle commenced about 2 P.M., with Cleburne's corps opening the fight and pushing into a portion of the Federal breastworks and capturing several guns. Lee, however, met stout resistance and his corps was unable to force the Union line and fell back in demoralized state. To bolster Lee, Hardee took a division from Cleburne but by this time dusk was falling and Hardee returned to his own breastworks and assumed the defensive.

Hood ordered the return of Lee's corps to Atlanta, but instructed Hardee to remain with his command at Jonesboro, where he would soon face the concentration of six Federal corps. Soon Hood realized he had to concentrate his own army, else he would soon have no army. And so he withdrew from Atlanta and marched south to join Hardee, who meanwhile, had reached Lovejoy.

Sherman, with a chance to crush Hood's much-depleted army, seemed content to occupy Atlanta and wire President Lincoln: ATLANTA IS OURS, AND FAIRLY WON. He called it quits and marched back to Atlanta.[45]

IX

The end of the Atlanta Campaign found both armies panting for breath. Four months of steady fighting, marching and countermarching had exhausted Sherman's troops as well as those of Hood. But when they both decided to make a move, one of the strangest operations of the Civil War developed, for Sherman marched his victorious Union army through Georgia to the sea, and Hood turned his back on his adversary and launched an invasion of Tennessee, which, if successful, could send the Army of Tennessee sweeping all the way to the Ohio River.

General Cleburne was not very happy as Hood's invasion began, because General Hardee was no longer with the army. At the end of the campaign, Hardee had reiterated his previous request for transfer from Hood's command and now Hood, who regarded Hardee as the cause of his failures at Atlanta, urged his removal. And so Hardee was sent to Charleston to command there and his old corps was placed under Major General B. F. Cheatham.

The removal of Hardee—"Old Reliable" his men called him—upset the corps, but Cleburne was particularly grieved and distressed, for practically all of his Confederate service had been under Hardee, for whom he had profound respect as well as a warm, personal feeling. Cleburne's adjutant, Captain Buck, states that Pat "was heard to say in substance, that but for his affection for his division, now the only tie that bound him to the Army of Tennessee, he would apply for service in Hardee's new command, even if he had to resign his major-general's commission and accept a staff position with him." But "Old Pat" remained with the men whose valor and spirit and high morale had made them the toast of the Army of Tennessee and helped to win for their gallant leader the title of "Stonewall Jackson of the West."

By slow stages, delayed by the gathering of supplies, Hood's army, now reduced to about 30,000 men, advanced into Tennessee. Meanwhile Sherman had determined to push his main force to Savannah, but when he realized Hood's intentions, he sent General George E. Thomas to Nashville with more than 8000 men and detached the Fourth Corps under General D. S. Stanley and the XXIII Corps under General John M. Schofield, a total of about 22,000 men, to Tennessee to keep tab on Hood's movements.

The two forces made contact on November 24, near Columbia, situated on the south bank of the Duck River. Fearful of being flanked, Schofield, after several days of skirmishing, crossed the river and drew up for battle on the north bank. Hood now had a bold idea. He would demonstrate with one of his corps in a noisy fashion in front of Schofield, while the other two corps and Nathan Bedford Forrest's cavalry, which had joined Hood, would cross the Duck River above Columbia and interpose themselves across Schofield's retreat route at Spring Hill, about a dozen miles north, on the road to Nashville.

On November 28, 1864, Hood turned over all his artillery to Stephen D. Lee, whose corps was ordered to make an active show against Schofield. With Forrest's cavalry in the van, the rest of the Army of Tennessee crossed the Duck River and took up the march to Spring Hill the next morning. If Hood could hold Spring Hill in strength, Schofield would be in a bad way, caught between two Confederate forces, Hood's main army and Lee's corps tagging on his heels from the Duck River.

Later on the morning of November 29, Schofield, just to play it safe, sent his wagon train back to Nashville with a division to guard it. Thus, unknown to each army, a race to Spring Hill along parallel routes was under way. The wagon train, on the more direct route won it, getting to Spring Hill just as elements of Forrest's cavalry unsuccessfully attacked a small Federal force in the town.[46]

Hundreds of thousands of words have been written about the "Mystery of Spring Hill," and most of the principals have recorded conflicting testimony of what happened or didn't happen and who was to blame. But, as a perceptive historian of the Army of Tennessee said: "The outstanding and undisputed fact is that Schofield, apparently caught in a trap, in some unexplained fashion escaped and got away. That there was some sort of tragic bungling in the handling of the Confederate forces is inescapable."

At about 4 P.M. Cleburne's division, leading Hood's army, was sent into action. Cleburne charged in the face of heavy fire and was partially successful, but when Forrest's cavalrymen, supporting Cleburne on the right, withdrew from the fight because their ammunition was exhausted, Cleburne had to reorganize his now disarranged line. He did this and was preparing to advance again, when orders came to attack no more that night. Between 4 P.M., when Cleburne opened the action, and midnight, there occurred a series of fatal misunderstandings in Hood's army which added up to perhaps the greatest of all the lost opportunities of the Confederacy. A single Union division was on the scene and yet, with Hood leading, planning and directing the Confederate operation, no attack in force was made. Schofield's force, although dangerously exposed, was allowed to escape. Union Colonel Henry Stone of General Thomas's staff says: "A single Confederate brigade . . . planted across the pike, either north or south of Spring Hill, would have effectually prevented Schofield's retreat, and daylight would have found his whole force cut off from every avenue of escape by more than twice its numbers, to assault whom would have been madness and to avoid whom would have been impossible."[47]

As divisions came up they were dressed on Cleburne's line, General Bate to the left, General Brown to Cleburne's right. Orders were that when Brown opened fire, Cleburne was to follow and Bate likewise when he heard Cleburne's rifles. Meanwhile, however, as he prepared to get into line, Bate detected Federal troops moving up the pike from Columbia. It was the advance of Schofield. Bate promptly fired on them, but orders from General Cheatham, given without knowledge of Schofield's approach, required Bate to change position. Why Bate didn't notify Cheatham of the changed condition on his front is a sub-mystery to the "Mystery of Spring Hill."

Having made his shift, Bate waited for the sound of Cleburne's firing. Cleburne, in his turn, waited for the sound of Brown's guns. But both waited in vain, for Brown, discovering he was dangerously flanked on his right, did not advance at all. Brown contended he was told to wait until General Stewart's corps came up. Cheatham claims he told Brown to refuse his right flank for protection and to charge as ordered. Hood states that he rode up to Cheatham at twilight, exclaiming: "General, why in the name of God have you not attacked the enemy and taken possession of that pike?" Cheatham said this "only occurred in the imagination of General Hood."[48]

Two amazing facts must be remembered: (1.) A little more than a single Union division at Spring Hill had paralyzed two-thirds of Hood's whole army; (2.) Schofield was moving slowly up the pike toward Spring Hill and the Confederates were doing nothing about it. Indeed, as Stanley Horn says, Confederate "ineptitude was . . . bountifully displayed" at Spring Hill.

But worse was yet to come. When Hood's troops went into bivouac for the night, "Schofield . . . with his heart in his throat . . . was quick-stepping his army silently down the turnpike, within sight of the camp fires of the slumbering Army of Tennessee."[49]

Perhaps the most exasperating mystery came after "eleven or twelve o'clock," according to Hood, or "late at night," according to his aide, Governor Isham Harris, who later said "at 3 A.M.," when a Confederate private came to Hood's headquarters with the news that Federals were passing on the turnpike. Hood ordered his adjutant, Major A. P. Mason, to send a message to General Cheatham to move down the road immediately and attack the enemy. Then Hood went back to sleep. Apparently Major Mason did too. Governor Harris, who told of the incident, definitely did. The next day, when Hood discovered Schofield had given him the slip, he was furious and sharply censured Cheatham, whereupon Major Mason confessed to Harris that he hadn't sent the message to General Cheatham. "I never sent him the order," he told Harris. "I fell asleep again before writing it." And yet General Cheatham claimed that "about midnight" he got a note from Major Mason telling of troops moving on the pike, but that investigation proved this untrue. How can this fantastic bungling be explained? Major Mason confessed he didn't send the order, but General Cheatham tells how he reacted when he received the order Mason didn't send![50]

x

Deep in thought, his expression sober almost to the point of grimness, Pat Cleburne rode at the head of his division shortly after daybreak on November 30, as Hood moved forward in pursuit of Schofield, determined to bring him to battle.

It had been a stormy breakfast at the home of Major Nat Cheairs at Spring Hill. Hood, bitterly chagrined at Schofield's escape, was "wrathy as a rattlesnake" and berated his generals in the course of a violent quarrel. "There were angry accusations of neglect, followed by flashing swords and demands for apology, as the edgy commanders stewed in impotent exasperation. In his blind anger, Hood lashed out viciously at his subordinates, placing the blame everywhere but where it belonged—on himself."

Cleburne brooded over the scene as he rode along and he must have come to the conclusion that General Hood held him responsible for the fiasco at Spring Hill, the previous night. He decided to talk it over with his friend, General Brown, and he sent a message ahead asking the latter for an interview. Brown wheeled his horse off the road and let his column pass on as he waited for Cleburne to ride up. The two left the pike and rode together through the fields.

"I have heard that the commanding general is endeavoring to place upon me the responsibility of allowing the enemy to pass our position last night," Cleburne told Brown, speaking with much feeling.

"I've heard nothing on that subject," replied Brown. "I hope you're mistaken."

"No, I think not," stated Cleburne. "My information comes through a very reliable channel. I cannot afford to rest under such an imputation. As soon as we are out of the presence of the enemy, I want the matter investigated to the fullest extent."

General Brown realized from Cleburne's words and tone that he was quite angry and deeply hurt by the conviction Hood had censured him.

"Who do you think was responsible for the escape?" queried Brown.

Cleburne criticized a command on the left of Hood's line, but quickly added: "Of course the responsibility rests with the commander-in-chief, as he was upon the field during the afternoon and was fully advised during the night of the movement of the enemy."

At this moment a courier rode up with orders for both generals. As Cleburne rode off, he called to Brown: "We will resume this conversation at the first convenient moment."[51]

None ever came, for three hours later Pat Cleburne was dead on one of the bloodiest battlefields of the war.

Some may deduce a premonition of death from Cleburne's words a few previous days as he reined his horse in front of the little Episcopal Church of St. John at Ashwood on the march to Spring Hill. Lingering a moment to contemplate the peaceful churchyard, with its lovely ivy-clad Gothic church, Cleburne turned to one of his staff and said: "It is almost worth dying for, to be buried in such a beautiful spot."

Although the bulk of Schofield's army had reached Franklin early in the morning of November 30, Hood came up on the Union rear guard at Winstead Hill, about two and a half miles from the town, in the early afternoon. Franklin, embraced by a big bend in the Harpeth River, lies south of the stream. Between the town and Winstead Hill was undulating meadowland through which the Columbia turnpike ran north and south, approximately across the center of the open space. The Lewisburg Pike, on Hood's right, and the Carter's Creek road on his left, also led to Franklin.

Schofield occupied crescent-shaped works which the Federals had erected when they had occupied Franklin previously and an advance entrenched position across the pike about half a mile in front of the main Federal line.[52]

Hood and his generals immediately gathered on Winstead Hill to survey the situation. All of them, except the commander-in-chief, were satisfied that it would be folly to launch a frontal attack, across more than two miles of open ground against such strongly held, formidable fortifications.

Hood put down his field glasses and announced: "We will make the fight."

"I do not like the looks of this fight," objected General Cheatham. "The enemy has an excellent position and is well fortified."

"I prefer to fight them here where they have had only eighteen hours to fortify, than to strike them at Nashville where they have been strengthening themselves for three years," declared Hood.

When he arrived, Cleburne examined the Union fortifications from the hill, resting his field glasses on a stump. After he had studied the enemy works carefully, he said: "They are very formidable."

General Hood, in his book *Advance and Retreat*, states that in a pre-battle conference, Cleburne spoke with "an enthusiasm, which he had never before betrayed in our intercourse."

"General, I am ready," Cleburne said, according to Hood, "and have more hope in the final success of our cause than I have had at any time since the first gun was fired."

"God grant it!" Hood says he replied.

A few pages further on in his book, Hood declares Cleburne knew "in what manner my orders at Spring Hill had been totally disregarded . . . It has been said he stated, upon the morning after the affair of Spring Hill, that he would never again allow one of my orders for battle to be disobeyed, if he could prevent it."[53]

Captain Irving Buck, Cleburne's adjutant, who knew him as well as any man, discounts Hood completely: "It seems incredible that as clear-headed, intelligent a soldier as Cleburne *could* have made such remarks at a time when any one above the degree of idiocy must have known that chances for final success of the Confederacy were desperate."

Besides, the evidence of Brigadier General Daniel C. Govan, one of Cleburne's brigade commanders, refutes it entirely. "General Cleburne seemed to be more despondent than I ever saw him," Govan wrote. "I was the last one to receive any instruction from him, and as I saluted and bade him good-bye, I remarked, 'Well, General, there will not be many of us that will get back to Arkansas,' and he replied, 'Well, Govan, if we are to die, let us die like men.' "[54]

Cheatham's corps was assigned the center of Hood's attacking line, with Cleburne's division to the right of the turnpike and Brown's to the left. At 4 P.M., the Confederates began their advance across the more than two miles of open space. "In the whole history of the war there was never such an imposing military spectacle as was here presented," wrote Stanley Horn, "eighteen brigades of infantry, with their cavalry support, marching in a straight line across an open field, in full view of their commanding general and of the entrenched enemy."

Startled rabbits fled before the advancing gray line and coveys of quail took wing from the grass and the waiting Federal troops were "for the moment . . . spellbound with admiration" as the Army of Tennessee moved resolutely forward as if on parade. As Hood's line came into range, the Federal artillery opened with canister and shrapnel, but although men dropped here and there as the shells burst, the ranks quickly closed and the advance continued. Cleburne's division and that of Brown made first contact with the enemy, quickly driving in the advance brigades deployed across the turnpike.

As the Union troops broke and ran for the main defense, the men of Cleburne and Brown followed, and soon they were in the Federal lines, engaged in bitter hand-to-hand fighting. But Cleburne's troops on the right were soon in trouble. Stewart's corps on their right had been repulsed and Cleburne was caught in a furious cross fire from Stewart's erstwhile adversaries. "I never saw men put in such a terrible position as Cleburne's division was for a few minutes," says a Federal participant in the battle. "The wonder is that any of them escaped death or capture."

Two horses were shot from under Cleburne, but on foot he moved forward, encouraging his men, waving his cap in his hand as he disappeared into the smoke of battle close to the Federal lines. A few seconds later, Pat Cleburne was dead.

The Battle of Franklin raged well past the sinking of the sun and desultory firing continued until after nine o'clock. When the day's bloody work was finally done, Hood had lost twelve generals, four others besides Cleburne killed, another fatally wounded, five others wounded and one captured, and more than six thousand of his men. The "heartbreaking, murderous, unnecessary battle that settled nothing" had cost the Army of Tennessee, and the Confederacy, dearly.[55]

Cleburne's division bivouacked that night with the dreadful knowledge that Old Pat was missing, and many prayers were offered that he may have been captured or wounded. But they found his body at dawn the next morning, 40 or 50 yards from the enemy's works. "He lay flat upon his back, as if asleep, his military cap partly over his eyes. He had on a new gray uniform . . . It was unbuttoned . . . a white linen shirt . . . was stained with blood on the front part of the left side, or just left of the abdomen. This was the only sign of a wound

. . . He was in sock feet his boots having been stolen," reported one of the men who found Cleburne.[56]

Cleburne was first buried in Rose Hill Cemetery at Columbia, Tennessee, along with others who had died at Franklin. General Lucius E. Polk, Cleburne's gallant brigade commander until disabled, then offered a plot in the family burial ground at St. John's Episcopal Church at Ashwood, and Cleburne and the others were re-interred in the quiet churchyard of which he had said it was "almost worth dying for, to be buried in such a beautiful spot." In 1869, Cleburne's remains were removed to Helena, Arkansas, from where the "Stonewall of the West" had started out as a private in 1861.

Many appropriate epitaphs can be found for Cleburne. To Robert E. Lee, he was "a meteor shining from a clouded sky." General S. B. Buckner "wept tears to [his] glorious memory." To a subordinate officer, he was "the perfect type of a perfect soldier." To a mere boy, in the 15th Arkansas, Old Pat was "the hardest fighter of the age." To a company commander Cleburne was "the idol of his command, and a better soldier never died for any cause."

President Jefferson Davis said that Cleburne's men followed him "with implicit confidence that in another army was given Stonewall Jackson, and in the one case, as in the other, a vacancy was created which could never be filled."

It remained, however, for General William J. Hardee to best perpetuate in words, the memory of Patrick Ronayne Cleburne:

". . . History will take up his fame, and hand it down to time for exampling wherever a courage without stain, a manhood without blemish, and integrity that knew no compromise, and patriotism that withheld no sacrifice, are honored of mankind."[57]

4

Confederate Corsair:

LIEUTENANT "SAVEZ" READ, C.S.N.

I

ROBERT E. LEE had surrendered, but the war wasn't over yet for Lieutenant Charles W. "Savez" Read, C.S.N.

He had orders from Confederate Secretary of the Navy Stephen R. Mallory to take the Confederate ram, *William H. Webb*, from Alexandria, Louisiana, on the Red River and to dash through the Federal gunboats in the Mississippi, past New Orleans and out to sea.[1] This was the kind of assignment that "Savez" Read relished. Throughout the war, he sought only action and here was one more chance for plenty of it.

At 8:30 P.M. on April 23, 1865, the *William H. Webb* steamed down the Red River and passed into the Mississippi unchallenged by the half-dozen Federal warships which kept guard there. Every ten or fifteen miles, Read sent a party ashore to cut the telegraph lines to New Orleans which the *Webb* approached by noon on April 24. Read hoisted an American flag at half-mast and, putting on all his steam, raced past the city at a speed of 25 miles an hour.[2]

The Federal gunboat *Hollyhock* gave pursuit, but the *Webb* distanced her. But Read's luck soon ran out. About 25 miles below New Orleans, the *Webb* came suddenly upon the *Richmond*, lying in the middle of the river, both its broadsides out.

Read ordered the *Webb's* speed reduced and then summoned all the officers in front of the pilot house. "It's no use," he said. "It's a failure . . . I think the only thing left for us to do is to set fire to the *Webb* and blow her up."[3]

And that's what "Savez" Read did, he and his men escaping into the swamps, soon to surrender or be captured by Federal troops. Thus ended the fabulous saga of "Savez" Read, "such an adventurous career that anyone reading an account of it would be justified in thinking that he was a creature of the imagination who had stepped bodily out of the pages of one of Dumas' novels."[4]

II

They called him "Savez" Read at the United States Naval Academy, because in four years as a midshipman he mastered only one word of French.

Never one not to employ his resources to the fullest, the young Mississippian exploited his linguistic skill at every turn. Read repeated his solitary French acquisition, *savez*, so often that it became a habit and seldom did he end a sentence without it.

The inevitable occurred and the nickname "Savez" was bestowed upon Read and it followed him through four years of fighting and then for the rest of his life.

"Savez" Read made no notable contributions to scholarship at Annapolis. In fact, he seems to have mastered no more than the barest minimum in all his subjects for, as one of his classmates said of him, "after a magnificent struggle extending over four years, 'Savez' Read triumphantly graduated at the foot of his class."[5]

Read was lazy and seldom opened his books. A distinguished American Naval hero, Admiral W. S. Schley, who was a classmate and friend of Read, said of him:

"The place he took in his class was in no sense the measure of his intellectual worth, but arose from his lack of application to study. He possessed in high degree common sense—or ought I to say uncommon sense, as everyone does not possess it—that underlies success in every calling . . . He had sublime courage, he had conspicuous dash, he had great originality, and was aggressive in all that he did."

Born in Yazoo County, Mississippi, on May 12, 1840, Read was barely sixteen when he entered the Naval Academy, where the qualities which Admiral Schley described soon won for him the affection of his fellows.[6]

"Savez" Read was not very formidable to look at. He was about five feet six inches tall and of slight, almost delicate, build. His features were undistinguished, his complexion fair, his hair sandy. He had a voice that bordered on the feminine and his manner was gentle and deferential.[7] His schoolmates at Annapolis found him "generous and loyal in character, firm in his friendships and decided in his opinions."[8]

Upon graduation in 1860, Read was assigned to the steam frigate *Powhatan*, then stationed at Vera Cruz, Mexico. On board the *Powhatan* he became a shipmate of the future Admiral George Dewey. When the word reached Read that his native Mississippi had seceded from the Union, he promptly tendered his resignation as midshipman in the United States Navy. It was not, however, until March 13, 1861, that the *Powhatan* returned to New York and Read could leave for the South. He went to Montgomery, still the capital of the new Confederate States of America, where his fellow Mississippian, President Jefferson Davis, with whom he was acquainted, asked many questions about the Naval Academy, and the naval service. "He said he hoped there would be no war," Read wrote many years later, "but if coercion was attempted, that the army of the South would be the place for a young man with a military education." Read also called on Secretary of the Navy Stephen R. Mallory who received him cordially and assured him that his services would no doubt soon be needed by the Confederacy.[9]

When the guns at Charleston ushered in the Civil War, Read's first impulse was to enter the Confederate Army. "It was, indeed, hard for me to keep from volunteering . . ." he wrote. "But I remembered that the South had but few sailors and would need them all on the water." Soon orders reached him in Mississippi and in response to them he reported to Captain Laurence Rousseau at New Orleans on May 1, 1861, for service aboard the Confederate steamer *McRae*.[10]

The *McRae*, formerly the *Marquis de la Habana*, had been taken by United States vessels near Vera Cruz on the charge that "she belonged to an unrecognized revolutionary government, and that she was a pirate on the high seas." The vessel had been recently purchased in England to aid the Miramón revolutionary movement. The *Marquis de la Habana* had been taken to New Orleans as a prize vessel and when the war came she was seized by the Confederates and her name changed.[11]

When Read reported to Lieutenant Thomas B. Huger aboard the *McRae*, the ship was being outfitted, along with another vessel, soon to win fame as the raider *Sumter*. Huger appointed Read acting sailing master of the barque-rigged and propeller-driven *McRae*. She was of about 600 tons and carried eight guns and it was planned for her to go to sea as soon as she was ready to raid the commerce of the United States.

But the *McRae* was not destined to go to sea. When she was fitted out, she dropped down the river to the Head of the Passes to await a chance to run the blockade. "The opportunity fortunately never occurred," wrote young Midshipman James Morris Morgan, "for the *McRae* would not have lasted a week as a commerce destroyer. At her top speed she could not make over seven knots, and her coal supply was very limited; worse than this, her engines broke down every time she was forced."[12]

Read, always eager for action, fussed and fumed at the delays. The shortcomings of the *McRae* didn't dampen his enthusiasm. To Midshipman Morgan, "Savez" privately confided what he would do if he were captain. He'd take a chance of getting the *McRae* through the South Pass where there were no blockaders. Reminded that the *McRae* drew 13 feet of water and that the pilot had insisted that there wasn't enough depth in South Pass for the vessel, Read scoffed. Pilot or not, he believed there was sufficient water for the attempt, and besides, the mud bottom was soft and oozy.

Read was keenly disappointed when the *McRae's* seagoing adventure was abandoned. The vessel returned to New Orleans, where it became the flagship of Commodore George N. Hollins, an old sea dog who had served in the United States Navy for nearly fifty years.[13]

Read did not have long to wait for action, but it came to him as a spectator, for with the *McRae* under steam, there wasn't much for the sailing master to do. On the night of October 12, 1861, Commodore Hollins attacked the Federal flotilla which had insolently taken up a position at the Head of the Passes, where it could more effectively blockade the multi-mouthed Mississippi.

The engagement, in which the Confederate ironclad ram *Manassas* rammed the *Richmond* and precipitated a flight of the *Water Witch*, *Preble*, *Vincennes*, and *Richmond* down Southwest Pass, was called "Pope's Run" in "honor" of the inglorious commander of the squadron, Captain John Pope. During the attempt to cross the bar, the *Vincennes* ran aground. The *McRae* engaged the *Richmond* at long range.

"Savez" Read stood on the poop deck, watching the action almost disinterestedly. He appeared oblivious to the shells from the *Richmond* which were exploding around the *McRae* or humming harmlessly by. Young Morgan joined him and Read complained that the *McRae* should run alongside the *Vincennes* and destroy her.[14]

Shortly after this, "Savez" was made executive officer of the *McRae*, succeeding Lieutenant A. F. Warley, a stern disciplinarian. Because they feared Warley, the crew had walked a chalk line, but when the mild-mannered Read took charge they decided to teach the young sprout a thing or two. Read reacted to their misconduct with mild reprimands and the sailors put him down for an easy mark.[15]

On the occasion when Captain Huger and all the officers except Read and two young midshipmen, one of whom was James Morgan, had been ordered ashore by the doctor to recuperate from fever, the crew decided to try out the young executive officer. Returning from shore liberty late one afternoon in an ugly mood, the crew was boisterous and insubordinate. Read, at first, chose to ignore their misbehavior.

Some of the half-drunken seamen declared that they wanted more liquor and that they meant to go ashore for it. When they made a move to lower a boat, Read beckoned to one of the midshipmen.

"Go below and put on your side arms and return to me," said Read softly. When the lad returned, "Savez," in a calm but loud voice, said: "Shoot down the first man who touches a boat-fall without my orders."

Astonishment enveloped the faces of men who heard the order. Could this be the placid little fellow they considered a soft touch? Moving away from the boats the men clustered in twos and threes, quite baffled by this unexpected turn of events. Read, ignoring the mutinous crew, sauntered casually around the quarterdeck, pausing frequently to contemplate almost listlessly the lights of the city which began to punctuate the oncoming darkness.

That night, Midshipman Morgan, who was only fifteen and small for his age, had the first watch. At seven bells he heard a considerable disturbance below. He stepped to the forward hatchway and commanded: "Silence! Fore and aft!"

"Ah, sonny, go and tell your mammy she wants you," yelled back a raucous voice. Boisterous laughter and jeers followed.

A second command for silence from young Morgan drew another round of jeers and abuse. The midshipman peered into the hatchway and saw that the sailors were not only not in their hammocks but, by the light of candles, were playing cards and were drinking, having discovered some whiskey aboard ship.

Unable to enforce his orders, Morgan went to "Savez" Read's stateroom and reported what had happened. Read was up in an instant and into his uniform and, buckling his sword belt on, was off on the run. Morgan's recollection of the incident is vivid:

"He fairly plunged down the hatchway when he got to it, and the next thing I heard was the ring of his sword blade as it came in contact with the heads of the mutineers. I also heard yells of pain and savage oaths, these latter followed by pleadings for mercy, and then I saw a stream of men scrambling up the hatchway, helter skelter, in a mad rush to avoid Read who was bringing up the rear, his sword working like a flail as it came down on the heads of the laggards. I expected to see much bloodshed, but he was only striking with flat of his blade."

The erstwhile gentle Read had turned demon and the mutineers, who had been filled with so much bravado only a few moments earlier, fled before him with genuine fear.

"Aloft! every mother's son of you!" Read roared.

Up the rigging scampered most of the men, but the few who hesitated quickly changed their minds when Read drew his pistol. When some of the men stopped in the lower shrouds, Read menaced them with his pistol and angrily ordered them to climb higher and higher. When they reached the top rigging, they complained piteously that there was no more room for more men. "Then lay out on the yards!" ordered "Savez."

With the unruly crew perched aloft, Read regained his usual composure and in his natural voice called out: "The first man who steps down a rattling, I will shoot the feet off him."

"And there they perched through the weary hours of the night like so many crows roosting on the limbs and vines which hung from dead trees," wrote James Morgan. "Daylight came to their relief at last . . .

Read ordered them down from aloft and the daily routine of the ship commenced . . . No further punishments were inflicted and no reference was again made as to the misunderstanding . . . and it was not very long before these same men fairly idolized their young executive officer."[16]

III

Early in 1862, the *McRae* was ordered upstream, along with four converted steamboats of the River Defense Fleet, to help in the defense of New Madrid, Missouri, and Island No. 10, Tennessee.

One day a Federal battery on shore opened up heavily upon the *McRae*. "Savez" Read, always itching for a fight, was impatient at the decision to fight the battery from a position in the middle of the Mississippi.

"If we stuck our nose into the mud in front of that battery we could drive those fellows out with canister," he suggested to Captain Huger.

"Yes, Mr. Read," replied Huger, "but they have canister as well as ourselves."

His enthusiasm for a bold move undampened, Read said: "Yes, Captain, but this canister game is one which always makes somebody tired and want to quit. Those soldiers in the battery can leave whenever they want to, but with as little power as this ship has, we would have to stay there until a towboat came and pulled us out of the mud, *savez?*"

Another of Read's bold ideas was overruled by Huger. "Savez" wanted *McRae* brought alongside the bank to let him carry a battery by "boarding." For three weeks the *McRae* was under almost continuous fire. When New Madrid and Island No. 10 were given up, Commander George N. Hollins, in charge of the little Confederate flotilla, decided, without orders from Richmond, to descend the river to New Orleans, now threatened by Farragut's formidable fleet from the Gulf.[17]

Although Hollins was ordered to Richmond, the *McRae* was rushed down to the forts to join the more or less improvised Confederate flotilla, which was to challenge Farragut if he succeeded in running the gantlet of the guns of Fort Jackson and Fort St. Philip.

On April 16, 1862, two days before David Dixon Porter's mortar vessels began the bombardment of the forts, the *McRae* arrived and anchored above Fort St. Philip. The Confederate naval force was one of the strangest ever assembled. There were three Confederate vessels—the *McRae*, the ironclad ram *Manassas*, and the unfinished (and hence immobile) giant ironclad *Louisiana*—under the command of Commander J. K. Mitchell. There was the State of Louisiana's gunboat, *Governor*

Moore. Also there were six converted steamboats known as the River Defense Fleet, commanded by steamboat captains, who refused absolutely to take orders from the Confederate Navy.[18]

During the six-day bombardment of the forts by Porter's mortar schooners, the *McRae* escaped damage. On the afternoon of April 23, "Savez" Read stood on the parapet of Fort Jackson with Colonel Higgins and the little he could see around the bend and downstream suggested to him that Farragut's attack would be made that night. Higgins entertained the same idea. Read returned to the *McRae* to prepare for imminent action. The *McRae's* cable was made ready for slipping and a man was stationed to unshackle it at a moment's notice. Moreover, half the crew was ordered on deck and the engineer was instructed to get up steam. The *McRae's* eight guns were cut loose and loaded.

"Savez" retired after midnight, but at 3 A.M. the officer of the deck sent him word that a steamer was coming up the river. In less than a minute, the *McRae* was under way, her guns firing on the advancing Federal vessels.

The so-called River Defense Fleet evaporated without a fight, some of the vessels fleeing, the others being run ashore and set afire, but none offering any resistance to the enemy.

Heavily engaged, however, were the *Manassas* and the *Governor Moore* commanded respectively by two officers from the old Navy, Lieutenant A. F. Warley and Lieutenant Beverly C. Kennon. And in the thick of the fight from the start was the *McRae.* "We had little trouble to find something to fire at, for as we were out in the river, the enemy was on every side of us," wrote Read, "and gallantly did our brave tars stand to their guns, loading and firing their guns as rapidly as possible."

Cool and fearless, Lieutenant Huger handled the embattled *McRae* superbly. When a shell from a howitzer fired from aloft pierced the *McRae's* deck and exploded in the sail room setting the ship on fire, Huger ordered "Savez" to inform him when the flames reached the thin bulkhead of 2-inch pine which separated the blazing sail room from the shell lockers. And then, as Huger continued to fight his ship valiantly, "Savez" worked desperately to quench the flames, conscious all the while that the *McRae* was in grave danger of being blown up.

Just as Read succeeded in extinguishing the fire, the *McRae* was engaged by four Federal vessels. One of them ranged alongside and delivered a broadside of grape and canister, mortally wounding Lieutenant Huger and the *McRae's* pilot, cutting away the wheel ropes and the signal halyards and taking the flag overboard.

"Savez" immediately assumed command and over Huger's gasping protests, insisted that the dying commander of the *McRae* be taken below to his cabin. Huger begged Read not to surrender the *McRae.* "I always promised myself I would fight her until she was under the water!" he exclaimed. "Savez" promised Huger he would fight the ship as long as she remained afloat.[19]

It was almost a miracle that the *McRae* was afloat at all, for it had undergone great punishment from the formidable guns of Farragut's fleet. Several large shells had penetrated the hull very near the water-line and the vessel was leaking badly. Her upper structure and rigging were shambles, and the smokestack was so badly riddled that it barely stood and provided so little draft that it was almost impossible to keep steam in the boilers.[20]

Nevertheless, Read headed the *McRae* upstream. Its tiller ropes had been by now replaced, and the little vessel's starboard guns blazed away at Federal gunboats that moved into range. When daylight broke, Read found his vessel about four miles above the forts and about to run smack into eleven of Farragut's ships, all out of range of the Confederate bat-teries in the forts.

"Savez" Read was a great gambler and he'd take any calculated risk or tackle any adventure in which there was some chance of success. But his battered ship, barely able to keep afloat, had no chance if he kept her on her course. Prudently, he turned the *McRae* downstream to return to the forts. Parting shots from the Federal ships again shot the tiller ropes away and the *McRae* ran into the bank and stuck fast.[21]

Meanwhile, Read spotted the *Resolute* of the not-so-resolute River Defense Fleet ashore with a white flag flying. He dispatched an of-ficer and twenty men to take charge of her. A tugboat, sent to the *McRae's* assistance, pulled her off the mud bank and Read dropped anchor close to Fort St. Philip.

For the next 24 hours, Read pondered a bold project which had come into his mind when he first spotted the *Resolute*, apparently in good shape. He wrote Commander J. K. Mitchell on April 26:

"I respectfully request permission to take charge of the Str. *Resolute* with a volunteer crew from this vessel, and proceed to sea.

"The *Resolute* is an Ocean Steamer and well supplied, mounts two long 32 pdrs—and has on board a sufficient quantity of ammunition for a cruise—She is remarkably fast and her engines and dependencies are in excellent order.

"I have reason to believe that but few of the enemy's vessels are below—that they will not be looking for anything from above—and as the *Resolute* is well barricaded she can succeed in running out to-night.

"I base my claim to that vessel upon the ground that I rescued her from being burnt and captured.

"The *Resolute* can be of little service on the river—but the history of privateering shows her value to our country on the ocean."

Mitchell replied that Read's proposition would be considered, but before "Savez" got approval from his superior, he got bad news from Lieutenant Arnold, aboard the *Resolute*. The previous day, two enemy ships had attacked and the *Resolute* received two shots in her hull, one forward, below the waterline when the vessel was afloat. It would take three days, Arnold estimated, to make repairs. And so Read's immediate scheme, which included raiding the New England coast, was abandoned. But "Savez" did not abandon the idea; he stored it in the back of his mind for future use.[22]

With Lieutenant Huger near death, and many of the crew of the *Mc-Rae* in need of medical attention, Read steamed up to the Quarantine Station, about five miles above the forts, to ask permission of the Union commander to proceed with the wounded to New Orleans.

This permission granted, "Savez" headed the *McRae* into the channel, but progress against the strong current was slow for the battered craft. About 11:30 A.M., on April 27, the *McRae* arrived in front of New Orleans and Read went on board Farragut's flagship *Hartford*, requesting that he be allowed to remove his wounded and then return to the forts, still under a flag of truce.

Read signed an agreement with Farragut that upon landing his sick and wounded, he would leave for the forts at 10 A.M. on the twenty-eighth with the *McRae* "in the same condition in every respect in which she came up . . . To the fidelity of which the commander of the said Confederate steamer pledges his word of honor."

"Savez" landed his wounded and saw that Lieutenant Huger was safely delivered to his home. Then he returned to the *McRae*, prepared to lift anchor in the morning and return to the forts. At 8:30 P.M., however, the *McRae* began to drag anchor, veering its cable its entire length, 50 fathoms. There was no other anchor to let go so Read started the engines and veered the *McRae* toward Slaughter House Point, about a mile downstream and across the river from the city, where the water was much less deep. In his official report, "Savez" described the *McRae's* predicament graphically:

". . . In going across the river the ship rested on something under the water, and swung entirely around several times, when she drifted off and brought up a short distance below. I soon ascertained that the ship was leaking badly. The donkey and bilge pumps were immediately started and kept going. At 11:30 the water had gained such a height as to put the fires out in the furnaces, thus stopping the donkey pump. I sent a boat on shore to ask assistance of the police or citizens. A lieutenant of the police with ten men came on board and assisted us in working the pumps. At 6 a.m. the water was 6 feet in the hold and gaining on us, the vessel was settling rapidly, and the water on the outside was only two inches below the shot holes in the ship's sides. The leak was not confined to any particular place, but the water appeared to come through all her seams. My men were exhausted, and I felt confident that further exertions were useless. I directed her injection pipes to be cut, so that she might sink as soon as possible, and got all hands ashore without delay. At 7 the ship went down."

Read immediately went on board the Federal flagship to explain why he could not fulfill his agreement with Farragut. The Flag Officer being absent, Read addressed himself to Captain T. T. Craven, who informed "Savez" that there was no way of getting down to the forts except by small boat. The Federal officer added that he supposed that Read could use his own option of returning or not, but that the best course would be to see the Flag Officer the next morning. But before "Savez" could get aboard the *Hartford* on the twenty-ninth, he learned that the forts had surrendered, and that the great, but unfinished ironclad *Louisiana* had been blown up. "I now considered myself and men at liberty to go where I pleased. . . ." reported Read. So without taking his leave of the Federals he proceeded to Jackson, Mississippi.[23]

Farragut was furious over what he considered a breach of faith by "Savez" Read in scuttling the *McRae*. In a sharp note to Commander J. K. Mitchell, then a prisoner aboard a Federal transport at the forts, the Flag Officer reproached Read's conduct: ". . . The rules of war . . . even of the most barbarous nations, recognize a flag of truce; and while it is flying it is the universal custom that all hostile operations cease . . . The written agreement, upon the solemn promise of the commander, was signed, by which pledge the vessel was to return in the condition in which she left by 10 o'clock the next morning, instead of which, at 8 a.m. she was discovered without the flag of truce flying, abandoned and scuttled. All of which goes to show a regardlessness of the usages of civilized warfare . . ."[24]

Evidence that probably never reached Farragut, or "Savez's" old friends in the U. S. Navy, substantiates Read's official report on the fate of the *McRae*. An entry in the Fire and Alarm Telegraph Message Book, dated April 27, 1862, reads: "11¼ p.m. The Gun Boat *McRae* has broke her moorings and drifting down the river leaking badly. Lieut. Brooks has sent 10 Workmen to render assistance."[25]

IV

Young Read's gallantry aboard the *McRae* at the battle at the forts had not gone unnoticed in Richmond. Secretary Mallory reported to President Davis that "the conduct of the officers and crew of the *McRae* . . . has rarely been surpassed in the annals of naval warfare."[26] Mallory marked Read as a man for dangerous enterprises.

Shortly after leaving New Orleans, Read reported to Mallory in Richmond and was promptly dispatched to join the Confederate fleet of makeshift rams on the Mississippi in the vicinity of Fort Pillow, Tennessee. The vessels, still known as "Hollins' fleet," although the old Flag Officer had been replaced by Commander R. F. Pinckney, were the subject of general ridicule and Read wasn't too happy about his assignment. "I was really ashamed to own that I was on my way to join it," he confessed later, "and it was only the hope of getting on detached duty that prevented me from throwing up my commission in the navy and joining the army."

Pinckney gave Read command of two heavy guns, mounted on a bluff five or six miles below Fort Pillow, but "Savez" was spared the chagrin of the evacuation without a struggle which soon followed for he had hardly established his battery before he was sent to Vicksburg to recruit sailors.

There was being built at this time at Memphis the ironclad gunboat *Arkansas*, 180 feet in length, displacing 800 tons, and mounting ten guns—six in broadside and two fore and aft. She had two engines and two propellers and "Savez" Read considered her "a very pretty little gun-boat." The *Arkansas* was unfinished when the news of the surrender of Island No. 10 reached Memphis and it was towed down the Mississippi and up the Yazoo River to be completed. The Confederate Navy Department detailed Lieutenant Isaac Newton Brown to get the *Arkansas* ready for service and to take command of it. And this energetic officer lost no time in getting the job done.

Always eager for action, "Savez" Read was soon in line for it, for he got orders to report to Brown for service aboard the *Arkansas*. It was characteristic of Read to chafe at delays. When things were ready to go, he wanted to go; this also seemed to be the state of mind of everybody else on the ship. "We had a full complement of officers and about two hundred men," Read wrote. "All were anxious for the time to come when we could show the enemy that he could not lay idly in our waters."

"Savez" and others must have shown their impatience for Lieutenant Brown later declared of his officers: "The only trouble they ever gave me was to keep them from running the *Arkansas* into the Union fleet before we were ready for battle."[27]

The Union fleet above Vicksburg was a sizable one, for it contained the river fleet under Flag Officer Charles H. Davis, which had fought its way down the Mississippi from Columbus, Kentucky, and Farragut's seagoing ships which had come up from New Orleans and had run past the Vicksburg batteries. At the mouth of the Yazoo River, the Federal vessels stood, blocking the way of the *Arkansas*, should Brown decide to dash into the Mississippi and try to make a run for the shelter of the Vicksburg batteries.

Read and the other officers were unanimous in urging an attack on the enemy fleet, but Brown was of the opinion that the *Arkansas* should stay up the Yazoo on the defensive to protect the river and its valley from which the Confederates drew considerable supplies. However, he agreed that if General Van Dorn, in command at Vicksburg, wanted the *Arkansas* to attack he was ready to do so. Brown sent "Savez" Read to Vicksburg to confer with General Earl Van Dorn. Riding all night, Read reached Vicksburg at 8 A.M. and soon was closeted with the general.

General Van Dorn weighed the matter for a moment, and although he appreciated the importance of holding the Yazoo, he felt that the *Arkansas* could successfully run by the gunboats above Vicksburg and attack the Federal mortar schooners below the town. Perhaps the *Arkansas* could even run down the Mississippi, destroying the Yankee gunboats scattered on the lower river and pass out into the Gulf and on to Mobile. Accordingly, he gave Read a message for Brown, urging him to move at once with his ironclad.

After leaving General Van Dorn, "Savez" proceeded up the bank with an Army officer to reconnoiter the Yankee fleet. He related what he saw:

"It was late in the afternoon before we got abreast with the fleet. The woods were so dense and entangled with vines and briars that we were obliged to dismount and grope our way through the best we could. I had a good field-glass, and watched the vessels carefully some time. Farragut's fleet consisted of thirteen heavy sloops-of-war, mounting tremendous batteries, and were anchored in line ahead near the east bank. I was satisfied that none of them had steam up. The fleet of Commodore Davis numbered over thirty ironclads and six or eight rams. They were moored to the west bank, nearly opposite Farragut's fleet. Below Davis's fleet were about thirty mortar-boats. Davis's vessels appeared to have steam up."

This information, together with Van Dorn's urgent requests, "Savez" brought back to Lieutenant Brown late the next day. The *Arkansas* was put into motion the following morning, heading for the Mississippi and the huge Federal fleet that lay near the Yazoo's mouth.

This high adventure was tempting to Flag Officer William F. Lynch, Confederate Naval Commander in the West. He arrived from Jackson and told Brown he was going along on the *Arkansas*. Unhesitatingly, Brown replied: "Well, Commodore, I will be glad if you go down with us, but as this vessel is too small for two captains, if you go I will take charge of a gun and attend to that."

"Very well, Captain, you may go," replied the old Commodore. "I will stay. May God bless you!"

On the evening of July 14, the *Arkansas* reached Haynes Bluff where it anchored. At 2 A.M., the ship cleared for action and got under way again. The memory of that scene was etched sharply in "Savez" Read's memory:

"The men of the *Arkansas* were all at their stations, the guns were loaded and cast loose, their tackles in the hands of willing seamen ready to train; primers in the vents; locks thrown back and the lanyards in the hands of the gun captains; the decks sprinkled with sand and tourniquets and bandages at hand; tubs filled with fresh water were between the guns, and down in the berth deck were the surgeons with their bright instruments, stimulants and lint, while along the passage-ways stood rows of men to pass powder, shell and shot, and all was quiet save the dull thump, thump, of the propellers. Steadily the little ship moved onward towards her enemies . . ."[28]

Shortly before daylight, Brown stopped his ship and sent "Savez" Read ashore to seek information of the enemy at a plantation. But it was a fruitless venture, for the sound of the steamer in the river had alarmed the people and they had taken to the woods, leaving an old Negro woman alone to protect the house.

Read inquired about the inhabitants. But the old woman didn't know anything about them. Where had they gone? She still didn't know.

"They have but just left," insisted Read, "for their beds are yet warm."

"Dunno about dat," replied the old Negress, "an' if I did, I wouldn't tell."

"Do you take me for a Yankee?" queried Read. "Don't you see I wear a gray coat?"

"Sartin you's a Yankee," the old woman exclaimed. "Our folks ain't got none dem gun-boats."[29]

At sunrise, as the *Arkansas* rounded a bend, three Federal vessels in line came into view, heading upstream under full steam. There were the ironclad *Carondelet*, and the wooden gunboat *Tyler* and ram *Queen of the West*, sent up the Yazoo to scout for the *Arkansas*. There must have been astonishment aboard all three vessels to discover the Rebel ironclad suddenly bearing down upon them. From a range of half a mile, the *Carondelet* fired a wildly aimed bow gun, backed around and headed downstream. The *Tyler* followed suit, and the stern guns of both retreating vessels began to pepper the *Arkansas*. The *Queen of the West*, displaying few regal qualities, had meanwhile turned and beaten a hasty retreat down the river.

Captain Brown held his fire with the *Arkansas'* bow guns, because he did not want to diminish the vessel's speed. He aimed to ram the *Carondelet*, using his broadsides to keep the *Tyler* from getting to his quarter, but the retreat of the two Federal ships down the Yazoo prevented this.

Now began a running duel with the enemy, whose well-directed shots began to ring on the *Arkansas'* iron front, while the *Arkansas'* guns delivered a raking, effective fire on the fleeing Federals. All this while, "Savez" Read, commanding the *Arkansas'* stern guns, chafed in silence. Here was a fight and, for all practical purposes, he wasn't in it.

But soon "Savez" was in action, for the *Carondelet*, its steering gear apparently shot away, had run aground. The *Arkansas* steamed abreast of her, blasting the Federal vessel with broadsides as the ships almost overlapped. As the *Arkansas* veered out into the stream, "Savez's" chance came and he blazed away at the *Carondelet* with his stern rifles, making good use of his opportunity.

The *Arkansas*, its progress slowed by shots through its smokestack, left the disabled *Carondelet* astern and gained the Mississippi, where, aided by the current, it moved down on the Federal fleet above Vicksburg. From his position topside the *Arkansas*, Captain Brown spotted the enemy—"a forest of masts and smokestacks—ships, rams, ironclads, and other gunboats on the left side, and ordinary river steamers and bomb vessels along the right."

A young Irishman, peering along his gun saw this immense force and exclaimed: "Holy Mother, have mercy on us; we'll never get through there."

"But we had ventured too far to think of backing out," said Lieutenant George W. Gift, who commanded the forward guns. "Through we must go."

Soon the *Arkansas* was in the thick of the Union fleet, all its guns at work, and the enemy responded with fury. Captain Brown told a graphic story of the unequal fight:

"As we advanced, the line of fire seemed to grow into a circle constantly closing. The shock of missiles striking our sides was literally continuous . . . we were now surrounded, without room for anything but pushing ahead . . . I had the most lively realization of having steamed into a real volcano, the *Arkansas* from its center firing rapidly to every point on the circumference, without the fear of hitting a friend or missing a foe."

"Savez" Read was in his element, his fire chasing off a Yankee ram which launched a feeble attack on the *Arkansas'* stern. But the Federal shots fell upon the *Arkansas* like sledgehammer blows and one ripped through a hole made by a previous shell and exploded with tragic effect, killing or wounding sixteen of the crew and setting the battered Confederate ironclad afire. Although the fire was quickly extinguished, more casualties were in store for the *Arkansas* as it ran the fiery gantlet.

But all the while, the *Arkansas* kept moving downstream. "Slowly we went," recalled "Savez" Read, "fighting our way right and left, until presently we passed our enemies and were received with loud hurrahs from the Confederate soldiers on the heights of Vicksburg."

But within and without, the *Arkansas* was a sorry sight.

"We got through, hammered and battered though," recorded Lieutenant Gift. "Our smokestack resembled an immense nutmeg grater, so often had it been struck, and the sides of the ship were as spotted as if she had been peppered. A shot had broken our cast-iron ram. Another had demolished a hawse pipe. Our boats were shot away and dragging. But all this was to be expected and could be repaired. Not so on the inside. A great heap of mangled and ghastly slain lay on the gun deck, with rivulets of blood running away from them. There was a poor fellow torn asunder, another mashed flat, while in the 'slaughterhouse' brains, hair and blood were all about."

"Savez" Read later recalled "the iron on her portside, though pierced but twice, had been so often struck with heavy projectiles that it was very much loosened. A few more shots would have caused nearly all of it to have fallen from the vessel."[30]

In a chagrin-tinged report to the Federal Navy Department, Flag Officer Davis reported that the *Arkansas*' "appearance was so sudden, and the steam of almost every vessel in the squadron was so low, or, in other words so entirely unprepared were we, that she had an opportunity to pass without positive obstruction, though she was seriously injured by shot."

Secretary of the Navy Gideon Welles did not disguise his disgust in his reply to Davis: "I need not say to you that the escape of this vessel and the attending circumstances have been the cause of serious mortification to the Department and the country. It is an absolute necessity that the neglect or apparent neglect of the squadron on that occasion should be wiped out by the capture or destruction of the *Arkansas*."[31]

Flag Officer David G. Farragut, through whose fleet the *Arkansas* had also fought its way to Vicksburg, was chagrined, too. "We were all caught unprepared for him," he wrote Davis the same day, "but we must go down and destroy him. I will get the squadron underway as soon as the steam is up . . . We must go close to him and smash him in. It will be warm work, but we must do it; he must be destroyed."

Farragut made a valiant effort, and passed the Vicksburg batteries a second time, but he and his vessels couldn't spot the *Arkansas* in the dark. "There was nothing to be seen of the ram," he wrote Davis. "I looked with all the eyes in my head to no purpose."[32]

Yet, as Farragut passed down the river, his "blind" shots dealt more death and damage to the *Arkansas*. A 160-pound wrought-iron bolt smashed through the armor into the engine room, disabling the engine and killing three men and wounding a fourth. It ripped through the dispensary, destroying the medicines there and caused a serious leak in the vessel.[33]

Despite the almost constant bombardment of Vicksburg by Commander William B. Renshaw's six mortar vessels below the city, the *Arkansas* was not struck by any of the lobbed shells. The work of repairing the vessel was pushed in anticipation of taking the offensive against Farragut's wooden warships and Renshaw's fragile mortar schooners below the city.

"Savez" Read, who never let bursting shells disturb him, was much amused at one of the volunteer doctors who had come aboard at Vicksburg. As the shells exploded close to the *Arkansas*, the doctor groaned: "Oh! Louisa and the babes!"[34]

When the *Arkansas* was deemed ready for action, Captain Brown started downriver to attack Renshaw's mortar boats, but before the *Arkansas* got into range, its engine broke down and it was only with great difficulty that it could return to its position in front of Vicksburg.[35]

On July 22, the *Arkansas* lay helplessly at its moorings, awaiting repairs to its ailing engine, while some of its officers and all but twenty-eight of its crew were ashore in hospital. Such was the *Arkansas'* condition as the Union ironclad *Essex*, commanded by William D. "Dirty Bill" Porter, moved to the attack, supported by the ram *Queen of the West*.

Captain Brown's narrative of the fight is graphic:

"We were at anchor and with only enough men to fight two of our guns; but by the zeal of our officers, who mixed in with these men as part of the guns' crews, we were able to train at the right moment and fire all the guns which could be brought to bear upon our cautiously coming assailants. With a view perhaps to avoid our bow guns, the *Essex* made the mistake, so far as her success was concerned, of running into us across the current instead of coming head-on with its force. At the moment of collision, when our guns were muzzle to muzzle, the *Arkansas'* broadside was exchanged for the bow guns of the assailant; a shot from one of the latter struck the *Arkansas's* plating a foot forward of the forward broadside port, breaking off the ends of the railroad bars, and driving them among our people; the solid shot followed, crossed diagonally our gun-deck, and split on the breech of our starboard after-broadside gun. This shot killed eight and wounded six of our men, but left us still half our crew. What damage the *Essex* received I did not ascertain, but that vessel drifted clear of the *Arkansas* without again firing, and after receiving the fire of our stern rifles, steamed in the face and under the fire of the Vicksburg batteries to the fleet below."[36]

The *Queen of the West* took a pass at the *Arkansas*, butting it gently, only to receive for its effort the full blast of three broadside guns at a range of fifty feet. The Yankee ram drifted astern of the *Arkansas*, whereupon "Savez" Read's stern guns pumped bolts into its protective coat of bales of hay. Soon, the *Queen of the West* had had enough, and beat a hasty retreat up the river, receiving a salvo from the broadside in passing the Rebel ironclad and a raking fire from the bow guns as it hurried back to the Federal fleet upriver.

"Thus closed the fourth and final battle of the *Arkansas*," wrote Captain Brown, "leaving the daring Confederate vessel, though reduced in crew to twenty men all told for duty, still defiant in the presence of a hostile force, perhaps exceeding in real strength that which fought under Nelson at Trafalgar."[37]

On July 24, both Union fleets got up steam and the *Arkansas* prepared for another attack. But, as Read reported it later, officers and crew "were agreeably disappointed" as the Federal fleets sailed off in opposite directions, abandoning the siege of Vicksburg and giving the battered Confederate ironclad a breathing spell. Mechanics, assembled from Mobile, Alabama, and Jackson, Mississippi, began repairing the *Arkansas*, during which time Captain Brown, having fallen ill, took leave to recoup his strength.

During Brown's absence, General Van Dorn ordered Lieutenant Henry C. Stevens, now commanding the *Arkansas*, to prepare to join General John C. Breckinridge's attack on Baton Rouge. Stevens, unwilling to move without authority from Brown, wired his commander, who was sick in bed at Grenada, Mississippi. Brown immediately wired orders to Stevens to remain at Vicksburg until he rejoined the *Arkansas*, and immediately left his bed to get back to his ship as best he could in a hurry. When Captain Brown arrived at Jackson, he learned that four hours earlier, Stevens had steamed downriver. The latter had been importuned by both Van Dorn and Breckinridge and it is entirely possible that "Savez" Read, always itching for a scrap and never wanting to be left out of one, and the other officers may have done a little persuasive urging. Read explained the departure by saying "no Confederate could refuse to comply with the wish of one so universally loved and respected."

And so, having acquired a new complement of men, the *Arkansas* cast off at 2 A.M. on August 4, and started down the river. The balky engines performed well and, aided by the current, the ironclad made about 15 miles an hour. As it steamed smoothly down the river the *Arkansas* received the cheers of people on the levee. However, the luck of the *Arkansas* ran out shortly after midnight on August 5, when one of the engines suddenly stopped about 15 miles below Port Hudson, Louisiana.

Read, who was officer of the deck, sought out the engineer, who informed him that the *Arkansas* could not proceed for some time. Read rounded the vessel to and dropped anchor. Work on the unreliable machinery was begun at once, but none of the engineers then aboard really understood the *Arkansas*' mechanism. Finally, by daylight, the *Ar-*

kansas was under way again and pushed on toward its rendezvous with General Breckinridge, whose plan was to strike by land at Baton Rouge while the *Arkansas* engaged the Federal gunboats.

But Breckinridge had already launched his attack and the sound of the firing reached the *Arkansas* as it sped on. "We could hear the guns of Breckinridge," wrote Read, "and we had hopes of being able to reach Baton Rouge in time to be of service." As the *Arkansas* rounded the point above Baton Rouge, the starboard engine stopped and, as the port engine continued to function at full speed, turned the vessel into shore where it wedged itself hard and fast among the cypress stumps.

All morning and into the afternoon the engineers labored, and still the faulty engine was not in operating condition. A courier arrived from General Breckinridge stating that he had driven the Yankees through the town and that they were on the river bank, protected by Union gunboats. If the *Arkansas* could get down by the next morning, Breckinridge's message said, he would attack again and probably bag the entire enemy force.

About sunset the *Arkansas* was afloat, its engines reported fit. Lieutenant Stevens decided to go upstream a couple of miles to take on coal and await the starting time. But as the ironclad made for the landing at the coal pile, one of the engines failed again and the ship ran aground. Two hours later the *Arkansas* was once more pronounced ready and it was soon afloat again.

At 3 A.M. on August 6, the *Arkansas* started down the river, everyone hopeful that nothing more would interfere with the co-ordinated attack on the Federals reportedly huddled on the Baton Rouge levee. But at the point above the town, once again the machinery gave way. Stevens, now satisfied that until competent engineers could be taken aboard, the *Arkansas* was useless as an offensive force, tied the ironclad to the shore in a good position for defense, determined to hold out as long as possible if attacked.

About 7 A.M. several Federal gunboats came up from Baton Rouge, approaching the *Arkansas* cautiously. About then the *Essex*, which had opened fire at extreme range, appeared and blasted away with three bow guns at a range of less than a quarter of a mile. At this juncture the senior engineer of the *Arkansas* came on deck and in a loud voice reported: "The engines are in good order, sir." A cheer went up from the crew, the order was given to cast off and the *Arkansas* moved out into the stream. The signal for "full speed" was given and the port engine responded well, but the starboard gave out again and the Confederate ironclad whirled into the bank, its stern guns bearing downstream.

"Savez" Read, who commanded the stern guns, was in his element as he opened up on the *Essex*. But after firing a few rounds, "Savez" was ordered ashore with his crew, for Lieutenant Stevens had decided to fire and abandon the *Arkansas*, whose thinly protected stern made the magazines and boilers extremely vulnerable.[38]

Thus ended the short but eventful life of the Confederate ironclad *Arkansas*, and with its destruction "Savez" Read sought a new theater of operations.

V

John Newland Maffitt, commander of the Confederate raider *Florida*, noted in his journal for November 4, 1862, the following: "Lt. C. W. Read, the last Lieut I personally applied for joined—this officer acquired reputation for gunnery, coolness and determination at the battle of N.O. When his Command [er] T. B. Huger was fatally wounded, he continued to gallantly fight the *McRae* until she was riddled & unfit for service. I am sorry to say the Gov. has not requited him. He is slow—I doubt not but that he is sure—As a 'military officer of the deck,' he is *not equal to many*." (Maffitt had written "by no means first rate," scratched it out and substituted the italicized words.) The entry closed with this sentence, "Time will reverse this," written in different ink, which indicates it was put down at a later date, after Maffitt had seen at close hand "Savez" Read's "daring beyond the point of martial prudence," as he put it.[39]

Read had jumped at the chance when he got orders to join the *Florida* in Mobile. "Being perfectly delighted with the prospect of getting to sea, I lost no time in reporting on board that ship," he wrote later.

The *Florida* was a trim, swift 191-foot three-masted, bark-rigged vessel, whose engines delivered 700 horsepower. Under both steam and sail, the *Florida* could do in excess of twelve knots. Her two funnels were hinged, and could be lowered out of sight to disguise the ship. Her armament consisted of eight guns, two pivot guns, and six in broadside.

"Savez," along with practically everyone else in the Confederacy, knew the story of the *Florida's* thrilling dash through the Union blockade fleet guarding Mobile Bay. Its rigging shot away, its boats damaged, its hull thoroughly peppered, the *Florida* (built in England as the *Oreto*) fought its way boldly through six Yankee warships to the safety of the guns of Fort Morgan.[40]

It was touch and go for the *Florida* to the end as the *Oneida* stationed itself across the narrow bar to block the entrance to the bay.

"Steer right for the bar," commanded Maffitt.

"That ship is in the way, sir," replied the pilot.

"Very well, sir, run him down," said Maffitt calmly.

Read, who got the story first hand after he joined the *Florida*, said that "the blockader . . . lost his grip" and moved out of the path of the oncoming Confederate vessel, which passed to the stern of the Union ship and so into the channel and safety.

Obviously, Captain Maffitt was the kind of officer under whom "Savez" Read loved to serve—a bold, daring, risk-taking officer.

And yet "Savez" fretted at the delay in getting the *Florida* to sea. For one thing, the vessel had to undergo extensive repairs and be refitted for combat. But when this was done, it became irksome to him for the *Florida* to lie calmly at anchor when the oceans were full of Federal commerce to be seized and burned. Years later Read wrote that although merchant steamers and schooners came in and went out of Mobile Bay, "Maffitt did not think that any of the nights were sufficiently dark to endeavor to go out with the *Florida*."[41]

Maffitt's entry in his journal for December 1, 1862, records the impatience of his officers and especially that of "Savez" Read: "Our tarry has far exceeded my expectation—and all hands are very restive, Lt. Read suffers particularly in this and has become somewhat bilious—Every passing squall is to him—a fine night for going out—even though it be of 50 minutes duration only—"[42]

Finally there came a night of heavy rain and squalls that suited Maffitt's fancy and the *Florida* dropped down to Fort Morgan. Unfortunately, the raider went aground and all the next day, which cleared, she was in view of the blockaders. "But our gallant little captain's blood was up," wrote Read, "and we were bound to go."

And go the *Florida* did in the predawn dark of January 16, 1863. "The ship fairly staggered under the pull of canvas," said Read. "The engines were working at full speed. Away we went with the black smoke pouring from the funnels, and rockets and blue lights went up all around us from the thoroughly aroused blockaders. At daylight, the *Florida* was well out to sea . . ."[43]

Three days later, the *Florida* seized its first prize, the bright new brig, *Estelle*, loaded with rum, honey, and sugar, and Maffitt ordered it set afire. Thus began, off the western tip of Cuba, the depredations on American merchantmen which soon made the name of the *Florida* as much feared in shipping circles as Raphael Semmes' *Alabama*.

The *Florida* roamed the Atlantic, from Cuba to the Delaware and back again, burning Yankee commerce and always avoiding combat with armed vessels of the United States Navy. Once, it appeared likely that, contrary to Maffitt's orders, the *Florida* would engage the Federal warship, *Sonoma*. "Everyone on board the *Florida* was eager for an engagement," Read wrote later. "Even Captain Maffitt looked as if he would like to have an excuse for disobeying orders."[44] But Maffitt's better judgment prevailed and he continued about the business of building "bonfires on the sea" out of Yankee cargo vessels, as one of his biographers picturesquely put it.[45]

One night while walking the deck with "Savez" Read, Maffitt said: "I've made up my mind to go to the East Indies and China. What do you think of it?"

"I think the Confederacy needs all her guns and men at home," replied Read. "And I can't see how the destruction of a few ships in the remote part of the world can in any way effect the war."

Read said that if Maffitt went through with his plan, he proposed to resign and return to the Confederacy and join the Army. Whereupon Maffitt agreed to give "Savez" the first small vessel he captured and let him take his chances of getting on shore somewhere on the coast of the Southern states.[46]

The following day, May 6, 1863, the *Florida* cruising off Brazil hailed the Yankee brig, *Clarence*, bound from Rio de Janeiro to Baltimore, loaded with coffee. Read promptly reminded Maffitt of his promise, but he had no idea now of hurrying back to the South to join the Army.

Read hurried down to his cabin and penned a note to Captain Maffitt:

"I propose to take the brig which we have just captured, and, with a crew of twenty men, to proceed to Hampton Roads and cut out a gunboat or steamer of the enemy.

"As I would be in possession of the brig's papers, and as the crew would not be large enough to excite suspicion, there can be no doubt of my passing Fortress Monroe successfully. Once in the Roads I would be prepared to avail myself of any circumstance which might present for gaining the deck of an enemy vessel. If it was found impossible to board a gunboat or merchant steamer, it would be possible to fire the shipping at Baltimore.

"If you think proper to accede to my proposal, I beg you will allow me . . ."

Maffitt replied almost immediately that "Savez's" proposal had been "duly considered" and that "it evinces on your part patriotic devotion to the cause of your country . . . I agree to your request, and will not hamper you with instructions."

Asserting that "this is certainly the time when all our best exertions should be made to harm the common enemy and confuse them with attacks from all unexpected quarters," Maffitt gave his blessing and pledge of support to Read's bold project:

"Act for the best, and God speed you. If success attends the effort you will deserve the fullest consideration of the Department, and it will be my pleasure to urge a just recognition of the same.

"Under all circumstances, you will receive from me the fullest justice for the intent and public spirit that influences the proposal.

"I give you a howitzer and ammunition, that you may have the means of capture if an opportunity offers en route . . ."

Maffitt implemented his agreement at once. He had all hands called

on deck and he asked for volunteers to accompany Lieutenant Read on
the *Clarence*. The entire crew volunteered so it wound up with "Savez"
picking his own men, four officers and sixteen crewmen.

"Within an hour of the time the order was given, I dipped my colors
to the *Florida* and squared away to the Northward and Westward," wrote
Read. ". . . The only gun we had was one of the *Florida's* six-pound
boat howitzers with two dozen rounds of shrapnel shell . . ."

And thus did "Savez" Read set forth on what his old Naval Academy
friend, George Dewey, later described as "a career up and down our
coast worthy of the days of Drake."[47]

VI

For a month, as it sailed for Chesapeake Bay, the "branch office" of
the *Florida* did no business. Off the Windward Islands, the *Clarence* gave
chase to several sails but the brig proved a very dull sailer due to the
copper on her bottom being loose.

"Savez" Read was disheartened by his vessel's sluggishness, and feared
the *Clarence* would run out of stores if it didn't soon make some captures.
Fortunately, Read fell in with a British ship and traded some of the *Clarence's* coffee for foodstuffs.

The *Clarence* had a large supply of spruce spars and Read had them
converted into Quaker guns and carriages, which made his one-gun ship
appear to be bristling with armament. "The guns when lackered [sic]
and polished were very fair imitations," Read recalled later.[48]

On June 6, Read made his first capture, the bark *Whistling Wind*,
loaded with coal, bound from Philadelphia to New Orleans. And thus
began a fantastic operation wherein in 19 days "Savez" captured 21
ships, throwing the Atlantic seaboard into a panic and causing President
Lincoln's Secretary of the Navy Gideon Welles one of his biggest headaches of the war.

Read captured another vessel, the *Alfred H. Partridge*, the next day
and added his third victim on June 9, the *Mary Alvina*, which he consigned to flames.

From papers which he found aboard these ships, Read became convinced that it would be impossible to carry out his original project as
no vessels were allowed into Hampton Roads unless carrying supplies for
the Federal Government. Moreover, vessels at the wharves above Fortress Monroe were guarded by a gunboat and sentries on the wharf.

"I then determined to cruise along the coast and try to intercept a
transport for Fortress Monroe," reported Read, "and with her endeavor
to carry out the orders of Commander Maffitt, and in the meantime to
do all possible injury to the enemy's commerce."

"Savez" Read's big day was June 12. He reported:

"On the morning of the 12th of June . . . captured the bark
Tacony . . . As soon as we had possession of her, a schooner was discovered which we stood to intercept . . . She proved to be the schooner
M. A. Shindler . . . The bark *Tacony* being a better sailer than the *Clarence*, I determined to burn the latter vessel and take the bark. While the
howitzer, etc., was being transferred from the *Clarence* to the *Tacony*,
a schooner was discovered coming down before the wind. Passing near
the *Clarence*, a wooden gun was pointed at her, and she was commanded to heave to, which she did immediately. She was found to be the
schooner *Kate Stewart* . . . As we were now rather short of provisions
and had over fifty prisoners, I determined to bond the . . . *Kate Stewart* and make a cartel of her . . . I bonded her for the sum of $7000,
payable to the President of the Confederate States thirty days after the
ratification of a treaty of peace between the Confederate States and United
States. The brig *Clarence* and schooner *Shindler* were then set on fire."

That business done, Read gave chase to another sail and soon captured the brig *Arabella*, which he bonded for $30,000 payable thirty
days after peace. "Savez" Read's score for the day was now four ships.[49]

The next day, June 13, word of Read's marauding reached the Navy
Department in Washington. Secretary Welles received a telegram from
E. Souder & Co., of Philadelphia: THE PIRATE CLARENCE CAPTURED, WITHIN
SIGHT OF CAPE HENRY, YESTERDAY MORNING, BRIG [schooner] SHINDLER
AND SCHOONER KATE STEWART AND BARK TACONY, OF THIS PORT. THEY ARE
USING THE TACONY FOR PIRATING FURTHER.

Welles instructed Assistant Secretary of the Navy Gustavus V. Fox
to order "every vessel in condition to proceed to sea without delay in
search of this wolf that is prowling near us." Fox kept the telegraph office busy. SEND OUT ANYTHING YOU HAVE AVAILABLE, he ordered
Rear Admiral S. P. Lee at Newport News. SEND WHAT VESSELS YOU CAN
IN PURSUIT, he instructed Rear Admiral H. Paulding at New York. CAN
THE SHENANDOAH GO IN PURSUIT? he queried Commodore C. K. Stribling
at Philadelphia.

Even President Lincoln expressed his concern in a message, June
14, to Secretary of the Treasury Salmon P. Chase: "You will co-operate,
by the revenue cutters under your direction, with the Navy in arresting
rebel depredations on American commerce and transportation and in
capturing rebels engaged therein."

On June 15, "Savez" Read made the front pages of the New York
papers and soon the entire Atlantic seaboard, from Chesapeake Bay to
Maine, was swept first with concern and then with near panic. The
New York *Tribune* contributed to this, with an item noting sudden
activity in the New York Navy Yard: "The cause is stated to be the
presence of some 15 Rebel privateers off the coast watching for ves-

sels coming in and going out of New York Harbor. There was considerable excitement in consequence."

In the same edition of the *Tribune*, Captain William G. Mundy of the *Tacony* described his adventure with the "pirate." The *Clarence*, he said, had hailed him, saying it was short of water, whereupon, on "this appeal to humanity" he hauled to to permit a boat from the *Clarence* to pull alongside.

". . . an officer and six men . . . came aboard. They told me they . . . would assist me in passing [the water] to the boat," Captain Mundy stated. "While taking the after hatch off I was confronted by the officer of the boat, who presented a pistol at my head, and stated that my vessel was his prize, a prize of the Confederate States . . ."

The excitement that "Savez" Read caused with his one little 375-ton bark, a crew of twenty and one gun, can be gathered from the news accounts and the outgoing and incoming telegrams in the Navy Department and the various Navy Yards.

The New York *Tribune*, on June 16, said: "The recent depredations on our commerce by the Rebel pirates have stirred up the Navy Department to such an extent that all the Navy Yards are perfectly revolutionized by the amount of work ordered to be done within a few days."

And on June 17, the *Tribune* said: "Yesterday the excitement at the Navy Yard continued unabated, orders arriving every hour directing some new movement."[50]

In less than three days from the reception of the news of the Confederate raider off the coast, 32 armed vessels were at sea searching for "Savez" Read. Every available Navy ship was employed in the search, other ships were chartered and armed and even the Naval Academy's midshipmen's practice ships and the racing yacht *America* joined in the hunt.

Within the next ten days, 15 more vessels, making 47 in all, would be out to bag "Savez" Read. During this time, urgent appeals and protests came from shipowners, underwriters, chambers of commerce, and city and state officials, all flooding into Gideon Welles' office.

Governor Edwin D. Morgan of New York asked that "iron-clads might be spared for defending the harbor of New York" and he added: "Our people are uneasy at the boldness of the pirates, and they will not rest much longer without efforts for more adequate protection for this harbor." Governor John Andrews of Massachusetts reported: "I am receiving representations daily, both oral and written, from towns and cities along the Massachusetts coast, setting forth their defenseless condition." Abiel A. Low, president of the New York State Chamber of Commerce, called on Welles to provide "convoy twice a month . . . from this port to the British Channel" and he pointed out that "the war premium alone on American vessels carrying valuable cargoes exceeds the whole freight in neutral ships."

Boston merchants volunteered to send out private vessels "to go for the pirate." Underwriters of Boston offered a bounty of $10,000 for the capture of the *Tacony* which in their resolution they called "*Florida No. 2*."

Meanwhile, "Savez" Read was capturing at a merry pace, burning some and bonding others. In 19 days, between June 6 and June 25, Read captured 21 vessels. As fast as the news reached port, more clamors for protection roared into Welles' ears.

One shipowner, victimized by Read, complained bitterly to Welles that a gunboat in the vicinity had not warned the *Goodspeed's* captain that privateers were on the coast. "If our Navy can not afford the commerce of the country the protection which is its due, we think its officers, while on the high seas, might at least put themselves somewhat out of their way to communicate information important to its safety."

When Welles ordered the ironclad *Roanoke* from New York, he was bombarded with telegrams. Mayor George Opdyke urged that the ironclad remain "until the city can devise other means of securing its safety from a naval attack." And General John E. Wool, Army commander at New York, warned Welles that "to take the *Roanoke* from this city at the present moment will produce a very great excitement from all classes, friends as well as foes."

Welles noted with contempt these importunities in his *Diary:* "The idea that New York is in danger is an absurdity . . . Morgan and Opdyke, Governor and Mayor, have responsibilities that are perhaps excusable, but not General Wool, who feeds on panic and fosters excitement."[51]

By now, "Savez" Read himself was informed about the frantic hunt for the black-hulled *Tacony*, for every outgoing ship that he seized yielded the latest newspapers. From them he learned of the constant departure of armed vessels joining in the search, and also of the state of alarm which gripped the New England coast

Since he was off New England, "Savez" decided to throw a scare into the mackerel fleet, fishing on Georges Bank. When he came upon the fishing vessels, he later wrote, he "would hoist the Confederate flag and fire a few shells amongst them and it was a sight to see them make for home. In this way, we not only 'raised Cain' but also the price of fish."

On June 24, "Savez" captured the schooner *Archer*, his twenty-first prize, and the next day, Read decided to baffle his pursuers by burning the *Tacony* and continuing his operations in the *Archer* "After dark the transfer was made," wrote Read, "and we sailed away feeling a bit sad as the flames consumed the good old bark with which we had been so successful."

As he sailed along in the *Archer*, "Savez" formulated a new plan: He would capture a coasting steamer, make a raid down the coast and run into Wilmington, North Carolina.

Outside the harbor of Portland, Maine, the *Archer* overhauled a small fishing boat with two men in it. "The fishermen were not very well pleased at being forced to come on board the schooner but a drink of brandy, a cigar each, and a couple of twenty-dollar gold pieces softened them perceptibly," wrote Read, "and loosened their tongues so that I readily obtained all the information that I desired. From them I learned that the only armed vessel in Portland was the revenue cutter, *Caleb Cushing*; that coasting vessels and fishermen were not boarded on entering the harbor."

From a newspaper which the fishermen gave him, "Savez" learned that a steamer from Bangor was due in Portland the next day. He would seize the *Caleb Cushing* that night and with it intercept and seize the Bangor steamer with which he would continue his raiding.[52]

The night of June 26, 1863, was clear and pleasant with the moon shining brightly. But there was one thing missing for "Savez" Read's purposes—there was no breeze.

Having passed the forts at the mouth of the harbor, "Savez" dropped anchor in the midst of the shipping about 4 P.M., and bided his time. It was not until after midnight that the pleasure boats, with laughter and music aboard, quit plying the harbor.

Read's own account of his daring operation is a colorless statement, or rather understatement, of fact: "When everything quieted down we manned our two boats and pulled alongside the revenue cutter *Caleb Cushing*, completely surprising and capturing her without anybody being hurt. She had a crew of forty men who were secured below . . ."

But not so Jedediah Jewett, collector of the Port of Portland. His report to the Treasury Department, based upon interviews with the cutter's crew, is a graphic picture of the seizure:

"At about 1 o'clock a.m., after the moon had set, the watch on deck, hearing boats approaching, at once called Lieutenant Davenport, but as the watch returned on deck, he found armed men pouring over each side of the cutter, variously estimated at from 25 to 40 men. They instantly seized the watch on deck, presented revolvers to their heads, and threatened to shoot them if they spoke or made any noise. The watch were put in irons and sent below, and, the main hatch being open a part of the attacking party rushed below and threatened to shoot the men asleep in their hammocks or just awakening, if they spoke. The men below were then ironed, and ordered not to look on deck at the peril of their lives. Four men seized Lieutenant Davenport as he attempted to come out of the cabin at the call of the watch and bore him below in the cabin and ironed him, ordering him to keep quiet as a prisoner."

Another account states that "Savez" Read recognized his old Annapolis classmate, Dudley Davenport, midshipman from Georgia, and took him to task for deserting the South. "Why, you ought to be ashamed of yourself," exploded Read and then left Davenport to get the *Caleb Cushing* under way.

The wind, which had been hardly a whisper, had now died out entirely so "Savez" put two boats ahead to tow the cutter out of the harbor. At 2 A.M., the *Caleb Cushing* passed Fort Preble, and about this time the breeze freshened and the *Caleb Cushing* moved up the coast.

But as the cutter left the harbor entrance, the Boston steamer, *Forest City*, due to dock at 4 A.M., but ahead of schedule, was encountered. Aboard her was Lieutenant J. H. Merriman of the U. S. Revenue Service, who was to take command of the *Caleb Cushing* the next morning.

According to Jedediah Jewett, he was not informed of the cutter's departure until ten minutes to eight the next morning. He at once sent to Fort Preble for guns and men and to nearby Camp Lincoln for the 7th Maine Volunteers. He chartered tugs and steamers and in quick order the pursuit of the Confederate corsair was on. ". . . in fifty minutes after I had learned of the capture of the cutter three steamers had left the wharf to overhaul her," Jewett reported.

Meanwhile "Savez" Read tried in vain to get the key to the *Caleb Cushing's* magazine, but Lieutenant Davenport steadfastly refused it. On deck were a half a dozen rounds of ammunition, certainly not enough for an adequate fight, if that cutter was pursued.

At 10 A.M., when about 20 miles off the harbor, Read knew that the pursuit was indeed under way. With his glass, he discerned two large steamers and three tugs under full steam. "Savez" ordered the cutter cleared for action and when the first steamer came into range, Read gave the order to fire.

"The shot ricocheted and, passing over him, just clearing his deck," Read wrote later. "Around he went and steamed back to his consorts. They remained together some little time and then the two larger steamers made a wide detour and getting well to seaward of us, turned and steamed directly for us—the three inshore tugs also made for us."

After firing five rounds from the pivot gun, Read was out of ammunition and he realized the futility of trying to put up any resistance to a simultaneous attack from all sides. Accordingly, he ordered the prisoners and his crew into the boats and set fire to a slow match leading to the magazine.

Hoisting a white handkerchief to the end of a boat hook, "Savez"

Read surrendered himself and crew to the *Forest City* at 11:30 A.M. At 12 noon, the *Caleb Cushing* blew up, the twenty-second and last victim of the Confederate Corsair.[53]

Excitement prevailed aboard the *Forest City* as "Savez" Read and his men came alongside. They were permitted to board the steamer only one at a time and as each reached the deck he was seized and his hands tied behind his back.

Nervous citizens of Portland and the Maine volunteers were all for hanging the "pirates" at once, but fortunately for "Savez" and his crew the regular soldiers aboard wouldn't permit it.

Fortunately, again, Read and his men were turned over to the commander of Fort Preble, Major George L. Andrews, for the temper of the people of Portland was such that their safety would have been very much doubted in the hands of the civil authorities.

Read recalled later the excitement that his presence and that of his men had on the people: "The officers and men of the fort belonged to the Regular Army and had served with McClellan in Virginia, and were therefore familiar with war and the sight of Rebels. But the volunteers and the people of Portland had never seen either and made every effort to have us turned over to the civil authorities to be tried and hanged as pirates."

Major Andrews was much concerned over the possibility of an attempt by the people of Portland to seize "Savez" Read and his men from Fort Preble, and string them up. He reported on June 29:

"You can form but a faint idea of the excitement now existing among the citizens of Portland and vicinity. Rumor follows rumor in rapid succession, and just before daylight this morning someone from the vicinity of the post went to the city with a fresh rumor which set the whole city in a ferment. The bells were rung and men, women, and children soon filled the streets, and were rushing hither and thither in aimless fright."

The major urged that "the prisoners be sent from here as quietly and expeditiously as possible, as I do not think it safe for them to be placed in the custody of the citizens." He added that during the prevailing excitement, he felt it necessary "to mount so large a guard that one-half of my force are on duty every night."

When Jefferson Davis heard in Richmond the rumor that "Savez" Read was to be hanged he flew into a rage and swore that if Read was so treated he would order the ten highest ranking Federal officers in Confederate prisons hanged in reprisal.

Read and his men were well treated by the officers and men of Fort Preble. Although their room doors were locked at night, they were allowed in the day the freedom of the parade grounds. Many curious people and newspaper reporters sought to see the Rebel prisoners, but

Major Andrews permitted no one to speak to them, unless they were willing. "Savez" was quite willing to receive Artemus Ward (Charles Farrar Browne) when he called upon him, for the humorist, Read related later, "presented me with a copy of his book and a gallon of good whiskey, both of which were highly appreciated."

Shortly thereafter, to the relief of the nervous citizens of Portland who, since they couldn't hang the Rebel pirate were happy to be rid of him, "Savez" Read and his men were transferred to Fort Warren in Boston Harbor.

From there, on July 29, 1863, Read wrote Secretary of the Navy Mallory, asking for money to purchase a change of clothing for his men "as all our clothing was distributed as relics to the people of Portland."[54]

VII

The one thing on "Savez" Read's mind when he arrived at Fort Warren was to devise some way of getting out. The chance of being exchanged at this stage of the Civil War was slight, and "Savez" didn't bank very much on the possibility. So he wasted no time in looking around for some means of escape.

When "Savez" found it, most of his fellow prisoners considered it a mad project. In the casemate in which Read was confined, there was a chimney leading to the parapet above. But the chimney, long in disuse, had been stopped with bricks and mortar and, to all appearances, was absolutely secure. But "Savez," using pocket knives, which had been overlooked when they were searched, and a rusty ice pick which someone had discovered in a crevice of the wall, began the painfully slow task of digging his way through brick and mortar.

The debris was spread about the stone floor and covered with the prisoners' clothes, the presence of which on the floor rousing no suspicion as there were no pegs in the cell on which to hang garments. Later, as the mortar dust accumulated, it was placed in and under the bunks.

Night after night, "Savez" stuck with his task, standing on the shoulders of his cellmates as he picked away at the mortar. When he had reached a sufficient height, he dug out a foothold in the chimney. No one in the group except the small, light, and wiry Read could have done the job, for the chimney was not a spacious one.

"Savez" worked under exasperating conditions, but nothing dulled his enthusiasm for digging his way to freedom, not even the lime that got into one of his eyes, causing him considerable pain. Obviously, Read couldn't seek medical attention without revealing his plot and so he kept on digging, suffering in silence. As a consequence, for the rest of his life, Read had an injured right eye.

Finally, Read dug his way into the open air and, climbing out of his narrow "escape hatch," "Savez" crouched behind the chimney, awaiting for the emergence of his companions. A young Navy lieutenant named Alexander followed "Savez" up the flue, but being a larger man than Read, he got stuck and he could go neither up nor down. In this desperate situation, the prisoners climbed upon shoulders and pushed Alexander up the chimney by sheer force. When the latter joined Read on the parapet, he had left much skin and nearly all his clothing behind him. Alexander's difficulty in getting through the narrow hole determined the course of action of the other prisoners: They would stay put.

When the sentry was farthest from their uncertain hiding place, Read and his companion crept out and made their way down to the beach. Anticipating the round of the guard, Read and Alexander ducked under some old sailcloth and other dunnage piled on the beach, biding their time until they would swim out to a small pleasure schooner, belonging to the officers of the garrison, and put out to sea. They were none too soon.

The footsteps of the guard approached. They heard one of the soldiers complain about the dampness and say that he was going to dry his bayonet in the sailcloth. A second later "Savez" Read experienced a sharp pain in his thigh, but he didn't utter a cry as the bayonet went deep into his flesh.

"You're a fool," said another soldier, as the man withdrew his bayonet from the pile. "That dunnage is wetter than the air. You'll have a time cleaning the rust off in the morning."

The soldier ran his hand over his bayonet, "It is wet," he said, but in the darkness neither he nor his companions realized that the blade was dripping with Read's blood.

"Savez" and Alexander waited for the footsteps of the guard to die away before they came from their hiding place. Then they swam to the little boat, similar to the fishing craft which abounded in the locality. It was "Savez's" idea to sail the frail vessel to Halifax, Nova Scotia, from where they would take a steamer to Bermuda and then run the blockade into a Confederate port.

At daylight their vessel was among several hundred fishing boats, and "Savez" felt that if they could remain undetected during the day, darkness would make their escape practically certain. Soon "Savez" saw warships prowling among the fleet of fishing boats, but he realized that they could not possibly stop and examine all of the craft before nightfall.

Read's wound was now paining him intensely and Alexander prevailed upon him to lie down in the bottom of the boat to try to get some sleep. Reluctantly, Read agreed. He stressed the importance of doing nothing to arouse suspicion, and cautioned his companion to watch the other boats and do exactly as they did. "Savez" had been asleep for a spell when something went wrong with the jib sheets. Alexander, not wanting to disturb Read, thought he could go forward, unfoul the jib and return to the helm before anything happened. But he was wrong; the boat flew up into the wind and went about quickly, before Alexander got back to the tiller. This unnautical maneuver was immediately spotted by a warship and "Savez" and his companion were soon taken in custody.

"Savez" and Alexander recognized an officer aboard the ship as one they had both known in the service, but when he asked their names, they stolidly replied "Brown" and "Jones" and claimed to be only "poor harmless fishermen."

"I thought you were my old shipmate, 'Savez' Read," replied the officer, "and I was going to treat you like an officer and a gentleman. But as you are only a common fisherman, into the 'brig' you go, in double irons, until further orders!"

This was too much for Read, who was suffering from his wound. "Sam, you are not going to treat an old shipmate that way, and me badly hurt, too?" he returned.

"Savez" was sent to "sick room" where his wound and his eye received attention. And in a short time, Read was back in Fort Warren, where he remained quietly, if not patiently, until exchanged.[55]

VIII

Young Jimmy Morgan was on deck of the *Patrick Henry* in the James River when a boatload of exchanged Confederate prisoners came alongside on October 18, 1864.

To his pleasure and surprise, he at once recognized an emaciated and disheveled little man who limped across the gangplank as his friend and shipmate on the *McRae*, "Savez" Read.

Despite his drawn features and prison pallor, "Savez's" spirit was unbroken and his boundless energy remained unflagged. Accordingly, he accepted the hospitality of wardroom officers for only a few days and hastened to get himself assigned again to active duty

Within ten days, Read was in command of Battery Wood, one of three naval batteries on the south side of the James River, below Richmond's chief river defenses at Drewry's Bluff.

Beyond taking potshots at Ben Butler's troops digging the Dutch Gap Canal across a narrow neck of land, there wasn't much to occupy

Read's restless spirit. But his eager mind was thinking bold and exciting thoughts.

He pondered over the possibility that the three Confederate ironclads, *Virginia, Richmond,* and *Fredericksburg* might attack the lone Union monitor at City Point, Grant's headquarters, and by seizing that place, not only raise the blockade of the James River, but perhaps relax Grant's pressure on Lee's lines at Petersburg. The time was propitious, for all the other Federal ironclads were engaged in the operation against Fort Fisher. The only question was the obstruction that Grant had ordered erected across the James at Trents Reach, about two miles by river, below Read's battery.

One night in mid-January there was a freshet on the James and a large amount of ice floated down the river. The next morning, from his battery, Read got the impression that a portion of the Federal obstruction in Trents Reach had been washed away. Read immediately went into action:

"I sent two master's mates in a dugout down to examine the obstructions. After carefully sounding, the mates reported 14 feet of water through the obstructions, of a width of about eighty feet. A boom consisting of a large spar lay diagonally across the entrance."

"Savez," on January 15, 1865, reported his information to Flag Officer John K. Mitchell, who commanded the James River Squadron, and then hurried off to pass on his idea to higher echelons:

"I went at once to General Pickett's Headquarters and reported the results of our observations. General Pickett directed me to hasten to Petersburg and advise General Lee. General Lee asked if I thought the channel sufficiently wide and deep to admit the passage of the Confederate ironclads. I replied that I had no doubt of it, and that at any rate, it might be tried. General Lee ordered me to go at once to the Secretary of the Navy, and ask that the ironclads be sent down that night. I rode as fast as possible to Richmond and went to see Mr. Mallory and explained everything to him, and without the least hesitation he wrote an order to Captain Mitchell . . . directing him to move as soon as possible if he deemed it practicable."

On January 16, Secretary Mallory wrote Mitchell:

"From Lieutenant Read I learn . . . it [is] probable that there is a passage through the obstructions, I deem the opportunity a favorable one for striking a blow at the enemy, if we are able to do so. In a short time many of his vessels will have returned to the river from Wilmington and he will again perfect his obstructions. If we can block the river at or below City Point, Grant might be compelled to evacuate his position . . . I regard an attack upon the enemy and the obstructions of the river at City Point, to cut off Grant's supplies, as a movement of the first importance to the country and one which should be accomplished if possible."

Mallory expected Mitchell to move at once and when, by January 21, the latter had not launched his expedition, the Secretary of the Navy made no attempt to conceal his impatience. YOUR MOVEMENT IS BEING DELAYED FATALLY, I FEAR, he telegraphed Mitchell. UNLESS YOU ACT AT ONCE ACTION WILL BE USELESS . . . YOU HAVE FULLY MY GENERAL VIEWS AND WISHES, AND YOU MUST ACT AT ONCE. I EXPECT YOU TO MOVE TOMORROW.

Not content with his telegram, Mallory dispatched an unofficial letter to Mitchell the same day. "You have an opportunity, I am convinced, rarely presented to a naval officer," wrote the Secretary, "and one which may lead to the most glorious results to your country. I deplore that you did not start immediately after the freshet, and have deplored the loss of every day since."

More delays, once by fog, ensued and it wasn't until the night of January 23 that Mitchell descended the river. On arriving at Trents Reach, the *Virginia* and *Richmond* anchored while the *Fredericksburg* proceeded to the obstruction, through which a reconnoitering party under "Savez" Read was preparing a passage. While Read supervised the cutting of the moorings of the spar, Mitchell satisfied himself that there was sufficient depth below the obstruction for his ships.

At 1 A.M. the *Fredericksburg* passed through the gap and Mitchell returned to the *Virginia*, where to his chagrin—he called it "my inexpressible mortification"—he discovered that the vessel was aground. To Mitchell's disgust, as vain efforts to float the *Virginia* were continued, word came at 3:30 A.M., that the *Richmond* also was aground, and two of the smaller ships, *Drewry* and *Scorpion* also. The *Fredericksburg* was now recalled to protect the grounded ships. When daylight broke, Federal sharpshooters and batteries, who had fired during the night with no success, began to find the range. The *Drewry*, from which its crew had left, was struck by a shell and blew up. The only Federal monitor in the river, the *Onondaga*, came to join in the fight. The *Virginia* was struck more than 70 times, but the *Richmond* escaped damage. Shortly after noon, both ships commenced floating and immediately steamed upstream, out of range.

At 9 P.M. on January 24, Mitchell ordered the Confederate flotilla downriver again for a second try at the opening in the barrier. However, the pilots of the *Virginia* complained that escaping steam from a damaged exhaust pipe and smokestack, together with the dazzling glare of a Drummond light with which the Federals lit the river, blinded them and they could not properly steer the ironclad. Mitchell brought the vessels to and called a council of war.

In vain did "Savez" Read, junior to all the officers present, urge an attack on the *Onondaga* at the break of day. "I advised an immediate attack on the monitor when we had the advantage of daylight to go through the obstruction," Read recalled, "and could see when to strike the monitor with our torpedoes, as each ironclad had a ship torpedo ready for action, and when the pilots could handle the ships so as not to get aground again." The council of war did what most councils of war do; it decided not to continue the expedition. Its decision coincided with Mitchell's own views and so the bold operation, born in the adventurous brain of "Savez" Read, came to naught.[56]

Not daunted, "Savez" came up with yet another scheme to destroy the Federal ironclads at City Point and thereby threaten Grant's supply base. An expedition, including wagon wheels drawn by mules, would transport overland four long boats, a supply of long beams with arrangements at the end for fastening torpedoes and a supply of the latter. The expedition would move around the left of Grant's army and by a wide circuit reach the James River above Hampton Roads.

Biding their time in their longboats, Read and his men would seize one or more of the tugs that plied the James on Army business and, having fixed the torpedoes to them, would ascend the river, without arousing suspicion and sink the Federal warships anchored at City Point.

Read was confident of success. After the war, he told one of the members of his party that he had counted upon surprise to make the adventure profitable. "I am sure," he said, "before they could possibly have known what was going on I could have run alongside and boarded a gunboat with my men, and, having thus captured the first gunboat, with this gunboat and my torpedoes, I could easily have sunk the rest of the gunboats . . . My plans were made known to General Lee, and were also approved by President Davis himself."

Early on February 3, 1865, more than a hundred men, armed with heavy cutlasses and pistols, and four wagons, each bearing a longboat, booms, and torpedoes, moved out from Drewry's Bluff under command of Lieutenant Charles W. Read on one of the boldest and most hazardous operations of the Civil War.

The first day's march, punctuated by dodging enemy columns, carried the band several miles west of Petersburg. The next day false alarms broke the march and sent the group hiding on several occasions.

Read sent a volunteer naval officer named Lewis ahead to reconnoiter the ford of the Blackwater. Lewis had been a mate on an American ship at Norfolk and, with secession, he had joined the Confederacy. He served faithfully in the Army, and later transferred to the Navy, being commissioned an acting lieutenant. Lieutenant Lewis was well regarded by all and Read considered him trustworthy for his important mission.

On the third day a sleet storm held up the expedition, the men taking shelter in a deserted farmhouse and there "Savez" Read received bad news. He learned that Lieutenant Lewis had deserted to the enemy and had a regiment of Union troops waiting for the expedition at the Blackwater Ford. One story says an exhausted courier from General Lee rode up on a spent horse with a message for Read that he had been betrayed by one of his men. The other story states that a young Confederate soldier, who had been a prisoner, heard Lewis reveal Read's plan to the Federal commander in whose custody he was, and that he escaped to warn "Savez" not to walk into a trap.

"Savez" ordered the party to hide in the woods and to await him until sundown the next day. If he were not back by that time, the expedition was to make its way back to Richmond, on the assumption that he was either dead or captured. At 4 P.M. the following day Read returned to his men with the confirmation of the betrayal. Not only was a regiment waiting at the ford, but the enemy cavalry was scouring the country. Reluctantly, "Savez" ordered a retreat.

Marching by night and hiding by day, the party picked its way through enemy-infested country and on several occasions it seemed certain that "Savez" and his men would be bagged. To escape the ever-tightening noose, "Savez" led his men through the waist-deep frozen waters of the Appomattox River, wagons and all, and when their clothes froze stiff on them as they emerged from the river, "Savez" doubled-quicked them to warm them up.

Finally, on February 13, eleven days after they had started out, suffering from hunger and exposure, the party was back at Drewry's Bluff, without the loss of a man (except the deserter Lewis), wagon, mule, or equipment. "The character of this expedition, involving so much peril and aiming at such grand results, entitles it to an important place in the history of the war," wrote a member of the expedition many years later, "and . . . Read, its projector, deserves to be remembered as among the bravest of the brave."[57]

IX

Although the Civil War was drawing rapidly to a close, with the hours running out for the hard-pressed Confederacy, there was still time for one more daredevil exploit by Lieutenant Charles W. Read.

Not many days after his return from the abortive James River raid, Read suggested to Secretary Mallory that the Confederate ram *William H. Webb*, on the Red River in Louisiana, be run to sea for the purpose of preying on American commerce.

And, of course, Read nominated himself to lead the mad dash by the

Webb from the Red into the Mississippi—a dash which called for passing through a Union squadron guarding the mouth of the Red, other Union warships at intervals down the river to New Orleans, and still another squadron at anchor at the Crescent City. After that, all the *Webb* would have to do was to pass the two formidable forts, 75 miles downstream, Fort Jackson and Fort St. Philip, and any other Union vessels that happened to be in the lower Mississippi.

Mallory not only showed enthusiasm for the bold operation, but he got the approval of President Davis and other members of his cabinet. He also sent a dispatch to James D. Bulloch, Confederate Naval agent in England, on February 17, 1865, which indicates that he had the expectation that Read would make the perilous run with the *Webb* a successful one. He wrote Bulloch: "Lieutenant Commanding Charles W. Read, C. S. Navy, is authorized to draw upon you for funds upon his cruise . . . to the extent of £10,000."[58]

Read picked a group of officers and men who had been with him in the James River expedition and promptly set out to reach Shreveport, Louisiana, where the *Webb* was last reported. Traveling by rail, sometimes, by wagon others, "Savez" and his party had to make frequent detours around elements of Sherman's army. A fruitless visit to Mobile in the hope of obtaining a couple of engineers further delayed the expedition. Finally, after more than a month on the road, "Savez" Read assumed command of the *Webb*, on March 31, 1865.

Built several years before the war the *Webb* was about 200 feet long, its 35-foot sidewheels being driven by two independent low-pressure engines. She was designed for heavy service in the Gulf and just prior to the war had been used as a towboat at New Orleans. As for speed, the *Webb* was just about the fastest vessel afloat. The Confederates converted her into a formidable ram and she had helped sink the Union ironclad *Indianola*.[59]

Read found the *Webb* unprepared for the service on which he was to take her. There was little or no crew; no guns, no fuel, and no small arms, except a few cutlasses.

For three weeks, "Savez" prepared his vessel for her madcap voyage. From General Kirby Smith he procured a 30-pounder Parrott for a bow pivot gun and two 12-pounders, and permission to recruit volunteers from the Army. Coal was scarce and after loading a day's supply of it, Read took on enough pine knots to last for four more days. He had the *Webb* whitewashed, because a white ship is harder to discern at night than a dark one. Almost 200 cotton bales were taken aboard and placed as a shield around the *Webb's* mechanism. A month's rations and water were taken on and by April 22, 1865—nearly two weeks after Lee's surrender at Appomattox—Read was ready to begin his dash.

Read wrote Secretary Mallory that day that he would sail after night-fall, to time his arrival at the mouth of the Red River for 8 P.M. on April 23. He described his plans:

"Off the mouth of the Red lies the *Tennessee, Manhattan* (monitor), and *Lafayette*, ironclads, and one boiler-iron plated gunboat, the *Gazelle.* The distance from the mouth of the Red to the mouth of the Mississippi is about 300 miles, and at regular distances in most of this length there are one or two of the enemy's gunboats. To be the first to notify these of my approach is my chief aim . . ."

Read outlined his plans to cut the telegraph wires along the way, not only to keep his coming unannounced in New Orleans, but also to prevent word from reaching Forts Jackson and St. Philip "as those formidable fortifications will have to be passed in daylight." Read concluded his report: "As I have to stake everything on speed and time, I will not attack any vessel in the passage unless I perceive a possibility of arresting my progress. In this event I am prepared with five torpedoes (100 pounds), one of which I hold shipped on its pole on the bow . . ."[60]

As the *Webb* edged toward the mouth of the Red River, all lights on board were screened, and with the engines idling, the vessel was allowed to drift down with the current. All about the *Webb*, as it moved silently into the Mississippi, were the dark outlines of vessels. Here and there lights showed on either side, as she passed among the Federal vessels, close enough for those on board the *Webb* to hear distinctly the striking of eight bells aboard the blockaders.[61]

The steam in the *Webb's* boilers was very high, and the engineer told "Savez" Read that they could not stand the pressure much longer without blowing up the vessel. At that moment a rocket shot skyward from one of the Federal blockaders, a clear indication that the *Webb* had been spotted.

"Let her go!" yelled Read.

Pilot William Biggio rang the fast bell. In the engine room the throttle was thrown wide open and the *Webb*, all atremble, leaped forward in the water.

"Keep her for the biggest opening between them," ordered Read and the pilot nodded in assent. Pilot Biggio years later recalled the exciting moment:

"By this time every whistle of the fleet was screaming, drums were beating, rockets were going up, and it seemed as if the very devil was to pay. I kept the *Webb* straight on her course, however, headed for the biggest opening, and before a gun was fired we had passed the blockade and had turned the bend and were making down the Mississippi River. A few futile shots, fired by the *Manhattan,* followed the *Webb* down the river and a couple of would-be pursuers were soon distanced by the fast-moving Confederate vessel."[62]

After steaming for about half a dozen miles, the *Webb* went close to shore and a rope from the ship was attached to the telegraph poles, which with their wires were then dragged into the river, thus cutting communication with New Orleans and intermediate points.[63] At regular intervals, about every five miles or so, the *Webb* passed Federal warships anchored in the river. As the *Webb* approached these vessels, they sent up signals. The *Webb* responded, with any kind of a signal, just to puzzle the other vessel, and continued steaming by, without the fraud being discovered. On several occasions throughout the night, the *Webb* slowed down while Read sent ashore to cut the telegraph wires. He didn't overlook a chance to prevent word of his coming to precede the *Webb* to New Orleans.

Early the next morning, near Donaldsonville, about 65 miles above New Orleans, "Savez" Read and his men had a scare. There before the *Webb* was a Yankee gunboat. The Federal ship ran up signals and at the same time ran out its guns. "Savez" breathed easier when the guns were run in and he realized it was only a drill. The *Webb*, meanwhile, signaled back and sped on.

"The Signals of the Federal boats were duly answered by the *Webb*, flags being used in the daytime in the same manner that lights were used at night," related Pilot Biggio. "We could have destroyed millions of dollars of property on our trip, but our sole object was to run the blockade."[64]

Despite Read's precaution of cutting the telegraph wires, word reached the fleet at New Orleans that a Rebel raider was loose on the river. The log of the *Lackawanna* shows that at 9 A.M. it was alerted as the *Webb*, now flying the U.S. flag at half-mast, steamed by the Federal fleet at New Orleans. The 24-gun *Lackawanna* fired at close range, "so close," said the *Webb's* pilot, "that a rock could have been thrown from one boat to another." One shot went through the *Webb*, well above the waterline, and landed in Algiers, across from New Orleans. The *Ossipee*, *Pembina*, and *Port Royal* also fired at the *Webb* and the *Hollyhock* and *Florida* took off in pursuit.

After the first shot, "Savez" Read ordered the American flag down and ran up the Confederate colors. ". . . He expected to see the *Webb* sunk right there," said Pilot Biggio, "and he wanted her to go down with her own colors flying."

The Federal ships were raining shot at the *Webb* and while some struck glancing blows, no serious damage was done and the vessel raced for the great bend in the river, at the lower edge of New Orleans. Ahead, in the middle of the stream, was a Federal ship believed to be the *Hartford*. Read tried to blow her up with his bow torpedo, but a mishap —a fortunate one it proved to be—occurred and the torpedo couldn't be exploded in time. Pilot Biggio related:

". . . The vessel proved not to be the *Hartford*, but the *Fear Not*, loaded with fixed ammunition. Had we run into her with the torpedo as we intended, the chances are that no one on either vessel would have lived to tell the tale."[65]

The mishap, however, was not without further danger to the *Webb*, for as the torpedo was being lowered to make contact with the Union ship, its pole snapped and the lethal charge fell into the water and under the *Webb's* starboard wheel.

"Stop the engine," shouted "Savez" Read, "and cut away the guy ropes." Instant response to both orders saved the *Webb*, as the torpedo dropped harmlessly to the bottom of the river.

Inasmuch as the *Webb's* presence was now known at New Orleans, and the ship was being actively pursued, albeit the Federal pursuers were easily distanced, "Savez" decided that it was useless to cut the telegraph wires to Fort Jackson. This stronghold and its companion, Fort St. Philip, would be prepared for the *Webb* and "Savez" decided he would just have to take his chances of running by them, as Farragut did almost three years earlier to the day.[66]

About 32 miles below New Orleans, the *Webb* cleared a point of land and there ahead of it, its guns out, the warship *Richmond* lay at anchor. Actually, the *Richmond* was at anchor to repair its engine and was not forewarned that the Rebel ship was coming down the river in a mad dash to escape to sea.

But to "Savez" Read, it appeared that the 19-gun *Richmond* was lying in wait for him. He summoned all the officers to the pilot house and addressed them.

"It's no use, it's a failure," he said. "The *Richmond* will drown us all, and if she does not the forts below will, as they have a range of three miles each way up and down the river, and they know by this time we are coming. Had we passed New Orleans without being discovered, I would have cut the wires below the city and we could have reached the Gulf with little trouble, as it is, I think the only thing left for us to do is to set fire to the *Webb* and blow her up."

The *Webb* was nosed into the mud of a shoal, life lines were thrown over the bow and "Savez" Read and his men left the ship, which had been set afire at many places with a slow match to the magazine.

From the swamps ashore, "Savez" watched the futile efforts of the *Hollyhock*, which had steamed up, to extinguish the flames and about 3 P.M., the *Webb* blew up.[67]

Thus ended the Confederate saga of "Savez" Read.

X

Picturesque, if slightly piratical, was the early postwar life of Charles W. Read, late of the Confederate States Navy. He had been captured on April 25 and sent first to Fort Columbus in New York Harbor and then to Fort Warren, Massachusetts, where he arrived on May 10. On July 24, 1865, Read gave his parole and took the oath of allegiance to the United States and he was released.

During the winter of 1865–66, Read called on his old friend James Morris Morgan, the little midshipman whom he had known first on the *McRae*, in New Orleans. He was broke, and told Morgan that he would probably have to go to sea before the mast to make a living. Other young Confederate officers, he said, had gone to sea as common sailors and he could too.

Morgan insisted that he should do no such thing and when Read spoke of an opportunity to buy a small brig and engage in the fruit trade with the Caribbean Islands, Morgan, who was one of the few ex-Confederate officers who had any money, lent him the necessary amount and in a week's time, Read had his brig fitted out and had sailed off in it.

For several months, Morgan heard nothing from "Savez" and then one day he walked into his office. He had given up the fruit business and his brig he had abandoned to Customs officials. Of the fruit business, "Savez" said "no man could make a living at it without going into *side lines*."

Morgan wrote of this meeting with his old shipmate:

"What 'Savez' had done to incur the enmity of the Custom officials he never would tell me; but I had my suspicions that the business on the '*side*' lines meant a little harmless smuggling. At all events we never saw his brig nor my money again."

Shortly after this another Read—E. G. Read—came into Jimmy Morgan's office looking for "Savez." This Read had waged a bitter duel with "Savez" for last place in the Class of 1860 at Annapolis, but he hadn't been able to uproot "Savez." He told of a big deal waiting for some enterprising souls in the Republic of Colombia where a civil war was under way. One faction had the money to buy a gunboat and wanted one badly. E. G. Read wanted "Savez" to join him in getting an old tub in New York, freshening it up, and delivering it in Colombia. He further explained that the boat he had in mind had been somewhat victimized by time and dry rot and getting authority to clear New York Harbor would be difficult. Accordingly, the vessel would have to be run out as if it were a Confederate blockade runner.

Morgan brought the two Reads together and "Savez" ever ready for an exciting project jumped at the chance and that night they left for

New York. The old ship was brightened up with a lavish application of paint and they procured several guns, considerable ammunition and, without troubling to tell Customs officials or port authorities about it, they put out to sea and eventually made their delivery to the Colombian authorities and received their price.

"Savez" did not pocket his share of the money and return home. Instead, he remained in Colombia and soon got into contact with the revolutionary leader. "Savez" pointed out the hopelessness of his cause, now that the government had a fine new warship. Then "Savez" offered for a fee to capture the "fine man-o'-war" and deliver it to the revolutionary leader. The offer was snapped up at once. One dark night "Savez" Read gathered a dozen of the wharf loafers hanging around, seized a shore boat and rowed out with his motley boarding party to the ship. In a moment the sleepy crew was overpowered before they knew what had happened and "Savez" sailed off to make his second profit on the "fine man-o'-war."

"Savez" then went to Trinidad where, from the safety of British soil, he wrote the President of Colombia, original purchaser of the ship, "expressing deep regret that circumstances 'over which he had no control' had compelled him to carry off the Colombian navy." "Savez" offered to recapture her and return her to Colombia for the same consideration. The President replied that if Read ever put foot on Colombian soil, he would hang him.

It took a little while for "Savez" to outlive the tendencies that he had developed as a Confederate raider, but he finally settled down, becoming a bar pilot at the mouth of the Mississippi River. Later, he was appointed one of the harbor masters at New Orleans. On January 25, 1890, he died in Meridian in his native Mississippi, at the age of forty-nine.

"Read had as kindly a heart and was as lovable a man as I ever knew," said his friend Morgan, "and he undoubtedly was the hero of the Confederate Navy."

The last time the two met was in 1883, when Morgan was a passenger on the steamer *City of Mexico* from Vera Cruz to New Orleans. At the mouth of the river, Read came aboard as pilot. He and Morgan had not met for years and they fell into each other's arms. Captain McIntosh, skipper of the *City of Mexico*, turned the ship over to Read and as the three were walking to the bridge, Read nudged Morgan.

"Jimmy, wouldn't she make a bully blaze?" laughed Read.

"I want you fellows to stop that kind of talk," broke in Captain McIntosh. "I don't care if the war has been over for years, I don't feel safe with you two pirates aboard!"[68]

5

The Cannoneer Wore Specs:

COLONEL WILLIE PEGRAM

I

W HENEVER curly-haired, bespectacled Willie Pegram galloped up, his guns rattling along behind him, one of Lee's rawboned, ragged Rebels was apt to shout to his comrades: "There's going to be a fight, for here comes that damn little man with the 'specs'!"

A private at nineteen and a full colonel of artillery at twenty-three, Willie Pegram had become synonymous with action in the Army of Northern Virginia. Where he was, the fight was usually torrid. General Ambrose Powell Hill noted this early in the war in a report: "Pegram, as usual . . . managed to find the hottest place." General Henry Heth said of him: "Pegram was one of the few men, who, I believe, was supremely happy when in battle." A friend and fellow officer compared him to Stonewall Jackson in combining "the strongest Christian faith and deepest spirituality with the most intense spirit of fight."[1]

Willie Pegram was the most unwarlike-looking officer in Lee's army. His beardless, boyish face belonged to a young schoolteacher or divinity student, not to an enthusiastic artillerist. He was so nearsighted that he was helpless without his thick-lensed gold spectacles. He was a poor horseman and sat his horse awkwardly. "Brought up in the city of Richmond, he was apparently as unfitted for army life as one could well be," wrote his friend John Haskell, himself a brilliant young artilleryman. ". . . The better I knew him the greater my wonder was to see how he could overcome his natural defects. But he did: and altogether because he had a character and will that were grand, a sense of duty never surpassed, and a determination to do his best, utterly regardless of his own safety or comfort."

To his physical appearance of a mousy little fellow, Pegram brought what appeared to be corroborating characteristics. He was shy, modest, quiet, sober, retiring, pious. Even Willie's most intimate friends were astonished when this almost shrinking lad developed immediately into a great soldier and won rapid and steady promotion as a Confederate artilleryman.[2]

From private up to Robert E. Lee, Pegram was the pride of the Army. "There was a certain magnetism about Willie Pegram that impressed all who came into his presence . . ." recalled a private who served his guns. "Never excited, possessing at all times that perfect equipoise so much prized in a commander, he embodied all the qualities of a soldier. While a strict disciplinarian, he was ever kind and thoughtful of his men."

A fellow officer, Robert Stiles, said that Pegram "as commander of an artillery battalion . . . built up a reputation second to none for effective handling of his guns, his favorite method, where practicable, being a rush to close quarters with the enemy and open at the shortest possible range."

His devoted friend and adjutant, Gordon McCabe, said that outside of Jeb Stuart, Pegram "had probably been under fire oftener than any man in the Army of Northern Virginia."

In official reports of the generals and colonels under whom he served Pegram's "indomitable energy and earnestness of purpose" were noted; his "ready cooperation . . . usual coolness, good judgment and gallantry" were commended; his "efficiency" praised. General Hill called him "My gallant Pegram," General Charles W. Field trusted that "the merits of this officer will not go unrewarded," and General Heth paid him the supreme compliment when he wrote: "When I was going into battle, I always applied for Colonel Pegram's battalion of artillery to accompany me."[3]

General Lee, at the time of Willie Pegram's death at Five Forks, a week before Appomattox, said of the young cannoneer: "Faithful in every position he had filled—brave, zealous, intelligent, he added modesty, courtesy & piety to every manly virtue." And, after the war, Lee said of Willie Pegram: ". . . No one in the Army had a higher opinion of his gallantry and worth than myself. They were conspicuous on every field."[4]

II

William Ransom Johnson Pegram was born in Petersburg, Virginia, on June 29, 1841, the third of five children of General James West Pegram and Virginia Johnson Pegram. On both sides of the family, Willie Pegram came of distinguished Virginia stock.

He had two older brothers, John and James West. The former, a West Point graduate of the class of 1854, became a Confederate brigadier general and was killed at Hatchers Run on February 6, 1865, just two weeks after he had married the lovely Hettie Cary. The second Pegram boy held a majority in the Confederate Army.

The two Pegram girls, Mary Evans and Virginia (Jennie) Johnson, both married Confederate officers, the former being the bride of General Joseph R. Anderson and the latter marrying one of her brother Willie's warmest friends and battlefield colleagues, artillerist Colonel David G. McIntosh.[5]

As a boy of sixteen or seventeen, Pegram joined the elite Richmond military unit known as Company F. When he was nineteen, in the autumn of 1860, Willie Pegram entered the law school of the University of Virginia. To his campus mates at Charlottesville, he appeared "reserved almost to shyness, grave and gracious in his manner, in which there was little of primness and much of charm, of old fashioned politeness." Among his close friends, young Pegram's shyness seemed to vanish; behind his quiet, sober mien was a keen sense of humor. When the university students organized two companies of infantry, Pegram participated eagerly in the project and he was appointed sergeant of the first unit to take shape, the Southern Guard.

The coming crisis for the South, with Abraham Lincoln's election, was discussed by the students at the University of Virginia with as much fervor as it was discussed by their parents and the Southern leaders. Willie Pegram had definite ideas on what would happen. Just a few days after Lincoln's election, Willie wrote his sister, Jennie, thanking her for slippers she had made him. "But I am afraid I will not have much time to wear them now for I look upon disunion as certain, and wouldn't be surprised if I were ordered away at any time." Pegram was still a member of the crack Company F, and if that unit were called for service by the Governor of Virginia, Willie would have to go along.

"It is perfectly dreadful to think of our disunited, afflicted Country," Pegram's letter to his sister went on. "On the one side we have a President, opposed to us in every way . . . while on the other side we have disunion, and that greatest of all evils, 'a civil war' staring us in the face. Isn't that perfectly dreadful? All we can do is to hope that 'that God of all nations' will direct all things for the best." Willie apologized for running on so about a political subject but he warned his sister that the subject called for serious thinking. "It is not a mere Jno. Brown raid," he said.[6]

A little more than a month later, Willie Pegram saw his prediction of disunion prove true. On December 20, 1860, South Carolina seceded from the Union. By February 1, Mississippi, Florida, Alabama, Georgia, Louisiana, and Texas had severed their ties with the Federal government and already acts of hostility had occurred in South Carolina, Georgia, Mississippi, Florida, and Louisiana. The Confederate States of America came into being and, on February 18, Jefferson Davis was inaugurated provisional president at Montgomery, Alabama.

A Virginia-called peace convention in Washington had failed but as yet the states of Virginia, North Carolina, Tennessee, Arkansas, Missouri, Kentucky, Maryland, and Delaware, all slave states, remained in the Union. Then on April 12, 1861, Confederate forces at Charleston fired on Fort Sumter and the long-iced "cold war" between the sections became hot. Virginia refused President Lincoln's call for volunteers to put down the rebellion in the South and on April 17, the Old Dominion State seceded, joining the Confederacy. Her step was soon followed by Tennessee, Arkansas, and North Carolina.

The next day, Willie Pegram was in Richmond with his old unit, Company F, which had been called out by Governor John Letcher. He was one of the first to leave the university. On April 18, he wrote to a friend, Charles Ellis Munford, inviting him and friends to hurry to Richmond to join the company. "There are about forty vacancies, as the Govr. has allowed us to take about a hundred and fifty men in the company."

Immediately, Company F was ordered to Aquia Creek. At Camp Mercer, near Fredericksburg, Willie Pegram was named sergeant major of the post, but he had his sights set higher. On May 3, in telling his sister Mary of his appointment, he added: "I wrote to Govr. Letcher . . . asking him for a lieutenancy in the Va. army, but, of course, have received no reply yet."

Willie didn't stay with Company F long, for he was assigned as a drill master to the Purcell Battery, a Richmond artillery group commanded by Captain R. Lindsay Walker. So fine an impression did he make as an instructor, Pegram was elected a lieutenant in the Purcell Battery. This famous artillery unit, wrote Gordon McCabe, was with Pegram "from the first battle of Manassas, through every general action in Virginia, to the trenches of Petersburg."

Captain Walker quickly discovered that his young subaltern was a "soldier's soldier," thorough, efficient, dependable. Generously, Walker conceded that Pegram spared him all trouble and that "commanding a light battery, one of the most troublesome things in the world, became a pleasure with such an executive officer."[7]

At the Battle of Manassas on July 21, 1861, the Purcell Battery was attached to the reserve brigade commanded by Brigadier General T. H. Holmes. During the actual fight it was not engaged, but when the partial pursuit of the fleeing Federals was undertaken late in the day, Holmes had a brush with Union General Robert C. Schenck's brigade at Lewis Ford. Lieutenant Pegram, although not named in any of the battle reports, shared in the terse praise which General Joe Johnston bestowed upon the Purcell Battery in his report: "His [Holmes'] artillery, under Captain Walker, was used with great skill."

The "terrible war," predicted by Willie Pegram in a letter to a friend in April had, in July, broken out in full blast. Lieutenant Pegram, now just twenty years old, was in it, though only briefly, at the beginning. For the next four years, Willie Pegram's history is, as Gordon McCabe aptly put it, "the history of the army to which he belonged."[8]

III

After Manassas, the "phony war" set in for many months and there was nothing to do in the Confederate Army except to drill and stand picket duty. An occasional brush with enemy pickets or scouting parties relieved the boredom of camp routine. Such was the case for the Purcell Battery, which was stationed, in August 1861, at Marlborough Point at the mouth of Potomac Creek.

In the late afternoon of August 23, the Federal steamer *Yankee* and a tugboat were seen at the mouth of the creek. Captain Walker's six-gun battery under Lieutenants Pegram, Hagerty, and Dabney was ordered to the point. As soon as Walker's guns opened, the Federal steamer *Release* stood in and engaged the battery. During the 45-minute duel, Walker's guns fired about 25 rounds; the enemy about twice that number. Although the Federal gunners showed good accuracy and many shells burst around Willie Pegram and his mates, no one was hurt. The Purcell boys thought that the *Yankee* was hit several times and the *Release* at least once, but they weren't sure. Captain Lindsay Walker had reason to be satisfied with the way his battery performed under fire and he could take pride in Colonel R. M. Cary's report that "the officers in charge of the pieces and the men behaved with proper coolness and deliberation."[9]

It was during these "do-nothing" days on the Potomac, that Captain Walker and his subordinates brought the Purcell Battery to the high degree of efficiency for which it became famous, as soon as the fighting broke out again. It was during these days that the young artillerymen mastered the art of gunnery and developed that fine sense of discipline and *esprit de corps* which caused Willie Pegram to say later: "The Purcell men are the coolest and most desperate men I ever saw in a tight place."

With the coming of spring, the long deadlock of idleness between the two armies was broken when, on March 9, 1862, the Confederate Army withdrew from the line of Bull Run and fell back to the vicinity of Richmond. The Purcell Battery went into camp near Fredericksburg.

On March 31, Captain Walker was promoted to major and given

command of an artillery battalion of which his old battery formed a part. Willie Pegram was promoted to captain and succeeded to the command of the Purcell Battery. How he felt, he told his sister Jennie on April 3:

"I have been so busy since my election to the captaincy that I have not had time to drop a line home . . . Tell Sister that I have grown six inches since my promotion, and that I have employed two barbers to keep my beard in trim, for fear my friends won't know me.

"I don't think I will ever get used to the title of Captain. When I hear myself called Captain, I generally look around to see if Capt. Walker is present.

"I certainly am very fortunate and have a great deal to be thankful for.

"The position is a very responsible one, but I would not exchange places with any body in the Confederacy.

"I have a hundred & fifty as high spirited, respectable, able bodied men as is found. I have six pieces, & about one hundred horses so you know my hands are full . . . I don't know yet where we will be ordered to . . .

"I don't intend to allow anything, except my duties to God, to interfere with my duty to my country . . ."[10]

With the coming of spring in 1862, Union General George B. McClellan launched his attack on Richmond by way of the peninsula between the James and the York Rivers. By slow stages he advanced up the peninsula with his army of more than 100,000, while General Joe Johnston, with a force of 60,000, fell back upon the defenses of the Confederate capital. On May 31–June 1, in a bloody two-day battle at Seven Pines, Johnston left his lines to attack the enemy. Although the forces actually engaged were about equal, almost 42,000 on each side, Johnston had an excellent opportunity to deliver a telling blow on the Federals. However, Johnston was wounded and his subordinates did not press the attack aggressively and the chance was muffed. Robert E. Lee arrived on the field about 2 P.M. on June 1, and succeeded Johnston in command of the army. He ordered the action broken off and the Confederates retired to their original prepared positions in front of Richmond.

Captain Willie Pegram and his Purcell Battery did not participate in the Battle of Seven Pines. They were attached to the brigade of Brigadier General Charles W. Field, which was part of a force of 10,000 guarding the "back door" to Richmond at Fredericksburg. When the Federals had advanced in strength on that place on April 17, Field evacuated the town, burned the bridges and went into camp on Telegraph Road about a dozen miles south of Fredericksburg.

Even if Pegram and his eager gunners had been at Seven Pines, they would have doubtless shared in the inexplicable artillery inactivity. E. Porter Alexander, expert Confederate artillerist, declared that the Federals "did not receive a single hostile cannon shot" from Confederate batteries. "We had no lack of batteries," he stated. "The roads were full of them, but there was no organization to make them effective."[11]

However, Captain Pegram and the Purcell Battery did not have long to wait for action of the hottest kind. After taking command of the Confederate Army between McClellan and Richmond, General Lee executed an audacious plan which he had already begun to develop while holding his desk job as President Davis's military adviser. Stonewall Jackson's Valley Campaign had admirably served Lee's purpose. With the little Valley Army, never stronger than 16,000 men, Jackson had paralyzed three Federal forces out to bag him and had kept reinforcements from joining McClellan. Now, Lee would spring his surprise. Jackson would presumably be strengthened, and troops were actually sent to join Stonewall, sent in such a way that the Yankee high command would be sure to get wind of it. But Jackson had his orders that when his "reinforcements" arrived to march at once to join Lee against McClellan, falling upon the Union right flank, while Lee attacked frontally.

And so the stage was set during June for the Seven Days' Battles, in which Lee maneuvered McClellan away from the gates of Richmond and forced him gradually down the Peninsula, ultimately to give up the campaign against the Confederate capital. In the opening scene of the drama, young Willie Pegram would play an important part and both he and his battery would capture the public imagination and hold it until the curtain came down at Five Forks for the cannoneer who wore specs.

At Mechanicsville on June 26 Willie Pegram's battery was in the forefront of the fight. Upon his six guns the Federal infantry poured a withering rifle fire while five Federal batteries—thirty guns to Pegram's six—engaged the Purcell Battery in an unequal duel. As the enemy shells burst all about them, Pegram's cannoneers stuck courageously by their guns, blasting away as long as the pieces were serviceable. The casualties in the little battery were terrific. Before nightfall, four of Pegram's guns had been put out of commission, and he had lost three officers, one killed and two wounded, and of the ninety men who had galloped into action early in the day, fully fifty were killed or wounded. The slaughter of Pegram's horses was frightful. With the coming of night, the battle died down elsewhere along the front, but Pegram's two remaining guns answered back the shot and shell that still pelted down upon his position. "Listen to the little gamecock crowing in the dark," exclaimed an admiring Rebel, as Pegram's weary remnants kept the two guns blazing. At midnight, all the guns were at last silent.

The story is told—perhaps glamorized, but basically factual—that at dawn on June 27, General A. P. Hill and his brigade commanders were mapping out the battle plan for the day in the headquarters tent.

"I think we can take it for granted that Pegram's battery was so nearly annihilated as not to be counted in forces available," one of the officers said.

At that moment, the tent flap was thrown back and the slight figure of a young captain wearing gold spectacles, his uniform dusty and smelling of smoke, his boyish face powder-blackened, was silhouetted on the firing line this morning.' "

"I am Pegram of Pegram's battery," he said. "I bring you a message from my men. It is this: 'In recognition of service done yesterday, what is left of Pegram's battery claims as its right the most exposed position on the firing line this morning.' "

Gordon McCabe, Pegram's adjutant and devoted friend, substantiates this story and said that during the night, Willie and his men thoroughly equipped the two guns that were not disabled and his request for a place in the advance was granted by General Hill.

There was no time for praise, now, but Pegram became a marked man in the eyes of his brigade commander, Brigadier General Field, and his division commander Major General Hill. They would not forget Willie Pegram when the reports were written. Of Pegram's activities in the bitter struggle of Gaines' Mill on June 27, General Hill wrote: "Pegram, with indomitable energy and earnestness of purpose, though having lost 47 men and many horses at Mechanicsville, had put his battery in condition for this fight also."[12]

And so it was throughout the furious fighting in the Chickahominy swamps during that bloody week before Richmond. At the final furious fight of the Seven Days at Malvern Hill, Pegram's battery "nobly did its work" as General A. P. Hill reported and Captain Pegram was among those whom Hill cited for "conspicuous gallantry."

Pegram was ordered up to the firing line about 11:30 A.M. and he opened a well-directed fire on the Federals, which, reported General A. R. Wright, "told with fearful effect on them." When a supporting battery, under Captain M. N. Moorman, was forced to withdraw, Pegram "was left alone to contend with the whole force of the enemy's artillery."

Undaunted by the unequal fight, Pegram's gallant gunners served their pieces with courage and determination, until, one by one, their guns were knocked out, and the loss in men sorely taxed their capacity to keep firing those that remained serviceable. Reduced to one single gun, Pegram nonetheless stood his ground and "continued to pour a deadly fire upon the enemy's line." Only when General Wright realized the utter hopelessness of the contest and ordered Pegram to cease fire, did he and his battered little band silence their smoking cannon.

At 3 P.M., another battery was moved up to support "the gallant Pegram," as General Wright called him, and Willie opened up again with his single gun, assisting himself in firing it.

Every general officer under whose gaze Willie Pegram's tireless activity came during the Seven Days had high praise for him. But no one better summed up what "the damn little man in specs" contributed in the furious fighting than his own brigade commander, General Field:

"The conduct of Captain Pegram's battery in the engagements excites my admiration. Always eager, always alert, Captain Pegram was in every action where opportunity offered, and always doing his duty, as the loss of every officer killed or wounded and sixty of about eighty men, sadly attests. I trust that the merits of this officer will not go unrewarded by the Department."

Soon after the Seven Days' Battles, Willie Pegram had become a hero in his home town. Wounded soldiers, convalescing in Richmond, spread the story of the valor of the Purcell Battery and its shy, boyish leader. Captain Pegram's name was on everyone's lips, even on the Richmond stage. An actor declared that the boy-captain fought his guns at such close quarters because he was so nearsighted that he couldn't see a dozen yards and never wanted to open fire until he saw what he was shooting at. "At this," said Gordon McCabe, "the bronzed veterans in the pit, with bandaged hands and arms in slings, rose and cheered lustily."

As for Pegram, he blushed furiously whenever anyone mentioned his battlefield conduct. He shunned adulation, and modestly remained in his camp except on the rare occasions when he rode into Richmond to see his mother and sisters.[18]

IV

For three weeks after the Seven Days' Battles, Captain Pegram was busy re-equipping his severely crippled battery and in recruiting new artillerymen to man its guns.

Meanwhile, Lee had sent Jackson off to Gordonsville to meet a new threat. General John Pope, newly arrived from the West, had taken command of the combined forces of Banks, McDowell, and Frémont, whom Jackson had recently hoodwinked in the Shenandoah Valley. McClellan's intentions were not clear at this time and Lee feared that Pope, with his 47,000 men, would march south to combine with McClellan in another attack on Richmond.

Jackson, who had only 12,000 men, realized that he was incapable of any aggressive action against Pope. He called upon Lee for reinforcements. On July 27, 1862, Lee dispatched General Hill's division in response to the request, and, on August 2, Willie Pegram found himself for the first time on the march with Stonewall Jackson. And he soon found out what that meant.

". . . We have been so constantly on the march, that I have not had time to write," he told his sister Mary, in a hastily penned letter from Orange Court House on August 8. ". . . I have made up my mind to the fact, that I will hear very irregularly and seldom from home, and this I consider to be the only drawback to being with Jackson . . ."

Apparently, Pegram had suffered a physical and mental letdown after his exciting experiences in the Richmond battles, for he reported to his sister that his "health and spirits" had improved since leaving tidewater Virginia for the hills. "You can't imagine how much I enjoy the pure air & fine scenery of the mountains," he wrote. "I have eighty-five men present, and not one on the sick list."

The Pegrams were a close-knit family and letters among them were frequent and numerous. But being on the march with Jackson cramped Willie's correspondence. "I will take every opportunity I can to write home," he said. "I don't know exactly how to direct you about directing your letters to me. I think the best plan is to direct them to me, Genl Field's Brigade, Genl Hill's Division, Genl Jackson's Army. That is pretty awkward, but I expect it is about the best plan."[14]

The next day, August 9, Jackson struck Pope at Cedar Mountain, not far from Culpeper. He had hoped to destroy the first Union corps with which he made contact, before the rest of Pope's army came up. Then, as he did in the Valley at Cross Keys and Port Republic, Jackson would attack the other corps in detail and deliver a crushing blow to the Federals. Unfortunately, things did not work out according to plan. Jackson's famous "foot cavalry" for once dawdled and as it approached the enemy on August 7, it covered but seven miles. The next day, due to a mixup in orders and some misinterpretations of instructions, Jackson advanced at a snail's pace, the head of his column making only eight miles and the rear of it only two miles. "Each Division," wrote E. P. Alexander, "was allowed to take its own wagon-train behind it on the road, instead of concentrating all three into one train behind the whole force." Jackson had to wait until 3 P.M. for the divisions of Ewell and Winder to form a battle line in front of Banks's corps. Hill's division was still moving up when Banks attacked vigorously after 5 P.M., throwing Winder's division into confusion. With the arrival of Hill on the field, Pegram's battery unlimbered and went into action against the Federal infantry. Soon the fighting was stabilized and Hill moved forward, pressing back the Federals. Willie Pegram gave the family a graphic description of his share in the fighting:

"In the afternoon my battery was on the field playing on the infantry, and I had good opportunity of seeing all the infantry movements on both sides. It was certainly a fine sight. At first our infantry behaved badly. My support ran, and the battery was charged by the enemy. I kept a sharp lookout, and played upon them with canister to the last, and then got out in time, with the loss of one man wounded, three horses killed and a caisson. After we drove them back, I got my caisson. But the hottest time for me, was that night. After whipping them, we cautiously advanced, my battery being in front. As we were advancing, General Jackson told me to shell some woods and a field. There was a great deal of the enemy infantry in the field, and we could soon hear them in confusion, the officers trying to make their men charge upon me, and the men running. They succeeded in getting three batteries upon me, when we had it until nearly 12 o'clock at night. If they had brought another battery by me, we could have whipped them . . . Longstreet's division has come up, and it is said that General Lee is certainly coming up. Hurrah! On to Philadelphia! I'll get you shoes &c."[15]

Once again Willie Pegram's superior officers sang his praises in their reports. Lieutenant Colonel Lindsay Walker said that Pegram's conduct and that of his men at Cedar Mountain "cannot be too highly commended." Stonewall Jackson commended Pegram's "well-directed and unexpected fire [which] produced much disorder and confusion." General Field reported: "I have taken occasion before to speak of the distinguished services of Pegram's battery. It is sufficient to say now that it fully sustained the reputation made on other fields."

The gossip around General Hill's headquarters after Cedar Mountain had it that Captain Pegram was headed for promotion. "Genl Field sent me an extract from his official report which I intended sending you, but lost it," Pegram wrote his sister Jennie. "He was very complimentary and asked for my promotion which I do want." One of General Hill's staff told Willie that the division commander had also recommended his promotion.

To the men of his battery Willie Pegram seemed to bear a charmed life. Though shells fell all about him in the Seven Days and his casualties were frightfully high, Willie escaped without a scratch. In the Cedar Mountain affair, the battery lost a brave and able officer, Lieutenant Mercer Featherston, who was killed along with two of the men. In addition, a dozen of the gunners were wounded. But the nearest Willie Pegram came to being hit was four bullet holes through the skirt of his coat. "One sharpshooter took deliberate aim at me eight or ten times," he wrote home, "and missed me." Pegram credited his safety to "an ever merciful God" and asked the family: "What have I to fear from Yankee bullets and shells, as long as I am under His protection?"[16]

Satisfied on August 13 that McClellan was leaving the Peninsula, Robert E. Lee decided to make a junction with Stonewall Jackson and together strike a powerful blow at Pope. Leaving 20,000 troops to protect Richmond, he set out with 30,000 men to join Jackson at Gordonsville, arriving on August 15.

A dramatic raid by Jeb Stuart—he was red-faced behind his bushy beard for having earlier been surprised by a Yankee cavalry party which captured his cloak and plumed hat and almost Stuart himself—had netted General Pope's private dispatch book, with copies of important correspondence with Washington. From this Lee learned that Pope had only 50,000 men, but was strengthening almost daily. With McClellan's troops hastening to join Pope, in the space of five days the Federals could have as many as 130,000 men in the field against Lee's 55,000. Even the addition of the 20,000 men at Richmond would put the Confederate Army at a decided disadvantage in a short time.

Lee decided upon an audacious move, which in a lesser man would have been folly. In the face of a superior enemy, he divided his army in half and sent Stonewall Jackson with about 25,000 men on a wide sweep to the left to get behind Pope and wreck his supply base at Manassas Junction. While Jackson was making his circuit to get to Pope's rear, Lee would maintain his line on the Rappahannock River and occupy Pope's attention.

Captain Willie Pegram by now had become accustomed to Stonewall Jackson's long and rapid marches and frequent skirmishes with enemy outposts or rear guards. From August 8, the day before the fight at Cedar Mountain, through August 24 Stonewall Jackson's troops had either fought or marched every day, and sometimes both. Pegram was never surprised at the hour of the day or night when "Old Jack" put his army into motion, or how far he marched it. "We frequently march eighteen out of twenty-four hours," he wrote his mother.[17]

On August 24, Pegram's guns with other Confederate batteries engaged the Federals in an all-day duel on the Rappahannock and despite the exposure to enemy fire, Willie reported only one fatal casualty in the Purcell Battery. That night, Jackson's troops were relieved, but not for rest. "We withdrew to Jeffersonville & made preparations for a march," Pegram wrote his sister. This was no ordinary Jackson march, this was "the most famous of his marches" as Stonewall's first important biographer Colonel Henderson, called it. Of Lee's bold operation about to unfold, Colonel Henderson delivered this critique:

". . . We have record of few enterprises of greater daring . . . It is easy to conceive. It is less easy to execute. But to risk cause and country, name and reputation, on a single throw, and to abide the issue with unflinching heart, is the supreme exhibition of the soldier's fortitude."

Willie Pegram wrote his mother a letter in diary form which enables one to follow Jackson's remarkable march and its brilliant consequences as the young cannoneer experienced it. After breakfast, on August 25, Jackson began his movement to the left. Willie reported that the army "marched rapidly until midnight, making a flank movement & crossing the Rappahannock above Warrenton, completely fooling the enemy and getting to their rear." Stonewall had the column on the march again at dawn on August 26, and the men "marched rapidly all day until late in the night." Jackson was now within six miles of Pope's supply depot at Manassas Junction. On the night of August 26, Old Jack sent General Isaac R. Trimble's brigade and Jeb Stuart's cavalry to swoop down upon the Junction. Jackson's ragged and hungry rebels beheld a sight that made their eyes pop out. E. P. Alexander said that "the supplies embraced everything eatable, drinkable, wearable, or usable in immense profusion."

Pegram's description of the scene is vivid:

"Made a dash upon Manassas, whipping and capturing greater portion of Taylor's New Jersey brigade . . . and two trains of supplies for Pope's army valued at several millions of dollars, consisting of everything that the human mind can imagine. Unfortunately, the enemy pressed upon us in heavy force, & we, having only twenty thousand men were forced to burn everything we could not carry off. Before doing so, however, the troops were allowed to go in & help themselves to everything they wished for. I got the following articles a first rate Yankee bridle and sabre, carbine, enough sugar & coffee to last me for six months a small tent fly which accomodates two or three persons, & can be carried behind the saddle with the blankets, a dozen cakes of nicest toilet soap & as many tooth brushes which I hope to send home—also a good quality of stationary (unfortunately the soap has been lost, however, we will soon be in Baltimore, & I'll get you plenty) and various other small articles. The troops supplied themselves with food enough for several days without which we should have starved.

"The enemy advanced in force in the afternoon & we were all placed in position in line of battle, awaiting their attack. Seeing this they held off, & after firing the train we retired in the night to Centreville."

The next day, August 28, Jackson's refreshed troops marched from Centreville to the old battlefield at Manassas where, with local superiority, Jackson attacked a Federal force near Groveton, with undecisive results. Stonewall then took up a line behind an unfinished railroad embankment and awaited the junction with Lee, elements of whose army under Longstreet were at Gainesville less than a dozen miles away. The Federals launched a strong counterattack on Jackson's right, aiming to cut off communications with the advancing Longstreet. "Our situation this and the next two days may be said to have been one of extreme hazard," wrote Willie Pegram, "and nothing but the most obstinate courage of our troops could have saved us."

In overwhelming force, the Federals pounded Jackson's line, attacking about 4 P.M. Pegram's guns fired continuously until at last the assault failed. "God assisted us and we drove them back with great slaughter," Willie told his mother. "I lost three men severely wounded."

It was August 29 that Willie Pegram suffered his greatest ordeal as the

Battle of Second Manassas roared on. "It was a repetition of the pre-ceeding day," he said. "The only change being that the fight was more severe, & lasted all day." With two of his pieces, Pegram, during the hottest part of the fight, engaged an entire Federal battery, until a shell burst in the midst of a gun crew. "It was the worst shot I ever saw," said Pegram, ". . . killing two of my best men, wounding two, stunning the remainder, killing three horses, disabling a wheel & cutting through a tree."

On this day, about 11 A.M. Lee came upon the field with Longstreet and the Confederates now had approximately 50,000 troops with which to oppose Pope's still numerically superior force. Pegram thought the enemy had double the Confederate number. Pope, who did not realize that Lee had performed the impossible of splitting his army into two and then reuniting it on the battlefield, attacked on August 30, confident that he had Jackson in a bad way. "We drove them 2 miles back, completely routing them," wrote Willie Pegram, "capturing six thousand prisoners, and any number of caissons, small arms &c."

Captain Pegram and the Purcell Battery won honorable mention, with other artillerymen, in General Hill's report on Second Manassas: "The batteries of Braxton, Pegram, McIntosh, and Crenshaw were gallantly served during this fight and did yeoman service."[18]

After the crushing defeat at Second Manassas, Pope retired into the Federal fortified positions around Alexandria. "The enemy having taken refuge within lines impregnable to assault, Lee had no alternative but to take the offensive elsewhere," stated E. P. Alexander. "He could not afford to sit down before Washington and await the enemy's pleasure."

On September 3, 1862, General Lee wrote President Davis that "the present seems to be the most propitious time since the commencement of the war for the Confederate Army to enter Maryland . . . The pur-pose, if discovered, will have the effect of carrying the enemy north of the Potomac, and if prevented, will not result in much evil."

And so early in September, Lee's Army of Northern Virginia marched to the fords of the upper Potomac and in three columns crossed over to the other side. It was a "grand . . . spectacle," Willie told the family:

"There was the river several hundred yards in width, the mountain scenery around, the troops up to their waist in water, the setting sun and the bands playing 'Dixie' and 'My Maryland.' But there was one thing wanted to complete the scene—that was a crowd on the opposite bank welcoming them as their deliverers. It seems a pity we could not have crossed at some other point. You could see disappointment written on the face of every man, on none more than the Marylanders who were in our army . . ."

On September 7, from Frederick, Maryland, Willie Pegram wrote his mother: "Here we now are lounging about, enjoying the respite al-

Collection of Ezra J. Warner, La Jolla, California

[1] *William Mahone.* Beginning slowly, this Virginia-born engineer and railroad president grew in military stature as the war advanced and at the end he was one of Lee's best major generals. He was one of the most picturesque figures in gray—small, skinny, and heavily bearded—and he had a sharp tongue and an iron will.

[2] *Turner Ashby*. Born to the saddle, Ashby was perhaps the finest horseman in the Confederate Army and his daredevil followers, sensitive to
discipline, eagerly followed him into a fight. He survived only the first
year of the war, but in that time he won his name as one of the best
fighters in the Southern army.

Courtesy
Confederate
Museum,
Richmond, Virginia

[4] *William Ransom Johnson Pegram.* One of the most dashing of artillerymen in the Civil War, Pegram always placed his guns where the fighting was thickest and hottest. The bespectacled young Virginian, resembling a divinity student more than a soldier, seemingly led a charmed life until a fatal day at Five Forks in the dying hours of the Confederacy.

Collection of
Ezra J. Warner,
La Jolla, California

[3] *Patrick Roynane Cleburne.* Irish-born, this Arkansas lawyer volunteered as a private and wound up a major general and some said that he would have become a lieutenant general but for his proposal that the slaves be recruited for the Southern army and promised their freedom with peace. One of the great division commanders of the war, Cleburne won the name of "Stonewall Jackson of the West."

[5] *Henry Hotze*. Although the youngest of all agents, Union and Confederate, Henry Hotze was one of the most able men sent to Europe during the Civil War. Skilled in diplomacy and a tactful handler of people, Hotze, a Mobile newspaperman, directed Confederate propaganda in England with the deft touch of Madison Avenue. As the founder and behind the scenes editor of *The Index*, Confederate propaganda organ, Hotze did a tremendous job for the Confederacy.

[6] *Lucius B. Northrop.* Petulant, irascible, stubborn in the belief that everybody else besides himself and Jefferson Davis was out of step, Commissary General Northrop quickly became the most hated man in the Confederacy. His job of feeding the Southern armies, in the light of lost territory and a breakdown in transportation, would have been difficult had his disposition been an amiable one, but to an impossible task he brought an impossible personality.

[7] *Richard Taylor.* One of the three Confederate lieutenant generals to come from civilian life—the other two were Nathan Bedford Forrest and Wade Hampton—Dick Taylor established himself as one of the South's finest fighting generals in Stonewall Jackson's Valley Campaign of 1862. Transferred to the Trans-Mississippi, Taylor distinguished himself in thwarting Banks's Red River Campaign in Louisiana in 1864. His *Destruction and Reconstruction* is among the best of the books produced by Civil War participants.

[8] *Edward Porter Alexander.* Bold, dashing, original, Porter Alexander was one of the most brilliant artillerists of the Civil War and every Confederate army commander requested his services. From Manassas to Appomattox, he made invaluable contributions to Southern arms and in his later years he wrote the finest critique of Confederate strategy and tactics ever produced in his *Military Memoirs of a Confederate.*

[9] *Charles W. "Savez" Read.* The only time during the war that "Savez" was inactive was when he was in a Yankee prison. Here he is—the little man seated in the middle, with mustache and goatee and derby hat— among fellow Confederate naval prisoners of war at Fort Warren, Mass.

lowed us from our truly hard labours preparatory to, as we suppose, another week of fatigue and danger . . ." Willie explained the lukewarm reception the army received in Maryland by the fact that "we have hit upon two Union counties." Pegram found even the Virginia side of the Potomac "much tainted," and complained that the reception in Leesburg "might have been much warmer than it was." The Southern sympathizers, Willie said, were restrained for they didn't know how soon they might again be inside Federal lines and the Union men were spies upon them. "It will take a good victory to bring them to our ranks," he said.[19]

V

To secure his supply lines and protect his rear as he pushed deeper into Maryland, Lee sent Stonewall Jackson to attack Harpers Ferry, where 12,000 Federal troops were posted at the confluence of the Potomac and Shenandoah Rivers.

Accordingly, Willie Pegram and the Purcell Battery didn't have much time to lounge about in Frederick for, on September 10, Jackson began to march. His corps recrossed the Potomac on September 11 and made for Martinsburg, from which the Federal garrison retired on Jackson's approach. Shortly before noon on September 13, the head of Jackson's column came into sight of the enemy drawn up on Bolivar Heights, above Harpers Ferry.

The Federal position, despite the size of the force, was not an enviable one. For General Lafayette McLaws with two divisions, and batteries, had routed a Union force on Maryland Heights and had taken possession of this commanding position which looked down from across the Potomac into the town. Similarly, General Walker had installed his division and guns on Loudoun Heights, another commanding position across the Shenandoah, also dominating the town. When Jackson launched his attack, the Federals would be under the fire of the guns of McLaws and Walker as well as under the frontal fire of Jackson's infantry and batteries.

General Hill, who was in the van of Jackson's force, received orders to move down the left bank of the Shenandoah on September 14, turn the Federals' left and enter Harpers Ferry. Hill immediately perceived that the Federals had a strong position on Bolivar Heights, having thrown up earthworks between the rivers. As he moved down the river bank, Hill spotted an eminence crowning the Yankee extreme left devoid of earthworks and held, not too strongly, only by infantry. Hill attacked at once with three divisions, seized the high ground and immediately had Lieutenant Colonel Lindsay Walker bring up his guns and establish them on the hill. Throughout the night of September 14, Willie Pegram and the other battery commanders, ably directed by Walker, got their guns into position. At daybreak, Pegram and the others opened a rapid enfilade fire at a range of about 1000 yards. Immediately the Federal batteries replied vigorously and for an hour the guns roared at each other. When the Federal fire died down and seemed to be silenced, Hill's infantry moved to the attack. But no sooner had the yelling Confederate foot soldiers begun to charge the works, than they met a galling fire of small arms and artillery.

Then it was that Willie Pegram got an order that he liked. The cannoneer with spectacles always wanted to see what he was shooting at. His battery and that of Captain William G. Crenshaw were ordered forward about 400 yards nearer the enemy's works and, as General Hill described it, "quickly coming into battery, poured in a damaging fire." Soon a white flag showed in the Federal position and the smoking guns of Pegram and Crenshaw fell silent, having delivered the *coup de grâce*.

Eleven thousand prisoners, 12,000 stands of arms, 70 pieces of artillery and a large number of horses and their equipment, many wagons and a great quantity of commissary, quartermaster's and ordnance stores fell into Jackson's lap with the capture of Harpers Ferry.

With Jackson's approval, Hill gave Union General Julius White liberal terms. A sentence in Hill's report amusingly reminds the reader a century later just what was meant by the statement that the Civil War was "the last of the gentlemen's wars." Hill did not write his report until February 1863, at which time he regretted to report that "this magnanimity was not appreciated by the enemy, as the wagons which were loaned to carry off the private baggage of the officers were not returned for nearly two months, and not until repeated calls had been made for them."[20]

Jackson left Hill at Harpers Ferry to receive the Federal surrender of troops and supplies and took off with the rest of his force to rejoin Lee in Maryland, where the Confederates had made contact with the Union Army, once again under the command of General George B. McClellan.

The stay afforded little rest for Pegram's gunners and the remainder of Hill's troops, for at 6:30 A.M. on September 17, Hill received an urgent message from Lee to move at once to Sharpsburg. Leaving a brigade to complete the removal of the captured property, Hill was in motion at 7:30 A.M., hurrying to join Lee, then under tremendous attack along Antietam Creek.

The head of Hill's column reached the battlefield at Antietam at 2:30 P.M., having marched seventeen miles. Hill immediately reported in person to General Lee, who ordered the division to take up position on the Confederate right. At about 3 P.M. Hill's batteries were up. Willie Pegram and Captain Crenshaw were ordered to go into battery on a hill from where, with a wide field of fire, they played upon the Federal infantry with furious rapidity. "My troops were not in a moment too soon," Hill later reported. At 4:30 P.M., one of Pegram's guns, together with Captain Braxton's, was moved to the extreme right, where they began to pour an enfilading fire. "From this point they were worked, with beautiful precision and great effect upon the infantry of the enemy until nightfall closed the engagement," reported Lieutenant Colonel Lindsay Walker. By now Pegram's men were exhausted from the march from Harpers Ferry and from incessant firing, and this gun was withdrawn.

Hill's arrival and the deadly work of his artillery probably saved Lee at Antietam. Tremendously outnumbered by McClellan, Lee had withstood five separate Union attacks, although hard-pressed. Hill came up in time to meet the fifth onslaught, Burnside's attack on the Confederate right. Hill fell on Burnside's flank and drove him back to Antietam Creek. McClellan had had enough and the bloody battle of Antietam, which the Confederates called Sharpsburg, was over.

Among the Confederate casualties was Willie Pegram. Hill thought enough of the young artillery captain to list him in his report along with generals and colonels who were killed or wounded: "My gallant Captain Pegram, of the artillery, was also wounded for the first time." A small shell fragment struck Pegram in the head, but it was a trifling wound. Pegram's friend, Lieutenant Ham Chamberlayne, wrote his sister: "Willie Pegram was hit at Sharpsburg, a moment after I had moved from him, on the head, not serious." Pegram refused to take leave, and within two weeks he was on duty once more with his battery. Meanwhile, Lee had recrossed the Potomac into Virginia and Pegram's battery went into camp with Hill's division near Bunker Hill, twelve miles north of Winchester.[21]

By this time nearly everybody in the Army realized Pegram's worth but apparently had not yet caught the eye of General William N. Pendleton, Lee's chief of artillery in the Army of Northern Virginia. For when asked by General Lee to list "captains of batteries who had distinguished themselves in the recent battles," Pendleton submitted a list of artillery captains in the order "of distinction recently earned" and Willie's name was thirteenth on the list of fourteen. Moreover, after Antietam, Pendleton, contemplating the remaining fragments of Pegram's battery, had recommended that the battery be disbanded and that the men, guns, and horses be distributed into other batteries. A. P. Hill wouldn't countenance the idea. He appealed to Lee and made good his point that if batteries had to be disbanded in the reorganization of the army that some outfit less distinguished than Willie Pegram's be dispersed. Lee, ever conscious of other people's feelings, "suggested" to Pendleton on September 23 that some other battery than Pegram's might better be broken up. Less than two weeks later, on October 4, Chapman's Dixie Battery, reduced to 32 men, was disbanded and the men and horses were assigned to Pegram.[22]

Pegram found remaining quiet in camp boring, he complained on October 7, 1862, to his sister Jennie:

"After an active campaign this seems very stupid and dull to a soldier. But we have not been idle. General Lee is getting rid of all incompetent officers and cowards, by a simple order relieving them from duty, without any Court. The result of it is, that the whole army is in a much better state of discipline than heretofore, and should we have any more fighting shortly, there will not be the same amount of straggling & cowardice that usually attends a large army."

About this time, Pegram fell temporarily out of favor with General Hill and he and Captain Crenshaw were charged with neglect of duty and placed under arrest. It seemed that their men had been stealing fence rails and burning them at their campfires, in violation of orders. (At the same time, in a brigade in General Dick Ewell's old division, every colonel was under arrest for the identical offense.)

Ordered to return to duty and released from arrest, Pegram and Crenshaw did not wish to accept the release, preferring to go before Court. But on inquiry they found that they had no option in the matter. Having in a previous letter told of his arrest, Willie, on October 24, related to his sister Jennie, how the case had been disposed:

"It seems a very hard case, that we should be charged with neglect of duty & placed under arrest, and then not even allowed the privilege of a Court. Capt. Crenshaw & I went to see Genl. Gregg, of S.C., to get some advice. As soon as we showed him the communications that had passed between ourselves & Genl. Hill, he told us that both parties had misunderstood each other & upon going to see Genl. Hill, he found that he was correct. Genl. Hill expressed his regret that the affair had occurred, & expressed the kindest feelings towards us all.

"Thus ended the matter. I regret very much that the affair ever occurred, but as it did occur, am sorry it ended so soon & without the decision of a Court.

"I met Genl. Hill yesterday. He was very cordial in his greeting . . ."[23]

After returning from the invasion of Maryland, Lee had again split his army. Longstreet was in the vicinity of Culpeper while Jackson remained in the Shenandoah Valley, based at Winchester. But when General Ambrose Burnside replaced McClellan as commander of the Army of the Potomac early in November 1862 and marched for Fredericksburg, Lee summoned Jackson out of the Valley and started Longstreet in motion for that place. Stonewall's "foot cavalry" marched 100 miles in ten days and Lee had his army together again by the end of November.

Meanwhile Burnside was throwing pontoons across the Rappahannock, under much harassment from the Confederates, in preparation for hurling his army of more than 100,000 against Lee's partially prepared line on the high ground south and west of Fredericksburg. Jackson, who had marched 15 miles down the Rappahannock to prevent Burnside from crossing there and turning Lee's right flank, had hurried back when it became apparent that the Union general would assault Lee frontally. A. P. Hill's division was the first of Jackson's force to arrive on the field, and shortly after dawn on December 12, Hill relieved John B. Hood's division and formed on the right of Lee's line, near Hamilton's Crossing. His division front covered about a mile and a half. Immediately, Lieutenant Colonel Walker located the division artillery. On a hill, crowning the right of Hill's position, and near the railroad, he placed Willie Pegram's battery, together with that of Crenshaw and sections of three other batteries—a total of 14 guns in all. It was a commanding position, with an excellent field of fire for direct infantry assault but it had the disadvantage of any fixed position that it would attract the concentrated fire of many guns. Moreover, the formation of the ground at the top of the hill did not give much cover to the gunners and practically none at all to the horses of the batteries.

Under orders from Stonewall Jackson's chief of artillery, Colonel Stapleton Crutchfield, Walker kept his guns as concealed as possible and he restrained the natural impatience of Pegram and the others to engage the enemy artillery. But Walker's orders were explicit: he was to disregard the fire of the enemy's batteries and to reserve his own fire for the Yankee infantry when it came into effective range.

About 10 A.M. on December 13, Federal guns, in a desultory sort of a way, began probing at Lee's position. About an hour later, when the enemy began to deliver a hot fire on Walker's guns, he reminded Captains Pegram and McIntosh to await an infantry movement before firing. This came about noon, when a division formed to attack the height. As the Federal line moved forward the signal came that Willie Pegram and Crenshaw had awaited. As the blue line moved into range, the fourteen guns cut loose with a murderous fire. The Federal infantry, swept by the rain of shells from the height, broke and fell back. Coincidental with the infantry demonstration, about 25 Federal guns concentrated a destructive fire on Pegram and Crenshaw.

Another and stronger massed attack, "in enormous forces," Colonel Walker reported, "moved forward rapidly, protected by a fearful fire from all their guns." As they advanced toward a point of woods in the plain, Confederates emerged from the trees, met and repelled the charge, while Pegram and Crenshaw, serving their guns rapidly, ripped huge gaps in the densely packed Union ranks. While Willie and Crenshaw were devoting their attention to the Yankee infantry, the Federal artillery again concentrated its fire on them, causing heavy loss. "But, as soon as engaged by our guns," reported Lindsay Walker, "their shots flew wide, though in weight of metal they much exceeded us."

By 3:30 P.M., after firing almost incessantly for more than three hours,

Captain Pegram became short of both men and ammunition and Captain Crenshaw suffered from similar disabilities. Moreover, one gun was disabled, a caisson and limber had exploded and many horses had been killed or wounded. Except for one section of Pegram's battery, which remained in position, Walker's weary gunners were relieved by other batteries.

When the bloody day was over, Burnside had been repulsed along the entire line with frightful loss. Of 106,000 Union troops engaged, casualties totaled nearly 13,000, while Lee lost about 5300 of his 72,000 effectives. The heaviest losses in Lee's army were experienced by A. P. Hill's infantry and gunners, more than 2122, or about 40 per cent of Lee's casualties, coming from the division. Eleven dead and eighty-eight wounded in Walker's batteries, attested to the intensity of the fight for Pegram and his fellow gunners. General Hill noted this in his report:

"Lieutenant Colonel Walker, assisted by Lieutenant Chamberlayne, directed the fire from his guns with admirable coolness and precision. Pegram, as usual, with McIntosh to help him, managed . . . to find the hottest place . . ."[24]

VI

The winter of 1862–63 was a dreary one for the Army of Northern Virginia. There was bitter cold, much rain, sleet and snow, and it was difficult to keep the men warmly clothed and shod and the horses fed.

There was considerable sickness in Lee's camps, although many of the men reported on the sick lists were actually too poorly clad to face exposure to the elements on the more miserable days. At an inspection in February 1863, Willie Pegram's battery of 171 officers and men reported 55 men sick.[25]

Pegram's battery, after Fredericksburg, was stationed at Bowling Green, on the railroad to Richmond, and frequently it was sent on picket duty to Port Royal on the Rappahannock. As usual, when he wasn't blazing away with his beloved guns, Captain Pegram was bored. "Every thing is quiet and dull in this region," he wrote his sister Jennie from the vicinity of Port Royal on January 8, 1863. He had hoped for a furlough to visit the family, "but General Lee is turning down all requests. I very cheerfully submit to this," wrote Willie, "for I know that General Lee has the interest of the service at heart & will do whatever is right." Having read the newspapers of that date, Willie made two astute observations to his sister. Speaking of the Battle of Murfreesboro, fought in Tennessee at the turn of the year, he said: "Bragg's victory, like all our western victories, turned out to be scarcely any victory at all." The other comment he made concerned European intervention on behalf of the Confederacy. "I see that the *Enquirer* of today is again trying to induce the people to believe that France is going to recognize us!" he wrote. "What a pity! I have always been of the opinion that we would be better off in the end, to fight the battles out ourselves . . . Louis Napoleon is not going to interfere unless it will benefit the French people more than any other . . ."

Despite—or indeed, because of—his aversion to the routine of camp life, Captain Pegram spent his time in looking after the comfort of his men in the cheerless weather. His close friend and later his adjutant, Gordon McCabe, described Pegram's camp activities, in that frightful winter:

"One of his first cares on going into winter quarters . . . was to assemble the men and say a few words to them concerning the importance of building a chapel and holding regular prayer-meetings. All these services he attended himself with earnest pleasure, and it was a common sight to see him sitting among his men in the rude log-chapel, bowing his young head reverently in prayer, or singing from the same hymn-book with some weather-beaten private, from whom he had ever exacted strictest military obedience. His discipline was, indeed, that of long-established armies. He justly considered it mercy in the end to punish every violation of duty, and he knew that men do not grow restive under discipline the sternest at the hands of officers who lead well in action. He performed with soldierly exactness every duty pertaining to his own position, held officers and men to a rigid accountability."[26]

During February, General Lee had a plan in his hands for the reorganization of the artillery of the Army of Northern Virginia. It had been prepared by General William N. Pendleton in collaboration with those two brilliant colonels of artillery, Stapleton Crutchfield and E. Porter Alexander. They proposed doing away with brigade batteries and division groups and arranging the artillery in each corps in battalions, which would have two field officers in command. A proposed schedule of organization was embodied in the proposal, with an alphabetical designation, for convenience, used for the various batteries. When he reached the Second Corps in the report, Lee read:

"Battalion L: Lieut.-Col. R. L. Walker, of Virginia, so justly distinguished for long and gallant service, has been recommended for the full rank of Colonel. He might justly receive it and have command of this battalion.

"Capt. W. J. Pegram, now commanding a battery in Gen. A. P. Hill's Division, has been recommended for promotion. He has also fully earned it by efficient service, and would no doubt be highly approved by Lieut.-Col. Walker and by Gen. Hill as the second Field Officer in this battalion. He is from Virginia."

On March 2, 1863, General Lee, having made some slight revisions in Pendleton's recommendations, forwarded them with his approval to

President Davis. On April 4, but with his rank to date from March 2, Captain Willie Pegram was promoted to major. The new artillery organization was authorized on April 16, 1863, by Special Order No. 106, Army of Northern Virginia, and Major Pegram found himself second in command of Walker's battalion in A. P. Hill's division in Stonewall Jackson's II Corps of Lee's army. Colonel Stapleton Crutchfield continued as chief of artillery for the corps. Walker's battalion consisted of five batteries: Pegram's old Purcell Battery, under Captain Joseph McGraw; Pee Dee (S.C.) Battery, under Captain E. B. Brunson; the Richmond Battery under Captain William G. Crenshaw; the Letcher Battery under Captain Greenlee Davidson; and the Fredericksburg Battery under Captain E. A. Marye.[27]

When the spring campaign opened in 1863, Lee had a new opponent, "Fighting Joe" Hooker, who had succeeded Burnside as commander of the Army of the Potomac late in January 1863.

To oppose Hooker's army of about 133,000 men, with more than 400 guns, Lee had fewer than 60,000 troops and about 228 guns. Moreover, Longstreet and two of his divisions were off foraging in the vicinity of Suffolk where they had been sent by Lee during the winter on the importunities of Secretary of War Seddon that the capital should be better defended. Lee had told Longstreet to be ready on a moment's notice to return to the Rappahannock should Hooker make an offensive move. But when Lee wanted Longstreet back, President Davis and Seddon still retained him in the vicinity of Suffolk.

On April 28, Hooker threw a pontoon bridge over the Rappahannock near Fredericksburg and began crossing troops. When Hooker, having built a second bridge and crossed a considerable number of troops, failed to demonstrate before the Confederate lines at Fredericksburg, Lee rightly surmised that a main Federal effort was being made elsewhere. Word reached Lee on April 29 that Hooker had also crossed the Rappahannock at Kellys Ford in force and that some of these Union troops, marching south, were crossing the Rapidan at Germanna and Elys Ford and descending upon Lee's left. Since the roads over which the Federals were advancing converged at Chancellorsville, Lee dispatched troops to that point to contest their progress, while he determined what the intentions of the enemy on his front at Fredericksburg really were. Their inactivity convinced Lee that his estimate was correct that Hooker's main attack would be on his flank and rear. "It was, therefore, determined to leave sufficient troops to hold our lines, and with the main body of the army to give battle to the approaching columns," reported Lee. And so he marched off to Chancellorsville with Stonewall Jackson on May 1, moving out with the last divisions of his corps.

When contact with Hooker was made, Lee realized at once that due to the strength of the Union position and Federal superiority in numbers a direct attack would be hazardous. "It was, therefore, resolved to endeavor to turn his right flank and gain his rear, leaving a force in front to hold him in check and conceal the movement," Lee reported. "The execution of this was intrusted to Lieutenant-General Jackson . . ."

And thus began, at dawn on May 2, Stonewall Jackson's dazzling flanking movement which sent the ragged Rebel foot cavalry swooping down upon Hooker's exposed right as a prelude to Robert E. Lee's greatest victory.[28]

Major Willie Pegram and Lindsay Walker's battalion of artillery marched with Jackson and played a tremendous part in the success of the audacious movement. During the action, when Colonel Crutchfield was wounded, command of the corps artillery developed upon Colonel Walker. Major Pegram, for the first time, assumed command of the battalion. And from his first report, the reader can follow his activities at Chancellorsville.

At 6:30 A.M. on May 2, Pegram was directed to advance as many rifled guns as could be employed on the road leading from the Confederate right to Chancellorsville to shell Federal infantry in the woods. As Major Pegram got his guns into position, two Federal batteries opened on him. "I kept some of the guns actively shelling the woods, whilst the others engaged the enemy's batteries," Willie reported. However, Pegram felt the long range at which he was firing did not justify the expenditure of ammunition and he communicated that fact to General Henry Heth, who directed him to cease firing and withdraw his guns.

In the afternoon Major Pegram took command of the battalion and at 7:30 P.M. he hustled four guns to support Generals Pender and McGowan, who were heavily engaged. Lieutenant Ham Chamberlayne opened on the enemy with his two guns, firing over the heads of the Confederates, inflicting upon the Federal infantry heavy damage. At 5 A.M., on May 3, Colonel E. P. Alexander, acting chief of artillery, called on Pegram for two batteries and Captain R. C. M. Page's battery to deliver an oblique fire on the Federal batteries with telling success, exploding several ammunition chests, killing a number of men and horses and driving the gunners from their guns.

About this time more guns joined Pegram—Colonel Alexander's own battalion under Major Huger—and Willie concentrated the fire of about 25 pieces on a large Union infantry force which emerged from some woods on Pegram's front. "A murderous fire was kept up on them," Pegram reported, "killing and wounding a very large number until our infantry came up on their flanks, and we drove them entirely off from this position."

Once during the action, his eyes gleaming with excitement through his spectacles, Major Pegram turned to Colonel E. P. Alexander and exclaimed: "A glorious day, Colonel, a glorious day!"[29]

By now Pegram had about 40 guns under his command. When three of his batteries expended their ammunition, he sent them to the rear to refill their chests and moved forward with one of his own batteries and the battalions of Carter and McIntosh to the position from which he had just driven the Federals. Major Pegram now opened heavily upon the enemy near the Chancellor house. "After a heavy cannonading of an hour, during which time we inflicted a heavy loss on the enemy, suffering but slightly ourselves, we succeeded in driving them entirely off the field." reported Pegram. "They left several guns and caissons on the field."

After this spirited fight, Colonel Lindsay Walker resumed command of his battalion, but that night he became ill and once again Willie Pegram was in charge. On May 4, the Federals opened with about eighteen guns on Pegram's position, but Willie's gunners replied immediately and silenced them. His guns remained in position until the Federals retreated. The great battle of Chancellorsville was over for the young cannoneer.

The battalion lost heavily, with 33 men killed and wounded, but it performed conspicuously in the eyes of its youthful temporary commander. "Throughout this series of engagements both officers and men have acted with great gallantry," Pegram reported. "The firing was the best I have ever seen."

Pegram's superiors had reason to think so too. Lee in his report noted the officers and men of the artillery were "deserving especial commendation." Colonel E. P. Alexander included Pegram by name among those to whom he felt a "deep obligation" for "earnest and efficient cooperation." He also singled out Major Pegram and Lieutenant Ham Chamberlayne as "due the credit of the first footing in the field on the right." General A. P. Hill reported that in giving credit for the victory at Chancellorsville "much is due the artillery." But perhaps the best praise of all for Major Pegram, came from some of his gallant boy-gunners. "Willy Pegram distinguished himself greatly," Lieutenant Chamberlayne wrote his mother after the battle. And Lieutenant John Munford wrote his cousin Sallie Munford:

"I expect by this time you have heard all about the last battle, well as usual we had our share of it, and were complimented by Maj. Pegram, he said he never saw men behave better or guns handled with such effect. This was the first battle Major Pegram commanded us in, he was everywhere on the field, encouraging and cheering the men to their duty, he is the bravest and noblest fellow I ever saw, has won the confidence & esteem of the whole command . . . Present my compliments to Mrs. Pegram when you see her & tell her Willie is the adoration of this Batt:

& of all who know him & if he had his deserts he would have three stars on his collar instead of one."

Chancellorsville always remained the high spot in Willie Pegram's mind, the thrill of his first command ever remaining vivid. Many months later, after many other fights, some of the young officers were amusingly discussing the happiest day of their lives.

"Well," someone asked Pegram, "what day do you reckon your happiest?"

"Oh!" replied Willie promptly, "the day I had sixty guns [he had about 40] under me at Chancellorsville, galloping down the turnpike after Hooker and his people."[30]

VII

The joy of Lee's great victory over Hooker was dampened by the death of Stonewall Jackson, who had been wounded in the dusk on May 2, 1863, when his own men mistook his party for Federals.

Throughout the army, there was unrestrained grief when word came on May 10 from Guiney Station, where Jackson had been taken, that Stonewall was dead.

In a letter on May 11, 1863, to his sister Mary, Willie wrote:

"There is quite a gloom over the army today, at the news of Jackson's death. We never knew how much we all loved him until he died.

"His death will not have the effect of making our troops fight any worse. Besides being the bravest troops in the world, they have the most unbounded confidence in their *great leader* Genl. Lee. It is feared that the Yankee troops will fight better, since they will not hear any more that Jackson is in their rear . . . Our troops will fight well under any body. Fortunately with us, the soldiers make the officers, & not the officers the soldiers."

In the same letter Willie reported that "every one here looks to A. P. Hill as the man to fill his place, & after he once gets a show, the enemy will fear him as much as they ever feared Jackson."

Pegram was not wrong in his forecast for when Lee reorganized his army three weeks after Chancellorsville, Lieutenant General James Longstreet retained I Corps, Dick Ewell was promoted to lieutenant general and placed in command of Jackson's II Corps. A new III Corps was created and A. P. Hill, on May 24, was also promoted to lieutenant general and named its commander. Hill promptly nominated Colonel Lindsay Walker as his chief of artillery and on June 2, Major Willie Pegram took permanent command of Walker's old battalion now known as Pegram's Battalion.[31]

Early in June, Lee moved from the Rappahannock with the I and II Corps, his destination Pennsylvania. Hill's III Corps remained temporarily to face Hooker's whole army at Fredericksburg. Pegram's Battalion was camped at Hamiltons Crossing when, on June 11, Willie came down with a high fever. Taken to the home of a Mr. Marye at the Crossing, Major Pegram was quite ill for several days and when he recovered he was permitted to go to his home in Richmond to recoup his strength.

On June 16, Hill pulled his III Corps out of Fredericksburg and picking up Lee's trail followed the army across the Potomac and into Pennsylvania. As the battalion marched along, Major Pegram's young officers thought a lot about him and hoped he wouldn't miss the fun. On June 23, from near Berryville, Lieutenant Ham Chamberlayne wrote his mother: "Give my love to Willy P. I hope he will be here shortly." Two days later from Shepherdstown, he wrote again: "Let me know always how Willy P. is and let him know when you hear from me, where we are—He must be anxious to hear . . . Tell him we need him, but he must be careful not to come before he is well: there is a stage . . . between Staunton and Winchester [and] he must come that way."[32]

Before those letters reached Richmond, Pegram was already on his way to join the army. He had left sometime prior to June 28 and, riding the last ninety miles in an ambulance, he had overtaken Hill's Corps at Cashtown, Pennsylvania, on June 30. Major Pegram was warmly received by his battalion and even General Lee, whom he encountered immediately upon his arrival, seemed pleased to see the young artillerist. A few moments later, Lee met A. P. Hill:

"General Hill," said Lee, "I have good news for you. Major Pegram is up."

"Yes," replied Hill, "that *is* good news."

When Willie heard of this from a member of Hill's staff, he was thrilled, because everyone knew that Robert E. Lee always weighed his words. Afterward, around a campfire, Major Pegram told Gordon McCabe that he valued, more than another star on his collar, those few words from the General of the Army and the General of his Corps.[33]

On July 1, 1863, at 5 A.M., Pegram's Battalion moved out of Cashtown toward Gettysburg, supporting General Heth's division. The battalion of his friend Major David McIntosh followed in support of General Pender. As Heth approached Gettysburg, he detected evidence that Federals in some force were in the town. Heth assumed it was mainly cavalry with perhaps a brigade or two of supporting infantry. When his column reached a ridge overlooking Willoughby Run, west of the town, Heth determined that the Federal force in and around Gettysburg was larger than he had anticipated and included artillery as well as cavalry and infantry. Heth formed his division in line of battle, brought up Pegram's guns and ordered Willie to fire at the Union cavalry videttes. Captain Marye's battery executed the order and thus Pegram's Battalion fired the opening shot of the Battle of Gettysburg. General Heth in his report erroneously states: "One of the first shots fired by Pegram mortally wounded Major General Reynolds, then in command of the force at Gettysburg." The gallant Reynolds, as competent as he was brave, was killed by a Confederate sharpshooter, not by artillery.

Heth soon became heavily engaged and Pender, who was marching behind him, came up and together they drove the Federals through the town. Pegram's Battalion continued actively engaged until the fighting ended. Heth, a great admirer of Willie Pegram, had high praise for Pegram's Battalion on the first day at Gettysburg. He reported:

"At the same time that it would afford me much gratification, I would be doing but justice to the several batteries of Pegram's battalion in mentioning the assistance they rendered during this battle . . . My thanks are particularly due to Major Pegram for his steady co-operation. He displayed his usual coolness, good judgment, and gallantry."

Early on the morning of July 2, Pegram's Battalion and the rest of the artillery took up position along Seminary Ridge. Pegram had 20 guns in his five batteries—ten Napoleons, four 10-pounder Parrotts, four 3-inch rifles, and two 12-pounder howitzers—and throughout the second day's fight, they were actively engaged. They fired at intervals on the Union line and when the Federals tried to concentrate their artillery on Lee's right, Pegram's guns delivered hot enfilading fire upon them.

On the third day at Gettysburg, July 3, 1863, when Pickett's charge swept up Cemetery Ridge and the high tide of the Confederacy lapped momentarily at its crest, Pegram's Battalion contributed to the terrific bombardment of the Union defenses preparatory to the grand assault. From 1 P.M., until Longstreet's reluctant, evasive signal to Pickett to advance, Pegram's guns roared. "The fire having been continued so long and with such rapidity," reported Colonel Walker, "the ammunition was almost exhausted."

With Pickett's repulse, the Battle of Gettysburg was over. Just how active Pegram's Battalion was may be gathered from the fact that his guns fired 3800 rounds during the three-day battle, more than half of the III Corps artillery's total. Pegram's Battalion lost heavily in horses during the Gettysburg campaign, but the official records show a discrepancy in the totals—in one place reporting 38 horses killed and in another 89.[34]

Lee began his dolorous retreat on July 4—a day of double celebration in the North, for even as Lee turned his defeated army back to the Potomac, Vicksburg, on the Mississippi, surrendered to U. S. Grant. By the next Fourth of July, Lee and Grant would be adversaries at the siege of Petersburg, after the bloodiest campaign of the war.

VIII

For more than six months the Army of Northern Virginia and the Army of the Potomac had faced each other on the Rapidan, but after Gettysburg it was as if both armies welcomed a chance to catch their breath.

Outside of a few skirmishes, some cavalry sorties and raids, very little fighting took place in Virginia in the fall of 1863. There was a sharp engagement at Bristoe Station in mid-October, but Pegram's Battalion took little or no part in it. In late November, Willie's guns were in place along Mine Run and while no decisive firing took place, there was, as General Hill reported, "some little artillery practice."

During the lull, Pegram got an unexpected trip to Richmond in early September. His health was much improved, thanks, he said, to the "fine country" where his battalion was in camp and the fact that the army was "faring better just now, than at any previous time." While Willie was in Richmond, part of Longstreet's Corps passed through, en route to Georgia to join Braxton Bragg. "There is a great deal of mystery about the movement but as Genl Lee seems to be at the bottom of it all, it must be right."

The army went into winter quarters in the general vicinity of Gordonsville and Pegram's Battalion camped near Cobham's and Lindsay's Depots on the Virginia Central Railroad in Albemarle County. Pegram wrote an interesting letter from camp on December 16, 1863, to his sister Mary, in which he told how he was going to consume the spare time that winter would provide:

"I look forward to passing the most of the time reading and studying. I have felt keenly during the past twelve months my ignorance, and shall, as far as possible, endeavor to make up for lost time. But I cannot entirely do this; for it will take several years after the war is over. If I can only keep my mind in training, so that when the war is over, I will not have a distaste for books, I shall think I am doing well."

Pegram revealed his awareness of the political implications of the campaign of 1864. "We must get a large number of men in the field by Spring, and have a successful campaign in the Summer and Fall," he wrote. "Lincoln's term of office and the power of the war party depends upon the campaign of 1864."[35]

In February 1864, Willie Pegram looked forward to leave in Richmond and he announced to his sister Mary that he intended to give himself up "entirely to pleasure" when he gets home. On his last leave, he was sick and concerned about his battalion, but things were different now. "I never felt more in the mood for recreation," he said, "for I don't think I have ever worked as hard in my life as during the past five months."

He told his sisters of the cares and anxieties of an artillery commander. The chief problem is the horses and keeping them up. "Mine, unfortunately, are at this time in low order, & I have lost many, owing to . . . an epidemic among them." What discouraged him most, Pegram said, was that "Genl. Lee regards the horses above everything else."

Major Pegram's letter reflected his usual impatience away from battle action:

"I am exceedingly tired of winter quarters and shall be delighted when the Spring campaign opens. I wish that when active operations once commence, they could continue until the war is brought to an end. Camp is getting to be insufferable. The music of a shell would be delightful. This idleness may have a good effect in disgusting all our soldiers with camp life, and make them more zealous to conquer the peace."

He feared, from reading the papers, that "Richmond must be getting fearfully corrupt." He would like to believe that the unseemly gaiety and corruption exists only among *parvenus* and newcomers, "but I am afraid that a great many formerly good people are being contaminated." He condemned the "bad taste and hard-hearted" conduct of half the community engaging in dances and festivities, while the other half are mourning for their friends. "I fear that God will not favor us as long as such is the case," he said. "I hope that the season of Lent will put a stop to it."

Willie told his sister of his disappointment that, when he recently proposed to his battalion to re-enlist, his old company, the Purcell Battery, refused. He wrote:

"Three companies did so. The fourth have to serve a year longer and would not do so until the end of that time. The fifth, the Purcell Battery, I am sorry to say, would not do so, with a few exceptions, on account of some dissatisfaction with some of their officers. I am still in hopes, however, that they will come around in a day or two. Men in the ranks are like children, and when they take up whims, it is hard to get them out of them. My battery is composed of three different companies, and I think this accounts for the dissatisfaction. They have an excellent set of officers. The old men that are left are all, I believe, in favor of reenlisting, and they all say that they will fight as hard for the cause as ever. I shall certainly give them the first opportunity for showing this."[36]

On March 12, 1864, Ulysses S. Grant became Commander in Chief of the Union Armies and immediately made plans for a powerful offensive against Lee in the forthcoming spring and summer. Two days after Grant was made a lieutenant general, Major Willie Pegram was made a lieutenant colonel. The long-awaited action that Willie craved was soon to come. On May 4, Pegram's Battalion marched out of winter quarters into the most furious month's fighting of the war—the Wilderness, Spotsylvania, the North Anna, Cold Harbor. Grant, with his overwhelming numbers, kept hurling fresh troops into the fight. Lee, with consummate skill, parried Grant's blows and thwarted every attempt for a break-through.

For the artillery, this meant almost ceaseless action. Jennings C. Wise, whose *The Long Arm of Lee* is the artillery classic on the Civil War, pointed out:

"From the day of the rapid concentration of Artillery along the Rapidan on the 5th of May, there was never an hour when every battery of Lee's Army was not either in position, in immediate support, or on the march and actually with the infantry divisions. Not one single instance of delay in the movement of the Artillery, or of a single battery, has been encountered, for the simple reason that the leaders the war had developed, always enabled the batteries to be in the first line."[37]

Pegram's Battalion was constantly engaged in the long shifting slugging match over wild and tangled terrain. His guns blazed in support of Longstreet's counterattack on May 6 in the Wilderness. And when the Federals tried to drive through a gap between two of the Confederate corps, Pegram's batteries "assisted materially in driving back the enemy." Several days later, Pegram's Battalion, several hundred yards from the courthouse at Spotsylvania, cooperated vigorously with Confederate cavalry until Lee's line could be stabilized.

When major action lulled, there were constant skirmishes and frequent sudden charges by the Federals which had to be met by ready artillery fire. On May 10, the Federals made a demonstration on the Confederate right, but the battalions of Pegram and Cutts "opened on them with vigor and speedily drove them back to the cover of their trenches." So day after day, week after week, from May 5 to June 18, 1864, when Lee established his line around Petersburg and Grant began the 10-months investment of the city, Pegram and all the artillerymen were almost constantly in action.[38]

IX

In the trenches at Petersburg, Willie Pegram saw more of the man everyone in the army idolized—General Robert E. Lee.

"My confidence in Genl. Lee increases daily, & I think our cause more than ever, under Providence, dependent upon him," Willie wrote his sister Mary on July 21, 1864. "He should certainly have entire control of all military operations throughout the Confederate States. In fact I should like to see him King or Dictator. He is one of the few great men who ever lived, who could be trusted."

Lee held the young artillerist in high regard, too. One day, in the fall of 1864, Major General Henry Heth pointed out to General Lee that one of his brigades was without a brigadier general and requested Lee to promote Lieutenant Colonel Pegram to that grade and put him in command of the brigade.

"He is too young—how old is Colonel Pegram?" Lee asked.

"I don't know, but I suppose about twenty-five," replied Heth.

"I think a man of twenty-five is as good as he ever will be," Lee declared. "What he acquires after that age is from experience; but I can't understand, when an officer is doing excellent service where he is, why should he want to change?"

After the war, Pegram's faithful friend and adjutant, Gordon McCabe, wrote to General Lee for information on the rumor that ran through the army that Pegram had been recommended in 1864 for a brigadiership, not only by General Heth but by General R. H. Anderson. Lee, from Lexington, replied on February 6, 1870:

"I do not recollect ever having rec'd recommendations from Gen'ls Anderson and Heth for the assignment of Colo. W. J. Pegram to the command of brigades in their Divisions. If I did, they were not denied for want of confidence in his ability, for no one in the Army had a higher opinion of his gallantry and worth than myself. They were conspicuous on every field . . . Col. Pegram had the command of a fine battalion of artillery, a service in which he was signally skillful, in which he delighted, and in which I understood he preferred to remain. I do not think under the circumstances that he could have considered the command of a brigade in 1865 as preferable to the position he held."[39]

Lee had plenty of opportunities to observe Willie Pegram at close range during the long siege at Petersburg. On August 11, Pegram and three of his batteries cooperated with Generals Heth and Billy Mahone in an attack on the Federals on the Weldon Railroad, three miles from Petersburg, and in three engagements, at Davis's house on August 19, at Poplar Spring Church on August 21, and at Reams' Station on August 25. "Success was marked on this occasion," General Pendleton, chief of artillery, reported, "and due in no small degree to the efficiency of Colonel Pegram and the good conduct of his officers and men." General Heth himself said: ". . . To Colonel Pegram I measuredly owned my success at Reams' Station." Pegram's friend, Ham Chamberlayne, wrote his mother that "in the last of these affairs . . . Willy Pegram especially distinguished himself & the arm which he directed."[40]

Frequent skirmishes and artillery exchanges took place as the siege wore on, but it wasn't until September 30, 1864, that Pegram was in the thick of things again. Sent to support an attack by Heth and Wilcox on the Federals opposite the Confederate right, Pegram established his batteries and then rode forward in the attack. As he advanced with the infantry he surveyed the field in case it should be possible for him to advance his guns.

Heavy Union support for their engaged line began slowly to push back McGowan's South Carolina brigade. Suddenly, Willie Pegram gave spur to his horse and galloping through the battle line he snatched the battle flag from the color bearer and drove his horse straight for the Federal lines. After he had ridden about 40 or 50 yards ahead, Pegram placed the staff in his stirrup and, turning in his saddle, shouted: "Follow me, men!" The Rebel yell on their lips, the South Carolinians surged forward and formed on the colors. Up to Pegram ran the young color bearer, tears in his eyes, crying out:

"Give me back my colors, Colonel! I'll carry them wherever you say!"

"Oh, I'm sure of that," smiled Pegram, handing the boy the battle flag. "It was necessary to let the whole line see the colors, that's the only reason I took them."

The next day, October 1, Willie Pegram suffered his second wound. As he rode along the skirmish line, a minié ball struck him in the leg, but he refused to leave the field. It was shortly after this that independently of each other Generals Heth and Anderson recommended Pegram be made a brigadier general. On Heth's recommendations, General A. P. Hill put an endorsement: "No officer in the Army of Northern Virginia has done more to deserve this promotion than Lieutenant Colonel Pegram."[41]

The report quickly spread. Ham Chamberlayne wrote his mother on October 31: "Willy Pegram will shortly be made Brigr Genl . . ." Pegram, in a letter to his mother on October 28, pledging the family to secrecy, revealed the news:

". . . I know it will gratify you, as much or more than it does me, because I feel confident of my unworthiness and the responsibility which I will have in case it goes through. General Archer recently died. Generals Heth & Hill have applied to have me made Brigadier General & placed in command of the Brigade.

"I think it very probable, however, that it will not meet with Gen. Lee's approval, on account of my age, and on account of his objection to irregular promotions, i.e. promoting . . . officers from one branch of the service into another. Gen. Heth told me this morning that he thought it would go through . . ."

That Pegram would have welcomed the promotion contrary to General Lee's assumption, even at the price of giving up his beloved artillery battalion, is evidenced by the length to which he went in discussing it with his mother. "If I do get it," he said, "I will take it with fear and trembling, trusting in God's guidance and mercy, and constantly praying to Him for help." He described the brigade in make up and size, said he anticipated trouble and work because of its "very bad state of discipline and organization," and cautioned his mother not to be disappointed "if Gen. Lee refuses to have me promoted. He will do whatever is for the good of the service and I had rather be in the ranks than have him do otherwise."

Willie's admiration and devotion to his brother, Brigadier General John Pegram, nine years his senior and a West Pointer, comes through in this letter to his mother:

". . . I sincerely hope that before I am promoted to that grade, if it is to be done, Brother will be made Major-Genl; for otherwise I shall not believe that they ever promoted according to merit. I know that he has as much military, and all other sense, in one minute, as I have in a year."[42]

In late January 1865, Willie was laid low with a slow, bilious fever and he was confined to his home in Richmond for several weeks. From the lines at Petersburg, Willie's brother John, sent news to cheer him up. On February 3, he wrote his mother: "I trust Willy is well, but if he is not, do not let him come back to the Army, for nothing is doing just at this time. Genl. Lee told me yesterday he sent Willy's name up for promotion in the Artillery, and expressed an earnest wish that Willy's health might be restored."

Three days later, on February 6, in a fight at Hatchers Run, General John Pegram was killed, a musket ball striking him near the heart. It was a terrific blow to the family—to General Pegram's bride of several weeks, the lovely Hettie Cary—and to Willie. The latter was back with his battalion in the last week in February, his heart still heavy over the death of his brother. "Whenever I meet anyone of Brother's friends, whom I have not seen, my grief breaks out afresh," he wrote his sister Mary. ". . . I do not like to annoy anyone here with expression of my grief, & it is such a relief to be able to give utterance to some one who sympathizes with it."

On March 10, Willie wrote his sister Jennie: "My commission of Colonel of Artillery has arrived at Army Hd. Qrs, and I will probably receive it tomorrow."[43]

The war was now entering its last phase and it was evident to anyone that Lee's thinning lines before Petersburg must inevitably break under Grant's relentless pressure. On March 30, Grant ordered Sheridan to seize Five Forks in an attempt to turn Lee's right and force him out of the Petersburg works and into the open, where the Federal superiority in numbers could have decisive consequence.

About 11 A.M. Pegram got orders to move with six of his guns to Lee's extreme right with Pickett's division to assist Fitz Lee, who was engaged with Sheridan's cavalry at Five Forks. About 4:30 P.M., Pegram reached Five Forks and went into camp. It was a cheerless night, with no food nor blankets and both men and horses were wet and cold and hungry.

On March 31, Pegram's guns moved out with the infantry and cavalry to Stony Creek, where a sharp engagement took place at the ford, which was successfully carried. Pegram, however, did not get into the action and at 2 A.M., on April 1, he was ordered back to Five Forks, arriving at the old camp at sunrise. Having nothing to eat, Pegram and Gordon McCabe took some of the corn from their horses' feed and parched it for breakfast. Pickett's men threw up breastworks along the White Oak Road and Pickett ordered Pegram to place three of his guns at the crossroads which gave the place its name, three on the right of the line.

At about 10:30 A.M. Federal cavalry appeared in front of Pickett's right and Pegram opened at once with his guns, the Union horsemen hurrying back into the woods from which they had emerged. Federal skirmishers now appeared and Pegram's three guns on the right tossed occasional shells among them. The sound of skirmishing toward the center of the line, brought Pegram riding up with McCabe at his side. He ordered the three guns at the forks to fire a few rounds and the skirmishing soon died down.

Pegram and McCabe then rode back to the right, dismounted and threw themselves on the ground under a tree to take a little rest. Willie Pegram had been in the saddle virtually 24 hours—he was exhausted, and soon fell asleep. McCabe was reading a Richmond newspaper, the cannoneers and troopers were lounging around, laughing and talking. The attack came with sharp suddenness at 4:30 P.M. and tremendous volleys of musketry indicated that the Federals had launched a determined drive on Five Forks. With the first blast, the men sprang to their posts. Colonel Willie Pegram and Gordon McCabe leaped to their saddles and galloped furiously toward the Confederate center. Pegram's three guns at the crossroads were already engaging the enemy, who were advancing in overwhelming numbers, their seven-shot Spencer repeating rifles keeping up a steady volley as they pushed on.

As Pegram and his young adjutant dashed up, the Federals in three or four lines of battle were only 50 yards from the guns. The Federal fire was terrific, but Pegram's gunners were exacting great toll from the advancing horde, delivering double canister at a rapid fire. Gordon McCabe recorded the dramatic moment:

"Our artillery officers were as cool as if on parade, and the men were serving their guns with a precision and rapidity beyond all praise. The enemy's loss must have been fearful. Their lines were masses, and we were pouring double canister into them at thirty yards, each gun three rounds to the minute. The officers saw that the odds were desperate and they did not grudge to expose themselves freely for the sake of example. But the men seemed scarcely to need it. There were no wild, irregular yells, as usual. It was grim, close, hot work, and I saw no man near the guns who seemed disposed to shirk his share of it."

Colonel Pegram, not yet twenty-four years old, rode up and down the line on his gray horse, encouraging the men, heedless of exposing himself. As the Federals moved closer, almost to the very guns, Pegram cried out: "Fire your canister low, men!" and a moment later he slumped from the saddle, shot through the left arm and side.

"Oh, Gordon," he cried, "I'm mortally wounded, take me from the field."

Young McCabe called for an ambulance, gave Pegram's last command to the battery, and then joined his wounded commander whom he loved as a brother. The Federals by now had gotten into the rear of the battery. McCabe ordered the ambulance driver to give whip to the horses as the vehicle careened between two parallel battle lines.

Grief-stricken, McCabe held Pegram in his arms to lessen the jolting of the ambulance. Once Willie took Gordon's hand and said: "Tell my mother and sisters that I commend them to God's protection."

He was in terrific pain and the doctor gave him some morphine. McCabe prayed audibly that Pegram's life be spared and he kissed him again and again. Once Willie broke in on Gordon's prayer: "If it is God's will to take me, I am perfectly resigned."

And then, when thoughts of home came to him, Willie repeated several times during the harrowing ride: "Give my love to Mother and both sisters and tell them I thought of them in my last moments."

The agony of it all, seeing the young man whom he loved, respected and emulated, sinking in his arms was too much for McCabe. They had been inseparable in camp and the respect, affection, and devotion were mutual. Pegram had once written his sister Mary: "I don't know any young man whom I admire altogether as much I do Gordon McCabe . . . His Christian character is beautiful."

McCabe cried out: " 'My God, my God, why hast thou forsaken me!' "

Pegram quickly protested: "Don't say that, Gordon, it isn't right."

"Willie," sobbed McCabe, "I never knew how much I loved you until now."

"But I did," replied Pegram, pressing McCabe's hand.

For ten interminable miles the ambulance rattled to Fords Depot on the Southside Railroad, Gordon McCabe easing Pegram's discomfort the best he could, and praying ceaselessly, while Willie responded with an occasional "Amen."

At 10 P.M., McCabe found a bed for Willie in the home of a Mr. Pegram, no doubt a distant kinsman of the dying artillerist. About midnight, when McCabe heard that the Yankees were approaching, he sent off their horses, sabers, and spurs to prevent them from being captured.

Pegram begged for morphine and McCabe, who had gotten some from the doctor before he left, administered it and Willie fell asleep. McCabe dressed his friend's wounds, moistened his lips and caressed him in sorrow as the hours ticked off. As Sunday morning broke, Willie Pegram died peacefully.

Gordon McCabe helped to dig Willie Pegram's grave, laid him out in his uniform and wrapped the body in a blanket and as it was commended to the earth he read over his friend the Order for the Burial of the Dead of the Protestant Episcopal Church.

And then, as some Union soldiers appeared and began firing at him, Gordon McCabe leaped upon a horse that was in the yard and galloped off to join Lee's army on the road to Appomattox.[44]

6

The Peevish Commissary:

COLONEL LUCIUS B. NORTHROP

I

IT CAN be said with little chance of contradiction that barely more than three people in the entire Confederacy had a kind word for the Commissary General, Colonel Lucius B. Northrop. One of these was Mrs. Northrop, the second was Jefferson Davis, and the third was Northrop himself.

Practically everybody else in or out of the Southern army blamed Northrop for most of the ills visited upon the Confederacy during the Civil War. And even the South's "solitary sainted figure," as Carl Sandburg once called Robert E. Lee, lost patience with the peevish commissary.

Colonel Northrop was unquestionably one of the three most detested of President Davis's appointees, but whether he outranked Judah P. Benjamin or Braxton Bragg in this respect must remain a matter of conjecture, tinctured with personal preference.

It is a fact, however, that Northrop got the jump on all potential challengers for the dubious honor of being the Confederacy's most despised figure. In August 1861, while the South still basked in the glory of the rout of the Yankees at Manassas, Mary Boykin Chesnut penned in her diary: "If I were to pick out the best-abused man in Richmond, now when all catch it so bountifully, I should say Mr. Commissary General Northrop was the most cursed and vilified. He is held accountable for everything that goes wrong in the Army."[1]

Northrop's task, under the most favorable conditions, would have made him, and perhaps any other man, a target for criticism. In the face of a shortage of funds, a depreciated currency, the early loss of food-producing territory and a poor transportation system steadily deteriorating under the attrition of war, the job of feeding the Confederate armies was a tremendous one. But to his assignment, Northrop brought a petulant personality, a jealous regard of every suggestion as interference, and an unswerving faith in his own infallibility. These added only fuel to the forensic flames sparked in the Confederate Congress against him and gave proof to popular opinion that the Commissary General was an incompetent, holding office only because he was President Davis's "pet."

Congressman Henry S. Foote of Tennessee denounced Northrop in Congress and out, calling him "coarse, overbearing . . . insulting . . . austere, crabbed . . . irritating . . . utterly ignorant of the duties of the post assigned him," and he said that in Charleston before the war, the impression was general that Northrop was "more or less disordered in mind." Although not prepared to "assert anything in regard to his pecuniary honesty," Foote employed a guilt-by-association technique in charging the Commissary General with engaging men of "notoriously bad character" as his purchasing agents. Foote condemned Northrop's "heartless tyranny . . . in connection . . . with impressment" and his "brutal indifference to the sufferings of Confederate soldiery," and summed him up as a "monster of iniquity."[2]

One would be inclined to dismiss Foote's demagogic invective as stemming from his utter detestation of Jefferson Davis and consider that the white-hot bolts of abuse fired at Northrop were in reality aimed at the President himself. But the violent opinions that the intemperate Congressman from Tennessee expressed so venomously were generally held throughout the South, both in and out of the Army, albeit not so vehemently.

The evidence is strong that Northrop was irascible, obstinate, condescending, fault-finding, contentious, secretive, indirect, eccentric. He quarreled with nearly every general in the Confederate Army and early in the war he developed for Generals P. G. T. Beauregard and Joseph E. Johnston a bitter hatred, the fires of which were still flaming almost thirty years after the war when Northrop went to his grave.

"This strange man, though he had the full confidence of Mr. Davis, had the singular faculty of keeping every army commander in a state of constant indignation," wrote Douglas Southall Freeman, biographer of Robert E. Lee. "He is, in fact, one of the few functionaries of the period whose letters . . . irritate if they do not actually outrage the historian. Convinced that his own methods were right and were thwarted by the stupidity or opposition of the generals in the field, he took refuge in interminable letters of explanation when he was asked why the army was starving. He seemed satisfied if he could demonstrate that he was on record as predicting what had come to pass. By his own enigmatic code, he had rather be consistent than efficient."[3]

But, despite all criticism of Northrop's administration, Jefferson Davis, with stubborn loyalty, retained him as Commissary General until the dying days of the Confederacy, when Robert E. Lee's voice, added to the general clamor, effected his removal.

Years later, when Davis's *The Rise and Fall of the Confederate Government* was published, Davis was still singing Northrop's praises as "a man of rare capacity and character" who administered the Subsistence Department with "practical sense and incorruptible honesty." He was, wrote Davis against a body of contrary evidence, "an able officer" with "well directed efforts . . ."[4]

II

Lucius Bellinger Northrop was born in Charleston, South Carolina, on September 8, 1811, and grew up in "an atmosphere of genteel poverty." When he was still quite young his planter-lawyer father died and his mother, with not much success, continued to operate the family plantation.

When Northrop was fifteen, John C. Calhoun, a family friend, secured for him an appointment to West Point, which he entered in July 1827. His career at the Military Academy could not be considered as brilliant for he was graduated twenty-second in a class of thirty-three in 1831 and his conduct standing among the entire corps of 219 cadets was 151st.[5]

At the time of his appointment as Commissary General of the Confederacy it was common gossip in Richmond that the only reason Jefferson Davis had appointed Northrop was that they had been classmates at West Point. Colonel Ambrosio José Gonzales, chief of staff of the ill-starred Narciso López in Cuba a decade earlier, wrote angrily to Davis on not being awarded a Confederate brigadier generalship, asserting that he probably would have gotten it had he been, as Northrop, Davis's classmate at West Point. Davis in a sharp note inquired who Colonel Gonzales was quoting as regards his West Point relationship with Northrop. Gonzales replied that he was quoting "the public voice only."

The truth is that Jefferson Davis was graduated from the Military Academy in 1828 and, accordingly, not only were the President and the Commissary General not former classmates, but they were together at West Point only one year. There is little reason to suppose that a warm friendship developed between a graduating cadet and a first-year man. One will have to look further for what Congressman Foote was pleased to call "the mysterious circumstances . . . (which) in some way, many years previous to the commencement of the war, established relations of special amity and consideration" between the two.[6]

Graduating as a brevet second lieutenant of infantry, Northrop first saw some service in the Seminole trouble. In 1833, Northrop transferred to the 1st Dragoons and was sent to Fort Gibson, in the Cherokee Nation, on the Western frontier. There he renewed his acquaintance with Lieutenant Jefferson Davis in 1834, but once again the two were not thrown together for a long period, for in 1835 Davis resigned from the Army.

On October 6, 1839, there began a chain of events which ultimately interested Davis, a decade later, in Northrop's career, and undoubtedly led to the close relations which induced the Confederate President to name Northrop the Commissary General. By the accidental discharge of his own pistol Northrop was severely wounded, the ball lodging in his knee, thus rendering him unfit for active duty.

Northrop remained on the inactive list for almost three years, turning in each month a certificate of disability and drawing his army pay. In July of 1842, his leg having improved, Northrop called on Adjutant General Roger Jones in Washington and asked for some duty adapted to his crippled condition until such time as he was able to rejoin his regiment. In October 1842 he was made an assistant commissary in the Subsistence Department and served in that capacity for six and a half months, from October 7, 1842, to May 24, 1843.

Obviously acting in good faith to give some services to the Army, Northrop was surprised to receive, on November 27, 1842, orders from the Adjutant General to report to his regiment at Fort Leavenworth "if able to perform any military duty" or to report monthly his condition as required by the regulations. What had happened was that Northrop's colonel, having noted his return to active duty, applied for him. "Because I could not do dragoon duty, I was by order stopped from trying any other," Northrop later wrote.

On December 6 and 7, 1843, Northrop addressed two letters to Adjutant General Jones, restating his case and declaring it was repugnant to him to be a burden on the service. He stated that he was determined to acquire another profession and asked for three years to qualify himself as a physician. On December 11, permission was granted, with the War Department seemingly understanding that at the expiration of the three years Northrop would resign from the Army if he could not resume his regimental duties. This, however, does not appear to have been Northrop's understanding.

Northrop studied medicine at Jefferson Medical College in Philadelphia, and then returned to Charleston to practice, all the while submitting his monthly certificates of disability.

On November 24, 1847, in a special report to Secretary of War William L. Marcy, the Adjutant General stated the facts in Lieutenant L. B. Northrop's case. He then pointed out that after nearly ten months had elapsed since the expiration of the three years, no word had come from Northrop other than his monthly disability certificates. Whereupon the Adjutant General had written Northrop on September 21, 1847, asking whether he intended to join his company or resign from the service. Northrop's reply was at variance with the Adjutant General's impression and that of the General-in-Chief "that Lieutenant Northrop would voluntarily leave the service at the expiration of the three years allowed him to obtain another profession, if he were then unfit for active military duty."[7]

Secretary Marcy read the report and, on January 8, 1848, authorized the dropping of Lieutenant Northrop from the Army rolls. It was then that Northrop appealed to his West Point schoolmate and fellow officer in the 1st Dragoons, Jefferson Davis, now a brand-new Senator from Mississippi, who, fortuitously for Northrop, had been made a member of the Military Affairs Committee.

On January 19, 1848, Senator Davis asked the Adjutant General for the facts and, having studied them, he talked to Secretary of War Marcy in Northrop's behalf. Apparently, he made no headway, for on May 5, 1848, he wrote Marcy:

"Some time since I called your attention to the case of Lieut. L. B. Northrop, 1st Dragoons, who was ordered to be dropped from the service. I stated to you that I felt convinced that the case had not been understood, further inquiry convinced me that the decision is less justified than was even supposed by me at the date of our conversation . . . When under apprehension that he would not again be able to render service, he applied for three years leave of absence that he might apply himself to the study of medicine, and mentioned his intention if permanently crippled, to retire from the army, if he should recover, the knowledge gained was spoken of as adding to his future usefulness. This the Adj. General has most strangely construed into a contract by which Lieut. Northrop was to surrender his commission at a fixed time . . . I ask you to examine this case assured that you will find a gallant officer and an honorable man has been unjustly deprived of his commission and if you agree with me as to the merits of the case I trust you will show the error of the Adjt. Genl's construction to the President that he may rescind the order dropping Lieut. Northrop from the rolls of the Army."

When Davis got no satisfaction from the Secretary of War Marcy he took the matter up directly with President Polk on June 23, 1848, because "a sense of duty, of obligation to an injured friend requires it." He stated the facts to the President, satisfied that they "have not been justly presented to you." He declared:

"I presented the case to the Secty of War hoping that upon an examination of the case he would correct the error of the Adj. Genl's conclusion and that the orders would be annulled by which Lieut. Northrop was deprived of his position in the army. In this I have been disappointed, the answer of the Secty does not go beyond the report and correspondence of the Adj. Genl., consequently does not reach the matter at issue . . . The only peculiarity in Lieut. Northrop's [case from that of other disabled officers] is that he expressed his unwillingness to remain an useless charge upon the Army, and asked to be permitted to qualify himself for civil life, that he might resign if permanently disabled. But for this avowal prompted by a delicate sense of propriety he might have continued unquestioned to make his monthly reports and draw his monthly pay. . . .

"Lieut. Northrop's wound has not been healed, the ball lodged in the knee, & has affected his general health, and he is unable as he had hoped to support himself by the practice of medicine. I ask most earnestly that you examine this case, and confidently believe that you will find it just to rescind the order by which Lt. Northrop was dropped from the Army rolls, that he may resume his position, and receive the benefit of any provisions which may be made for officers retired from the Army on account of disability from wounds &c."

Two weeks later, on July 6, 1848, the voice of John C. Calhoun was added to that of Davis. From the Senate chamber, the South Carolinian penned an urgent request to President Polk to give "favorable consideration" to "this gallant, honorable and unfortunate officer."[8]

On August 12, 1848, Northrop got the good news. He not only was reinstated in the Army, but was promoted to captain as well. Northrop's boundless gratitude to Jefferson Davis never left him and his loyalty, friendship, and devotion were evidenced throughout the Civil War and the long, bitter years that followed.

During the next dozen years, Captain Northrop continued as a disabled officer, at the same time practicing medicine in Charleston to help provide for his family. He had married in 1841 Maria Euphemia Joanna de Bernabeu, daughter of the Spanish Consul at Charleston, and by 1860, they had six living children.

When his native South Carolina led the parade of Southern states out of the Union on December 20, 1860, Lucius Bellinger Northrop was a man of some substance, owning property worth $65,000. He apparently had made a success as a physician, despite later scornful comments of his enemies that he was a "vegetarian" and a "pepper doctor."[9]

III

On January 8, 1861, less than three weeks after South Carolina seceded, Captain Northrop resigned from the United States Army. Six days earlier, he had written a friend that he intended to take that step. "The Govt is virtually exploded *now*," he wrote, "and a southern confederacy is the only hope of order now left." His old friend, Jeff Davis, he said, was "the man the time & the occasion [required] as leader of the South."

Less than a month later, the Confederate States of America came into being at Montgomery with Jefferson Davis as the provisional president. One of Davis's early acts was the commissioning of Northrop as a lieutenant colonel and assigning him to the Subsistence Department. On March 27, Northrop was named Acting Commissary General; on June 21, he was promoted to colonel and Commissary General, both rank and title to date from March 16, 1861.

Northrop, seemingly, had to be persuaded to take the post, for Davis, in their postwar correspondence, wrote him: "I remember that you did not want to be Commissary General, and I still think it was good for the country that you did not have your own way."

It is clear, however, that Secretary of War Leroy Pope Walker did not see eye to eye with Davis on Northrop's appointment, or, at least, at the time he considered it only a temporary one. On April 9, 1861, he wrote Captain William Maynadier of the United States Army in Philadelphia, offering him the post of Commissary General in the Confederacy. Maynadier could not reconcile "the dictates of conscience, of honor, and of duty" with the offer and turned it down. Northrop, of course, knew nothing of this, for not many weeks later he assured Catholic Bishop Patrick N. Lynch of Charleston that "I jog along pretty well, and have my own way. Mr. Walker understands me and is an upright straight forward man not because he understands me however."¹⁰

Northrop prepared for the Secretary of War estimates of appropriations for the Subsistence Department, and the Confederate Congress appropriated $5,464,258.80 for the purchase of subsistence stores and commissary property for 100,000 troops during the fiscal year ending February 1862.

The Commissary General became incensed when by mid-May bills began to pour in for meals served troops traveling by railroad to the various theaters of war and he refused to honor most of them. "I am making enemies as usual," he wrote Bishop Lynch, "for I am refusing to pay many bills that ought never to have been contracted." He complained that although troops were equipped with haversacks and canteens to carry cold provisions on the march, the officers have been letting them off to eat at railroad stations at the cost of fifty cents a meal. "Before long War at that rate had better be settled by just seeing who has the most money and the weakest purse submitting on a show of hands," he wrote.

Even before the war had fairly begun, before the Subsistence Department and the Commissary General became Congress' favorite targets, Northrop showed his contempt for the legislative branch of the Confederate government. "I wish Congress would vote an enormous money bill," he wrote on May 17, 1861, "and then adjourn and let Jeff Davis call them when the money fails or make him Dictator until the war was over." Eight months later when he was under Congressional fire, Northrop openly thumbed his nose at Congress: "I have had one sort of compensation & that was to tell the Congressmen that I cared not a snap of a finger for them or their commission. I told the Military Committee so repeatedly . . . and this has been the burden of my intercourse with them . . . The chairman . . . informed me of the nature of their report. I told him to remember distinctly that I never tried to conciliate one of them; he said that it was well understood. They have in Congress charged me with rudeness to them. I consider rudeness a crime but am glad that they do understand that if I am confirmed it is because they want me."[11]

Whatever early criticism was leveled at Northrop, it all added up to only a trifle compared to the abuse that was aimed at him following the Battle of Manassas on July 21, 1861. A question frequently asked throughout the South after the rout of the Yankees in the first big battle of war was: Why didn't the Confederates pursue the panic-stricken Federals to the gates of Washington?

The conclusion soon reached, from reports and rumors and letters from Manassas, was that a lack of food and transportation prevented a Confederate advance following their smashing victory. Mrs. Chesnut summed up the Richmond gossip in her diary entry for August 1: "They say Beauregard writes that his army is upon the verge of starvation . . . and now they say we did not move on right after the flying foe because we had no provisions, no wagons, no ammunition, and so on. Rain, mud, and Northrop; these restrained us."

General Beauregard sent a letter to W. Porcher Miles, complaining of the things the army at Manassas lacked and it was read in Congress. Whereupon Davis wrote a chiding letter to Beauregard: "Some excitement has been created by your letters. The quartermaster and the commissary generals both feel that they have been unjustly arraigned. As for myself, I can only say that I have endeavored to anticipate wants, and any failure which has occurred from imperfect knowledge might have been avoided by timely requisition and estimates."

General Joseph E. Johnston complained directly to Davis that the food situation at Manassas was intolerable, declaring that the army "never had a supply for more than two days, sometimes none."[12]

The complaints from the generals in the field, highly critical of Commissary General Northrop, not only caused sharp irritation in Richmond among President Davis, Secretary of War Judah P. Benjamin and Northrop himself, but proved the basis for the life-long hatred that the latter held for Beauregard and Johnston.

Strong denials, of course, came from Northrop and Quartermaster General A. C. Myers that they had been negligent in supplying the army. Joe Johnston, anxious to get the facts, organized a board of officers, composed of Major W. L. Cabell, representing the quartermaster's department; Lieutenant Colonel Robert B. Lee (a cousin of General Robert E. Lee), representing the commissary department; and Major John D. Imboden, representing the line.

Organized early in August, the board made an exhaustive investigation and a detailed report. It found that on the morning after the Battle of Manassas, there was not one full day's ration for the army and that on no single day during the next two weeks was there as much as a three-day supply of food. The board concluded that there were insufficient wagons and teams to have transported three days' rations for the troops. It found that General Beauregard for weeks before the battle had been "urgent and almost importunate" in his demands on the quartermaster and commissary general for adequate supplies. In conclusion, the officers found that "Colonel Northrop . . . had not only failed to send forward adequate supplies for such an emergency as arose when General Johnston brought his army from the Valley, but that he had interfered with and indicted the efforts of officers of the department who were with Beauregard to collect supplies from the rich and abundant region lying between the hostile armies."

After stating the facts, the board unanimously agreed that they proved that the immediate pursuit of the fleeing Federals on July 21 was impossible. Several days after the report had been forwarded to Richmond, it was returned by Secretary of War Benjamin with an endorsement to the effect that the board had exceeded its powers in expressing an opinion on what the facts did or did not prove and ordered curtly that the opinion be removed and the facts only be returned to the War Department.

"We met and complied with this order, though indignant at the reprimand, and returned our amended report," wrote Imboden. "This was the last I ever heard of it. It never saw daylight. Who suppressed it I do not know."[13]

That may have been the last Major Imboden heard of it, but it wasn't the last for Lieutenant Colonel Robert B. Lee. After twenty days' service as Chief Commissary of the army at Manassas he was superseded by an officer of inferior rank on August 10. Lee's written request for the causes of his removal elicited from Northrop the information that he was sending Lee's letter to the Secretary of War. Colonel Lee then wrote Adjutant General Cooper asking for an investigation of his removal "after a brief service of twenty days." A penciled endorsement, uninitialed, on Colonel Lee's letter states: "Investigation refused. No charges were made agt the officer and no right is recognized in a subordinate to require reasons for the action of Superior officer in assigning him to duty or removing him from duty."[14]

Colonel Northrop, meanwhile, had come to his own defense in a letter to President Davis on August 21, 1861. He asserted that meat, which took twenty to thirty days to get from Nashville to Richmond, was spoiled in the closed freight cars. As for the Manassas situation, he claimed that "plenty of provisions were awaiting transportation" in Richmond, while there were "plenty of cars at the other end detained as is alleged, for 'storing baggage' and as 'store houses' . . ." The Commissary General painted a dark picture of the future: "The real evil is ahead. There are not enough hogs in the Confederacy sufficient for the Army, and the larger force of plantation negroes. Hence competition must be anticipated by arranging for the purchase of the animals and getting the salt to cure them. Furthermore, beeves must be provided for the comeing [sic] Spring; cattle must be collected from Texas before the rains set in, and be herded in ranging grounds convenient to the Mississippi."

Not quite a month later, the question of the holding of boxcars at Manassas came up again and President Davis, on September 18, 1861, telegraphed General Joe Johnston: IT IS REPORTED THAT CARS ARE DETAINED AT MANASSAS FOR STORAGE, SO AS TO RENDER IT IMPOSSIBLE TO FORWARD FROM THIS PLACE SUPPLIES FOR YOUR COMMAND. Secretary of War Benjamin followed this telegram with a letter pointing out "the necessity of promptly discharging and returning the cars of the railroad company as soon as they can be unloaded."

There were two enclosures in Benjamin's letter to Johnston, one from Colonel Northrop stating that a thousand barrels of flour had been requested to be sent to Manassas from Richmond but that "the Central Railroad writes that it is impossible to transport the flour." The second enclosure, from the railroad agent, stated why: "The Confederate States have all our cars at Manassas and Millsborough. We cannot get them back. We have only two cars now in Richmond. Our depot is blocked up. If you send the flour today we shall be compelled to store it out of doors, and the Confederate States must take the risk."

General Johnston wired back that the cars were never unnecessarily detained at Manassas, whereupon the Secretary of War wrote Quartermaster General Myers to make an immediate investigation and report. "The contradictory statements now reported to me officially demand that I should know which of the officers has made a report unfounded on fact."

On September 21, Myers reported "as far as I can discover, there is a mistake in the report of the detention at Manassas. The Superintendent of the Central Railroad in his reply . . . concludes with these words: 'I have been misinformed.'"

"You have ascertained that the blame was not attributable to the officer at Manassas," Benjamin replied. "Who was the delinquent, I must insist that the investigation be pursued until the question is satisfactorily answered."

Meanwhile General Johnston had presented substantial proofs to Davis that the charge was untrue and he sent copies to Benjamin on September 22 with "the hope that they may convince you that the negligence with which we are charged does not exist." Benjamin replied: "I was gratified to ascertain before receiving your reply that there was no truth in the assertion that the delay was caused by the detention of the cars at Manassas . . ."

Colonel Northrop, inasmuch as he had launched this hassle, surely must have known that the War Department had absolved Joe Johnston completely. Yet, years later, in correspondence with Jefferson Davis, on at least two occasions, he repeated the charge of loaded railroad cars standing idle at Manassas for weeks.[15]

IV

Before 1861 was out, the Commissary General had developed a feud with Generals Johnston and Beauregard; had brought upon himself and his department a Congressional investigation; had embroiled himself with General John H. Winder on the question of feeding prisoners of war; had already begun to have his war-long difficulties with the Treasury Department in the matter of getting cash for foodstuffs; had established two packing plants in Virginia; and had proposed purchasing salt meat behind Union lines, a suggestion upon which Mr. Davis frowned.

Northrop's feud with Johnston and Beauregard lasted until the breath left his body. To his dying day they both were "charlatans" and "scoundrels" and "paltry fellows" and Johnston was a "calumniator" and Beauregard "the vainest liar I have met." Johnston's book was "contemptible trash," and Beauregard's book "a tissue of calumnies and false pretenses . . ."

The Commissary General successfully weathered the Congressional investigation, the report of which, presented on January 29, 1862, declared:

". . . We have had our Army well fed, and with an amount on hand, so large as to place us beyond the reach of want for the ensuing campaign, and trusting in a kind Providence for our usual seasons and the preparations that are made throughout the Confederacy for the next crop, we need fear no coming want."[16]

At regular intervals Northrop's bête noire, Henry S. Foote, would call for other investigations of Northrop and the Commissary Department, but Northrop survived them all until the closing weeks of the war.

When Northrop was appealed to for food for the Yankee prisoners taken at Manassas, his response was: "Chuck the scoundrels in the river." However, after the responsibility for feeding Federal prisoners of war had been passed around the various bureaus it finally came to rest permanently in the office of the Commissary General and the "scoundrels," despite their own disbelief, were fed just about as well as the Confederate soldiers. On two occasions in May 1863, and in March 1865—

charges of mistreatment and starvation of Yankee prisoners were investigated and proved groundless.

As early as August 19, 1861, Northrop complained to Secretary of War Walker that "The efforts of this department, hitherto successful, will be abortive unless funds of a character such as will be received by dealers are furnished from the Treasury."[17]

Making full allowances for Northrop's personality quirks and his constant irritation of generals in the field and members of Congress, it is very evident that even a man of unchallenged ability and amiable disposition would have found his job almost an impossible one.

The stringency of the blockade, the inadequacy from the beginning of the Confederate rail system which steadily deteriorated during the War, the loss of food-producing areas in the West, the depreciation of Confederate currency and the difficulty of getting it to the Commissary Department's purchasing agents in the field provided Northrop with one headache after another.

The loss of Middle and West Tennessee in the late winter of 1862, preceded by the destruction of huge amounts of supplies at Forts Henry and Donelson, Bowling Green, Columbus and Nashville, deprived the Commissary General of an important source of food. And the fall of New Orleans in late April all but cut off sugar and molasses, Texas beef, and Louisiana salt from Northrop's access.

Northrop was now desperate for cash. "Unless my requisitions can be filled promptly and to an adequate amount in current funds, not bonds (which latter are at a heavy discount)," Northrop wrote the Secretary of War on April 29, 1862, "it will be almost if not absolutely impossible for this department to feed the armies of the Confederacy."

Procedures of the Treasury Department were indeed exasperating, as Northrop had quite properly pointed out to the Secretary of War many months earlier:

"The delay which sometimes occurs before an officer can use the funds called for could without injury be prevented. A requisition being made from this office—for an officer—it goes through the War & Treasury Depts and a Warrant is sent to the Officer, if he happens not to be where there is an assistant Treasurer. He has to endorse the Warrant and send back to the Treasurer before the notes are sent to him—or bonds . . ."

Northrop, in the spring of 1862, still chafed under the Treasury Department's rule that requisitions be paid half in bonds and half in Treasury notes. At his instigation, Secretary of War Randolph wrote President Davis: "As the very existence of our armies is involved . . . I respectfully submit that a larger proportion of Treasury notes should be issued, or that authority be obtained for the Secretary of the Treasury to sell the bonds at their market price and current funds be furnished to the Commissary Department. The impossibility of using bonds of larger denominations in the purchase of livestock, and the evils of making every commissary and contractor an agent for the sale of Government stocks, are shown clearly . . ."[18]

At this time, Colonel Northrop found himself again embroiled with Johnston and Beauregard, now separated by the width of the Confederacy. Ironically, whereas the first bone of contention of the generals had been the lack of food at Manassas, Johnston now complained that "the accumulation of subsistence stores at Manassas is now a great evil." The withdrawal of the Confederate Army from the line of Bull Run to that of the Rappahannock River had been contemplated for some time and Johnston asserted that more than once the Commissary General had been requested to suspend shipments. Johnston also complained that the meat-packing plant Northrop had established at Thoroughfare had become "a great encumberance." He stated that much commissary supplies would have to be sacrificed in the contemplated movement.

President Davis replied, urging Johnston to furnish definite information as to his plans of withdrawal, so that "the subsistence stores should, when removed, be placed in position to answer your future wants." He added that the Commissary General had previously stopped further shipments to Johnston's army and "gives satisfactory reasons" for establishing the packing plant at Thoroughfare.

When Johnston pulled back from Manassas, early in March 1862, vast commissary supplies were destroyed. At the meat-packing plant, Northrop years later told Davis, preparations well in advance were made to remove the goods. Platforms, level with the car doors, were built along the tracks and the meat was piled high waiting for transportation, which Johnston had promised but which never came. And so the torch was put to 2,000,000 pounds of cured meat and hides and oil from more than 11,000 beeves. The Commissary General told Mr. Davis he believed Joe Johnston "*wanted* the public property to be destroyed both at Manassas and Thoroughfare . . ."

Northrop's memory was bad, apparently, for Major B. P. Noland, his agent at Thoroughfare, reported in March 1862 that 369,819 pounds of meat were given away and destroyed before the plant was abandoned, and only 500 hides were burned.[19]

The Commissary General's trouble with Beauregard began after the Battle of Shiloh and his own vindictiveness had a lot to do with initiating it. Beauregard's Chief Commissary was Lieutenant Colonel Robert B. Lee, the same officer who had been Chief Commissary at Manassas and who had been summarily removed by Northrop after participating on the board that reported critically upon the Subsistence Department and its chief. On April 16, 1862, Beauregard complained to Adjutant General Cooper about the Commissary General's treatment of Colonel Lee:

"I fear that Colonel Northrop, Chief of the Subsistence Department, is disposed or determined to ignore the presence with these headquarters of Lieutenant Colonel Lee, of his department, the officer next in rank in it to himself, and one of the largest experience in our service, sent here, as you are aware, on my application, because of that experience. Circumstances convince me that I am not mistaken, and that unless Colonel Northrop is led to change his course the service and the country will suffer. His attempts to communicate directly with subordinates of Colonel Lee and not to communicate at all with Colonel Lee are palpably disrespectful to the authority that sent the colonel to my staff as well as to me, and I trust Colonel Northrop will be brought to understand this before he can do any material mischief."[20]

Beauregard won his point and Colonel Northrop began to address his messages to Colonel Lee, but one so directed on April 29 started another argument. Beauregard had just prepared a general order regulating the subsistence of his army, when a telegram from the Commissary General came reducing the daily ration to half a pound of bacon or pork and one pound of beef, and no more than one and a half pounds of flour or corn. This was well below the ration prescribed by Beauregard. "In the name of my men I must respectfully but urgently protest against such a reduction of the substantial part of the ration," he wrote Adjutant General Cooper. ". . . I shall carry out the orders inclosed until otherwise instructed by the War Department."

Beauregard, of course, had simply ignored the Commissary General's reduction of the ration, sent in the name of the Secretary of War, and he had tossed the matter right back onto the latter's desk. On May 27, Beauregard telegraphed his reasons for not complying with the order, and Northrop, to whom the telegram was sent by Secretary Randolph, challenged the general on every point. The ration, which he had set and Beauregard had disregarded, was "sufficient for robust men at hard labor and is abundant for an army ration." Beauregard's claim that much of the salt meat was bad and that scurvy had broken out prompted a medical dissertation by the Commissary General on the relationship of salt to scurvy and he said Beauregard's reasons "are fatal to what they are intended to support." The general should cut out the meat and in the absence of vegetables, more bread should be given the men, as potash is the sole specific for scurvy. Beauregard's army was getting a ration larger than allowed by regulations and was being fed far better than the army in Virginia "which without a murmur acquiesces in the obvious necessity of curtailing the meat." On April 17, Beauregard's army had 1,300,000 half rations of coffee while the rest of the forces were without it. "General Beauregard has reiterated his apprehensions of starvation, while he gives actually more than the regulation ration or than is necessary," commented the Commissary General.[21]

V

His enemies to the contrary, the Commissary General did not just flounder around in his office purposelessly. He had a plan for operating the Subsistence Department, but whether he followed it faithfully is another thing. "This Bureau has been conducted on the principle that essential duties of its chief are to ascertain and to anticipate the present and future wants of the commissariat in general and particular," he wrote Secretary of War Benjamin on January 18, 1862, "thereon to apply to the Secretary of War for the means, and to appoint the agents deemed most competent to accomplish these objects; then to effect them."

Difficulties from without as the Confederates fortunes ebbed, and his own peevishness and obstinate insistence in proving himself right in any clash that came up, constantly put obstacles into the smooth operation of Northrop's well-stated policies.

Before the Confederate government shifted from Montgomery to Richmond, Northrop had realistically recognized that adequate food supplies, especially salt meats, would have to be obtained in the enemy country. He took immediate steps to procure them, and, as a consequence, such a quantity of bacon and pork was acquired—at half the 1862 rates—that it was still being distributed in early 1862.[22]

In the fall of 1862, the first great food crisis developed in the South and Northrop looked to trading with the enemy to solve the problem. Just how critical the situation had become was disclosed on October 18, when the Commissary General's chief assistant, Lieutenant Colonel Frank G. Ruffin, made the startling declaration that throughout the Confederacy there was only a 25-day supply of meat for 300,000 men. "As we feed by rough estimate not less than that number, including prisoners, and we cannot expect to commence on the new hog crop before the 1st Jany, the condition of the Commissariat is well described . . . as 'alarming,'" Ruffin informed Northrop.

About this time, an offer to supply the Subsistence Department with 30,000 hogshead of bacon and salt meat in exchange for cotton, pound for pound, was made by Dr. Jephtha Fowlkes and Northrop quickly seized upon it. The meat, to be obtained within Union lines, would be exchanged through a Confederate supplier at Memphis for the much-sought cotton. R. M. Davis, president of the Bank of Louisiana, who acted as agent in the matter, assured Northrop there would be no difficulty in executing the contract and the only objections would be "of our own people which I do not consider either valid or entitled to the least consideration." The banker Davis might have been thinking the Commissary General's own thoughts when he added: "I cannot reconcile a policy which would doom our cotton to destruction, or our army to starvation and disbandment and our country to subjugation merely because a few crazy legislators imagine that cotton is of paramount importance." Unfortunately, President Davis did not feel the same way about the proposal as did banker Davis.

The Commissary General wrote Secretary Randolph immediately, urging strongly the acceptance of the proposition, adding that without it, it would not be possible to feed the Army. Northrop said that the cotton to be used would otherwise either be burned or fall into the enemy's hands and he asked the Secretary's sanction for it to pass through Confederate lines. On October 30, Secretary of War Randolph wrote the President, not only approving Northrop's scheme, but extending it to include shoes and blankets for the Quartermaster General. He enclosed the letters of Fowlkes and Northrop for the President's perusal. On November 1, President Davis returned all the papers to the Secretary of War with his veto of the proposal.

"He hesitates, and does not concur," recorded J. B. Jones, War Department clerk through whose hands the documents passed. "But says the secretary will readily see the propriety of *postponing* such a resort until January—and he hopes it may not be necessary then to depart from the settled policy of the government—to forbear trading cotton to the Yankees . . ."

War Clerk Jones commented in his diary for the same date:

"Mr. Benjamin, Secretary of State, has given Mr. Dunnock permission to sell cotton to the Yankees and the rest of the world on the Atlantic and Gulf Coast. Can it be that the President knows nothing of this? . . . We have acres enough, and laborers enough, to subsist 30,000,000 of people; and yet we have the spectacle of high functionaries, under Mr. Davis urging the necessity of bartering cotton to the enemy for stores essential to the maintenance of the army!"[23]

The situation worsened in November and Secretary Randolph, shortly before he resigned on November 15, 1862, urged the President again to permit the Subsistence Department to trade with Union sources for food supplies. Davis replied with a request for a "comparative view" study of the Confederate supply situation.

Davis had wanted a report based on accurate figures and this the Commissary General could not supply because, as Lieutenant Colonel Ruffin later testified, the Adjutant General "had never been able . . . to furnish any information sufficient to guide the Bureau of Subsistence in its estimates of purchases . . ." The President returned the report and asked for details of all available sources of supply inside the Confederacy and detailed reasons why supplies should be sought within the Federal lines.

Northrop gave three cogent reasons in his second report why trading with the enemy was absolutely essential to feed the Confederate Army.

The first and most important reason, he stated, was that in all areas of the Confederacy sources of supply were either exhausted or were rapidly becoming so. Secondly, the 22,516,194 available rations were by no means assured to the Subsistence Department because of the transportation crisis, the critical shortage of salt for curing meat, and the rapid depreciation of Confederate currency. And, finally, pointed out the Commissary General, the Army would need 500,000 hogs shortly and only one third of that amount was obtainable by the Subsistence Department.

The President studied the report and then authorized the new Secretary of War, James A. Seddon, to contract for purchases within the Union lines should it be indispensable. He made it clear to Seddon, however, that he himself did not consider it indispensable at this time. The new Secretary of War, seemingly, took his cue from the President and subsequent proposals to trade within enemy lines were rejected.

Enemies of Northrop, who asserted he held office only because he was the President's "classmate" at West Point, generally did not know of the Commissary General's proposal to trade with the enemy nor of Davis's opposition to it. If they had known, they would have been hard-pressed to explain why the President did not support his "pet's" project in so vital a matter as feeding the Confederate armies.[24]

The postwar correspondence of Davis and Northrop reveals that the Commissary General was not adverse to ignoring, after a time, the interdiction and to go quietly about his way making purchases where and how he could. Two examples demonstrate this:

"Arrangements for trading for cotton with the enemy were made in several quarters with Lincoln's consent I doubt not. He wished to satisfy the North and quiet England from uniting with France in recognizing us and breaking the blockade . . . I recommended it, it was not permitted on the policy I think of increasing the want of cotton in England and the north."[25]

"In regard to trading with the enemy, it might have been elaborated indefinitely. Butler's offers were unlimited . . . Flour bacon coffee and tea with clothing and &c would be given for cotton . . . My agents were trading all around Va. and N.C. by my authority alone—*sub silentio*, and this became a very large business; there were nearly 30 little agencies around Va trading yams and tobacco for bacon and on the Blackwater in N.Ca. 1500-2000 bales of cotton I think were traded every month. At length an arrangement with Baltimore was made; six steamers were engaged to run regularly, one or two cargoes were delivered but Grant found it out and stopped it. That Lincoln approved is certain, but he did not dare to order Grant to permit its re-establishment. The Sec. of War officially knew nothing about these latter arrangements but they supplied Lee with meat."[26]

There were, indeed, many transactions as the war wore on, in which

Confederate cotton was bartered for foodstuffs and other supplies. And before the war was over, Northrop was authorized to purchase United States currency for the use of the Subsistence Department. This was, in all likelihood, the first instance in history "in which one belligerent has bought the money of the enemy in order to purchase food."

But by far the oddest proposition was recorded by Robert G. H. Kean, head of the Bureau of War, who noted in his diary the following piece of intelligence: "A queer contract has been made; a fellow has been found who *contracts to be captured* with a cargo of supplies."[27]

VI

The year 1863 had barely begun before the Commissary General found himself embroiled with Generals Johnston, Beauregard, Bragg, Pemberton, and, of all people, Robert E. Lee.

Moreover, Congressman Henry S. Foote, ever ready to believe the worst about Northrop, insisted that Congress investigate a deal for flour which the Commissary General had made with the Richmond firm of Hoxall, Crenshaw & Co. The loose-talking Tennessean made no attempt to disguise that he sniffed fraud in the transaction.

To add to Colonel Northrop's already highly developed natural talent for making people angry, a new means of irritating citizens and spreading bitterness throughout the Confederacy was placed in his hands, when Congress passed the Impressment Act in March 1863.

"Northrop was Lee's one outspoken critic in the administration," said Douglas Southall Freeman. "Most of the others were his open admirers." The Commissary General's grudge against Lee stemmed from the latter's refusal to reduce the army ration as Northrop desired. Then there was the matter of a rebuff that Northrop felt Lee had given a civilian whom he had sent on an important mission to the general, armed with a letter of introduction from the Secretary of War.

In vain did Northrop urge Lee to use his authority to impress foodstuff for his army. "I tried to persuade Lee to act up to his powers, by two letters and a special messenger . . . He replied that it was not his place to get provisions," claimed the Commissary General.

Early in January, the Commissary General informed General Lee beeves on hand would hardly carry his army through the month. Lee complained to Secretary Seddon that because of difficulty of finding grazing land, the beeves he had were a sorry lot. He suggested that these be fattened for the spring and that salt meat be sent the army in their stead. "I hope the chief commissary has enough on hand to supply the army until we can again procure beeves in proper condition for use," he said.

About this time, Colonel Northrop sent James B. Crenshaw to General Lee to inform him personally that 300,000 or more bushels of wheat were available provided wagons to transport it and cavalry to protect it could be obtained. Crenshaw bore letters from both Northrop and the Secretary of War to General Lee and these he turned over to Lee's adjutant general, General Chilton. He then asked for a personal interview with General Lee. The Commissary General read what happened and became furious. Crenshaw reported:

"When I arrived, I was informed by General Chilton that General Lee was at that time engaged with General Stuart, but he supposed would be through shortly . . . After some two hours' delay, I was informed by General Chilton that General Lee declined seeing me."

Northrop, on receiving Crenshaw's report, wrote a long endorsement on it and forwarded it to the Secretary of War on January 13, 1863, complaining that Crenshaw, because of Lee's refusal to see him, had not been able to get to the most important business, namely the deficiency in transportation. ". . . The . . . inevitable deficiency of transportation by wagons . . . had been long foreseen and commented on by this Bureau; therefore, the efforts to get teams and use every means to accumulate supplies at Richmond . . . were unintermitting," stated the Commissary General. "Had teams been procurable in any other way, General Lee would not have been applied to. This Bureau will continue its efforts, but will accomplish but little, it is feared."

And then, in exactly a dozen words, Colonel Northrop washed his hands of the whole matter: "The Commissary General hereby absolves himself from all responsibility attending this deficiency."[28]

On January 20, Lee proposed to the Secretary of War that his commissary be permitted to trade sugar for bacon to citizens on a basis of one pound of sugar to two of bacon. "By offering sugar in small quantities at a time, many thousands pounds of bacon can be obtained . . ." wrote Lee. Secretary Seddon passed it on to the Commissary General with his sanction. But that did not induce favorable response in Northrop, who returned it to the Secretary of War with this endorsement:

"It is not proposed by the Bureau to diminish its supplies or resources by barter; it is better to use the sugar, and to impress all the bacon that can be found, consistently with leaving a supply for the family; after that, barter would be beneficial."[29]

At the end of the month, when the predicted meat crisis developed, Northrop blamed it on railroad delays and also because General Lee had not accepted his suggestion, made a year earlier, that the necks and shanks of beeves, usually excluded by regulations, be used to stretch the supply of meat. The Commissary General seemed to justify the situation by stating that on several occasions "General Lee was notified of impending want, so that it has long been understood . . . These significant facts must have prepared all persons to whom they had been stated for the present condition, which General Lee seems now to realize."

Colonel Northrop complained that Lee had for three or four months not observed an order to reduce the meat ration. "But for the violation of the . . . order and the failure to economize beef, the supplies for General Lee's army would have lasted several weeks longer." He declared that "all the transportation that can be begged will be needed to get wheat to be converted into flour for the same army that now wants meat." Of General Lee's suggestion that an appeal be made to the citizens to forward supplies, Colonel Northrop stated that "it is noted by this Bureau, and is not approved." The Commissary General closed on an "I-told-you-so" note, saying that the defects in the transportation system, "with their inevitable result have been repeatedly pointed out by the Bureau from a period which dates as far back as June, 1861."[30]

The insufferable Foote was again moved in mid-January, 1863, by "painful rumors" concerning the Subsistence Department to demand that Congress investigate the purchase of a large quantity of flour from Hoxall, Crenshaw and Co. The latter promptly offered to open their books to the investigators.

If the Commissary General fed on controversy, he was well nourished in 1863. In February, Joe Johnston complained that Bragg's Army of Tennessee was suffering from an excess of salt meat. He urged that fresh beef be procured in northern Georgia. Northrop promptly replied that the Army of Northern Virginia was in a critical state and all of the Georgia supplies were for its use. Eventually, Johnston would order the commissary officer in Atlanta to ship no foodstuffs to Virginia until Bragg's army had been supplied.

In mid-February, it was Beauregard's turn to arouse the ire of the irascible Commissary General. He had arrested Major A. C. Guérin, post commissary at Charleston, for corresponding directly with the Subsistence Department and not through the general's headquarters. Apparently there must have been considerable talk about the affair in the War Department, for the Chief of the War Bureau, Robert Kean, noted the incident in his diary for February 15:

"Beauregard has got into another controversy with the Government . . . Colonel Northrop got the President to order the release of Guérin. Beauregard sends a very angry and impertinent letter on the subject, which cannot fail to widen the old breach. Colonel Northrop backs up his subordinate and throws the weight of his influence against Beauregard in this matter. The fact is the General is wrong. He insists that all the officers of the staff departments in his military department shall correspond with their chief of bureau through his headquarters. This pretension is not supported by the army regulations, or by common sense."[31]

The Commissary General, almost without exception, considered unsolicited suggestions as implied criticism of him or his department and just as readily turned down proposals of Robert E. Lee as those of his subordinates. J. B. Jones, the very articulate war clerk whose diary is a source book for wartime Richmond, submitted to President Davis on February 19, 1863, a plan to ease the food crisis. He urged that the parents and sisters of soldiers be called upon to make "patriotic contributions" of foodstuffs and that the army furnish transportation to collect the provisions. Davis sent the proposal to Northrop, who dismissed it with this indorsement: "The Commissary General has no experience as to this mode of raising supplies and does not think it a promising one . . ."[32]

Later, in February 1863, General John Pemberton got into an argument with Northrop over the accumulation of sugar and molasses at Vicksburg. The Commissary General had just learned that commissary stores were being mismanaged at Vicksburg and Port Hudson and that 50,000 bushels of corn had spoiled from being exposed to the weather. Accordingly he was in one of his less congenial moods when Pemberton, on February 25, 1863, wrote Richmond for authority to keep huge amounts of sugar in his department. Northrop indorsed the request: "It is not proper that his army should have more than a due proportion of sugar and molasses, & anything beyond that is protested against."

Pemberton telegraphed back the same day that he was obliged to retain three thousand hogsheads of sugar. The Commissary General commented: ". . . Protest against it." In a third telegram, Pemberton showed the necessity of keeping the three thousand hogsheads at Vicksburg, at least to his own satisfaction. But not to Colonel Northrop's. "If the supply of sugar was unlimited, then trade for bacon would be wise," he penned. ". . . The sugar *should* be sent . . ."[33]

With the approach of the spring campaign, General Lee questioned the Commissary General about prospects of subsisting the army. Lee asserted the rations were not sufficient for the health of his troops and, as the symptoms of scurvy were appearing, he was detailing men to search for sassafras buds, wild onions, garlic, lamb's quarters, and poke sprouts. Northrop, and perhaps with some accuracy, replied blaming the short rations on the railroads which, he claimed, preferred private freight to government shipments.

When it became evident to the Commissary General that there was bitter competition among the services for supplies, he urged that the purchase of subsistence stores be accomplished by a single authority. He also came up with the scheme in mid-April to reorganize the purchase of food for the armies. Under the existing system, each army had been subsisting on the territory in which it was operating. The Chief Commissary with the army was the purchasing agent, while the Subsistence Department made general purchases of meat and breadstuffs. As a result, while some armies lived well at times, others were on the verge of starvation. Northrop's new project was to have a Chief Purchasing Commissary in each state, with the subdivision of the states into districts each under a Commissary, and the districts further subdivided and agents placed in charge of each subdivision. This "grass roots" procurement of food, an officer of the Subsistence Department claimed after the war, "enabled the armies to exist for a longer period than it would have been possible under the old system." Whenever food became scarce thereafter, "it was the cause of much dissatisfaction with and criticism of the Bureau," wrote the same officer, "especially as each General felt morally sure that the old system was the best."

About this time, Northrop received word that bacon was plentiful north of Cumberland Gap in Kentucky and that commissary agents could probably collect between half a million to a million pounds on a barter basis of one pound of cotton for three pounds of bacon. Once again the Commissary General sought War Department approval of this contraband trade, but once again the proposal drew official frowns.

The meat shortage became so acute in the late spring of 1863 that Colonel Northrop wrote gloomily to the Secretary of War, on June 4, urging a cut in the ration. "The dream about the oceans of cattle in East Florida has no foundation," he told Seddon. "Importations from abroad were looked for by the last of May. A few mouthfuls have come." The Commissary General told Seddon that the meat would not last until the new bacon came in. He urged that "throughout the whole army the ration of salt meat be reduced to one-third of a pound for all troops not engaged in actual movements, to one fourth of a pound for all troops garrisoning forts, or manning permanent batteries or intrenched camps, and the ration only to be raised to one-half of a pound of bacon when on active duty."[34]

The dual July disasters of Lee's repulse at Gettysburg and the loss of Vicksburg were a great concern to the Subsistence Department. Lee's early return from enemy soil found the Subsistence Department with only 500,000 pounds of meat on hand for the weary soldiers of the Army of Northern Virginia. Northrop urged Lee to reduce the meat ration to one-fourth of a pound. Noting this in his diary, Robert Kean exclaimed: "This is a most alarming state of the supply question. God help this unhappy country!" With the fall of Vicksburg, Northrop's food supply suffered a staggering blow, for the last important connecting link with the Trans-Mississippi theater was snapped. Moreover, during the Vicksburg campaign, huge supplies of commissary stores had been abandoned at Jackson. Another setback for the Subsistence Department was the excessive rain in Virginia in July which damaged the wheat crop.

Throughout the summer of 1863, protests from generals in the field poured in on Northrop. Braxton Bragg was first in line, submitting a statement from his Chief Commissary, Major Giles M. Hillyer, on August 25, to the effect that there was no reasonable expectation of feeding his army with meat after the last of September, "and that only with the most rigid care and economy." He called for drawing on the cattle of Florida and southwest Georgia and for a general impressment of all stock.

Bragg indorsed the statement on August 26: "This paper treating a matter of such vital importance is submitted for the information of the War Department. The morale of this army is being seriously injured by this cause principally, and desertions, some to the enemy, are not uncommon."

When the document reached Northrop's desk, the Commissary deftly put Bragg in his place. His indorsement, dated September 4, 1863, states:

"General Bragg admits serious demoralization in his army; he attributes it to the prospect of impending want of subsistence one month ahead; consequently his judgment of the true causes is legitimately contradicted by my judgment in support of a different explanation. The reserves at Atlanta were intended for the east, it being justly supposed that the armies of the West and Southwest could hold the country, which was amply sufficient to subsist them . . . Twice within two months the stores at Jackson, Miss., have been destroyed . . ."

General Joe Johnston provided a mild headache when he sought clarification as to whose authority it was, his or Northrop's, to control purchasing commissaries in his theater. Northrop lost no time in telling Johnston that the control was his, not the general's.[35]

To add to the problems in the Subsistence Department, many of Northrop's men in the field, civilians, were removed by the conscription officers. A plan to take all of the Commissary General's able-bodied men for the army and to replace them with disabled officers and men met his stubborn opposition. Northrop argued effectively that it was impossible for anyone to be useful to the Subsistence Department unless he were healthy and active.[36]

VII

". . . Northrop! What a bone of contention he is! Even if the army is mistaken, and Northrop is not inefficient, still something ought to be conceded to their prejudice," Mary Boykin Chesnut confided to her diary in October 1863. "One day, I saw Mr. Northrop at the President's. He is an eccentric creature. He said newspapers were not without some good uses. He wore several folded across his chest under his shirt, in lieu of flannel. He said they kept out the cold effectually. Think of him with those peppery articles in the *Examiner* next to his heart. There is abuse of Northrop in some of those papers, that would warm up the spirit of the Angel Gabriel."

Abuse was coming in on Northrop from all directions and for many reasons. One was impressment, which Congress had enacted, but the burden of which fell upon the Subsistence Department and its agents throughout the Confederacy. Northrop reportedly once declared that impressment was not intended to please the people, but to secure all necessary army supplies.

Congress was bombarded with tales of woe of distressed constituents who felt they had been unjustly treated and some Congressmen themselves had personal grievances against the "pressmen." North Carolina's John A. Gilmer stormed and fumed when impressment agents took a large amount of his whiskey and he raised such a furor that it was replaced, despite the Commissary General's insistence that the whiskey was "needed as a stimulant" for the Army of Northern Virginia.

Another heated controversy developed in the President's official family when a commissary agent in Alabama exchanged sugar for flour and rice with a merchant, and then after a month or so impressed the sugar. The merchant got a favorable opinion from the Confederate Attorney General and this was approved by the Secretary of War, who issued an order to release the sugar to its owner. Northrop challenged the "good sense" of such a decision, asserting that nothing should be exempt from impressment under any circumstances when needed to continue the war. Moreover, Northrop claimed, according to War Clerk Jones, "that the way to success is to do justice to the whole country—and not to please the people. Northrop insisted that if the sugar were released, it will be done against his judgment."[37]

Although impressment had been forced upon the Confederacy in some instances by military necessity as early as 1861, there was no legality in it until 1863, when Congress enacted complicated legislation. In such a war, fought under such conditions, there were bound to be inequities and abuses. But the Southern opposition to impressment and the indignation and resentment against the Commissary General and his agents were almost universal.

One Southern historian, E. Merton Coulter, has summed it up neatly: "The ubiquitous activities of the 'pressmen,' who conducted veritable raids on the private property of Confederate citizens, stirred up a storm of bitterness as they seized food, horses, wagons, and anything else they wanted, and too often left worthless promises to pay. It has been estimated that at the end of the war the Confederate government owed its citizens $500,000,000 for property it had impressed. Occasionally impostors claiming to be impressment agents carried off much property and left in exchange worthless receipts. This interference with the normal rights of the individual struck a fatal blow at the morale of the people."[38]

The price of meat in Richmond in October 1863 fluctuated between 75 cents and $1.25 a pound and one observer sensed that the community was "in an inflammable condition, and may be ignited by a single spark." The indignation was as much the result of a rumor of a speculation for personal profit by one of the Subsistence Department's agents as it was for the exorbitant price of beef. The commissary agent bought beef cattle at 18 to 22 cents per pound and sold it to the butchers for 45 to 55 cents per pound, War Clerk Jones heard. "If this be so," the latter wrote in his diary, ". . . a great profit is realized by the government or its agents at the expense of a suffering people."

Few of the complaints that came to the War Department reached Seddon, for his subordinates disposed of them, being under orders not to disturb the Secretary with matters of secondary importance. The day after the rumor was circulated, Jones saw Colonel Northrop and the Commissary General admitted that the speculator was one of his men, a man named Moffit. "And so we have a government agent a speculator in meat, and cooperating with speculators," noted the Richmond diarist. "Will Mr. Secretary Seddon permit this?"[39]

The question of what department would feed Yankee prisoners had been finally settled and on October 31, 1863, the Commissary General assumed the responsibility. On November 11, however, Captain J. Warren, assistant commissary at the prisons, informed the Secretary of War that there was "not one pound of meat on hand for 13,000 prisoners." Mr. Seddon, the next day, reminded the Commissary General that "such supply as is given to soldiers is by law required to be given to prisoners." Years later, Northrop would remember the incident and write Jefferson Davis that "Warren was a spy" whose "vengeance prompted refusing the food for the departing prisoners and avarice selling the best of the rations to the officers."[40]

As 1863 drew to a close, the Commissary General tried to convince Robert E. Lee that he should impress food for his army, but Lee balked at this, considering that he had no legal authority to do so. On November 22, 1863, Northrop explained the law to the general: "Your proposition that the Secretary of War should issue appropriate directions to the generals commanding is beyond his power . . . legality [is] . . . in the hands of the generals commanding."

Lee replied on December 7: "I . . . am unable to take the view entertained by you of my powers under the impressment act . . . The power that you desire rests, in my opinion, with the War Department; was intended by Congress to be exercised by the Department excepting in casual emergencies . . . I regret to learn that the necessity for impressment by commissaries of armies has, in your opinion, arrived. I shall endeavor to collect all the supplies for this army that I can legitimately do, and keep it on the best conditions I can. But unless it is supplied with food, it will be impossible for me to keep it together."

Colonel Northrop sent Lee's letter to the Secretary of War with this notation: "The power of meeting the present crisis, as far as possible, rests somewhere because that necessity is absolute which has no law to limit it."

Mr. Seddon read the general's letter and the Commissary General's indorsement and he added an indorsement of his own: "I know, as an officer, no greater necessity than to obey the law."[41]

VIII

War was at a standstill as a cheerless Christmas was followed by the New Year of 1864. The severe cold had imposed a stalemate on both the Confederate and Union Armies in northern Virginia. At Dalton, Georgia, General Joe Johnston was reorganizing the Army of Tennessee after Bragg's debacle at Missionary Ridge. In East Tennessee, Longstreet's Corps, which would later march eastward to rejoin Lee, was immobilized by bad weather, miserable roads, and shoeless soldiers. At Charleston the Yankee siege dragged on.

"Such is the scarcity of provisions," wrote War Clerk J. B. Jones in his diary, shortly before Christmas, "that rats and mice have mostly disappeared, and the cats can hardly be kept off the tables."

The new year started bleakly for the Subsistence Department. On January 3, the entire stock of breadstuffs in Richmond was exhausted and the Commissary General was unable to supply Lee. Flour and hard bread reserves had been used up and the daily arrival of corn was inadequate to the needs. In North Carolina, accumulations of commissary stores at Greensboro and Charlotte just sat there because the railroad couldn't move them.[42]

Meanwhile, General Lee had reported on January 2 that he had only one day's supply of meat for his troops and he expressed the grave doubt of his ability to retain the army in the field. The Commissary General's response to this was to compile a chronological list of his letters to General Lee and others predicting that if certain things were not done, some day the army would come to want. Northrop, recorded Diarist Jones, took "great credit for his foresight."

It was inevitable that the situation would bring Congress's number one Northrop hater, Henry S. Foote, to his feet, ranting and raving. His resolution to remove the Commissary General from office "in order to secure the comfortable subsistence of our valiant armies and to allay certain discontents . . ." was tabled by a 48 to 20 vote.

The turn of events was embarrassing to President Davis, who was in a quandary about submitting Northrop's name to Congress for recon-firmation along with other officers who had been confirmed by the Provisional Congress. Robert Kean, in the Bureau of War, noted Davis's dilemma in his diary on February 10, 1864, and offered a solution: "If he is nominated he will certainly be rejected—a deep mortification to the President and himself; if he is not, the President will have put himself in a false position in order to save his friend. The true solution is for Colonel Northrop to resign."[43]

Meanwhile, not without some justification, Northrop blamed his inability to concentrate food reserves in Richmond on the obvious transportation deficiencies. To all complaints, however, that poured in his chief answer was that he had predicted the present crisis long ago. When a dispatch arrived from General Lee's chief commissary, on February 29, 1864, stating the army had only enough bread to last till March 1, and that meat was again scarce, Northrop indorsed the paper to the effect that he "foresaw" and frequently "foretold" precisely what had come to pass. War Clerk Jones says that the Commissary General's face "was lit up with triumph, as if he had gained a victory." Northrop claimed he predicted the crisis because he had not been authorized to impress all the food in the country. "And now he has no remedy for the pressing need," observed the War Clerk. "But soldiers won't starve, in spite of him."

By mid-March there was no improvement in the situation. Lee's army was out of meat and had only one day's ration of bread. "All the Armies," noted Jones, "are in the same lamentable predicament—to the great triumph of Col. N., whose prescience is triumphantly vindicated!"

From all sides Northrop was involved. Beauregard complained of lack of rations; Generals Jones and Imboden placed an embargo on food supplies being shipped from their districts; Joe Johnston stated that all that was needed to secure much food from Mississippi and West Tennessee was proper management. Northrop indorsed Johnston's telegram with the charge that it was inconsistent and exhibited a heedless disregard of the facts. The Commissary General, a few weeks later, clashed with Johnston and General Polk regarding the duties of the Chief Commissary of an army in the field.

The summer of 1864 was a decisive one for the Confederacy. Lee had gone into the trenches at Petersburg after the blood baths of the Wilderness and Cold Harbor, and the ten-months' siege was under way. Sherman, relentlessly pushing back Johnston's outnumbered Army of Tennessee, was closing in on Atlanta. Soon the Confederacy would be severed a second time. Loss of territory, destruction of commissary stores on retreat and the cutting of the railroads seriously aggravated the Commissary General's already mounting problems. The depreciated Confederate currency—in July 1864 wheat was selling for $30 and corn $20 a bushel—and the Subsistence Department's lack of credit increased Northrop's difficulties.[44]

About this time, the government finally condoned trading behind enemy lines and Northrop was authorized to purchase United States currency for that purpose. However, the Commissary General still insisted, and with logic, that cotton should be used as the medium of purchase abroad because cotton was worth six times as much as gold and 120 times as much as Confederate money.

As the Confederacy's fortunes in 1864 continued to ebb, the crisis in food increased. And with both there came a great lowering of morale in the civilians and soldiers. But the Commissary General never felt for a moment that he shared in the responsibility for the situation. His unfailing confidence that everyone in the Confederacy was out of step save the Subsistence Department is reflected in a letter to Secretary of War Seddon on July 26, 1864:

"In response to a letter addressed to you by General R. E. Lee, dated 21st inst. & referred to me for consideration, I have the honor to say that the present state of privation was foreseen by this Bureau, from the beginning of the War. Hence the efforts to economize, & save supplies from waste & heedless condemnation by incompetent Boards of Survey &c have been constant, and the destruction caused by the retrograde movements of our armies, have always stimulated these efforts. The information *now* given by Gen. Lee, of the importance of a regular supply of provisions, and the effects to be feared from a deficiency, has constantly been before my eyes. Over two years ago, a restriction on the meat ration was attempted, and Gen. Lee had had pressed on *him* by *me*, substantially the views herein stated by him . . ."[45]

On September 15, the grim facts of the situation were unminced in a report to Northrop by Major S. B. French, one of his assistants. There was less than fifteen days' supply of meat in Richmond, French stated. And there were no reserves accumulated anywhere which could be drawn upon. The results of a month's efforts to collect meat from all sources would not subsist Lee's army a week. Major French blamed the lack of funds "to purchase, liquidate accrued indebtedness and thus restore public confidence" for the impairment of the Subsistence Department's operation. And impressment had proved a signal failure because payment was required when goods were impressed . . . "Our restricted means will not enable us to offer currency, and the mass of people refuse to accept 6 per cent certificates and non-taxable bonds." The major declared that in all the Confederate States, impressments are evaded "by every means which ingenuity can suggest, and in some openly resisted." The Army of Tennessee, within thirty days, will have consumed the present meat supply. In conclusion, Major French told Northrop:

"Our officers in all of the States are fully alive to the interests of the Department, but the difficulties which beset them are insurmountable, and must receive due consideration in connection with the present condition of the Commissariat."[46]

A month later, the Commissary General had only 41 days' supply of beef for 100,000 men and only 34 days' supply of bacon and pork. Combined, the resources would provide only 25 days' rations for 300,000 men.

To add to this distressing condition, the Subsistence Department was $30,000,000 in debt by the end of October 1864.

Despite the storm that raged around him, Northrop was promoted to brigadier general on November 26, 1864, but Congress never confirmed him and there is considerable doubt as to whether President Davis ever submitted the Commissary General's name.

The Senate investigated, in December 1864, the Army's daily food ration and Northrop admitted that for two years past he had been unable to issue rations in quantities assigned by regulations. His excuses were familiar, and not without some validity; the almost valueless currency, difficulties in transport, lack of cooperation from the people, conscription of Subsistence Department personnel, and the refusal of the government to use cotton as a medium of exchange.

Josiah Gorgas, Chief of the Ordnance Bureau, wrote in his diary on December 26:

"A despondent Christmas has just passed, yet people contrived to eat hearty and good dinners. The soldiers, unfortunately have not even meat, and have had none for several days. The Commissary General has signally failed in his duties."[47]

Early in January, heavy rains washed out sections of a railroad needed to supply Lee and Secretary of War Seddon wrote the general on January 11: "I fear the extraordinary powers reposed in commanding generals of impressing without limit will have to be resorted to by you." Lee immediately replied: "There is nothing within reach of this army to be impressed; the country is swept clear . . . We have but two days' supplies."

Seddon answered on January 12 that he had ordered both the Commissary General and Quartermaster General to send out officers to all railroad lines to round up whatever food they could. He also enclosed a letter which Northrop had sent him, urging that Lee send officers broadcast asking the people in his name to contribute for the army. ". . . Never can there occur a more critical moment or occasion in which General Lee's popularity or hold on the confidence of the people . . . can find a more fitting opportunity for testing its efficiency in saving the cause . . . I am willing to do all I can, but I urge that General Lee act also."

On January 12, the Secretary of War, in a special order, called for "extraordinary means" to meet the "present emergency" and instructed Northrop to "impress for immediate use of the army" whatever subsistence supplies were needed by Lee. Eight days later, with the crisis weathered, the order was revoked.

Less than a month later, another food crisis developed while Lee's right wing operated against the Federals at Hatchers Run in miserable February weather. On February 8, Lee reported that "some of the men have been without meat for three days, and all were suffering from reduced rations and scant clothing, exposed to battle, cold, hail, and sleet . . . Colonel Cole . . . reports that he has not a pound of meat at his disposal . . . If some change is not made and the commissary department reorganized, I apprehend dire results. The physical strength of my men, if their courage survives, must fail under this treatment."

Several days before Lee's letter reached the War Department, James A. Seddon had resigned as Secretary of War and General John C. Breckinridge was named his successor. Breckinridge and Northrop were in conference when Lee's dispatch arrived and the former handed it to the Commissary General to read. The Commissary General's reaction was recorded by Robert Kean in his diary:

" 'Yes,' the old stoic remarked: 'it is just what I predicted long ago.' And he went on to rehearse the record without a single suggestion of relief. General Breckinridge inquired, 'But Colonel what shall we do?' 'Well I don't know. If my plans had been carried out instead of thwarted etc. etc.' "

When the President got Lee's letter it was the last straw. He penned this indorsement on it: "This is too sad to be patiently considered, and cannot have occurred without criminal neglect or gross incapacity. Let supplies be had by purchase, or borrowing, or other possible mode."[48]

This was the end of Davis's old friend.

On February 16, 1865—less than two months before Appomattox— Lucius Bellinger Northrop was removed. Brigadier General Isaac M. St. John became Commissary General of the Confederacy in its dying days.

He had performed with distinction as head of the Nitre and Mining Corps and he brought quick and effective measures into action, appealing to the people for contributions as an auxiliary to the regular operations of the commissary service. General St. John, of course, was too late—too much time had run out for the Confederacy. But he acted with energy from the beginning and Lee hastened to express his gratification of his "prompt and vigorous measures."

On February 27, 1865, War Clerk Jones wrote in his diary: "I saw Col. Northrop, late Commissary-General, today. He looks down, dark, and dissatisfied. Lee's army *eats* without him . . ."[49]

IX

After his dismissal as Commissary General of the Confederate States of America, Northrop apparently felt that he had no further military responsibilities. And so he left Richmond for his farm in North Carolina, about forty miles from Raleigh.

In the dying days of the Confederacy, President Davis learned that Northrop regarded himself out of the service and, in the hectic flight of the government from Richmond, Davis took time to dispatch to him a telegram from Danville, Virginia, on April 7, 1865: ARE YOU NOT AWARE THAT YOUR COMMISSION REMAINS IN FORCE, MAKING YOU ASSIGNABLE TO DUTY ANYWHERE IN THE SUBSISTENCE DEPT.?

Two days before Appomattox, the question was purely academic and there is no evidence that Northrop made any attempt to answer it. By that time he and his family had surmounted difficulties of food and lodging and, despite the fact that his horses and provisions had been stolen, he and his son got in a crop.

And then on June 30, Yankee troops came and plucked the former Confederate Commissary-General off his farm and from his family and tossed him into prison in Richmond on the charge of willfully starving Union prisoners. Assailed by dyspepsia and other disorders, Northrop's health in prison was bad. "I have had much inconvenience from confinement and bad fare," he wrote his friend, Bishop Lynch. ". . . I am, of course, not depressed for God's will is my will I trust." The charges against Northrop did not stand up and at last, after more than four months in prison, he was paroled on November 2, 1865. He did not return to North Carolina, but settled himself and family on a farm near Charlottesville, Virginia, and began raising cattle.[50]

For a quarter of a century Northrop bred cattle and fed his bitterness against generals and politicians in a voluminous correspondence with Jefferson Davis. His hatred toward Generals Joe Johnston and P. G. T. Beauregard, previously noted, became an obsession and barely a letter that he wrote Davis failed to denounce both men. Davis, during a greater part of the correspondence, was preparing his book, *The Rise and Fall of the Confederate Government* and Northrop frequently encouraged him to light into the miscreants: "Johnston must be discredited if your book is to be accepted as authority"; "If Bgd. is demolished, many will be glad . . ."; "Do tell me confidentially must you not discredit both Johnston and Beauregard as preliminary to commanding the confidence of the country in your statements?"[51]

The desire for self-justification was still strong though the years passed rapidly on. "From the beginning I knew that failures in all other Depts would by reflex action cripple mine, so I ever tried to get unity and co-operation . . ." he told Davis. He still expressed confidence in his "methods and system which were unchanged because unimprovable."

He professed a contempt for practically everything except his family, his farm, and Jefferson Davis. "I did my part from no love of the people or any patriotic ardour, but from duty," he once wrote Davis. On another occasion he wrote: "Having no respect for the judgment of the people, I was indifferent to their opinions of me." And a third time; "I have now an impartial contempt to all politicians; and indifference to Americans generally . . . I have . . . the most profound pity for Americans in particular. The love of comfort, sensualism and money being omnipotent."[52]

Twenty years after the war, Northrop was, as far as he was concerned, a man without a country, "with an impartial aversion to all parties and no spark of patriotism or obligation." Still a prisoner on parole, he reported monthly for a long time to the military commandant of Virginia, but "the commandant having vanished, that obligation ceased." "I abhor the U. S. Govt. and Americans generally . . . This nation is incorrigible, so may be allowed immunity until like the great Empires of antiquity the destruction becomes necessary for cosmic plans," he predicted.

There is something pathetic about these two old men, sharing their bitterness and their hatreds and sustaining each other with their mutual regard and friendship. "I . . . puzzle to discover what there is in me to attract such steady affection as you have retained through so many years," Northrop wrote Davis in 1882. And three years later, he penned: "You are my only living friend except one in Carolina so I cling to you." A few days after that Davis provided, perhaps, a key to their friendship: ". . . You showed extraordinary capacity, but, like myself, were wanting in the quality to conciliate men who had private ends to serve, or who were vain enough to believe that they could teach us about things on which we had labored exhaustively, and of which they were profoundly ignorant."[53]

This similarity of their two natures, as expressed, by Davis, suggests other character comparisons between the former President and the Commissary General of the Confederacy. Both were stubborn, both were humorless, both were keenly sensitive to criticism, and both wrote interminable letters to prove that they were always right.

A convert to Catholicism, Northrop tried to convert Davis by mail. Referring to Davis's religious confirmation while in Richmond, he wrote: "It grieved me then, and still does, that the key which opens the mysteries of life is not in your possession, and the veil of doubts which hang over every one outside the R. C. Church still invests you." On another occasion he told Davis that he had settled in his mind all the problems of the present and future life. "In fact," he declared, "an intelligent honest Catholic can't be unhappy or disquieted."[54]

Year after year, the letters passed between Charlottesville and "Beauvoir," Davis's last home on the Mississippi Gulf Coast. On September 15, 1889, in a letter full of venom for Beauregard and Johnston, Northrop added a postscript: "I am 78 you must be 82 or 3. Your hand and style are unchanged. You have outlived your country." Davis noted on the letter that he had answered it on September 20.[55] What he said, apparently, has been lost. This appears to be the final exchange between the two. Less than three months later, on December 6, 1889, Jefferson Davis died. Earlier in the year, Northrop had lost his wife. With her and his dear friend both gone, Northrop had little to live for now. Frequently bedridden in his later years, he finally became paralyzed in 1890.

Four years later, on February 9, 1894, Lucius Bellinger Northrop, helpless and friendless, died in an old soldiers' home at Pikesville, Maryland.[56]

His epitaph might well be what he once wrote of himself to Jefferson Davis: "I am as God sees me, and I try not to care what man thinks."[57]

7

Every Inch a Soldier:

GENERAL BILLY MAHONE

I

THE Yankee officer asked: "Which one is General Mahone?" The Confederate officer pointed out a veritable bantam of a man, small and skinny, with a long pointed beard.

"Not much man," observed the Federal officer, "but a big general."

A Confederate soldier summed up Billy Mahone even better than that: "He was every inch a soldier, though there were not many inches of him."

The dying message of a member of Mahone's brigade to his friends proclaimed: "Billy Mahone is the biggest little man God Almighty ever made."[1]

Everybody agrees that Major General William Mahone, CSA, was small, but no two agree on whether he was a mere five feet or whether he soared to five feet, five inches or five feet, six inches. And as to his weight, there are various estimates, none of them higher than 125 pounds and at least one below 100 pounds.

That he was just about skin and bones is evident from a story that made the Confederate rounds after Mahone was pinked by a Federal bullet for a severe wound at Second Manassas. When the news was carried to Mrs. Mahone, the bearer, to reassure her, stressed the general had received only a flesh wound.

"Now I know it is serious," exclaimed Mrs. Mahone, "for William has no flesh whatever."

Sometimes General Mahone's attire corresponded to the correct Confederate gray with the proper trimming. But generally he effected unconventional military garb. One of his brigadiers recalled that on a hot summer day, Mahone wore a "plaited brown linen jacket, *buttoned to trousers*, of same material, like a boy's; topped by a large Panama straw hat of the finest and most beautiful texture . . . and . . . he looked decidedly comfortable."

A young Confederate officer remembered Billy Mahone as "the sauciest-looking little manikin imaginable" and "the oddest and daintiest little specimen" he ever saw. He recalled Mahone's wardrobe as follows:

". . . He wore a large sombrero hat, without plume, cocked on one side, and decorated with a division badge; he had a hunting-shirt of gray, with rolling collar, plaited about the waist, and tucked into his trousers, which were also plaited around the waist-band, swelled at the hips, and tapering to the ankle; while he wore boots, his trousers covered them; those boots were as small as a woman's . . ."

On some occasions, Mahone wore a linen duster which was so long that it almost hid his sword. When so dressed, and walking back and forth in front of his tent as he often did, little Billy Mahone made almost a comic figure. "He looked the image of a bantam rooster or gamecock," said a Confederate veteran.[2]

Mahone had a well-shaped head and his bright, restless blue eyes were deeply set beneath bushy brows. His prominent nose was straight. He wore his hair long, and a long drooping mustache of rich chestnut color and a flowing beard of the same shade obscured his lower features. His complexion was sallow; his voice high and piping, like that of a falsetto tenor.

He suffered from dyspepsia, and lived often only on milk which was always available because he had brought into the army with him an Alderney cow that walked along on the march tethered to one of the General's headquarters wagons.

A bundle of nervous energy, Mahone was quick-tempered and an eloquent "cusser," and some thought him excessively irritable and even, at times, tyrannical. At the time the Civil War broke out, Billy Mahone, a native Virginian, was thirty-five years old and a highly successful railroad man, being president, chief engineer, and superintendent of the Norfolk & Petersburg Railroad.

Of him, Douglas Southall Freeman has written:

"Billy Mahone's is as strange a rise to fame as the Army witnesses in devastating 1864. After the war, when his ambitions soar, his henchmen will say he has been a great soldier from the first. The reports do not show it. As a brigadier he is not lacking in diligence, but he is without special distinction. A dozen of his rank might be named before him. Promotion transforms him. Dispute and caution give place to fierce action. His men become the most renowned shock troops of the Army. In the last phase of the war, when he boasts the age of 38, he is the most conspicuous division commander. Small, and as lean as a starvation year, he lives in unconcealed comfort and does not hesitate to question even the commanding general. Men do not always like him or take him at his own estimate, but they have to admit that he knows how to fight."[3]

When the cause to which he bravely lent his sword was lost, Billy Mahone realistically sought to adjust himself to the political winds and tides of the postwar period. And in doing so he alienated practically all of the old Confederates. As he rose to be the Republican political power in Virginia, "he became the most hated man in the state as time moved on."

To an old comrade in arms, General Thomas T. Munford, William Mahone, in 1882, explained the course he charted for himself on the road back from Appomattox:

"I have thought it wise to live for the future and not the dead past and, while cherishing honorable memory of its glories, I have thought that we should look to the future for life, power and prosperity . . ."[4]

II

William Mahone's ancestral roots in America go back to the late Colonial or early Revolutionary period, his Mahone ancestor having come over from Ireland and settled in Surrey County, Virginia.

Billy Mahone was born in Southampton County on December 1, 1826, at Jerusalem, where his father, Fielding J. Mahone—known to everybody in the county as Major Mahone—kept a tavern. In its environment, the youngster developed an independent spirit along with a taste for tobacco, a skill in poker, and a fluency in profanity. If an article in the *Boston Traveller* in 1886, when Mahone was still alive, can be taken at face value, he was the neighborhood "hell-raiser" as a lad. The article described him as "a sandy-haired, freckled-faced little imp who hung around the store in Jerusalem, and was a devil on wheels. He smoked, chewed and cussed like a pirate, gambled like a Mississippi planter. He was the leader in all the deviltry, and the terror of all good country mothers whose boys occasionally went to town. Every good boy was cautioned to look out for that 'bad little wretch, Billy Mahone.' "

Young Billy held horses for patrons of the tavern, delivered drinks to the hard-swearing gamblers, and picked up tips which he did not hesitate to bet on cock fights or horse racing. He owned a speedy quarterhorse himself, and he was ever ready to race it and back it with whatever money he possessed. Mahone saw a great deal of liquor drunk at his father's bar, and considerable gambling in the tavern and, although quite young, he frequently took a hand in the game.

One day, according to a story which Mahone himself told, a handsome carriage, with a fine pair of horses driven by a Negro servant, drew up at the tavern and a man of elegance went in to the bar. Before long, the guest and Major Mahone had begun gambling; as time went by, the elder Mahone, in a losing streak, had dropped most of his money. He called Billy and told him to take his hand, that he was going to sleep. When he came back from his nap, Major Mahone discovered that Billy had won all the man's money, his horses and carriages as well, and that they were then gambling for the servant. Major Mahone asked his son for the money. "Here is what you lost," replied Billy Mahone. "I am going to keep my winnings and educate myself."[5]

Mahone's education as a boy cannot be called a solid one, for when he was almost eighteen, and went to Virginia Military Institute on a legislative scholarship, he found college work difficult to master. "I had a hard time there," Mahone later wrote a friend, "The first year especially, from the want of previous preparation . . . However, I pulled through not without some credit to myself."

One who knew Billy Mahone well described him as "a youngster of precocious judgment, boundless enterprise, great ambition to win at any game he played, and indomitable grit." He had an amazing faculty for making friends, and many people who recognized in Billy "elements of unusual power" interested themselves in his success. The boy certainly was father to the man, for Billy Mahone carried these traits into the business world, into the Confederate Army, and into postwar politics.

Mahone was graduated in the class of 1847—the last of the three-year classes at VMI—and as a State Cadet he fulfilled his obligation of teaching school after graduation. While on the faculty of Rappahannock Academy, Mahone, who excelled in mathematics, decided to study engineering. In July 1849 he was appointed a surveyor for the Orange & Alexandria Railroad, then locating its route. In 1852, the twenty-six-year-old Mahone was appointed chief engineer for the Frederick and Valley Plank Road Company. While fulfilling this function, Mahone's legislative friends sought for him the post of chief engineer for the newly chartered Norfolk & Petersburg Railroad. In April 1853 he was elected chief engineer by the board of directors at a salary of $3500 per year, and for eight years, until the war interfered, he advanced steadily in his profession and with the railroad. By 1858, the road was completed, Mahone's most notable contribution to it being the laying of the roadbed through the almost bottomless Dismal Swamp. And when the offices of president and chief engineer of the railroad were consolidated into one position, William Mahone, only thirty-three years old, was elected to the new position.

Meanwhile, in February 1855, Mahone had married Otelia Butler, and had settled in Norfolk. Their union produced thirteen children, only three of whom lived to maturity.[6]

As the war clouds gathered over Virginia after the firing on Fort Sumter, opinion was by no means unanimous for the state to leave the Union. True, the ordinance of secession presented on April 17 passed, 88 to 55, but that vote clearly indicated a divided opinion in Virginia. Not so with Billy Mahone; he was an ardent secessionist, and warmly urged that his native state quit the Union.

Mahone was in Richmond when the ordinance passed. Governor John Letcher summoned the young railroad president and ordered him to seize the Gosport Navy Yard at Norfolk with the volunteer companies from Petersburg, Portsmouth, and Norfolk. But General of Militia William B. Taliaferro claimed the command of the operation, and Mahone volunteered to help him. General Taliaferro appointed Mahone to a committee of three which called upon Federal authorities at the navy yard to surrender the facility. They were promptly turned down.

At the very time that Mahone and the others were reporting the Federal refusal to Taliaferro, word came to headquarters that several boats had left the navy yard and were moving up the South Branch of the Elizabeth River, doubtless sent out to destroy the railroad bridge over the stream. When Mahone heard this, he didn't hesitate a moment. The Norfolk & Petersburg Railroad used that bridge and, if it were destroyed, Norfolk's rail communication was broken.

Mahone urged Taliaferro to give him a company with which to defend the bridge, should the Federals attempt to blow it up, and then rushed down to the railroad station to prepare an engine and flatcar for the operation. When the company arrived, the engine and flatcar were waiting, but the company commander balked at the proposal that his men board the "train," and refused to proceed any farther. Disgusted, Mahone was no less determined to defend the bridge that linked Norfolk with the rest of Virginia. He and his assistant, Henry Fink, both heavily armed, climbed into the engine cab and headed for the bridge.

It proved a false alarm. They found no naval units on the river. A run as far as the Dismal Swamp revealed that everything was clear and calm, so Mahone and Fink turned back. On the return run to Norfolk, Mahone hit upon a stratagem which would be used again and again as the war progressed. He gave orders to the engineer to blow the locomotive whistle and ring the bell in the manner of a train arriving in the station. Throughout most of the night, the engineer came clanging and whistling into the station, backing out for another "arrival" a little later. At intervals, Mahone sent messages to the navy yard, announcing that large numbers of troops were arriving from South Carolina and Georgia and would assault the navy yard if it were not surrendered.

Mahone's ruse worked, for on April 20 the Federal force evacuated the Gosport Navy Yard and, with its occupation by the Virginia troops, considerable war material fell into Confederate hands.[7]

III

The first military assignment that Billy Mahone received brought him to Richmond to head the Quartermaster's Department, but, eager for active service, he quickly resigned. On April 29, Governor John Letcher appointed him a lieutenant colonel of infantry in the Virginia volunteer service, and three days later, on May 2, he was promoted to colonel and assigned to the command of the 6th Virginia Infantry in the defenses of Norfolk.

Mobilization was very slow and, on May 8, Colonel Mahone reported that he was not yet in possession of the companies comprising his regiment. Ten days later little progress in this respect had been made, and Mahone complained:

"The ten companies constituting my proposed Regiment were designated to me but a few days ago. Seven of them have not in fact yet passed under my control. They are on detached duty at the various posts around. The other three . . . came under my command but yesterday. They are undisciplined and undrilled—and only this morning got arms."

Mahone's regiment was incorporated into the brigade of Brigadier General Benjamin Huger early in July 1861, and it was stationed in the defenses of Norfolk when General Irvin McDowell made his move against General P. G. T. Beauregard's line behind Bull Run on July 21, 1861. Thus Billy Mahone and his men missed the fight at Manassas, the first big battle of the war.[8]

In October, when Huger became a major general, Colonel Mahone commanded the Second Brigade under him, and on November 16, he was promoted to brigadier general. In his new rank, Mahone retained the Second Brigade, and the defense of Norfolk and its approaches became his responsibility until the spring of 1862.

During his long stay at Norfolk, General Mahone doubtless found time to direct the operations of the Norfolk & Petersburg Railroad. At any rate, on May 1, 1862, orders from Secretary of War George W. Randolph instructed Mahone to have his superintendent take charge of shipping at once certain war materials at Norfolk when it was decided to evacuate that city. This would suggest that Mahone had at least supervisory contacts with his railroad, if not the direct operation of it.[9]

After General George B. McClellan launched the Peninsula Campaign against Richmond in the spring of 1862, the Confederate authorities considered Norfolk no longer tenable. General Mahone's brigade was ordered to Gordonsville on May 9 to reinforce General Dick Ewell's division, which was on its way to join Stonewall Jackson in the Shenandoah Valley. But Mahone never got to the Valley. On May 14, General Robert E. Lee telegraphed General Huger to SEND IMMEDIATELY GENERAL MAHONE WITH HIS BRIGADE, OR PART OF IT, TO DREWRY'S BLUFF. A follow-up telegram from Secretary Randolph stated that GENERAL MAHONE . . . WILL ASSUME THE COMMAND ON HIS ARRIVAL THERE. In a letter on the same date, Randolph was more explicit:

". . . General Mahone . . . will find Captain Farrand, of the Navy, in charge of the battery and the obstruction. The President wishes General Mahone to superintend the engineering operations and to cover the battery with his brigade. He will have an engineer officer assigned to his command, and will cause the obstruction to be completed as rapidly as possible by the deposit of loose stone. He will have guns mounted and the batteries casemated . . ."

Drewry's Bluff, about eight miles below Richmond on the right bank of the James River, was an important bastion in the defense of the Confederate capital. General Mahone and most of his brigade reached Drewry's Bluff late on May 14 and, the next morning, they came under the fire of five probing Federal warships, which retired after dueling the Confederate shore batteries for about four hours.[10]

On the same day General Lee wrote Mahone to "make such use of your troops and resources as may be best calculated to prevent the ascent of the river by the gunboats of the enemy." Lee instructed Mahone to push the work of obstructing the river with "ceaseless vigor" and to complete the batteries "with all possible dispatch." General Lee urged Mahone to "harmonize" the several operations with the Navy and to "give vigor and energy to the whole."

Mahone reported to Lee on May 19 that he considered the river obstruction at Drewry's Bluff inefficient, and Lee, the next day, authorized him to take whatever measures were necessary to strengthen it. Meanwhile General Lee's brother, Captain Sidney Smith Lee of the Navy, had received orders on May 15 from Secretary of Navy Mallory to relieve Commander Farrand in command of the naval defenses of the James River at Drewry's Bluff. Captain Lee's instructions, in part, read:

"General Mahone has been assigned to the chief command, but the naval force is expected to fight all the batteries, complete the obstructions and mount additional guns where you may deem them necessary . . . Consult freely with General Mahone and defend the river to the last extremity."

It was obvious to General Mahone, when Captain Lee arrived, that there was a conflict of authority. General Lee had tried to obviate this by sending his brother a copy of Mahone's orders and by declaring that "there will be no interference with the naval forces under your command by the land forces serving in conjunction with you" and by urging the two branches to "harmonize perfectly in the duties that have been assigned them."[11]

On May 25, when the dual authority began to irk him, the outspoken Billy Mahone wrote Secretary of War Randolph:

"It is important to harmonize the operations of the Navy and Army I well understand, and so far as in my power this shall be done where no sacrifice to the service is to be the cost, but I cannot be responsible in any co-partnership authority.

"There has been no difficulty between the two arms of the service, but interferences have occurred in the prosecution of the works to the prejudice of the common object.

"I have therefore to inquire to what extent it is intended that I shall be relieved of the command and responsibility, as prescribed in your letter to General Huger, by the chief naval officer at the post.

"If I am to be responsible for the manner and energy of the works at this post I would thank you to make this understood with the Navy Department, as also the official relation of the Navy with my command, and that the engineers be directed to report to me and made subject to my directions . . . I am sure you will appreciate and understand the motive which prompts me to address you this paper. I desire simply to exercise authority where I am held to account."

The same day General Huger arrived at Drewry's Bluff and took the command from Mahone, thus relieving the latter of any further responsibility. Huger agreed completely with Mahone on the question of conflicting instructions to the Army and Navy and he wrote General Lee, on May 26, to that effect. "I consider these letters are conflicting," he said. "I ask that these conflicting instructions be reconciled or be withdrawn altogether."[12]

IV

By the end of May 1862, McClellan's snail-paced advance up the Peninsula between the York and James Rivers had reached to within six miles of Richmond. General Joseph E. Johnston decided to attack the Union army at Seven Pines, near the railroad station of Fair Oaks.

As he made his plans to attack on the morning of May 31, a torrential rainstorm turned the roads into quagmires, which would impair the progress of the assault, and caused the Chickahominy River to overflow, which would hinder Federal reinforcements from coming up.

Johnston joined battle, and for two days, May 31–June 1, the issue hung in the balance. Confusion caused by the severe wounding of Johnston on May 31 and the indisposition of General G. W. Smith, who succeeded to the command on June 1, led to an uncoordinated Confederate effort.

General Billy Mahone's brigade, on June 1, was caught in a terrific Federal attack aimed also at the brigades of Armistead, Pickett, Pryor, and Wilcox. General D. H. Hill, in his report of the battle, wrote:

"Armistead's men fled early in the action, with the exception of a few heroic companies, with which that gallant officer maintained his ground against an entire brigade. Mahone withdrew his brigade without my orders."

When Armistead's troops broke, this exposed the left of Pickett's line to a flank attack, and General Hill ordered Mahone's brigade forward to fill the gap. A sudden volley from the Federals threw Mahone's troops into disorder and then into panic, and they gave way to flight, seeking the safety of a roadside ditch.

In vain did Hill storm and threaten and plead with the troops to quit their shelter and fight like true Southerners, but Mahone's Virginians ignored his commands.

Hill called to the commander of the 13th North Carolina Regiment: "Colonel Scales! Come and occupy the position that these cowardly Virginians have fled from!"

Scales's men moved forward, obeying literally Hill's order to "run over the cowards," and as they marched into position they walked over the backs of the prone soldiers.

When word reached General Mahone that General Hill was insulting his troops, he rode up to Hill, protesting: "You should not abuse my men, for I ordered them out of the fight."

"Why did you do so?" Hill demanded. "Do you not see that you left a gap open for the enemy to pass through and break our line in two?" Before Mahone could reply, Hill continued with scathing scorn: "But if you ordered them out, I beg the soldiers' pardon for what I said to them and transpose it all to you."

Hot-tempered Billy Mahone went white with fury, but the heat of a hot battle was no place to vent it. Moreover, having rallied his troops, Mahone got them up on Pickett's right, where, under heavy fire, they held on valiantly until Pickett, the enemy having desisted in his attack, withdrew to the Confederate lines of the previous night. The Battle of Seven Pines was over.

The next day, Billy Mahone's rage against General Hill was unabated. He asked General Roger Pryor to carry his challenge to Hill. "Mahone," declared Pryor, "you are a — fool." Pryor, with cogent arguments, talked Mahone out of the idea of a duel. Mahone could only damage his reputation by challenging Hill, he pointed out. Everybody in the army knew of Hill's moral scruples against dueling and at the same time everyone knew of Hill's fearless courage in action. Accordingly, Mahone, knowing in advance that Hill would refuse the challenge, would lay himself open to the criticism of having made a cheap, unbecoming gesture. Mahone quickly appreciated the common sense of Pryor's argument, and he dropped the idea of a duel. But he never lost his bitter enmity for Hill.[13]

After Seven Pines, Mahone's brigade took position on the Charles City Road; its left connected with Wright's Brigade, but its right was wholly unsupported. His brigade, reduced to about 1800 officers and men, had a long line to cover, which, Mahone reported, "imposed constant and vigilant exertions." During four weeks of inactivity by the enemy, "the laborious duties" of this outpost duty "were cheerfully and faithfully performed by the troops," Mahone reported.

Mahone's men had several skirmishes with Federal scouts during this period, but it was not until June 25 that the brigade did any fighting of consequence. When the Federals attacked Wright's position, Mahone moved three of his regiments and the battery of Captain Carey F. Grimes to strengthen Wright, whose flank, apparently, the Federals were trying to turn. After a lively engagement, "the enemy fled precipitately," said Mahone. His brigade casualties were 32 wounded in this engagement known as French's Field.

In the early phases of the Seven Days' Battles, Mahone's brigade remained in its position on the Charles City Road until June 29, when it was ordered to join in the pursuit of the retreating enemy south of the Chickahominy. In the course of this operation, Mahone's men engaged in a number of skirmishes before they arrived, on July 1, at Malvern Hill, where the bloody Seven Days came to an end.

Under orders of General Huger, his division commander, Mahone reported to Major General John B. Magruder. The latter ordered the brigade to take position in the immediate rear of Wright's Brigade, already poised for a charge which would be made simultaneously on front and flanks against the Union batteries. Yankee sharpshooters, firing from behind wheat shocks, bedeviled Mahone as he got his men into line. At 5 P.M. the signal to move forward came. Mahone reported that his men "responded . . . with spirit and alacrity." Over a succession of steep hills and ravines the men of Mahone and Wright pressed forward until they were within a few hundred yards of the Federal left batteries. There, under cover of these guns, and in a strong position behind the crest of hills, Federal infantry was in force. Mahone related what happened:

"At this time there were no other troops engaging the enemy in our view or in supporting connection, and here for about two hours the fire and fury of battle raged with great obstinacy and destruction on both sides, our men finally succeeding in driving the enemy from the heights occupied in our front and immediately under his guns and upon his reserves at that point, and occupying the position from which he had resisted our advance with such obstinacy and deadly effect."

Night was now close at hand, but in the gathering dusk the enemy could be discerned moving troops from his right to enfilade the position of Mahone and Wright. Soon the Confederates were suffering severely from the intense flank fire. "Opportunely for our protection and perhaps rescue from utter destruction, our troops came upon him from the right of the line," reported Mahone, "disconcerting this plan of his and driving him back with great slaughter, upon his line of artillery and reserves." In the meanwhile, the portion of Mahone's command that had driven the Federals from their front had pressed on and were closely engaged with the enemy, "many," reported Mahone, "falling side by side with his men and near his batteries." Mahone's report tells a vivid story:

"Utter darkness now covered the scene, and the tragedy closes, leaving General Wright and myself with the remnants of our shattered brigades in possession of the ground which they had at a heavy sacrifice of kindred blood, but with spirit and gallantry, won. General Wright and myself . . . arranged and positioned for the night all the various troops which were now within the reach of our authority, first establishing our picket line, and then giving attention to the wants of the wounded around us as our capacity and resources would admit."

The two generals then made a reconnaissance and discovered that the Federals, in good order, but nonetheless rapidly, were abandoning their lines, and this intelligence was immediately communicated to General Magruder. The next morning, Federal cavalry appeared along the line which the Federal artillery had occupied the previous day. The Union horsemen, obviously shielding McClellan's withdrawal, made no offensive moves and then rode off. When the work of caring for Confederate wounded and gathering scattered arms and equipment was completed, Mahone turned over the field to fresh troops. "I withdrew my small band," he reported, "which was now in much need of rest and food."

Mahone went into the Battle of Malvern Hill with 1226 officers and men. His casualties were 329—39 killed, 166 wounded, 124 missing—or more than 26 per cent of his command. In his report, General Magruder listed Mahone and Wright first in declaring that he could not "speak too highly of the conduct of the officers and men of the brigades attacking the front."[14]

After the Seven Days' Battles, Robert E. Lee reorganized the Army of Northern Virginia, and Brigadier General Billy Mahone's brigade was assigned to the division of Major General Richard H. Anderson in Longstreet's command. Mahone's brigade was composed of the 6th, 12th, 16th, 41st, and 39th Virginia Regiments.

In the second Battle of Manassas, on August 29–30, General Mahone was severely wounded in the chest, but before retiring from action he and his brigade had fought well. General Longstreet, in his report, listed Mahone among the officers of his command "most prominently distinguished" in the bloody two-day fight.[15] While recuperating from the wound—described to Mrs. Mahone as "a flesh wound," thereby evoking her comment that it must be serious for the general didn't have any flesh—Mahone missed the invasion of Maryland and the tremendous battle at Sharpsburg on Antietam Creek.

When Lee retired into Virginia and took up his line on the Rappahannock, General Billy Mahone returned to his command in time to participate in the campaign at Fredericksburg in mid-December 1862.

This was familiar ground to Mahone. He was fighting in his own backyard, for he had surveyed the country around Fredericksburg when he was chief engineer for the Frederick and Valley Plank Road Company.

V

When Lee took up his position at Fredericksburg on the high ground to the south and west of the Rappahannock, Longstreet delegated to Billy Mahone the job of constructing and running the line of fortifications on his entire front.

General Mahone moved his brigade to its assigned position immediately in the rear of the selected line of battle at the first alarm on December 11, 1862. While the brigade as a whole remained under arms in its position with Longstreet's command on Lee's left during Burnside's tremendous assault on December 13, Mahone always had one, and sometimes two regiments, in advance of the Confederate batteries on the front. Although exposed to enemy artillery fire, casualties were strangely light. In his report, Mahone proudly credited his men with "much work in the erection of batteries and rifle-pits" during the battle. "Among these works," Mahone reported "may be mentioned the one as a special advantage in dislodging the enemy from behind the hills on the right of the Plank Road." Mahone's commander, General Anderson, noted this valuable contribution to the Confederate success in his report:

"It is due to Brigadier-General Mahone to say that he discovered and pointed out the important position for a battery, which enfiladed the slope upon which the enemy formed his battalions before and after his attacks on Marye's Hill, and that he rendered very efficient service, assisting in the construction of the battery which drove them from their place of shelter."

While Billy Mahone was no political general—he could qualify militarily on his VMI training, his engineering, his railroading—the little scrapper was not above having his military interest looked after by his politician friends.

A month after the Battle of Fredericksburg, thirty-five Virginia legislators—16 Senators and 19 Representatives—addressed themselves to
President Jefferson Davis as follows:

"We the undersigned members of the General Assembly of Virginia
do most cordially recommend to your Excellency for promotion Brig
Genl William Mahone, who is an educated & accomplished officer. Since
he has been honoured with your commission as Brigadier General we
most earnestly ask you to refer to his immediate Commanders . . ."[16]

Governor John Letcher appears to have thrown his influence behind
the campaign to get Mahone promoted, for his aide-de-camp, Colonel S.
Bassett French, sounded out both Generals Longstreet and Dick Anderson, Mahone's commanders, on the subject. On February 9, 1863, Longstreet wrote to Colonel French:

"Your letter of the 5th inst. is received. I have more than once thought
of recommending Brig. Genl. Mahone for promotion; but there is no
command for him that I know of. And I do not think that the President
will make a promotion unless there is a command for the officer. Genl.
Mahone is one of our best Brigadiers and is worthy of promotion. It has
been my intention to recommend his promotion as soon as I could see an
opportunity to give him a command."

On March 30, General Anderson wrote Colonel French that Mahone's
services "to his country during the past twelve months richly entitled
him to promotion." Anderson went all out in his praise of Little Billy's
military virtues:

"He is a thorough disciplinarian and unites to a military education
great skill and untiring activity in the field—quick perception, energetic
execution and in short all the qualities of a superior general officer . . .
His activity and engineering skill were noticed in my report of the part
taken by my Division in the battle of Fredericksburg.

"His constitution is not strong but it is supported by an indomitable
spirit . . . Heartily wishing you success in your purpose to secure his
promotion."[17]

The same day that General Anderson addressed his letter to Governor
Letcher's aide, he also wrote Adjutant General Samuel Cooper: "I have
the honor to recommend Brig. Genl Wm. Mahone for promotion to the
grade of Major General," and he repeated more or less the same praise
of Mahone that he had put into his letter to Colonel French. On April 4,
General Longstreet added his endorsement to Anderson's recommendation: "I can cheerfully endorse this recommendation in favor of Genl.
Mahone." When the recommendation reached General Lee, he added the
following endorsement on April 8 before sending it to Richmond: "Respectfully forwarded, as an evidence of merit of Genl. Mahone. I concur
in the commendation bestowed by Genls. Anderson and Longstreet."
But Lee then reminded the Richmond authorities that they might pro-

mote Billy Mahone right out of the Army of Northern Virginia: "There is no command in this army for Genl. Mahone, if promoted."[18]

Sixteen months would pass before Billy Mahone's promotion would come through—and when it did it would be a battlefield promotion, bestowed by Robert E. Lee himself.

Meanwhile, after Fredericksburg, Lee's army remained on the south side of the Rappahannock, while the Federals held their position north of the river, opposite the town. Mahone's brigade guarded the United States Ford as the bitter winter months dragged into spring. In late April, the winter deadlock of inactivity was broken when "Fighting Joe" Hooker, now in command of the Union Army, set the stage for the Battle of Chancellorsville by launching a wide-sweeping operation to the right aimed at striking at Lee's left flank and rear. Lee anticipated Hooker's intentions and moved towards Chancellorsville to meet the threat head-on.

On April 29, Mahone received word that Federal troops in considerable force had crossed Germanna and Ely Fords on the Rapidan River, and were marching on the Confederate flank and rear. "This appearance of the enemy . . . rendered our position at the United States Ford no longer tenable," Mahone reported, "and with a view to checking his advance upon the flank of our army, as was now clearly discerned to be his aim, the two brigades, General Posey's and mine—were immediately placed in a position near Chancellorsville, so as to cover the roads from the Germanna and Ely crossings of the Rapidan and that of the United States Ford, uniting at Chancellorsville."

Mahone and Posey held this position until the next morning, when General Dick Anderson came upon the field and assumed command of his two brigades. He ordered them to fall back, during which process Mahone's rear guard had a lively brush with Federal cavalry, which after "a precipitate advance . . . was repulsed, and so effectively," Mahone declared, "as to leave us free from any further annoyance during the change of position."

After taking up his new position at the intersection of the Mine Road and Orange Turnpike, Mahone braced for an attack when a considerable force of Union cavalry and infantry appeared on the turnpike. But nothing occurred except some skirmishing with Yankee sharpshooters and reconnoitering parties.

On May 1, Mahone's brigade, on the Orange Turnpike, led in the general Confederate advance and, encountering both Federal infantry and artillery, had "quite a brisk little engagement," Mahone reported. After repulsing the Federals and making captures, Mahone pushed on in line of battle to a point on the turnpike about a mile and a half west of Chancellorsville. All that day Mahone's battle line faced the Federals, but on May 2, the brigade was moved to the front line, to the left of the Plank

Road. "In this position we continued up to the fall of Chancellorsville engaging the enemy more or less warmly as the progress of General Jackson's operations on his flank and rear seemed to call for, and as the range of his [General Jackson's] enfilading fire would allow," reported Mahone.

It was during this phase of the fighting that skirmishers from Mahone's 6th Virginia Regiment, under the command of Captain Carter Williams, made a bold sortie, charging over the enemy's abatis, firing upon him in his rifle pits, capturing a few prisoners and the colors of an Ohio regiment, and then returning safely to the brigade lines.

When Stonewall Jackson's flank attack had driven the Federals from their position at Chancellorsville, General Billy Mahone's men were sent with another one of McLaws' brigades to meet the threat of Union General John Sedgwick, who was advancing rapidly from Fredericksburg. The two brigades were joined by Wilcox's Brigade at Salem Church and by General McLaws with the rest of his division. "My brigade, in the spirited fight at this place, occupied the extreme left of the line, lying wholly in the woods," reported Mahone, "and participated in the successful resistance made to the enemy's very determined effort to break our lines at that point." Upon the conclusion of this action on May 5, Mahone rejoined Anderson's division. In his report, Mahone bestowed "high commendation" upon his officers and men "in bearing the hardships and privations attending eight consecutive days of exposure and excitement as well as in battle." Once again, Mahone's losses were heavy —24 killed, 134 wounded, and 97 missing, for a total of 255.

General Anderson in his report highly commended "the gallant conduct of the division which I had the honor and good fortune to command," and General Billy Mahone's "bold, skillful, and successful management, so well seconded by his brave Virginians."

Mahone's able biographer, Nelson M. Blake, states that, after Stonewall Jackson's death in the twilight of the great victory of Chancellorsville, "General Mahone came more and more to occupy the place in Lee's regard which Jackson formerly held." The only evidence he presents, however, is a quotation from the Mahone family papers and some fulsome verse recited in 1876 at a reunion of Mahone's brigade. Had Billy Mahone indeed taken Jackson's place in Lee's regard, the fact would have long since been established. That Lee thought highly of Mahone there can be no doubt, and that he considered him in the final year of the war one of his most able division commanders is also certain. But evidence is lacking that Mahone ever filled Stonewall Jackson's place in Robert E. Lee's regard.

Shortly after Chancellorsville, Mahone was elected to the Virginia State Senate by the city of Norfolk to fill the vacancy occasioned by a resignation. This in no way interfered with Mahone's military activities, for the Virginia General Assembly did not convene until December 7, 1863, and he actually did not take his seat until March 1, 1864, just ten days before adjournment. Accordingly, Mahone led his brigade into Pennsylvania when Lee crossed the Potomac for the second time in June 1863.[19]

In the three-day Battle of Gettysburg, July 1–3, 1863, Billy Mahone's brigade took little part. His report in the Official Records requires only a dozen lines to tell how his troops were occupied, mainly as skirmishers, during the battle. The brigade was not engaged on the first day of the fight. "During the days and nights of July 2 and 3, the brigade was posted in line of battle immediately in front of the enemy, and in support of Pegram's batteries," Mahone reported. "In this front its skirmishers were quite constantly engaged, and inflicted much loss upon the enemy . . ." After the repulse of Pickett's Charge on July 3, Mahone maintained his position. The brigade was exposed to the terrific Federal shelling of the second and third days at Gettysburg. His losses—8 killed, 55 wounded, and 39 missing—were mainly sustained during the Federal artillery activity.[20]

In the reorganization of the Confederate Army after Chancellorsville, Anderson's division had been placed in Lieutenant General A. P. Hill's III Corps, and thus it was in Hill's Corps that Mahone fought at Gettysburg. Mahone's brigade shared in the general inactivity that followed Lee's return to Virginia. But on October 14, when Hill attacked the Federals at Bristoe Station, Mahone's troops participated in the sharp encounter, and in the campaign at Mine Run, late in November, Mahone's brigade saw service, too.[21]

Shortly thereafter, Lee went into winter quarters and serious fighting was held over until the following spring.

During the lull, Billy Mahone's political friends renewed their efforts to get him promoted to major general. On March 8, 1864—while Mahone was sitting briefly in the Virginia Assembly—twenty-five senators signed a petition to President Jefferson Davis in his behalf. They reminded Mr. Davis that Mahone was "a distinguished graduate" of Virginia Military Institute and had spent his whole life in civil and military engineering. At the moment he was the ranking brigadier in the Army of Northern Virginia and had but one senior in the whole Confederate service.

"There have been several promotions over him from among his *juniors* in service," declared the petition. "Of this we do not complain, as we know it was done, if intentional, for the good of the service in your judgment. We have only alluded to this, to show that, although apparent injustice may have been done him in this respect, yet he did not complain; for, trusting in that lofty and disinterested patriotism, sound judgment and strict impartiality that has always characterized your public career, he cheerfully submitted to your better and more enlightened judgment."

The petitioners called attention to the recommendations of General Lee and General Longstreet of more than a year previous and extolled Mahone as "a gentleman of enlarged and comprehensive views; of the greatest industry, and indomitable will—a brave and chivalrous man, and will distinguish himself as a Division commander, as he has done as a brigadier." The petition asserted that it was "beyond dispute" and "universally conceded" that Mahone had the "best disciplined and trained brigade in the Army of Northern Virginia, and is so openly pronounced by Gen. Robert E. Lee himself." The twenty-five senators hoped Mr. Davis would find it consistent with his "views of official propriety" to nominate "this worthy son of Virginia" and place him in a position which "will equally redown [sic] to his own distinction and renown, and to the good and welfare of the country."[22]

VI

The Wilderness was a wide tangle of stunted trees, thick undergrowth, and uneven ground, an area about 16 or 17 square miles, between Fredericksburg and Orange Court House. It was everything its name implied— desolate, rough, uncultivated. This was the stage upon which the next act in the drama would be played—an act in which one important new character would be introduced into the play, General U. S. Grant, commander-in-chief of all the Union Armies.

Early in May 1864, Grant made his move toward Richmond, aiming at getting around Lee's right flank. Lee, however, was ready for Grant, and battle was joined in the rugged wilderness.

General Billy Mahone's brigade broke camp at Madison Run Station, near the Rapidan on May 4 and guarded the crossing of the left and rear of Lee's army near Willis' Ford. On May 5 Mahone rejoined the rest of the army, which by now was facing Grant in the Wilderness. Mahone's brigade encamped that night near Verdiersville, and early the next morning took up position on the Orange Plank Road in support of part of General Longstreet's line. Mahone reported:

"We . . . very soon after were ordered to join and cooperate with Anderson's and Wofford's brigades, of that corps, in an attack upon the enemy's left flank. As the senior brigadier, I was by Lieutenant-General Longstreet charged with the immediate direction of this movement. Wofford and Anderson were already in motion, and in a few moments the line of attack had been formed, and the three brigades, in imposing order and with a step that meant to conquer, were now rapidly descending upon the enemy's left."

"After going some distance through the thicket," recalled one of Mahone's troopers, "we encountered the enemy apparently bivouacking and little expecting any attack from that direction. They fled pell-mell before us, leaving their light camp equipage scattered in every direction, making scarcely any resistance until they reached the Orange Plank Road; when, having a natural fortification, strengthened hurriedly by them, they stoutly resisted us."

Young Lieutenant Colonel Moxley Sorrel of Longstreet's staff had been sent to gather what brigades he could for this move against the exposed Federal left. Longstreet had quickly sensed a great opportunity. To Sorrel he had said:

"Colonel, there is a fine chance of a great attack by our right. If you will quickly get into those woods, some brigades will be found much scattered from the fight. Collect them and take charge. Form a good line and then move, your right pushed forward and turning as much as possible to the left. Hit hard when you start, but don't start until you have everything ready . . ."

And so it was that Hancock's left was rolled up "like a wet blanket" as he later admitted to Longstreet. At one point in the action, after the Federals had stabilized their line behind natural cover, Colonel Sorrel galloped up to the color-bearer of the 12th Virginia Regiment of Mahone's brigade, and reached for his colors to lead the charge. The youngster steadfastly refused to release his hold on the staff. "We will follow you," he shouted to Sorrel, holding on to his colors. Mahone's battle line moved forward, and the two brigades on either side kept pace and in a moment the Federals broke and fled. Mahone described what followed:

"The movement was a success—complete as it was brilliant. The enemy were swept from our front on the Plank Road, where his advantages of position had already been felt by our line, and from which the necessity for his dislodgment had become a matter of much interest. Besides this valuable result the Plank Road had been gained and the enemy's lines bent back in much disorder; the way was open for greater fruits. His long lines of dead and wounded which lay in the wake of our swoop furnished evidence that he was not allowed time to change front, as well as of the execution of our fire."

General Longstreet, with fresh troops, had followed the advance closely, and was preparing to strike the enemy again when his party was mistaken for Yankees. There was a rattle of fire from the Confederate line. Longstreet was hit in the neck, General Micah Jenkins was killed, and other staff officers were wounded. Curiously enough, Longstreet was shot by his own men, almost a year later to the day, and not far from the place where Stonewall Jackson fell under similar conditions. It would be almost six months before Longstreet would return to the army.[23]

The next day, May 7, 1864, General Lee assigned Major General

Richard H. Anderson to the temporary command of Longstreet's I Corps and, in the same order, he instructed Brigadier General Billy Mahone to assume command of Dick Anderson's division during his absence.

Grant, after his repulse in the Wilderness, did an amazing thing for a beaten Union general—he didn't fall back. Instead, he gathered his battered forces and determinedly pushed southward, still trying to get around Lee's right. The two armies engaged again at Spotsylvania Courthouse and, between May 8–19, furious and almost continuous fighting and skirmishing ensued.

Mahone's division was active in the heavy fighting around Spotsylvania. Late in the afternoon of May 8, Mahone's old brigade struck the Federals near the courthouse and drove them back on their main line. In a sharp skirmish on May 14, Mahone took a number of prisoners from the Union II Corps on Grant's left. When A. P. Hill's Corps checked Union General Gouverneur K. Warren's advance after he had crossed the North Anna on May 23, Mahone's division participated in the action. The next day, at Taylorsville, when the Federals probed feebly at the Confederate lines, Mahone followed up their repulse by driving three Union regiments across the river, capturing some prisoners and a stand of colors. On June 1, Major General John C. Breckinridge's and Mahone's divisions threw the Federals on their front back across the Totopotomy, taking about 100 prisoners during the sharp engagement.[24]

In his brief period as a division commander, barely three weeks, Billy Mahone ably demonstrated his capacity to lead larger units than a brigade. Of Mahone's development, Douglas Southall Freeman has written:

"Many officers who were competent, even conspicuous, at a particular rank in Confederate service failed when they were given larger duties. Mahone reverses this. A Brigadier of no shining reputation, with achievements scarcely above the army average, he proved himself—within three months—one of the ablest divisional commanders the Army ever had. He appears in the records as a man never aroused to his full potentialities until he felt he had duties that challenged all he knew, all he could learn, all he could do."

On June 4, 1864, Lee appointed Mahone a temporary major general, but Little Billy, probably piqued at the temporary nature of his new grade, declined to accept the appointment and continued as a brigadier general to command Dick Anderson's division.[25]

Meanwhile, the bloody battle of Cold Harbor had been fought on June 3. Grant's operation against Lee's prepared positions, begun on May 31, reached their peak that day. A. P. Hill's Corps held the extreme right of Lee's position, except for Heth's division, which held the extreme left. Mahone's division was in reserve, supporting Hill's divisions on the right end of the line, which was anchored on the Chickahominy.

Billy Mahone represented Lee's sole reserve force. A modern student of the campaign, Clifford Dowdey, stated Lee's gamble neatly:

"Only on the overshifted right was there a supporting force, Mahone's . . . [elsewhere] not a regiment was held in reserve. Lee staked the defense of Richmond on the powerful field fortifications and 'the steady valor of his troops under conditions which required of them no extensive physical exertion nor of their leaders any cooperative maneuver.'"

At daybreak on June 3, Grant made his grand assault on Lee and suffered the greatest losses in a corresponding period of time in the entire Civil War. Up and down the Confederate defenses, the Federal attackers melted before the blistering fire power of Lee's men. In less than an hour, the deadly fire from the entrenched line took a toll of more than 7300 bluecoats. The attack, Lee reported to Richmond, was "repulsed without difficulty." There was, however, a small Federal penetration on Breckinridge's front, at a boggy section where only a picket line manned the breastworks. But Finegan's Brigade of Mahone's division rushed up and, with help from the Maryland Battalion of Breckinridge's command, wiped out the salient, driving the Federals back with severe losses.

From June 4 through June 12, the front was quiet except for occasional skirmishing and picket line fire. On June 13 Lee discovered that the Federals had left his front. Grant, for the first time, had given his brilliant adversary the slip. Lee, after pushing skirmishers ahead for a couple of miles without contacting Grant's army, put his own army into motion "to conform to the route taken by him."[26]

Although Grant had stolen something of a march on Lee, the latter on June 11 had told President Davis that he expected Grant to move the bulk of his army to the James River. Accordingly, when he found Grant gone, Lee crossed the James himself and marched to Petersburg to place his army once more between Grant and the Confederate capital. Meanwhile General Beauregard, who had bottled up Union General Ben Butler at Bermuda Hundred, was feeling the weight of Grant's new pressure. Until Lee arrived with his army, Beauregard's undermanned force was the sole defense of Petersburg, the southern approach to Richmond. On June 18, Lee wrote President Davis that he had received information that "Grant's whole force had crossed to the south side of the James River." A four-word postscript set the stage for the great siege which was to follow: "I go to Petersburg."[27]

VII

The siege of Petersburg by Grant's superior force began on June 19, 1864, and it continued for almost ten months, until Lee ordered the evacuation of the city on April 2, 1865.

It was during the investment of Petersburg that General Billy Mahone reached his military peak and, from the Wilderness to Appomattox, his reputation and that of the division he led grew steadily.

Lee's entrenchments around Petersburg assumed the shape, roughly, of a question mark. The top of the "?", anchored on the Appomattox River, encircled Petersburg on the east and south, crossing the Weldon & Petersburg Railroad about two miles south of the city and running west to the Boydtown Plank Road. There the lower half of the "?", generally paralleling the Boydtown Plank Road, ran mainly southwestward for about five miles to Hatcher's Run, about a mile and a half east of Burgess' Mill.

Around Lee's defenses, Grant cast a semicircle, more or less regular in form, his right resting on the Appomattox, while his exposed left pushed toward the Weldon Railroad.

On June 22, officers in the headquarters of General Henry Wise at Petersburg commented on the sound of distant guns to the south.

"There has been heavy firing on the right this afternoon, General," said Colonel Alfred Roman of Beauregard's staff.

"Yes," replied General Wise. "Grant is evidently trying to extend his left as far as the Weldon Railroad. I met Mahone today, who said that he and Wilcox were moving out to intercept him. Whenever Mahone moves out, somebody is apt to be hurt . . . Since the death of Stonewall Jackson, the two men who seem to me to be the most gallant, enterprising and 'coming' soldiers of Lee's army are this little fellow Mahone and young Gordon, of Georgia."

That day, when Mahone moved out, the Yankees were indeed hurt. Grant had sent a cavalry raid swooping to the south to cut the Weldon Railroad and continue on a circle to reach the Richmond & Danville line. Meanwhile he sought to extend the Federal infantry line toward the Weldon Railroad. Billy Mahone, who was riding the line with Lee, suggested that he take three brigades and strike at the exposed Federal left. Lee assented. Mahone moved the brigades of Sanders and Wright and his old brigade, commanded by General Weisiger, over a covered route, formed them in battle "and, with a wild yell which rang out shrill and fierce through the gloomy pines," his troops took the Federals in flank. Gordon McCabe, Colonel Willie Pegram's dashing young adjutant, has given a vivid picture of Mahone's charge:

". . . Mahone's men burst upon the flank—a pealing volley, which roared along the whole front—a stream of wasting fire, under which the adverse left fell as one man—and the bronzed veterans swept forward shriveling up Barlow's division as lightning shrivels the dead leaves of autumn; then, cleaving a fiery path diagonally across the enemy's front, spreading dismay and destruction, rolled up Mott's division in its turn, and without check, the woods still reverberating with their fierce clamor, stormed and carried Gibbon's entrenchments and we seized his guns."[28]

That night, at 7:20 P.M., Mahone dispatched a report to General A. P. Hill that he had taken more than 1600 prisoners, four pieces of artillery, and a large number of small arms and tools. "We have pushed the enemy back for more than a mile to his trenches on the [Jerusalem] Plank Road, where I find he is more strongly fortified." Mahone told Hill that he was occupying the enemy's trenches less than a quarter of a mile from the Jerusalem Road, but he added: "Do not think the position we occupy desirable to hold."

Billy Mahone didn't have time to hold it if he had wanted to, for when word came that Union forces were tearing up the Weldon Railroad farther south, Mahone struck hard again on June 23. General Lee reported the results to Secretary of War Seddon:

"Yesterday the enemy made a demonstration with infantry upon the Weldon Railroad, but before he had done much damage was driven back by General Mahone with a portion of his command. About 600 prisoners and 28 commissioned officers were taken . . ."[29]

Apparently the tireless bantam, General Mahone, had the idea of continuing his pressure on the Federal left, despite almost two days of steady fighting. General Hill reported on June 24: "Have stopped Mahone. Mahone's men have been without sleep now two nights."

Five days later, at Reams' Station, Billy Mahone and his brigade distinguished themselves again. On the night of June 28, Mahone, with the brigades of Finegan, Sanders, and Perry, marched out from Petersburg and by daylight of the following day they were in position from which they struck General Wilson's cavalry, back from his fruitless raid on the Richmond & Danville Railroad. Fitz Lee's cavalry had first blocked his plan and then had harassed him and Brigadier General August Kautz as the latter pair fell back upon Reams' Station on the Weldon Railroad. And that's where Mahone struck them. Union Major General Phil Sheridan's report described what happened:

"General Wilson . . . was met by three brigades of infantry and surrounded. He then fell back, burning wagons, caissons, and abandoning artillery, which got tangled in the woods. As soon as the shells exploded, the enemy charged the rear guard and dispersed it. General Kautz, swinging off to the left, came in. The rebels continued after Wilson's column, charging it, and officers and men report a complete rout."

Fitz Lee and Wade Hampton, by turning the left of the Union cavalry, had herded Wilson into Mahone's trap. The fury of Mahone's attack had brought disaster to Wilson's horsemen, all of those who escaped having trudged into the Federal lines on foot, having lost their mounts in action or having abandoned them in crossing the swamps.

Lee reported to Richmond that at Reams' Station, the Confederates had taken a thousand prisoners, thirteen pieces of artillery, thirty wagons and ambulances, large quantities of small arms and ordnance stores, many horses and several hundred slaves which the Federals had picked up on their march.[30]

For the next few weeks, Mahone's division was in line along the Weldon Railroad and elements of it patrolled as far as Reams' Station to protect the tracks. Mahone moved around so much, apparently, during this period, that all kinds of confusing information as to the whereabouts of his division reached Union headquarters. To show General Grant "how conflicting is the information we receive," General Meade stated that "Mahone's division . . . has now been positively placed on our front, on our left and rear, and on its way to Pennsylvania."

Lieutenant General James Longstreet, recuperating from his painful neck wound at the Battle of the Wilderness, heard, of course, of Billy Mahone's exploits at Petersburg. He dictated a letter to Adjutant General Cooper on July 14, 1864, once again urging Mahone's promotion:

"At the battle of the Wilderness, May 6, I directed an attack to be made on the enemy's left, by a portion of the troops of the corps under my command and the brigade of Brig. Gen. William Mahone, to whom as the senior officer of the flanking column was intrusted its immediate direction. The success of the movement met my fullest expectation, and for the distinguished skill and gallantry displayed in its execution, I respectfully recommend Brigadier-General Mahone for promotion to the rank of major general. I desire to add that a painful wound received by me on the same day has delayed until now this recommendation, and although still unable to write I conceive it unjust to defer it longer . . ."[31]

In subsequent years, the question would be raised as to whether "West Pointism" had anything to do with the delay in promoting Mahone. There is certainly no reason to suspect that he encountered such a prejudice where none existed in the advancement of non-West Pointers as Lieutenant Generals Dick Taylor, Nathan Bedford Forrest, and Wade Hampton, and Major General Pat Cleburne. Moreover, Mahone's warm recommendations for promotions came from such West Pointers as Lee, Longstreet, A. P. Hill, and Dick Anderson.

There was no response from the War Department to Longstreet's reiterated recommendation that Billy Mahone be promoted to major general. There was one more test he had to meet, apparently, and that was not long in coming.

VIII

At 4:44 A.M. on July 30, 1864, there was a terrific explosion in the Confederate lines at Petersburg. First the earth trembled, then rocked as if it were an earthquake. Then came the tremendous blast, as a column of earth and smoke and flames leaped heavenward carrying more than

250 men to their destruction. Some were torn apart by the explosion, some were buried in the dreadful shower of stones and clay and shattered timbers and human limbs that roared down.

The Elliott Salient, barely a mile from the outskirts of Petersburg, had been ripped wide open by a Federal mine, and a jagged and irregular crater, 135 feet long, 97 feet wide, and 30 feet deep now existed where Captain Dick Pegram's battery and its infantry support had been. On either side of the chasm, the men of Elliott's Brigade fled the trenches in terror.

Poised a few hundred yards away was a Federal assault force of 15,000 men under General Burnside, ready to pour through the gap and into Petersburg.

The Confederates had known throughout the month of July that the Federals were engaged in a mining operation of some sort, and the subject was freely discussed and accepted by the Confederate troops.

"For some time the reports about the mine were exceedingly vague," recalled one Confederate veteran, John S. Wise. "More than one Union picket had hinted at a purpose to 'send you to Heaven soon,' or threatened that they were 'going to blow you up next week.' "

The Confederate engineers began countermining to determine the location of the Federal mine, and several areas were considered as likely, including the Elliott Salient. The men of Elliott's Brigade, according to Wise, were convinced their sector was the Yankee target. He wrote:

"Whatever doubts the engineers may have felt, the privates knew where the works were being mined. Elliott's men told the fellows on the left of our brigade all about it long before the explosion. Our men would go down there, and, lying on the ground with Elliott's men, would listen to the work going on below, and come back and tell all about it."

The ingenious project was the idea of Lieutenant Colonel Henry Pleasants of the 48th Pennsylvania Regiment, a unit made up largely of coal miners. Pleasants, himself, was a mining engineer. On June 23, Pleasants, from a rise in ground behind his line, was studying the Elliott Salient. Just the day before he had remarked to another officer: "If we could only knock out that fort, the rest would be easy." He was doubtless thinking about the salient, when a Union soldier, whose name is lost to history, spoke out: "We could blow that damned fort out of existence if we could run a mine shaft under it."

Pleasants developed the idea, convinced Burnside of its practicality, and the work was started at noon on June 25, 1864. Two hundred and ten men, two at a time, worked around the clock. By July 23, the job was finished. The main gallery was 511.8 feet in length while lateral galleries on right and left were 38 and 37 feet respectively.[32]

By sunset of July 28, everything was ready. Eight thousand pounds of powder—320 kegs of 25 pounds each—were in place, fuses were spliced and the tamping with 8000 sandbags, was completed. The mine was ready to be exploded.

Meanwhile, Grant had launched a diversionary attack on Richmond, and Lee, to meet it, had stripped the Petersburg defenses. On the morning of July 30, when the Federal mine exploded, Lee had in line along the ten-mile defenses of Petersburg only three divisions—Hoke's, Bushrod Johnson's, and Mahone's, a total of 18,000 men at the most. Grant had more than 60,000 men in front of Petersburg. With the shattering of the Confederate line by the mine, the road to Petersburg was open.

Fortunately for the Confederates, the Union assault troops were poorly led. Startled, or fascinated, by the explosion, the leading brigade froze in its place, and soon supporting troops crowded in on the first wave. When the Yankee line finally moved out, regimental and company organization was quickly lost and Federal officers had no control of their troops. Plunging forward, the confused Federal mass crowded into the huge pit as Elliott's survivors poured a hot fire upon them from the rim of the Crater. More than 12,000 Union troops, white and black, huddled in the Crater, as Confederate artillery, under the dashing young John Haskell, began blazing away with his guns and some eight-inch mortars, which lobbed shells into the swarming mass of bluecoats in the pit.[33]

Federal bungling and the gallantry of the Confederate artillery, although subjected to a frightful bombardment by Union guns, saved Petersburg in that perilous first hour. General Lee, who was across the Appomattox when the explosion came, hurried to General Bushrod Johnson's headquarters near the catastrophe, dispatching Colonel Charles S. Venable to General Billy Mahone with orders to rush two of his brigades to the support of General Johnson. Such was the urgency, Lee told Venable, the order did not have to go through General A. P. Hill, but could be delivered directly to Mahone.

Meanwhile, in Mahone's lines, the explosion, "sounding like a nearly simultaneous discharge of several pieces of artillery," had summoned the troops to the breastworks. So when Colonel Venable galloped up to Mahone's headquarters about 6:30 A.M., Mahone's men were standing at their arms. Orders were quickly issued and then, to prevent detection by Yankee observers in lookout towers of any troop movement from the lines, the men of Mahone's old brigade, commanded by Colonel D. A. Weisiger, and General A. R. Wright's Brigade, began to drop back from the breastworks, one by one, into a cornfield behind the line. Only when they were well out of sight of the Federals did the columns form and move out, with Weisiger's Virginians in the lead, marching up a ravine which gave them cover from the Federals' view.[34]

General Mahone rode at the head of the column with Colonel Venable, alternately giving instructions to his officers and inquiring of conditions at the Crater. After marching a while Mahone called a momentary halt and had the men divest themselves of their knapsacks and blanket rolls and prepare for immediate action. While the men were relieving themselves of their burdens, Mahone turned to Venable and said:

"I can't send my brigades to General Johnson—I will go with them myself."

As the head of the column neared the entrance to a covered way which approached the Crater, General Mahone rode on to General Bushrod Johnson's headquarters, hoping to find General Hill. Hill wasn't there, but General Beauregard was and, to Mahone's surprise, so was Bushrod Johnson, on whose front the disaster had occurred. "I did not of course expect to find Gen. Johnson anywhere else than on the ground where the front had been pierced," Mahone wrote many years later. ". . . Johnson . . . appeared to be about ready to take his breakfast . . ."

"General, you had better turn over any outlying troops you may have to Gen. Mahone, and let him make the attack," Beauregard said to Johnson, who assented.

"What frontage on the line does the enemy occupy?" Mahone asked. "I want to . . . determine the face of my attacking force."

"About a hundred yards," replied Johnson.

Mahone asked Johnson to show him the way to the Crater, whereupon the latter assigned a young officer to the job. In a few moments Mahone, having dismounted, followed his guide up the covered way into a ravine which led into a depression or swale along a little creek. At a glance, Mahone saw that the course of the depression just about paralleled the hundred yards or so of Johnson's line, to the left or north of the Crater and that it was about two hundred yards behind, or to the west, of the shattered line.

The young lieutenant pointed to a rise of ground. "If you will go up that slope there you can see the Yankees," he said. Mahone climbed the slope quickly. He later wrote:

"I found myself in full view of the portion of the salient which had been blown up, and of that part of the works to the north of the salient, and saw that they were crammed with Federal soldiers and thickly studded with Federal flags . . . I stood where I could keep one eye on the adversary whilst I directed my own command, which every moment was in fearful peril if the enemy should advance whilst the two brigades were moving, and the larger part of them were still in the covered way.

"A moment's survey of the situation impressed me with the belief, so crowded were the enemy and his flags—eleven flags in less than one hundred yards—that he was greatly disordered but present in large force. At once I sent back to my line in the trenches, full two miles away for the Alabama brigade to be brought to me quickly . . ."[35]

Returning to a covered position, Billy Mahone gathered his officers about him and delivered a short talk. "The enemy have our works," he said. "The line of men which we have here is the only barrier to the enemy's occupying the city of Petersburg. There is nothing to resist his advance. Upon us devolves the duty of driving him from his strong position in our front and re-establishing the Confederate line. We must carry his position immediately by assaulting it. If we don't carry it by the first attack we shall renew the attack as long as there is a man of us left or until the works are ours. Much depends upon prompt, vigorous, simultaneous movements."

As the men moved into position, Mahone spoke words of encouragement as they filed by. Some he slapped on the shoulder as they passed, some he called by their first name and called out: "Give 'em hell, boys!"[36]

The morale of Mahone's old brigade was high, as one of its members who filed by him into position to storm the Crater testified:

"Mahone, cool, courageous and able, was by nature fitted for generalship as few men are, and none knew this better than the men of his command. Wherever he led or placed them, they always felt a moral certainty that they were being properly led or placed, either to inflict the most damage on the enemy or to have the enemy inflict the least damage on them. Accordingly, on the morning of the charge of the Crater, there was not a man in the brigade, knowing that General Mahone was present, personally superintending and directing the movement, that did not feel that we were to be properly and skillfully handled, and would be put in just when and where the most effective service could be rendered."[37]

By now it was nearly 9 A.M. as Colonel Weisiger, at the head of Mahone's old brigade, formed the line of charge, the men being cautioned to hold their fire until they reached the brink of the ditch. The Georgia brigade began to form on Weisiger's right. Suddenly, a Federal officer in the occupied Confederate works appeared on the parapet, with colors in his hands, exhorting his men to charge.

"General!" shouted Captain V. J. B. Girardy to Mahone, "they are coming!"

Mahone saw the Federals jumping out of the breastworks and come forward in a desultory line to charge his two brigades. He raised his voice, so that the whole Virginia brigade heard him and shouted back to Captain Girardy: "Tell Weisiger to forward!"

Years later there would be a controversy as to who gave the order, "Forward!" Mahone and his friends contended that it was Mahone, and Weisiger and his friends claimed it was Weisiger. And, in a different political climate, the controversy became acrimonious, and bad blood was created between Mahone and Weisiger.

But regardless of who gave the order on that hot July morning, it was a valorous sight in the eyes of those who witnessed it. Generals Lee and Beauregard and Lieutenant Gordon McCabe, who was with Willie Pegram in the Gee House, 500 yards away, saw Weisiger's Virginians rush forward to meet the charging Yankees. McCabe wrote of it:

". . . the whole line sprang along the crest, and there burst from more than eight hundred warlike voices that fierce yell which no man ever yet heard unmoved on the field of battle. Storms of case-shot from the right mingled with the tempest of bullets which smote them from the front, yet was there no answering volley, for these were veterans, whose fiery enthusiasm had been wrought to a finer temper by the stern code of discipline, and even in the tumult the men did not forget their orders. Still pressing forward with a steady fury, while the enemy, appalled by the inexorable advance, gave ground, they reached the ditch of the inner works. Then one volley crashed from the whole line, and the [men] . . . clutching their empty guns and redoubling their fierce cries, leaped over . . . and all down the line the dreadful work of the bayonet began."[38]

General Lee, watching the charge, remarked: "That must have been Mahone's old brigade." When the confirmation came that it was, Lee said: "I thought so."

In the furious fight in the Confederate lines to the left of the Crater, Weisiger's Virginians sent the Federals in headlong flight and recaptured the positions. Meanwhile Wright's Georgia brigade had encountered heavy fire to the right of the Crater and its efforts to break through the line were repulsed. Federal artillery fire concentrated on them and they were pinned down. Shortly after 1 P.M., Sanders' Alabama brigade, called up from its trenches by Mahone, swung into action. With a frightening yell upon their lips, Sanders' men pressed resolutely forward in the face of searing fire. Supported by Confederate artillery and mortars whose lobbed missiles worked havoc in the seething Crater and Federally held Confederate works, they stormed the line, planting their tattered standards upon the ramparts.[39]

All the while the action on the right was going on, the brilliant artillerist John Haskell, in charge of the Confederate mortars, moved them to a ditch not many feet from the Crater and kept delivering overhead fire upon the huddled mass in the pit. Haskell cut down his powder to an ounce and a half and his shell barely soared fifty feet in the air before raining down on the unfortunate Federal troops. Confederates in the works near the Crater picked up abandoned muskets with bayonets attached and hurled them like spears over the crest of the Crater. The Yankees promptly hurled them back.

"The crater fight was not only one of the bloodiest, but one of the most brutal of the war," said John S. Wise. "It was the first time Lee's army had encountered negroes, and their presence excited in the troops indignant malice such as had characterized no former conflict . . . Our men, inflamed to relentless vengeance by their presence, disregarded the rules of warfare which restrained them in battle with their own race, and brained and butchered the blacks until the slaughter was sickening."

Other Confederate witnesses testify to the brutality of the fighting. First Lieutenant P. M. Vance of the 11th Alabama Regiment wrote: "Words fail me to describe the scene that followed. Gen. Mahone had told the soldiers of the brigade that negro troops were in possession of the Crater and had come in yelling, 'No quarter for Rebels!' He didn't say, 'Show no quarter,' but Sanders' men decided their point." Another Alabama trooper, B. F. Phillips, remembered General Mahone walking in front of the line and telling the men that the negroes in the Crater had yelled: 'Remember Fort Pillow! No quarter.' Mahone said it was a life and death struggle 'and go among them and give them hell.' Phillips said: "We tried to obey orders. Just before the job was completed, General Mahone sent orders to us not to kill quite all of them."

Major Smith Cleveland, adjutant of the 8th Alabama, standing among the carnage in the Crater as the Alabamians came over the crest, shooting, bayoneting, and swinging their muskets as clubs, was sickened by the sight.

"Why in the hell don't you fellows surrender?" he called to a Federal colonel who was close to him.

"Why in the hell don't you let us," shouted back the colonel.

Moments later, the white flag went up and the Battle of the Crater was over. The Confederate line was restored, 1100 Federal prisoners were taken, four guns recaptured and many stands of colors seized. As for the Federal dead and wounded, they ran into the thousands, various estimates running from Union General Meade's 4400 to General Mahone's 5240, which included prisoners in both cases.[40]

The Crater itself was a horrible sight, piled high with dead bodies of Federals, white and black, and the Confederates who were blown up when the mine was fired, or who were killed in the last desperate moments of the bloody struggle.

"To think of it makes me recoil even now," recalled Colonel George T. Rogers of Mahone's old brigade thirty years after the fighting at the Crater. ". . . The trenches were filled with the dead—in many places they lay heaped and there was literally no place on the ground for the feet . . ."

The smoke of battle hadn't cleared before General Lee sent a hastily scribbled note to Mahone—a "very gratifying note," Mahone said years later, but its contents "no eye ever saw while it was in my possession." The note was among his papers captured in the retreat to Appomattox, and its message apparently is lost to posterity.

Perhaps General Lee told Mahone that he was bestowing on him a battlefield promotion to major general. This he conferred upon Little Billy later in the day.

On August 2, President Davis made it unanimous in a telegram to Lee: HAVE ORDERED THE PROMOTION OF GENERAL MAHONE TO DATE FROM THE DAY OF HIS MEMORABLE SERVICE, 30TH OF JULY.[41]

IX

After the Federal failure at the Crater, the two armies settled down to trench warfare at Petersburg and the siege wore on, month after month.

". . . Attacks upon our [Confederate] lines were now abandoned for a succession of feints, first upon one flank and then upon the other, by which our lines were extended at both ends to the point of breaking," states General E. P. Alexander.

Lee, despite his shrinking army, made a number of aggressive counter-movements and Major General Billy Mahone's division played an active part in these offensive-defensive operations. General Mahone's brigades occupied the entrenchments on Lee's right, but during the maneuvering several of them were placed for a time in the Bermuda Hundred area, on Union General Ben Butler's front.

On August 19, 1864, Lieutenant General A. P. Hill struck the Federals severely with parts of the divisions of Heth and Mahone—a total of five brigades—supported by Lieutenant Colonel Willie Pegram's batteries, and captured 2700 Yankees. Two days later Mahone hammered the Union left flank, but could not dislodge it. On August 24, at Reams's Station, Hill dealt the Federals another sharp blow, taking 2150 prisoners, 3100 stands of small arms, nine guns, and twelve stand of colors.[42]

During September, both the attrition of battle and daily desertions thinned Lee's ranks. Two Southern deserters from Mahone's division reported to the Federals on September 4 that "the brigades of Mahone's division do not average 800 men . . . The brigades of Lee's army . . . will not average 1000 men." Barely ten days earlier, Lee had reported to Secretary of War James E. Seddon the critical manpower shortage in the Army of Northern Virginia: "Our numbers are daily decreasing . . . Without some increase of our strength, I cannot see how we are to escape the natural military consequences of the enemy's numerical superiority."

Near the Burgess's Mill, on October 27, three of Mahone's brigades attacked the Federals on the Boydtown Plank Road, capturing 400 men. Reporting the action, Lee said: "In the attack subsequently made by the enemy General Mahone broke three lines of battle . . ." In a night attack on October 30, Mahone swept through the Federal picket line for half a mile, retiring with 230 prisoners, without the loss of a man.

Shortly thereafter, Mahone went into winter quarters and his division began constructing shelter huts.[43]

Winter came and went, and with it the weakening of Lee's army, living on short rations and opposing the rigors of the bitter cold with threadbare clothing. Lee called for a reorganization of the Commissary Department and warned the War Department on February 8, 1865: "You must not be surprised if calamity befalls us." But Lee staved off the calamity for almost two months.

On April 1, there came the Confederate debacle at Five Forks when Sheridan crushed Pickett on Lee's right in the last pitched battle in Virginia. When General Lee learned the full extent of the disaster, he had only one course: Petersburg and Richmond had to be evacuated.

When the long siege ended, Billy Mahone had been for some time holding the Howlett line, heavy works with naval and siege artillery which extended for five miles between the James and Appomattox. For every mile of his thinly held line, Mahone had only 740 men, or a rifleman about every seven feet.

Lee sent out marching orders for 8 A.M. on April 2 for the several corps, instructing them to concentrate at Amelia Court House. "General Mahone's division will take the road to Chesterfield Court House, thence by Old Colville to Goode's Bridge," Lee's orders stated. "Mahone's wagons will precede him on the same road or take some road to his right." Shortly before dawn on April 3, Mahone's division was on the march to Goode's Bridge over the Appomattox.[44]

The next day, April 4, Lee, not having heard from Lieutenant General Dick Ewell, therefore not knowing what route he had taken from Richmond, ordered Mahone to remain at Goode's Bridge. When Lee finally got a note from Ewell late that day, he dispatched a message to him at 9 P.M.: "Notify General Mahone of your crossing, who is preserving the bridge at Goode's Ferry only until he shall hear you do not require it. He has orders to destroy the bridge as soon as he hears you do not need it. I wish you would give him the earliest intelligence."

Ewell effected his crossing, notified Mahone, and the latter, after destroying Goode's Bridge, marched toward Amelia Court House. The next day, April 6, Lee received word of a disaster at Sayler's Creek. The Federals had fallen on Ewell and Anderson, bringing up Lee's rear, and had cut them to pieces, capturing the wagon trains and many high-ranking officers and much of their commands—Generals Ewell, G. W. C. Lee, Corse, and Hunton among them.

General Lee was talking with Billy Mahone—remonstrating with him for the sharp tone of a note the latter had written objecting to Colonel Charles Marshall's interference with his division on the previous night —when Lee's aide, Colonel Venable, rode up asking if Lee had received his message.

"No," replied Lee, whereupon Venable told him of the shattering loss at Sayler's Creek.

"Where is Anderson?" exclaimed Lee. "Where is Ewell? It is strange I can't hear from them."

Turning to Mahone, Lee said: "General Mahone, I have no other troops, will you take your division to Sayler's Creek?"

Mahone immediately wheeled his troops to the left and marched them towards the scene of the disaster, Lee riding at his side at the head of the column.

Mahone provided a vivid picture of what he and Lee beheld as they reached the south crest of the high ground overlooking the creek:

". . . The disaster which had overtaken our army was in full view, and the scene beggars description—hurrying teamsters with their teams and dangling traces (no wagons), retreating infantry without guns, many without hats, a harmless mob, with the massive columns of the enemy moving orderly on. At this spectacle General Lee straightened himself in his saddle, and, looking more the soldier than ever, exclaimed, as if talking to himself, 'My God! has the army dissolved?' As quickly as I could control my voice I replied, 'No, general, here are troops ready to do their duty'; when, in a mellowed voice, he replied, 'Yes, general, there are some true men left. Will you please keep those people back?' "

Mahone quickly placed his division in position, during which time Lee had secured a battle flag, which he held in his hand, still in the saddle. Mahone rode up to Lee and requested him to give him the flag. Lee did, and then asked Mahone for a suggestion on how to get away.

"Let General Longstreet move by the river road to Farmville," replied Mahone, "and cross the river there, and I will go through the woods to the High Bridge [railroad bridge] and cross there."

Lee nodded and Mahone then asked for instructions about the bridge after crossing it.

"Set fire to it," ordered Lee.

Mahone pointed out that destruction of a span would serve the purpose of delaying the enemy as well as destroying the whole bridge. He then asked Lee to summon Colonel Talcott of the Engineers Regiment and personally give him his order, which Lee did.

Billy Mahone then turned to the task Lee had assigned him to "keep those people back." How well Mahone did it is told in the report of Union General Thomas C. Devin:

". . . We found Mahone's division of infantry in position, with artillery covering the crossing. On attempting to force a crossing the enemy opened a heavy fire of musketry, shell and canister at short range, and, in accordance with instructions, the division was retired one mile . . ."[45]

At 11 P.M. Mahone withdrew through the woods, made his way to High Bridge and before daylight had his command across the river. The engineers detailed to destroy the railroad bridge and the wagon bridge as well, awaited Mahone's order to fire the structures. When no orders came they sent to find him. General Mahone gave the order and the engineers set the railroad bridge aflame, but before they could get the fire going well on the wagon bridge, the Federals were upon them. "Whether Mahone forgot to give the orders earlier or assumed the engineers would act when he marched off, it is impossible to say," commented Douglas Southall Freeman.[46]

At Farmville, on April 7, when Colonel William T. Poague's artillery was under heavy pressure, with no infantry support, one of Mahone's brigades rapidly deployed to protect Poague's guns. "This performance of Mahone's men was as fine a piece of work as ever I saw," Poague later recalled. "His skirmishers deployed at a run and moved forward like a lot of sportsmen flushing partridges and old hares among the broomsedge and scrub pines. The enemy made no further demonstrations at this point."

Later, Colonel Poague looked up General Mahone to thank him and his men for their gallant aid at a critical moment. He found him dodging a thundershower under a sheltering tree. Billy Mahone was, said Poague, "in a towering passion abusing and swearing at the Yankees, who he had just learned had that morning captured his headquarters wagon and his cow, saying it was a most serious loss, for he was not able, in the delicate condition of his health, to eat anything but tea and crackers and fresh milk."

On April 7, General Grant had sent a note to Lee by a flag of truce pointing out "the hopelessness of further resistance." Lee denied this in his reply of the same day, but reciprocated Grant's "desire to avoid useless effusion of blood" and asked for Grant's terms on condition of surrender.

The next day there was another passage of notes between Grant and Lee. The latter still evaded surrender, but the exchange of messages between the two great leaders undoubtedly brought them nearer their historic meeting in the McLean House at Appomattox Court House.

Although Lee still tried to avoid the inevitable, reports on the morning of April 9 were bad. General John B. Gordon had fought his corps to a frazzle and called for support from Longstreet. But Longstreet was under heavy pressure himself and could offer no support.

In answer to a summons, Longstreet rode up to the campfire where Lee was standing. The commander-in-chief, Longstreet noted, was resplendent in a new uniform, wearing sword, sash, and embroidered belt, boots, and gold spurs, but "the handsome apparel and brave bearing failed to conceal his profound depression."

Lee outlined the situation and asked for Longstreet's views.

"Will the bloody sacrifice of your army in any way help the cause in other quarters?" asked Longstreet.

"I think not," replied Lee.

"Then," said Longstreet, "your situation speaks for itself."

Lee then turned to Mahone and stated the situation to him. In the damp, raw early morning, Mahone was quivering like a leaf in a breeze.

"I don't want you to think I'm scared," Little Billy told General Lee. "I'm only chilled."

Mahone asked several questions in response to Lee's request for advice. Little Billy agreed with Longstreet that Lee should call on General Grant.[47]

When the end of the Army of Northern Virginia came a few hours later, it had melted almost away. On the morning of the surrender Lee could summon only 7892 infantry with arms into his lines and the cavalry available added 2100 more effectives. His artillery numbered 63 guns at the end.

"When the army surrendered," stated John S. Wise, who was at Appomattox, ". . . Mahone's division was in better fighting trim and surrendered more muskets than any other division of Lee's army."

On April 10, General Billy Mahone marched his men into the open end of an otherwise rectangular formation of Federal troops. There were thousands of Union soldiers, in serried ranks, with arms at shoulder, flags flying and officers in place. Profound silence reigned—no cheering, no orders given, no murmuring from the troops.

Riding proudly at the head of his columns the bantam general waited until his last ranks had entered the enclosure of troops before halting them. Facing his men to the left, he ordered them to close up ranks and, when this was accomplished, he gave the order to stack arms. Surgeon H. A. Minor of the 9th Alabama gave a vivid picture of the solemn moment which ended the war for Billy Mahone and his gallant men:

"It must be known that on such occasions it is usual to have the men 'ground arms'—that is, to lay them down on the ground. But here we had no such humiliation. We stacked arms 'on the color line,' hung our colors on the center stacks, then fell back in line. We looked at our guns, then with eyes blinded with tears we looked for the last time at our colors, the old rags that had been flags. Ragged, yes, ragged from shell and shot. In place of the original staffs were sticks, makeshifts, for the shafts had been shot off. There we stood.

"What of the Federals? General Grant and his men treated us nobly, more nobly than was ever a conquered army treated, before or since . . . As the head of the column entered . . . every flag in that great Federal army came to and was held in salute. Every officer's sword was drawn and held in salute, and every man who carried a gun brought and held it at salute as long as we remained there."[48]

Appomattox found Billy Mahone at the height of his military fame and skill and the admiration and affection of his men were shared by the people of his native Virginia.

It would not be always thus, as other days and other times came upon Billy Mahone and upon Virginia.

Of him, at the end of the war, Robert E. Lee had the highest praise. After the war, Lee reportedly said that, among the younger men of his army, "William Mahone had developed the highest qualities for organization and command."[49]

X

Immediately after Appomattox, General William Mahone set about regaining the presidency of the Norfolk & Petersburg Railroad, which had suffered considerably during the war. Re-elected to the post, he began rehabilitating the line. Before the year was out, stockholders of the Southside Railroad, which ran from Petersburg to Lynchburg, elected him president of that line. And so eight months after Lee's surrender, Billy Mahone was back in business as a railroad president, not of one, but of two railroads.[50]

This dual presidency provided the impetus for Mahone to launch a scheme for consolidation, not only of the two roads he headed, but with a third railroad included—the Virginia & Tennessee, which ran from Lynchburg to Bristol. There was considerable opposition to the plan by stockholders of the latter company, so Mahone and his friends began buying up that company's stock. Before the end of 1867, Mahone was strong enough to be elected president of the Virginia & Tennessee Railroad. From that position, along with his other two presidencies, Mahone brought off the consolidation, creating the Atlantic, Mississippi & Ohio, with himself as president at an annual salary of $25,000, as much as the President of the United States received. The railroad's initials, A. M. & O., were facetiously interpreted by Mahone's enemies to mean "All mine and Otelia's." Mahone remained in control until a combination of the panic of 1873 and the revolt of British bondholders against his leadership forced him out.

Mahone turned to politics and in 1878 sought unsuccessfully the Democratic nomination for governor of Virginia. He stood for a strong public school system and for a readjustment of the staggering public debt that Virginia had incurred during the war years. Accordingly, he became one of the founders of, and a tremendous power in, the Readjuster Party, which eventually controlled the state. The Virginia Assembly, with Readjusters holding fifty-six of the one hundred seats in the House of Delegates and twenty-four of the forty-four in the Senate, sent Billy Mahone to the United States Senate in 1881. By degrees, the ex-Confederate major general eased into the Republican Party. In 1884 and 1888, he led the Virginia delegations to the Republican National Convention and in 1889 he ran for governor of Virginia as a Republican and was defeated.

By now, he had alienated many of his old friends and even comrades in arms. One of the latter, commenting years later on Mahone's heroic rear-guard operations on the retreat to Appomattox, said: "Pity for his honor and glory he had not died there." A Confederate woman, in her old age, declared: "General Mahone was a little man, but he was a big little man and just as brave and gallant as he could be. It was such a pity he became a Republican after the war." And still another woman of Virginia said: "Mahone lost caste with his friends; but we honor him for honoring once the Southern Gray."

There were no ifs, ands, and buts in the comment of Lucius Bellinger Northrop, the Confederate Commissary General, whose embittered life was drawing to a close. Writing Jefferson Davis on September 15, 1889, he said: "A political hum is now booming in Va. . . . I shall take the trouble to vote against Mahone . . ."[51]

In his able biography of William Mahone—the only full-length study of this remarkable little man—Nelson M. Blake dwelt a bit on Mahone's "abrupt and dictatorial manner." He summed up Billy Mahone's political career deftly:

"There can be no question but that he displayed many of the characteristics of an autocrat. His experiences as a self-reliant youth, a successful civil engineer, a brilliant general and an influential railroad president had developed his organizing and administrative ability to a marked degree but given him none of the tact and suavity so essential to a political leader . . . In running a convention and in carrying out a political campaign Mahone commanded rather than advised . . . To account for Mahone's dictatorial manner one must remember that he possessed unbounded confidence in himself and in the justice of the measures for which he fought . . . Accordingly, he was slow to accept advice from his friends and absolutely unwilling to compromise with his enemies."

Billy Mahone continued for some time to wield powerful political control inside the Republican Party in Virginia. In his last years, Mahone made his home in Washington, where he died, October 8, 1895, leaving behind the reputation of having been "the most influential political figure which Virginia has produced since the days of Thomas Jefferson."[52]

8

Rebel Propagandist:

HENRY HOTZE

I

I F Henry Hotze had been born a hundred years later, he could have been one of Madison Avenue's bright young men in gray flannel suits.

Failing this he could have become a distinguished American diplomat or one of the influential editorial voices of the United States.

Or, to place him more closely to the field in which he distinguished himself during the Civil War, he could have been the director of the Voice of America.

And yet, until Hotze's correspondence with the Confederate State Department was published in the Naval Official Records in 1922, practically nothing was known of this amazingly gifted young man who served the South so brilliantly abroad.

". . . Mr. Hotze, who is he?" asked Rebel War Clerk J. B. Jones in Richmond, in November 1863, nearly two years after Hotze had launched his Confederate propaganda campaign in England.[1]

Of Hotze, Frank L. Owsley, in *King Cotton Diplomacy*, states:

". . . He was a very able man—as able as any agent who went abroad during the Civil War. He showed more insight into public opinion and tendencies than did either [James M.] Mason or [John] Slidell, and his fastidiousness, his deftness, and his lightness of touch in a delicate situation was remarkable. His resourcefulness had a masterly finesse that would have done honor to Cavour or Bismarck. Finally he was intellectually honest and unafraid to face the facts."[2]

Another historian, Burton J. Hendrick, in *Statesmen of the Lost Cause*, said of Hotze:

". . . He possessed a suavity, a subtlety, and silence in method that would have distinguished an experienced diplomat. As far back as 1862 he introduced into publicity procedures those 'psychological methods' upon which so many modern exemplars pride themselves . . . No press

agent quite so noiseless as Hotze ever plied his trade . . . In comparison
with Hotze's suppleness and comprehension, James Murray Mason appears a slow-witted blunderer and even John Slidell looks like an unscrupulous marplot."[3]

For three years—from May 1862 to August 1865—Henry Hotze edited *The Index*, which he founded ostensibly as a weekly English journal,
but which was subsidized by the Confederate government. Always in
the background, and not identified with *The Index* publicly, Hotze edited it with adroit skill, sound judgment, and a brilliant pen.

Of *The Index*, Douglas Southall Freeman, in *The South to Posterity*,
declared:

"This remarkable publication, into which every student of Confederate
history should dip, is a reminder that propaganda is not a new art . . .
Admirably printed, *The Index* is a unique Confederate publication and
must have been one of the most effective of all organs of propaganda
before the period of the World War."[4]

Such briefly is the man and his work, a truly "forgotten man" of the
Civil War. Henry Hotze, even today, is little known except among Civil
War historians, a handful of graduate students, and comparatively few
of the enthusiasts for the struggle of 1861–65.

II

Very little is known about the life of Henry Hotze before he became
a citizen of the United States in Mobile, Alabama, in 1855.

Born in Zurich, Switzerland, in 1834, he was twenty-one years of age
when he was naturalized. But when he came to the United States, and
whether his parents accompanied him or not, can only be conjectured.
The only known obituary of Hotze, in the Mobile *Daily Register*, May 11,
1887, makes no mention of his family. Nor do the 1850 census records
for Mobile show anyone named Hotze living in the city. Because of the
five-year residence in the United States required of aliens seeking citizen-
ship, Henry Hotze would have had to come to this country no later than
1850 to be naturalized in 1855. Whether he came to Mobile several years
before his naturalization can only be guessed.[5]

From Hotze's correspondence and literary efforts, it is quite evident
that he had received a broad, liberal education and that his incisive,
logical, and brilliant mind had been thoroughly disciplined. He was only
twenty-two when his marked gift for writing was first demonstrated in
an adaptation and translation of Count Arthur de Gobineau's *L'Inégalité
des Races*. Hotze's version of this book, published in 1856 under the
title, *The Moral and Intellectual Diversity of the Races*, bears his name

as editor and contains a long introduction from his pen. In it, Hotze expressed the traditional Southern views on the racial question.

Whether the young Swiss was accepted because of his Southern orthodoxy or through the charm of his own personal gifts, Hotze moved in the select social and intellectual circles of ante-bellum Mobile.

That he had made an impression on the community despite his youth can be gathered from the fact that Mayor J. M. Withers (later to become a Confederate general) appointed Hotze to the Mobile delegation to the Southern Commercial Convention in Montgomery in May 1858. There he met such well-known spokesmen for the South as William L. Yancey, Roger A. Pryor, and Edmund Ruffin, among others. Shortly after the convention, General E. Y. Fair of Alabama was named United States Minister to Belgium. He took Hotze to Brussels as secretary of the legation and during his year's tenure, the young man also served as chargé d'affaires. Failure of Congress to provide funds for the post resulted in Henry Hotze's return to Mobile in 1859.

Hotze then joined the distinguished editor and diplomat, John Forsyth, on the Mobile *Register*, and acquired, as associate editor, the invaluable journalistic training which added to his natural bent for writing would stand him in good stead when the Civil War came. In the same year, Hotze was appointed secretary to the newly established Board of Harbor Commissioners, a post wherein he acquired considerable knowledge of maritime affairs.[6]

The day before the firing on Fort Sumter, Hotze, on behalf of a group in Mobile which wanted to seize the transport *Illinois*, entered into correspondence with Secretary of War Leroy Pope Walker to get Confederate commissions for the leaders of the proposed expedition. Although authorized by Walker, there is no evidence that the expedition ever materialized. It appears that Hotze's interest in the project does not seem to have gone beyond acting as the go-between.[7]

With the outbreak of the war, the Mobile Cadets, composed of young men of the best families who had "united for purpose of military amusement," put the company at the services of the Governor of Alabama. Hotze, a member of the Mobile Cadets, provided a delightful commentary on Army life in the early days of the war in "Three Months in the Confederate Army," which he ran serially in *The Index*.

On April 23, 1861, the Cadets steamed up the Alabama River to Montgomery, leaving the landing amid "the solemn toll of church bells, the booming of salute guns, cheers after cheers from thousands of lungs, waving of hats and handkerchiefs . . ." At several stops up the river, rural companies joined the elite Cadets and Hotze, with snobbish condescension, said they had the "appearance of good humored savages." Upon reaching Montgomery, these and other companies were grouped into a regiment, the 3rd Alabama Volunteers. Hotze's friend, Mayor Withers of

Mobile, a West Pointer and veteran of the Mexican War, was elected colonel of the regiment.

In due course, with pretty girls feeding them delicacies at every stop en route and cordial men offering "hospitality . . . in the shape of unlimited drinks at the neighboring barrooms," the 3rd Alabama reached Lynchburg, Virginia, where it was mustered into the Confederate service. In camp at Lynchburg, many of the men were visited by chiggers or red bugs, and they resorted, said Hotze, to bathing the bites with whiskey, but they eventually experimented "on an extensive scale, to discover whether its internal application might not prove equally efficacious."

On May 4, Hotze and his comrades were sent to Norfolk, where inactivity, other than the routines of drill, guard duty, parades, details and so on, soon produced utter boredom. "A sort of demoralization not in the worst meaning of the word, but still serious enough to be painfully felt" spread through the 3rd Alabama.[8]

At the end of May, Hotze was made a clerk in the regimental headquarters and in July he was back in Mobile, presumably on leave. He was still in Mobile on August 31, when orders came from Secretary of War Walker for Hotze to go to Europe to speed up the purchase and shipment of arms and munitions, for which purpose agents had already been sent to England and France. After stopping in Richmond for additional instructions and messages, he experienced many delays in getting to Canada, from whence he sailed for England. The delays, occasioned by slow trains, long stopovers, and a wreck, gave Hotze ample opportunity to study public opinion in the North concerning the war. His keen, perceptive mind noted that the Northerners had "absolute confidence, amounting almost to indifference" in the outcome of the war. He scornfully characterized the Federal soldiers he saw as coming from "the lowest walks of life." He saw posters deploring slowness in volunteering while also observing large numbers of young men about barrooms, saloons, and country stores.

Henry Hotze reached London on October 5 and delivered his messages to William L. Yancey, Pierre A. Rost, and A. Dudley Mann. He remained abroad barely two weeks and was back in Richmond on November 6. He reported to the new Secretary of War, Judah P. Benjamin, and was discharged from the army.[9] A young man with such energy, poise, confidence, and readily obvious qualities of mind and manner could serve the Confederacy in other and better ways than carrying a rifle.

Perceptively, he had recognized in his short stay abroad that the Federal Government had a monopoly on all the news that reached England from America. Southern news, the Confederate story, was not getting through to the British press. He formulated a plan for the Confederacy to send an agent to London to attempt to stem this adverse propaganda tide and to redirect its flow toward the South. And he nominated himself as the agent.

Secretary of State R. M. T. Hunter was much impressed with Hotze's proposal. Benjamin apparently thought highly of it, too. Between them they didn't take long to enlist President Davis's support and secure his approval. On November 14, 1861, Henry Hotze received his commission as a Commercial Agent for the Confederacy in England.[10] This was only a front for Hotze's true purpose in going to London. In his instruction to the young propagandist, Secretary Hunter made it very clear that his mission was to keep the State Department "advised of the tone of the English Press" regarding the war and to transmit "with appropriate comments . . . extracts from the printed journals as you may deem to have an important bearing upon the question."

Hotze was to be "diligent and earnest" in persuading British public opinion of "the ability of the Confederate States to maintain their independence." He was to have published any information which would show the South's "ample resources and vast military strength," and tend to raise the Confederate States' "character and government in general estimation."

Hunter instructed Hotze to "zealously strive" to dispel foreign fears "as to the reconstruction of the Union," and to emphasize "the universal sentiment" of the Southern people "to prosecute the war until their independence shall no longer be assailed."

The Confederate propagandist was to "keep constantly before the public . . . the tyranny of the Lincoln Government, its utter disregard of . . . personal rights . . . and its notorious violations of the law." These Hotze was to contrast with the "peace and order" that prevailed everywhere in the Confederacy, where "the laws have been instantly and impartially administered."

And, finally, the Secretary of State told Hotze to dangle free trade before the British people, assuring them "of the almost universal opinion in the Confederate States that as few restrictions as possible should be imposed upon that trade and those only for revenue purposes."

This was quite an assignment for a young man of twenty-seven, but Hunter expressed confidence in Hotze's "address and dispatch," although the meager funds allotted him—a salary of $1500 a year and a $750 contingent fund—might readily suggest the contrary. "In the light of Hotze's accomplishment" says Frank L. Owsley, ". . . the stipend and expense money . . . seem like a jest."[11]

III

When the Civil War broke out, the narcotic influence of cotton on the Southern mentality had lulled Southern statesmen into a false sense of security.

"Cotton is king," was on every Southern lip, the inference being that because European mills needed Southern cotton, a split of the Union would bring England and France to the side of the South in the event of war.

"Let any social or physical convulsion visit the United States," prophesied the *London Economist* in 1853, "and England would feel the shock . . . The lives of nearly two million of our countrymen are dependent upon the cotton crops of America; their destiny may be said, without any kind of hyperbole, to hang upon a thread." In the years leading up to 1861, Southern writers and politicians had embroidered upon the theme, so that it became an almost universal Southern belief.

When William H. Russell of the *London Times* visited the South during the early days of the war, he heard on every side that when England felt the pinch for cotton it would intervene to get it. "We know John Bull," he was told at a Charleston club, "he will make a great fuss about non-intervention at first, but when he begins to want cotton he will come down off his perch." Southern people, universally, "believe in the irresistible power of Cotton," Russell told his *Times* readers. To a man, they boasted to the British correspondent that they were "masters of the destiny of the world. Cotton is king—not alone king, czar."

Mrs. Jefferson Davis in her *Memoirs* stated the Confederate President was convinced that the power of cotton would bring foreign recognition. "The president and his advisers," she wrote, "look to the stringency of the English cotton market, and the suspension of the manufacturies to send up a ground swell from the English operatives, that would compel recognition."[12]

In March 1861 the Confederacy sent William Lowndes Yancey, Pierre A. Rost, and Ambrose Dudley Mann to Europe as commissioners, "armed," says Owsley, "with a dissertation on state sovereignty in their right pockets and a sample of New Orleans middling upland cotton in their left." Their mission was a failure, as it figured to be. Yancey, for all his personal amiability, eloquence and poise, was known internationally as a "fire-eating" champion of slavery; Rost, a French-born Louisiana judge, had no known qualifications as a diplomat; and Mann, a pleasant windbag, was an incurable optimist who lived in a sort of "never-never land" of international politics. Eventually, Yancey returned to the United States, Mann went to Belgium, and Rost to Spain, and

James M. Mason and John Slidell were dispatched to Europe to represent the Confederacy in England and France respectively.

The day after Henry Hotze had reported back in Richmond from his brief trip to Europe, Mason and Slidell, with their secretaries and Mr. Slidell's family, sailed from Havana aboard the British steamer *Trent* for Saint Thomas, where they were to take another British steamer for Southampton. On November 8, the *Trent* was halted by the USS *San Jacinto*, whose commander, Captain Charles Wilkes, seized the Confederate envoys and took them to Fortress Monroe, Virginia, from where on November 18 the news of their capture went out to all parts of the country.

The North exulted and Wilkes became a hero; the South was indignant. And when the news eventually reached England, a diplomatic crisis between that country and the United States developed over Captain Wilkes' violation of the British flag. United States Secretary of State Seward hastened to apologize and adroit diplomacy by Charles Francis Adams, American Minister to England, smoothed ruffled feelings. Mason and Slidell were released and were returned to Saint Thomas to continue their voyage to England.

Meanwhile, during the height of the "Trent Affair," Hotze, after several false starts, succeeded on December 22 in running the blockade from Mobile to Cuba. After a nine-day voyage he reached Havana, from where he reported to Secretary of State Hunter that he had procured in Mobile the latest charts on the Atlantic and Gulf coasts and harbors which would provide useful information for the blockade runners. He sent the secretary a list of vessels which had successfully run the blockade from Cuba and suggested that Havana would be an ideal "entrepot where our small craft can seek the necessaries we require from Europe in exchange for our commodities."[13]

Hotze sailed from Havana on December 31, 1861, for Saint Thomas, where he met Mason and Slidell, who had recently arrived. He sailed for England with the two commissioners, the party reaching London on January 29, 1862. Although he had been in London only three days, Hotze availed himself, on February 1, of William L. Yancey's imminent departure to dash off a report to the Confederate Secretary of State. Admitting that "it would be premature . . . to venture upon an expression of opinion on the tone of public sentiment," Hotze nonetheless said that "the impression left on my mind is favorable without warranting any sanguine hopes."

The young propaganda agent told Secretary Hunter that he could find no complaint in the London press's attitude toward the Confederacy, but "an indefatigible and unscrupulous agency is ever ready to seize the slightest opportunity for damaging us in public estimation." This malevolent Yankee force, he discovered, was directed by the well-known New

York publisher and politician Thurlow Weed, who, along with his colleagues, employed methods "most repulsive to English tastes and habits." Hotze concluded that Weed "injures most the cause he wishes to serve." From Thurlow Weed's example, Hotze got a warning: "I cannot be too cautious and circumspect. I shall not venture to write until I feel the ground firm under me." Accordingly, he would "have little to transmit of my own composition for three or four weeks." He promised Hunter he would survey the field "for an intelligent estimate of the relative importance of conflicting interests and views."[14]

IV

For three weeks Hotze did nothing but cultivate the British press, meeting editors and writers of the leading London papers and he also came into contact with many influential men in public life through the so-called "Southern lobby"—a group of English sympathizers with the Confederacy. "I have been fortunate enough to gain almost immediate access to a higher social sphere . . . than I hoped to attain in so short a period," he reported to Secretary Hunter. This, he said, would give him "a wider range of influence and immeasurably greater facilities for usefulness." He extended his acquaintances slowly, but "in the best possible direction" and daily he was applied to "for facts and arguments to be used in our favor."

On February 23 he happily reported that on the previous day, the *Morning Post*, organ of the Prime Minister, Lord Palmerston, had carried a composition of his as its leading editorial. He enclosed a clipping from the paper, but cautioned Hunter to make "due allowances for the necessity under which I felt myself, of studiously maintaining an English point of view, and not advance too far beyond recognized public opinion." Hotze's topic was the inauguration of the permanent Confederate Government which, he told Hunter, he felt should not "pass wholly unnoticed by the London press (which otherwise would have been the case)."

Opening with a tribute to George Washington, he said his birthday "continues to be honored by both fragments of the severed nation," but the North had "forgotten the lessons of his example and the spirit of his teachings." He recited evidences of the South's strength and unanimity of resistance. Withdrawal from the Union had been performed effortlessly and the South shook off "the old Government . . . with as much ease and unconcern as a worn out garment would be by its wearer." The South had created a new nation, but like an infant, it needed care "to ripen into vigorous life." Usually, this care had been provided to "nascent nations by the self-interest, the policy or the ambition of older sisters."

Hotze pointed out how France had aided the American Colonies. In conclusion, he suggested difficulties ahead for England if the South lost the war, for "who can doubt that Democracy would be more arrogant, more aggressive, more levelling and vulgarizing, if that is possible, than it ever had been before."[15]

To Hotze's surprise and delight, the editorial was a sensation in the London clubs and coffee houses and he reported to Hunter that the "deep impression" his "leader" had made resulted from the belief that it was "unmistakably an emanation from Lord Palmerston himself." Hotze professed to have gotten a tremendous lift from the initial publication of his work, and he had every reason to. But, when one considers his poise, tact, agile mind, education, personable nature, self-assurance, energy and confidence, it is hard to accept at face value this protestation:

". . . arriving here, the advocate of our case through the most fastidious press in the world, a stranger, with barely a few friends or introductory letters, with no extensive literary reputation to precede me and smooth my way, I felt almost disheartened."

Nothing in Hotze's record indicates that he was ever disheartened and his tremendous capacity to make friends quickly insured him a ready entrée into any circle with which he made contact.

In asking Hunter for more funds for expenses, Hotze stressed the necessity of adequate living quarters, for "I cannot hold conversations on confidential topics in the common drawing room of a boarding house, nor can I receive a Peer of England in a third story bed chamber." Conceding that such visitors would never be numerous, he mentioned that Lord Campbell was a frequent caller. "My intercourse with him," he told Hunter, "altogether unsought by myself, is likely to have important results . . ."[16]

During his early days in London, Hotze felt that he had correctly sensed the pulse of British public opinion as being pro-Southern, but after a month's stay it occurred to him that the only opinions that he was getting were those of the Southern lobby. On February 28, he wrote Secretary Hunter:

"It is true that we have many friends and well-wishers here, but the intercourse of a Southerner being mostly with that class, he is liable to mistake the exception for the rule. I plead guilty to having myself not been wholly exempt from that error on my return from my former brief visit to London. The thoughtful observation of a month convinces me that most of us have been too rapid in our conclusions and too sanguine in our expectations as regards the policy of Europe and especially England."

He analyzed British attitude as "not . . . hostile, but . . . cold and indifferent." The English people, he said, would prefer to see "the permanent disruption of an overgrown rival power" which would open the most profitable market in the world. But they don't prefer this, wrote Hotze, "sufficiently . . . to come to our aid."

With penetration and astuteness which would have reflected commendably upon a seasoned diplomat, Hotze skillfully diagnosed the British position. First of all, the dread of war had become "the national bugbear" and repugnance to slavery—"our institution," Hotze called it—had by now become a part of "the national conscience and therefore an honest article of the national creed."

What upset Hotze was to find that the national political parties were not split on the "American Question" which he had "confidently expected," and there was no chance of an immediate alignment. For either party to take a side, he said, would "insure its crushing defeat." The Opposition leader, Lord Derby, accordingly carefully avoids "advancing one inch beyond the position which Lord Palmerston is supposed to hold." Also, contrary to his calculation, "the manufacturing interest affords little, if any reliable support."

Hotze found only two men of any importance in Parliament who were declared foes of the Confederacy. These were the Foreign Secretary, Lord Russell, "who had lately made himself the apologist of the federal Government in the House of Lords," and John Bright in the House of Commons, who "represents or leads no party but himself."

Continuing, Hotze told Secretary Hunter:

"Conscious as I am that my pen can be useful to our cause and country only when it is controlled by an imperturbably calm temper . . . I find it difficult at times to restrain the expression of pain and indignation at the gross, callous, undisguised selfishness and almost brutal indifference with which the great spectacle on the other hemisphere is viewed on this . . . On the other hand it may be truly stated that if we have gained little, the enemy has gained less . . . I could not have arrived at a more opportune time, and I have so far succeeded beyond my expectations and perhaps yours."[17]

With the skill of a master poker player, Hotze played his cards with admirable restraint. Although more and more columns of the London papers were opened to his pen, he determined to use "the privilege moderately, neglecting no opportunity nor seeking to create artificial ones."

Two of the most zealous supporters of the Confederate cause, Hotze soon learned, were James Spence, author of the pro-Southern *The American Union*, and Lord Campbell, with both of whom he soon became on good terms. He considered Spence's book, then in its fourth edition, "permanently valuable" and compared it favorably in "acuteness of penetration and closeness of reason," with de Tocqueville's *Democracy in America*. Lord Campbell called on Hotze to supply him with the latest information on the blockade and to jot down the strongest arguments against its efficacy. Campbell revealed that he planned a speech in the House of Lords on recognition of the Confederacy and asked Hotze to write out the points of argument for him. The young man eagerly seized the opportunity and devoted ten days to preparing the paper for Lord Campbell.[18]

When news of the fall of Forts Henry and Donelson to the Federals reached London in early March 1862, Hotze hastened to underrate the importance of the border states in conversations with British writers:

"Our constitution was framed and our Government organized for the States comprised in the cotton region proper," Hotze explained to his editorial friends. "The territory which now forms the theater of the war was acquired by us after that war was declared . . . Even should the North succeed in overrunning the great States of Virginia, North Carolina, Missouri, Kentucky, and Tennessee, the Southern Confederacy would be precisely what Mr. Lincoln found it on the day of his inauguration."

Hotze's British friends seemed to have found no flaw in his argument, for several editors took the idea and developed it in their paper. The *London Times* used his exact words.

When the debate on the blockade opened in the House of Commons on May 7 and in the House of Lords on May 10, Hotze was in the visitors' gallery. No attempt was made to bring the question to a vote, but Hotze was gratified to note that Lord Campbell's address, for which he had supplied data, drew the reluctant admission from Lord Russell that "a reconstruction of the American Union was not possible."

Simultaneously with Lord Campbell's speech, Hotze tried a bold stroke and failed. In a piece written for Lord Derby's *Morning Herald*, he tried to commit the paper to an open attack on Lord Russell. "I should have produced no small political effect, had I succeeded," Hotze wrote Secretary Hunter. The editor, alert to the situation, used the piece, not as an article, but as a letter to the editor, which lessened its significance.

One of the Confederate propagandist's greatest needs was news from the South. He wanted badly the files of important Southern newspapers which he could clip and transmit to the London press. "If I had Southern intelligence, though ever so sparingly or irregularly," he told Hunter, "I should wield a real power in journalism here, which even my unremitting labor and hitherto singularly good fortune will not give me."

In mid-March, Hotze arranged with Lord Palmerston's organ, the *Post*, to run a series of letters on recognition of the South. The day after his first letter was published, the *London Times* ran a letter on the same subject by James Spence. Confederate friends in Parliament had assured Hotze that the letters would pave the way for a concerted effort to be made by them after Easter, or earlier, if an important Confederate victory occurred. Hotze was delighted. "I am for the first time, almost sanguine in my hopes of speedy recognition," he wrote Hunter.

In April 1862 the cotton famine, which the Southern leaders had long felt would bring England to the aid of the South, broke over the land, with, reported Hotze, "all its train of destitution and ruin." He predicted that the British government would be compelled to act, but felt an agitation, which he would consider undertaking had he £100 at his disposal, would hasten matters. It was obvious that he preferred not to employ such questionable means.

On April 25, Hotze wrote the State Department that, in his opinion, "recognition . . . has now become . . . only a question of the opportune moment." On that very day Flag Officer David G. Farragut's fleet appeared before New Orleans, the fall of which dealt a terrific blow to Confederate hopes of European intervention.[19]

Although additional newspapers put themselves at Hotze's disposal—notably Lord Derby's *Herald* and the *Standard*—an idea that had been maturing in his mind for some weeks was soon to become a reality.

In his April 25 letter, Hotze revealed his plan and purpose:

"I have now, after mature deliberation, concluded to establish a newspaper wholly devoted to our interest, and which will be exclusively under my control, though my connection with it is known only to a few initiated, and will not be suspected by the public at large . . . You will see from the prospectus which I enclose my plan for making the paper a machine for collecting, comparing and bringing before the public with proper comments the vast amount of important information which is received in Europe through private channels. This was most difficult to accomplish, and I did not seriously contemplate the new publication until I had assured success."

Two friends, H. O. Brewer of Mobile and A. P. Waters of Savannah, supplied funds, and Hotze contributed from his private resources, to insure publication "in a manner worthy of the cause" for a period of three months. "I hope to cause you an agreeable surprise with the first number of *The Index*." Hotze wrote the Secretary of State.[20]

V

The first issue of the Confederate propaganda organ, *The Index*, came from the press on May 1, 1862. Subtitled "A Weekly Journal of Politics, Literature and News," it contained 16 pages and was sold for sixpence. Publication time was Thursday afternoon, until its final issues, which came out on Saturday.

What did the name *Index* signify? Hotze explained it in the first issue: "Our Name . . . If *The Index* should be fortunate enough to point the way to a more speedy settlement of the unfortunate American War, or if it should serve as guide to a better understanding of the real character of a greatly calumniated people, we might well congratulate ourselves on the choice of our title."

Having explained the name of his paper, he then went on to state that its object was threefold: to put the Southern people back in contact with their kinsmen of England, from whom the blockade had separated them; to bring England news, which, due to "another rigid blockade," is censored in the North; and finally:

". . . When we state that the leading object of this journal will be to advocate the cause of the Southern Union, let it not be assumed that will be done in the spirit of heated partizans. We believe it to be the cause of justice and truth, and hold that it cannot be served by suppressing truth or distorting it. Our columns will be open to any writers of ability on the other side. The defects and shortcomings of the Southern States we shall make no attempt to conceal; on the contrary, we propose to call an error an error, and a defect a defect; taking as a guide the last message of the Southern President to its Congress, in which facts greivously depressing are stated in simple English, with that manly candour which is above the fear of shrinking from the truth."[21]

In its third issue, on May 15, 1862, *The Index* editorially minimized the fall of New Orleans, and in so doing Hotze ran counter to the general Southern opinion, privately held, but not expressed, in London. "Among the latter," he wrote Judah P. Benjamin, now Confederate Secretary of State, "I regret to find that this event is deemed to be fraught with far more disastrous consequences than I anticipated." In *The Index*, he admitted the loss of the South's greatest city "in its moral effects . . . as a severe blow to the Confederate cause." But in its practical aspects, one should "correctly distinguish between the great commercial importance of New Orleans, and its comparative insignificance attending the present war." He ventured to agree with those who claimed that the South gained by the loss of New Orleans because the fall released important troops to fight important battles. "The independence of the South does not depend on its seaports . . . New Orleans might safely and wisely be left to no other defense than the climate and the yellow fever—deadlier and surer weapons than cannon-ball or bayonet."[22]

As the weeks went by, Hotze was delighted at the way *The Index* had given him the chance of "multiplying" himself in discharging his duties as Confederate propagandist. Leader writers for many of the London papers came to him for information on the South, its armies, its resources, etc. And since a writer usually submitted material to several papers, Hotze's information was frequently multipled in presentation in print. He elaborated on this to Secretary Benjamin in September 1862:

"The establishment of *The Index* enabled me on occasion to assume the position of employer of the pens of some of these gentlemen. Thus, at least half the articles in *The Index* are written by Englishmen, who, only a few months ago, had but imperfect knowledge of and little active sympathy with the South. It is my object and hope, by this means, to found a school of writers whose services in the moral battles we still have to fight will, from their positions, be more valuable to those of the ablest pens of our own country."

The first of the English contributors to *The Index* was James Spence, whose book Hotze so highly praised. He was happy to have Spence as a leader writer, but after three issues, Spence ceased to contribute. Many months later, Hotze explained that he was frightened by Spence's ideas on slavery wherein he had "rendered the idea of ultimate emancipation unduly conspicuous." He told Secretary Benjamin: "I almost dread the direction his friendship and devotion seem about to take."

Another important English writer who wrote for *The Index* was Percy Greg, a regular contributor to the *Manchester Guardian, The Saturday Review,* and *The Standard.* Hotze hailed him as "one of the most talented leader writers in London, who besides being a valuable contributor to *The Index,* is one of our most efficient supporters in the columns of *The Saturday Review* and other literary and political journals of high standing."

Hotze did not confine his correspondents to England. In the United States he had journalists writing for *The Index* in the North as well as the South, from New York, Brooklyn, Washington and Philadelphia, as well as from Richmond and Norfolk, and even occupied New Orleans. From France and Italy, and to a lesser degree, from Germany, came articles from journalists that Hotze had on his payroll.[23]

Hotze was gratified, months later, when Secretary Benjamin's approval of both his own work and of *The Index* reached him.

"Your dispatches continue to afford interesting and gratifying proof of the intelligent zeal with which you are performing your duties . . ." wrote Benjamin. ". . . I have had occasion to examine *The Index* more particularly since I last wrote, and observe a progressive and marked improvement in its contents." Benjamin found Hotze's plan of engaging British writers and at the same time "educating" them in Southern affairs to be "judicious and effective."

Although *The Index* commented on many topics, defending the South, criticizing the North, chiding Lord Russell's "masterly inactivity," exulting in Confederate victories, minimizing Confederate defeats after frequently preparing a cushion for them in advance, there was one central, all-pervading theme to the paper's editorials: Recognition of the Confederacy. This was the do-all and be-all of Henry Hotze's mission to England and he never for a moment forgot it. A few random quotes from *The Index* readily demonstrate this.

On May 22, 1862, *The Index* pointed out that recognition did not mean intervention. On June 19, 1862, it declared that "Recognition of one nation by another is . . . the mere acknowledgement of an existing fact . . ." "The Recognition . . . of the Confederate States as an independent nation—nothing less, nothing more—is what the present situation in American affairs requires," *The Index* urged on July 17, 1862. As the war went on, Hotze never dropped the subject. On March 19, 1863, *The Index* declared that the Confederacy was "recognized on the Stock Exchange, recognized by common parlance and by public opinion the world over . . . (and) is unknown and unrecognized only by the diplomatic ceremonial." On June 2, 1864, *The Index* declared: "While we refuse to recognize the existence of any government in that country [Confederacy] . . . everything wears the air of complete organization and accomplished national independence." As late as January 26, 1865, with all signs pointing to Appomattox, *The Index* gave another variation on its well-known theme: "The true obstacle to recognition by England is not slavery (for in the height of the Abolitionist agitation she readily recognized Texas), but the apathy, or rather lack of initial power by her present government."[24]

If recognition of the Confederacy was *The Index's* number one topic to which it often and regularly returned, financing the propaganda journal was Hotze's number one recurring problem, for obviously, with a circulation that never exceeded 2500, and limited advertising, it never was, or could be, self-supporting.

VI

The Index was launched on borrowed money and for a long while it appeared as if the propaganda journal of the Confederacy was living on borrowed time.

Hotze's ridiculous contingent fund of $750 was tapped, and he secured support of friends, in addition to his own personal contributions to the paper's operation. It cost about £40 a week to produce *The Index* and its income from subscriptions and advertising never exceeded £20 a week. So a £20 subsidy was required each week.

He literally begged money from Benjamin in nearly every dispatch, he sought the assistance of Mason and Slidell and when, in the fall of 1862, Edwin De Leon arrived with $25,000 for Confederate propaganda work in France, Hotze sought his financial assistance. De Leon, an experienced journalist and former United States Consul-General in Egypt, was a personal friend of President Davis, but even this was no adequate reason why he should go forth from Richmond so well fortified with money while Henry Hotze, young though he was, held an equally important assignment on a pittance.

De Leon, who had stopped in London on his way to France, quickly recognized that Hotze was an able man and that Confederate propaganda was in good hands in England. But he took a dim view of *The Index*. On October 1, 1862, in reply to Hotze's request for financial aid, De Leon wrote:

"With regard *The Index* I will speak to you with the frankness of a friend. I do not think it can be sustained; the tax of £40 per week being too heavy to be long continued and temporary aid doing no good . . . Moreover in the *Herald* & *Standard* you have daily organs of wide circulation representing Political English Parties while the correspondence of the *Times, Post, Telegraph*, throw a flood of light on our affairs. With a weekly paper and the limited circulation you can get . . . you cannot hope to rival your native competition.

"I therefore do not feel at liberty to divert the funds under my control for the direction as suggested in your letter . . . Consider therefore whether you feel conscientiously bound to continue such a thankless and terrible labor, as the conduct of *The Index* involves, and whether now (whatever was the case when you established it) your time and talents and energy could not better be bestowed upon Papers of wide circulation in England or in contributions to German journals or periodicals. My judgment may be erroneous, but I have given you my convictions, and you will bear me witness that I have not intruded unasked advice and that no one acknowledges your services to the Cause more fully than myself . . ."[25]

De Leon had missed entirely the purpose of *The Index*. It was not aimed at the general public and Hotze had no intention of trying to compete with the great English journals. Its purpose was to present the Southern case to writers, newspaper editors, cabinet and government officials, and diplomats—the opinion makers in England.

Hotze then turned, in December 1862, to James Mason stressing that *The Index* was "the cheapest, the only honourable, and the most effective way or mode of subsidizing a foreign press," and pleaded for help else he would have "no choice but to suspend its publication." Under the joint recommendation of Messrs. Mason and Slidell, De Leon sent Hotze £250 "for the support of *The Index* during the next two or three months."

Edwin De Leon's views on *The Index* weren't the only criticism leveled at Hotze. Early in the paper's existence Slidell was impatient that *The Index* didn't attack the British cabinet and repeatedly urged Hotze to do so. Also, Hotze's tone of "studied moderation" which he had imposed upon himself and *The Index* was mistaken by many Southerners in Europe for "lukewarmness, timidity, or lack of spirit." One

Confederate, Paul du Bellet, who contributed to *The Index* from Paris, was sharp in his criticism. "Mr. Hotze," he wrote, "made a very fine use of his editorial scissors, too much indeed for the cause he pretended to represent."

Clement C. Clay, who was influential in Confederate affairs, as late as 1864 considered *The Index's* stand wishy-washy on many points concerning the Confederacy. On June 11 of that year, he wrote Benjamin:

"I apprehend *The Index* has but few readers besides its patrons and our open and active friends, and does not reach the minds of the great body of the English public opinions. Moreover, it has not met the oft recurring questions of public law where our rights and interests have been disregarded with requisite promptness and force. I have in memory several instances . . . where the wrong done by the English Government was palpably and not strongly presented for us."[26]

Once again Hotze's self-imposed "Olympian serenity" had been misunderstood. Hotze had designed *The Index* to be "in appearance and contents acceptable to English ideas," and it was essential, he told Benjamin, "to avoid the great error of American journalism, that of mistaking forcible words for forcible ideas." It was necessary, went on the young propagandist, "to draw a marked contrast between *The Index* and the popular idea of an American paper."

That Richmond approved of this is quite evident from Benjamin's letter to Hotze on September 19, 1863. Noting the regular arrival of *The Index*, Benjamin expressed satisfaction at the "tact and vigor" with which Hotze and his staff maintained Southern rights in its columns. "The paper being to a certain extent an English journal, although devoted to our defense," wrote the Secretary, "the moderate and temperate tone in which it is conducted is not only necessary but eminently judicious."[27]

While everything he did or wrote or published was ultimately aimed at securing recognition from England for the Confederacy, Hotze did not hammer exclusively on that idea. A brief chronological survey of *The Index* shows his treatment of continuing subjects and topical news impinging upon the Confederacy. As an ostensible English journal, *The Index* frequently discussed the inefficiency of the blockade or the repeated Federal insults to the British flag. Frequently it touched on the "cotton famine," deploring the great distress in Lancashire caused by the closing of the cotton mills. And it interpreted the war news from both the North and the South, never distorting facts, but presenting them in a light favorable to the Confederacy.

After the Seven Days' Battles, *The Index* spoke of the "collapse" of the Federal Armies; after Antietam it scoffed at Union claims of victory. Lincoln's Emancipation Proclamation Hotze called "a sop to Europe," and pointed out cleverly that Mr. Lincoln "does not promise to liberate the slaves in those states which are still occupied by Federal troops and subject to Federal rule, but only to emancipate those who are beyond his reach . . ."

When William E. Gladstone made his famous Newcastle speech in mid-October 1862—"Jefferson Davis and the other leaders of the South have made an army; they are making, it appears, a navy; and they have made what is more than either—they have made a nation"—*The Index* shrewdly warned that although "Mr. Gladstone's language is significant rather as indicating what the great majority of capable and impartial public men in England think, than as affording a clue as to what the English Ministry intends to do."

Lincoln's dismissal of General McClellan was politically inspired "as a defiance of the Democrats," *The Index* asserted.

The Index scored the British Foreign Office for turning down two proposals by France to mediate the war, the first reported in November 1862, the second in January 1863. "The policy of Lord Palmerston's Cabinet favours the aggressive, insolent, and worthless North; the sympathies of England are heartily with the gallant people who are defending, against overwhelming odds, the honour and the independence, the homes and the altars of the South."[28]

When on March 23, 1863, Lord Campbell made a brilliant plea in the House of Lords for recognition of the South, all it elicited from Lord Russell, said *The Index*, was a "reiteration of his policy of procrastination." Stonewall Jackson's death at Chancellorsville was a sad loss, but not an irreparable one, claimed *The Index*. "The great cause will go on and prosper, though Lee and a hundred other of the dead hero's comrades share his fate."

The twin Confederate defeats at Gettysburg and Vicksburg, early in July 1863, found *The Index* "not disposed to underrate the importance of the reverse that has befallen the South." But three months later the Southern victory at Chickamauga caused the paper to enthuse: "The South has again proved that with anything like equal terms it is far more than a match for the invader, and that the work of subjugation is more hopeless than ever." *The Index* rationalized Braxton Bragg's defeat at Missionary Ridge and retreat into Georgia in late November 1863: "That Bragg has sustained a serious reverse, we fear cannot be doubted. That his army is flying, scattered, and in hopeless panic, we utterly disbelieve."[29]

General U. S. Grant's appointment as commander in chief, said *The Index*, was "another of those clever dodges of 'Honest Abe Lincoln' by which a dangerous rival . . . is to be got out of the way." Mr. Lincoln's administration had to carry on two wars in 1864, Hotze wrote: "It has to subdue the South in order to carry the Presidential election; it must win the Presidential vote in order to beat the South." *The Index* accurately assessed Banks's Red River fiasco in Louisiana and said that the Confederate victory under Richard Taylor "has scarcely received the attention that it deserves in this country."

On June 23, 1864, *The Index* printed Admiral Raphael Semmes' report on the *Alabama's* fight with the *Kearsarge*, and commented: "The *Kearsarge* possessed every single advantage in this unequal fight—speed, strength, numbers, and weight of metal . . . The Federals have gained no glory by their success. The Confederate flag has sustained no dishonour."

Lincoln's re-election in November 1864 was characterized by *The Index* "as little else than an abdication by the American people of the right of self-government, as an avowed step towards the foundation of a military despotism."

As 1864 came to an end, Henry Hotze summoned his last reserve of optimism. *The Index* proclaimed on December 29:

"The Confederacy is at this moment stronger at every point than she was twelve months ago. Her armies are more numerous as compared with the Northern hordes; her material is more abundant and more perfect; she has undergone such a system of organization that her territory is a camp and her people an army; her finance is being managed with such skill that if the war continues but one year more, the reestablishment of a sound condition may be coincident with the collapse of her enemy, while her moral position in the eyes of Europe stands out with improved solidity. It is not only that her military successes have gained her respect, but that the tranquillity and unanimity of her citizens, the regard for the law and the cohesive power of her constitution have extorted acknowledgement even from those that pray for her destruction."[30]

VII

"My plan has been to abstain from attempting to do too much at once, but as soon as one position was secured to use it for attaining another," Hotze wrote Judah P. Benjamin. "Thus the establishment of an organ was at one time the great end, but when established it became the means to carry out other plans."[31]

Some of these other plans included pamphleteering. Even before *The Index* was launched, Hotze decided that James Spence's *The American Union* was too valuable a propaganda work to be confined only to the English language. Accordingly he had it translated and published in German at a cost of just under $200. A French translation of Spence's book was also prepared under Hotze's sponsorship. "If the translation have but a little of the success which the original has justly achieved," he told Benjamin, "the Southern Confederacy, when it formally takes its place among the nations of the earth, will not come as a stranger among them."

In 1863, Hotze reprinted Frank Key Howard's *Fourteen Months in American Bastilles*, first published in Baltimore. Distribution of this narrative of Federal cruelty to Confederate prisoners was undertaken at the request of James Mason. This indicates the propaganda value of atrocity stories was known before the twentieth century. That same year, Hotze achieved a tremendous propaganda coup as a result of an *Address to Christians Throughout the World*, prepared by a conference of Southern clergymen at Richmond early in 1863. Hotze printed it in full in *The Index* on June 11, 1863. Despite disclaimers by the 96 Southern Protestant ministers who signed the document, the "address" was definitely political in tone, with the defense of slavery woven into the arguments. Hotze, editorially, praised "the calm dignity of tone, the moderation of language, the absence of any reference to purely political topics," but he nevertheless jumped enthusiastically at an unusual opportunity to give it the widest possible circulation in the English-speaking world.

The Presbyterian publishing house of Nisbet & Co. suggested to the Confederate propagandist that the address be reprinted as a pamphlet which could be stitched inside the cover of the next issues of the *Quarterly Review*, the *Edinburgh Review*, and "every respectable religious publication" in England. "A quarter of a million copies of the address are by this means brought under the eyes of between one and two millions of readers in every part of the world where the English language is spoken," Hotze told Benjamin. Because the publishing firm agreed to do the work without compensation, Hotze was able to report to the Secretary of State that the deal would cost less than £250. The actual cost for the printing of 200,000 pamphlets was just under $1500, half of which Edwin De Leon volunteered to assume.

The publication of the ministerial address provided Henry Hotze with a much-needed propaganda crutch, because the fall of Vicksburg and Lee's repulse at Gettysburg had "spread very general dismay" among Confederate sympathizers in England. "The situation calls for extreme exertion . . . here," he wrote Benjamin, ". . . it is necessary by acts even more than by words to sustain the courage of our friends and supporters. A more than ordinary moral fortitude is demanded of the representatives of Southern views. The merest quaver of nerve on their part would be deemed a symptom of despair."

In *The Index* of November 5, 1863, Hotze printed in full a lengthy reply to the Confederate ministers by more than a thousand Scottish clergymen. The latter charged:

"Apologists for slavery, attempting to shelter themselves and it under the authority of God's word and the Gospel of Jesus Christ, are to be denounced as really, whatever may be their intention, the worst enemies of both."

Hotze replied editorially to the Scottish ministers with studied calm, noting that although they used strong language, it is "the earnest language of men who, from the depths of an honest conviction, protest and exhort against what they believe to be a most heinous and deadly sin." He charged them with "injustice to their fellow Christians in the Confederate States," while hastening to absolve them of "any willful intention of doing so." The injustice, Hotze insisted, is not "theirs, but rather that of a falsely informed but honest public opinion." Hotze expanded on this theme:

"This injustice consists in charging the Southern people with the defence or justification of wrongs or crimes which they would be the first to denounce and as sincere as their accusers in abhorring . . . The signers evidently take for granted that the struggle of the South for independence has no other object than to perpetuate slavery; apparently forgetting that a vigorous people of eight millions, of English blood, inhabiting half a continent, and differing, as this war has shown, so widely from their late associates, might have abundance of better reasons for desiring to live under a government of their own choice."[32]

Hotze's reply to the Scottish ministers reveals how scrupulously he adhered to his policy that *The Index,* in its advocacy of the Confederate cause, "should never lose its English tone, and above all never its temper."

When the design of the new Confederate flag, adopted May 1, 1863, reached Hotze about the time of the launching of his religious press operation, it struck him as a good idea "to placard every available space on the streets of London with representations of our newly adopted flag, conjoined to the British national ensign." He planned this solely as a " 'Demonstration' to impress the masses with the vitality of our cause." The colored posters, which cost Hotze $521.98, went up not only in London, but in other principal towns and in railroad stations.[33]

Throughout the rest of his propaganda career, Hotze did considerable pamphleteering, sometimes secretly preparing pamphlets himself. One such was *La Question Mexicaine et la Colonisation Française,* which he put together aided by an able translator. It was aimed, Hotze wrote, at having some bearing on the debate on Mexico in the French chamber. He had it ready for distribution before the debate opened, but French censorship held it up until the debate was over. On February 13, 1864, Hotze sent Benjamin a copy of the French pamphlet, with the above comments. Continuing he said:

"This leads me to the subject of the French press. I have been informed through Mr. Slidell of the recall of Mr. De Leon, but as I have had no communication from you or Mr. De Leon, I am uncertain what your intentions may be. My original instructions contemplated France as within the probable sphere of my duties, but I should not venture on an extensive plan of operation without your orders."

Pointing out to Secretary Benjamin the importance of developing in Paris a staff of well-trained native writers as he had done in London, he observed: ". . . It is not one newspaper article, nor a dozen, but hundreds that affect public opinion at large." And with keen foresight, in which he anticipated modern advertising practice, he told Benjamin: "Reiteration is the most powerful argument with the hundreds of thousands who take their opinions at second hand."[34]

VIII

Ever since his arrival in Paris in the early summer of 1862, Edwin De Leon had been *persona non grata* with John Slidell. Aboard the steamer to England, De Leon had had the effrontery to open sealed dispatches for Slidell from Judah P. Benjamin. When Slidell got the dispatches with the seals broken he fumed in private, held his tongue and restrained his pen.

But Slidell let De Leon know quite plainly what he thought of him, by refusing to associate with him socially or to introduce him officially in Paris. Eventually De Leon overstepped diplomatic propriety again and he wrote letters to Secretary Benjamin highly critical of Slidell and of the French people and government.

Unfortunately, De Leon's abusive letters were intercepted by the Federals and printed, to the great discredit of the Confederacy, in the New York *Tribune*. De Leon's recall and dismissal from the Confederate service followed immediately. Only then did Slidell break his silence and tell Benjamin of De Leon's opening of his dispatches. Benjamin mildly rebuked Slidell:

"While appreciating the motives which induced your forbearance from complaint, I can not but think that the Department ought to have been apprised earlier . . . as to his opening, without the slightest warrant of authority, the sealed dispatches addressed to you, and committed to his care. This fault was of so very grave a nature that it alone would probably have sufficed to put an end to Mr. De Leon's agency, and we should thus have been spared the annoyance of the scandal created by the interception and publication of the objectionable correspondence which caused his removal."[35]

When it became evident to Henry Hotze, early in 1864, that active direction of propaganda in France must now devolve upon him, he outlined to Secretary Benjamin the differences "in theory and in practice" of his propaganda techniques and those of Mr. De Leon. "Of course, I think mine the best," he told the Secretary. Neatly, he summed up for Benjamin his analysis of the British and French press:

"I act by means of persons rather than things, and therefore rely more upon the play of self-love, ambition, enthusiasm, admiration of our cause, and other passions than upon the power of money. But for this the English character, which is singularly earnest, affords me materials that are wholly lacking in the French. There is cynicism under the graceful drapery of French character which makes it far less easy to win honest converts, and devoted advocates. An English journalist, as a rule, writes, if not from conviction, at least not against it; the French journalist regards his profession as purely that of an advocate who earns his fee. It remains to be seen, therefore, whether my tactics will be as successful in the French press as in the English."[36]

In late March 1864, Hotze went to Paris to survey the ground and to confer with Slidell, under whose advice and orders he placed himself. Slidell was delighted with the young man, sensing, it seems, at a glance, that Hotze was many cuts above De Leon in intellect, talent, and finesse. "Mr. Hotze is here on a short visit," he wrote Benjamin on April 7. ". . . I think that you could not have selected a more suitable agent for the duties assigned to him, but it seems to me that a greater portion of his time could be beneficially employed here, and I shall so advise him."

Hotze, for his part, was pleased with the reception he got from Slidell and George Eustis, Slidell's secretary, both of whom demonstrated "the most energetic and efficient support" for his efforts, in addition to placing at his disposal their "extensive social relations." In the ten days he surveyed the Paris press, Hotze saw to what extent De Leon had used monetary persuasion to make the French journals "very accessible and amenable to reason," as the latter had explained it to Benjamin. From his predecessor, Hotze got no information on the status of Confederate relations with the French press, but on his own initiative, he obtained "sufficiently accurate and comprehensive knowledge of what had been done and attempted heretofore."

Disclaiming any criticism of De Leon, Hotze declared: "French journalists may or may not be more mercenary than the English, but certain it is that had I been preceded here [England] by an agent disbursing large sums of money in the manner in which they have undoubtedly been spent in France, I should have met English journalists of a very different stamp of those I found and made friends of." He told Benjamin he would have to exercise caution with the French press "lest bought friendships become suddenly converted into formidably hostile disappointments."

Hotze's financial problems, ameliorated from time to time by increases from Richmond, had by the time of his French mission disappeared. His contingent fund had been raised to $10,000 and eventually this was raised to $30,000 to take care of his many propaganda projects, over and above the publishing of *The Index*. But, desiring that his French account be kept separate from his English fund, Hotze asked Benjamin for $5000 for the undertaking.[37]

On May 7, 1864, Hotze sent Benjamin visual evidence of the work he had done in the limited time he had been in charge of Confederate propaganda in France. He enclosed clippings from the Parisian papers, marking the ones furnished by him and "which would not otherwise have appeared." But what was even more important was the manner in which Hotze had secured their publication with "no pecuniary consideration either present or prospective, direct or indirect, in it." It was perhaps the outstanding propaganda feat of Henry Hotze's career, next to launching and sustaining *The Index*.

He had met M. Auguste Havas, head of the great Havas-Bullier Telegraphic and Correspondence Agency, which supplied French papers with news. M. Havas, Hotze told Benjamin, was "both a man of honor and a gentleman." The young propagandist, with his amazing gift for making friends with important people, quickly won the confidence of the Frenchman, and soon was supplying him with Confederate news "which secures a hearing in journals of every shade of opinion, even those most fiercely opposed to us." Hotze expanded on the operation:

"Mr. Havas . . . professes no partiality for our cause. His business, he reasons, is to supply reliable interesting intelligence impartially, to express no opinion of his own. For this intelligence he goes to the best sources, and the sources he trusts according to his experience of their reliability. On my part, my object is to obtain in the Parisian press what we have never had before, a space proportionate to our importance among nations. If the public will only occupy itself about us and hear the truth, we may safely leave them to form their own opinions . . . He has never had a retraction to make, of anything I gave him, nor has he ever been charged with partiality. I rarely communicate a fact except by quotation of some recognized authority and even when the fact is exclusively my own, I take care that it is printed in some prominent journal before sending it over the wires. I always quote fairly and repress the temptation to comment. So it has happened, I think to the credit of both of us, that Mr. Havas never has refused a single thing I have sent . . . I pay the cost of transmission and this is all."

The effectiveness of Hotze's arrangement with Havas as regards the dissemination of Southern news he revealed in a subsequent letter to Secretary Benjamin. Drawing on his American correspondents to *The Index*, Hotze was able to furnish "an abundance of well-authenticated and valuable information." He thus had the satisfaction of seeing the columns of the French papers filled with correspondence from Richmond, New Orleans, and New York. He noted that "even enemies publish valuable facts for the purpose of controverting them." He was happy to see the "French writing world occupying itself sedulously with our affairs."

The temptation to open a Paris *Index* was for a time attractive, especially when a daily Parisian paper was offered him for a price. On mature reflection, Hotze turned it down. He also discontinued at his earliest opportunity, a subsidy which had been received under arrangements with De Leon. "A paper thoroughly devoted to us and representing our political philosophy in all its bearings might, indeed, perform the same functions here as *The Index* in England, but this would be too serious an undertaking for me to attempt a second time," he told Benjamin. "But a paper undertaking the advocacy of our cause by contract and as a means of adding to its revenue, is . . . an ally of questionable utility."

By the middle of September 1864, Hotze had done his work in France so well that he could say, with pardonable pride, that the Confederacy occupied "a dominant and almost impregnable position in both the English and French press." But Henry Hotze was too much of a realist to practice delusion upon himself. Useful as his press efforts were, not only for the present but for the future, he realized that his success was only theoretical; the practical criterion of success, recognition of the Confederacy, had eluded him. "I cannot blind myself to the fact that the immediate object toward which our efforts were directed has failed," he reported, "and whatever may be our triumphs in the arena of public opinion we no longer expect the political action of these governments of western Europe to have any direct influence upon the issue or duration of the war."[38]

IX

In the fall of 1863, and continuing into the summer of 1864, Henry Hotze had another country to concern himself with, but to a lesser degree. The Confederate government had noted the sharp rise in Irish immigration into the United States—in 1862 there were 40,000 Irish immigrant arrivals, whereas in 1863 there were 110,000—and Secretary Benjamin asked Hotze to look into it, to see if these Irish were being recruited for the Union Army. Hotze reported that a detective he had hired discovered beyond question that there was a violation of the British Foreign Enlistment Act, but, he pointed out, it would call for gathering evidence to prove it.

On the strength of Hotze's report and the growing number of Irishmen in the Northern Army, the Confederate government sent a number of agents abroad, all of whom reported to Hotze, who was assigned the general supervision of the operation by Secretary Benjamin. The first Confederate agent was an Irishman in the Confederate service, Captain J. L. Capston. He was followed by Father John Bannon, Irish-born Confederate chaplain, and the third was Captain J. P. Lalor. Their cumulative efforts were negligible. Although Father Bannon worked effectively with the Catholic priests in Ireland, the wave of Irish immigration and subsequent induction into the Union Army continued. In June 1864, Father Bannon asked for relief of duty so that he could go to Rome, but Capston and Lalor stayed on. In March 1865, as the Confederacy's hours ticked off, Benjamin wrote to Hotze to retrench and Hotze, on April 6, 1865, suggested dropping the Irish project, or at least recalling either Lalor or Capston. The latter, he wrote Benjamin, "is probably the more useful or less useless."[39]

In 1864, Hotze turned his attention to Germany, upon the suggestion of Samuel Ricker, *The Index's* correspondent at Frankfurt. At first lukewarm to the idea of trying to influence the German press, Hotze later saw possibilities in it, despite his own personal repugnance. "I feel conscious of lacking that sympathy or those points of mental and moral conduct with German thought which seems indispensable to influencing even in a slight degree the public opinion of a great people," he wrote Benjamin.

Still, Hotze made a trip to Germany and launched propaganda against German immigration to the United States, pointing out that most of the immigrants would wind up in the Union Army. In September 1864 he urged Benjamin to appoint an agent for Germany, because everything indicated that the war would last another year, and the Confederates had "interests to protect in Germany of vastly greater practical importance than either in England or France." He referred to German investments in United States bonds and the increasing recruitment of Germans for the Union Army.

Hotze's interest in Germany ceased, however, when Benjamin notified him that no special agent would be sent to that country because of the expense and the absence of a metropolitan center from which the press could be controlled. Hotze replied that henceforth he would treat Germany as a "dependency, incidentally included in my operations on the continent."[40]

By now the war was hurrying to its end, although the time lag in getting news to Europe prevented the full appreciation among Southern sympathizers of the approaching collapse of the Confederacy. The frantic, last-minute mission of Duncan F. Kenner to Europe, promising emancipation of the slaves in return for British and French recognition, came too late.

More than a year earlier, in 1863, Hotze, himself one of the zealous protagonists of slavery, had written an editorial in *The Index* on "Arming the Negroes." He had discussed it in advance with the Confederate finance agent, Colin McRae, a fellow Mobilian. McRae wrote Hotze: "I am anxious to see your article on the Negro soldiers if you have been able to make a few articles on that subject you are the most ingenious newspaper man in Europe."

Hotze tackled the subject in the September 10, 1863, issue. In part, he wrote:

"We have, in the various rumors that preceded this last direct announcement, so many indications that the question of arming the slave population has been under careful and serious consideration in the Confederate counsels. It is also certain that the same subject has been frequently discussed by the Confederates and their friends in Europe within the last few months. The Southern mind, therefore, on both sides of the ocean, has been ripening for this step, and, if not already taken, is prepared to take it.

"Intelligent observers of the struggle have long been aware that as a last resort the South possessed an element of latent strength which, whenever called forth, would at once shift the numerical superiority to the side which has hitherto been the weaker, and thus end the conflict. Those who know the temper of the Southern people knew that, if the alternative were fairly presented between independence and the maintenance of Negro slavery, it would not hesitate an instant to sacrifice the latter to the former."

When McRae read the piece, he wrote Hotze in admiration: "Your article 'Arming the Negroes' is admirably written & fully sustains the credit I gave you as a writer . . . The policy of arming the Negroes has not in my opinion, and will not be adopted by our Government . . . I am afraid your article was premature but nevertheless it was devilish well done."[41]

Hotze reported the rumor to Benjamin in his dispatch of September 26, 1863: "A short time since the whole of Europe was startled by the announcement, made in the most positive terms through Northern sources, that the South had decided upon arming immediately 500,000 of its slaves," he wrote. He said that Southerners abroad neither credited nor discredited the rumor, for the topic had been discussed among some of them in recent weeks and its possibility was admitted. What startled Hotze, however, was the equanimity with which he and his fellow Southerners accepted this proposed social change:

"I have been surprised, both at myself and others, how composedly an idea was received which two years, or even one year ago would not have entered into any sane man's mind. If the measure were really required—and no one presumed that otherwise the President would propose it—and if the alternative were once forced upon us of choosing between independence and the maintenance of our domestic institution,

I feel that I represent the views of the most loyal and most enthusiastic of its admirers when I say that we are not prepared to pay even this fearful price."

It is interesting to note that Hotze's piece on arming the slaves was printed in *The Index* almost four months before Major General Pat Cleburne urged the idea in a paper presented at General Joe Johnston's headquarters at Dalton, Georgia, on January 2, 1864, and more than two and a half years before the Confederate Congress finally authorized, on March 13, 1865, the employment of slaves as soldiers in the Southern Army.

Even before Duncan Kenner arrived in Europe early in 1865, Hotze had returned to the theme of making soldiers of the slaves. On November 10, 1864, *The Index* declared: "There is now no doubt that the people of the South have fully made up their minds, in the event of the war being continued beyond the present unfinished campaign, to throw into the scale the enormous latent strength so long held in reserve . . ." Two months later, on January 19, 1865, *The Index* said: "The Confederate press is inflicting cruel tortures upon the Northern War Christians by talking of emancipating the negroes . . . Emancipation, in the opinion of New England, is a most holy work when employed as a war measure for the purpose of exterminating the Southern people; but it is a wicked, and most damnable proceeding when suggested as a means of aiding the Confederates to defend their liberty, their lives, and their country."[42]

Had the Confederacy armed the slaves when Hotze first suggested it in September 1863, or when General Cleburne urged it in January 1864, it would have had a chance of establishing its independence. But when Congress finally acted, the Confederate cause was irretrievably lost.

Hotze was too intelligent, too shrewd, too much of a realist, in his heart of hearts, to feel that the Confederacy had any chance of survival as the early months of 1865 passed. He must have even smiled sadly when the perennially optimistic A. Dudley Mann, from his rosy cloud of make-believe, wrote him on January 26, 1865: "My confidence in our complete success continues unbounded . . . I believe that we shall 'hold our own' even better this year than we did last year . . ."

Still, in *The Index*, he kept up a brave front. On February 27, 1865, he said that the war was nearing its end, "but we await the result with confidence." The loss of Charleston was "a grave misfortune," *The Index* conceded on March 9, but it was now "one city less for the Confederate army to defend, and one fortified position the more for the Federal troops to hold." *The Index* predicted on March 16 that if Lee retired to the mountains "the war may be carried on for twenty years." At the end of March, *The Index* warned that the Federals "revise and prepare all the war news that reaches Europe." On April 6, three days before Appomattox, *The Index* confidently expected Robert E. Lee to "break the net which is said to be closing around him, and once more and finally destroy the Northern illusion of reunion." Two weeks later, when reports of the fall of Richmond reached England, *The Index* made no "attempt to underrate the gravity of its blow," but it urged its readers to wait "patiently and without despondency the arrival of Southern news that may place the evacuation of Richmond and Lee's retreat in a very different light."[43]

When the news of Appomattox arrived, Hotze doubtless felt as his friend James D. Bulloch, Confederate Naval agent abroad, did in a letter on April 25: ". . . The Confederacy cannot recover the shock of Lee's surrender . . . So long as the President holds out, I will, but I fancy he will in time be forced to acknowledge the inevitable result. I hope you will be able to keep up *The Index* . . ."

Such, indeed, was Hotze's intention. He wrote a correspondent on June 1, 1865: "*The Index* will, of course, continue to vindicate the true history of the struggle and the principles which though overcome by force still survive, but it will be less exclusively Southern than heretofore . . ."[44]

For four months after Appomattox, Hotze valiantly produced *The Index*. But the inevitable happened, and on August 12, 1865, Henry Hotze and *The Index* bade farewell to their readers:

"This is the last number of *The Index* . . . The blockade of the South rendered it necessary, for the representative of the Confederate Government, to have some avowed channel of publication; and, naturally, this position developed upon this journal. Under such circumstances, though we regretted, we had no right to complain, that in Europe we were looked upon as the mere organ of the Confederate Government, and that we were described in the United States as 'the rebel organ.'

". . . It did not, and indeed does not, occur to us that the downfall of the Confederacy deprived us of a field of usefulness . . . Unfortunately, we find our usefulness marred by the general impression that this journal has been nothing more than a Confederate organ. We might have battled against this impression and removed it, but circumstances have come to our knowledge which forbid this attempt. It is impossible not to see that the public on both sides of the Atlantic regards *The Index* as a kind of protest against the decision of Providence and as the organ of a new Secession party. It is needless for us to declare that such assumptions are entirely false, but we are unable to add they are manifestly unreasonable. To suppose that the continued publication of *The Index* has a political significance and that it must needs be hostile to the United States is natural, and almost inevitable. We have then no choice. We have sought to do the South good, and we cannot harm her to further our own views. We therefore suspend publication. *The Index* shall not be the excuse, the plausible excuse, for perpetuating a contest which can only aggravate the miseries of the conquered and disarmed.

". . . We are strongly tempted to address a few last words to our Southern readers . . . The long agony of the South will not be without a reward. Though defeated, the South is not dishonoured. The history of her independent existence does not exceed four years, but it is a complete and brilliant record that will endure so long as virtue and heroism are venerated . . . The Southern Confederacy has fallen, but her gallant sons have not died in vain. Whatever flag waves over her capitols the South will be free. Under whatever Government her people live, their influence will be felt . . . Time will obliterate the ravages of the fierce conflict, and the South, chastened by the will of God, and exalted by her chastening, will yet be happy and prosperous as in bygone days . . . It is with a good heart, though with personal pain, we bid our Southern friends farewell.[45]

Thus died *The Index* in its 172nd issue. It had been a remarkable experiment undertaken by a remarkable young man who, when the South, which he loved with a passion, was finally conquered, was only thirty-one years old, perhaps the youngest of all highly placed Confederates in civil affairs.

X

Henry Hotze disappeared from history with an abruptness which corresponded to his entry. Practically all the known activities of the brilliant young journalist-propagandist—one might well call him a quasi-diplomat—which can be documented, fall within a period of a decade.

From his naturalization in 1855 until he bade farewell to the readers of *The Index* in August 1865, his remarkable record is there to be dug out or pieced together. Most of his 52 official reports to the Confederate State Department have been published in the Official Records (Series II, Volume III of the Naval Records contains the Confederate diplomatic correspondence) and those which had not been found at the time of publication, later turned up in Hotze's manuscript dispatch book, now in the Library of Congress, where also to be found are his private letter books and miscellaneous other papers by, to, or about him.

And, of course, the complete file of *The Index*, readily obtainable either in the original or on microfilm at many libraries in the United States, admirably mirrors Hotze and his work, and the political climate in which he labored for the Confederate States of America.[46]

However, one searches in vain in the authoritative *Dictionary of American Biography* for an outline of Hotze's life. His name does not appear. Nor is his name or that of *The Index* to be found among the several thousands of listings in Colonel Mark M. Boatner's excellent *The Civil War Dictionary*.

Hotze lived twenty-two years after the war, but with the collapse of the Confederacy, he imposed upon himself self-exile and never returned to the land of his adoption. Only the barest fragments of information have survived the intervening century. At an undetermined date, he married Ruby Senac, daughter of Felix Senac, Confederate naval paymaster at New Orleans and later a Southern purchasing agent and paymaster abroad. Continuing his career as a journalist in Europe he reportedly was highly commended for his literary labors. At fifty-three, after some years of bad health, he died in Zug, Switzerland, on April 19, 1887.[47]

Henry Hotze's total effort, remarkable in itself, is all the more to be marveled at when one considers the maturity and experience of most of the Southern officials with whom he associated in his three years as Confederate propagandist. Before Hotze was born, Benjamin was a prosperous lawyer and John Slidell was a power in Louisiana and national politics. William Lowndes Yancey, approaching his majority, was tentatively trying out his forensic wings, and James M. Mason, at thirty-six, was on the threshold of a notable career in the United States Senate and House.

Thrown into contact with these older and more experienced men, with only two or three years of journalistic training behind him, Henry Hotze was never outshone on his mission to Europe. His perception, penetrating judgment, infinite patience and soft approach made him a special kind of diplomat, a prototype of Americans who would move noiselessly behind the scenes in other crises. Indeed, the effectively quiet techniques of Henry Hotze would have done credit to a Colonel House or a Harry Hopkins.

9

The Articulate Artillerist:

GENERAL E. P. ALEXANDER

I

ALREADY, by 8 o'clock on the morning of July 21, 1861, the sun was blisteringly bright in the cloudless Virginia sky.

Young Captain E. Porter Alexander could feel its heat upon his back as he stood with glass to his eye scanning the country to the north and west.

From the signal station he had erected on the hill on Josiah Wilcoxen's farm, about a mile east of Manassas Junction, the twenty-six-year-old Confederate engineer officer had a clear sweep of the defense line Brigadier General P. G. T. Beauregard had established along the twisting banks of Bull Run.

General Joe Johnston had arrived from the Shenandoah Valley with 11,000 troops, having given the slip to the aged Union General Robert Patterson, and he was in command of the combined Confederate forces now numbering about 30,000, approximately the same size as General Irvin McDowell's Union army at Centreville.

Beauregard had planned an offensive blow at McDowell's right for the morning of July 21, and Johnston had approved the plan and agreed that Beauregard should direct the attack. McDowell, however, did not wait for Beauregard to attack him, but himself launched an attack shortly after dawn, with artillery preparation and noisy demonstrations on the Warrenton Pike in front of Stone Bridge and on the road from Centreville to Blackburn's Ford.

After breakfast Captain Alexander had ridden out with the two generals. About 8 o'clock Beauregard instructed Alexander to take a courier and return to Wilcoxen Hill and remain in general observation of the field, sending messages of anything he noted.

"I was far from pleased at the receipt of the order," Alexander later said, "for I had hoped to accompany the generals throughout the day."[1]

So, reluctantly, Captain Alexander rode back to Wilcoxen's farm, climbed the hill and joined his men on the signal tower about 8:30 A.M. For three hours, since the first streaks of dawn, they had kept a constant watch but had seen nothing. Alexander resigned himself to inactivity, for the opportunity to render some service seemed indeed slight.

The line of sight from Wilcoxen Hill was good in all directions and, in his glass, Captain Alexander easily picked up the signal station he had set up on a bluff in the rear and to the left of Stone Bridge, six miles away. Beyond, the more or less level valley of upper Bull Run, with its fields, fences, and pastures, was foreshortened in his glass into a narrow band of green.

For fifteen minutes, Alexander made a close study of the whole field and then he fixed his glass upon the Stone Bridge station, while one of his men wigwagged flag signals, asking for information on developments of the morning. His glass was focused on the distant signalman when suddenly he became one of the principal actors in the first great dramatic moment of the Civil War. Alexander described what happened:

"While I was reading the motions of his flag, the sun being low in the east & I looking towards the west, from up the narrow band of green above the flag, the faintest twinkle of light caught my eye. My eyes were always remarkably quick and good, & I had had long training with a glass. It was but a single flash, but the color was that of brass & the shape a horizontal line. It could be nothing but the reflection of the morning sun from the side of a brass gun. I brought my glass very carefully to bear exactly, & presently made out a little swarm of still fainter glitters of bright musket-barrels & bayonets."

Captain Alexander at once grasped the significance of what he had seen—McDowell, by a wide circuit, was about to turn Beauregard's left flank and take him in the rear. All the noise at Stone Bridge and the movement towards Blackburn's Ford were merely diversions, while the bulk of the Union attacking force made its flanking march through the woods, north of Bull Run.

Immediately Alexander signaled to Colonel Nathan G. "Shanks" Evans at Stone Bridge: "Look out for your left; you are turned." Then he hastily wrote a message to Beauregard and hurried off the courier with it:

"I see a body of troops crossing Bull Run about two miles above Stone Bridge. The head of the column is in the woods on this side. The rear of the column is in the woods on the other side. About a half mile of its length is visible in the open ground between. I can see both infantry and artillery."

At the same time that a courier from the signal tower brought Alexander's warning to Colonel Evans, another courier from the Confederate pickets at Sudley Ford reached him with the report that the head of a powerful Federal column was crossing Bull Run at that point.

Evans, upon the advice of Major Roberdeau Wheat of the Louisiana Tigers, left only a token force at Stone Bridge, and with 1100 rifles marched to the rear to meet the onslaught of McDowell's attack. As soon as Beauregard received Alexander's message, the commands of Barnard Bee, F. S. Bartow, Wade Hampton, and Thomas Jonathan Jackson were rushed to the support of "Shanks" Evans' hopelessly outnumbered little band. In the bitter day-long fight, before victory was snatched from defeat, the first two would die gallantly in action, the third would render distinctive service and the last would win an immortal name.

In his glass, Captain Alexander followed the troop movements on the field as the Confederates desperately tried to stem the sweeping tide of Federals descending upon them from Sudley Ford. At 10:30 A.M., as the heat became almost unbearable, he spotted a tremendous column of dust developing about ten miles to the northwest. What did it mean? Was it Patterson's army from the Valley, following Johnston?

Alexander decided to be his own messenger with this information and, as he explained, "perhaps to point it out to the generals as it had now risen to a high altitude." There can be little doubt, also, that the young captain was hankering for a little of the action he was missing in his distant signal tower.

His news, for a time, as General Johnston reported, "excited apprehension of General Patterson's approach." Fortunately, it proved to be Joe Johnston's wagon trains, plodding along from the Valley. "I afterward acquired more experience with army dusts than I then possessed," Alexander wrote later, "but never during the war did I see a dust cloud tower higher or rise more densely than this."[2]

Captain Porter Alexander made his first contribution to the Confederacy by introducing battle-employment of wigwag signals at the intoxicating Confederate victory at Manassas. And he made his last at Appomattox around the dying embers of Lee's campfire and of the Confederacy. In the four intervening years, he rose from a captain of engineers to a brigadier general of artillery. From the privates who manned his guns to the commander-in-chief himself, Porter Alexander earned respect and admiration by his versatility and energy; by his imperturbable poise and unfailing self-confidence; by his quick and sound judgment and coolness in crisis; by the brilliant qualities of his intuitive and keenly perceptive mind; and, above all, by his extraordinary skill as an artillerist.

One of his closest friends in the army, General G. Moxley Sorrel, fittingly summed up what Alexander's contemporaries in the Confederacy thought of him:

"His was the happiest and most hopeful nature. He was sure of winning in everything he took up, and never did he open his guns on the enemy but that he knew he should maul him into smithereens . . . He was often called on both by Lee and Longstreet for technical work . . . Longstreet thought so well of his engineering and reconnoitering abilities that he kept him very near headquarters . . . He was a many-sided character—an engineer of the highest abilities, an artillerist of great distinction, a good reconnoitering officer and an enthusiastic sportsman besides."[3]

Modern students of the Civil War, a century later, still put the same evaluation on Porter Alexander that Robert E. Lee did when the young Georgia aristocrat was a conspicuous officer in the Army of Northern Virginia.

Douglas Southall Freeman placed Alexander "among the most scientific and resourceful" of all of Lee's officers. Alexander was, said Freeman, "a man of the sort on whom a busy commander safely may rely." Clifford Dowdey said that Alexander came "fairly close to the elusive category of genius" and was "the most brilliant cannoneer ever in the Army of Northern Virginia and one of the instinctive soldiers in the war." Fairfax Downey goes even further than Dowdey and asserts that Alexander "rates as the South's most brilliant artillerist."[4]

In the twilight of his years, after four decades of distinction as an educator, insurance executive, planter, railroad president, and international arbitrator, Porter Alexander brought a perceptive and articulate pen to the chronicling of the gallant saga of the Army of Northern Virginia to which he had lent a valorous sword.

His *Military Memoirs of a Confederate*, published in 1907 when Alexander was seventy-two, is probably the most frequently quoted authority for the Civil War in Virginia, including Lee's two fruitless invasions of the North.

II

Edward Porter Alexander was born in Washington, Georgia, on May 26, 1835, to a well-to-do and distinguished Georgia family of the planter class.

At eighteen he entered West Point and in 1857 was graduated third in a class of 38. Because of his high scholastic standing Cadet Alexander was assigned to the Corps of Engineers as a Brevet Second Lieutenant and detailed at West Point as an instructor in the Department of Practical Military Engineering.

For three years after his graduation, Alexander generally served at the Military Academy, except for two special details, which took him from the West Point classrooms for a period of about six months each. In January 1858 he was sent to Utah to participate in the Mormon War, but by the time he got there the war was over and so he returned to

West Point. In October 1859 he was again detached from teaching to participate in experiments which, in less than two years, would have momentous significance to Second Lieutenant E. Porter Alexander.

Early in 1859, Assistant Surgeon A. J. Myer had offered to the War Department a system of military signals which he had devised. It was based upon Baine's telegraphic alphabet in which only dots and dashes were used to form the letters, which would be indicated by waving flags in the day or lamps at night.[5]

Dr. Myer appeared three times in March before a Board of Officers headed by Brevet Colonel R. E. Lee to explain his signals. The board found the surgeon's system "simple in theory, clear and well arranged, and its use can be readily imparted to an intelligent person in the course of a few hours' instruction. In its application to practical purposes, however, there are apparently many difficulties." The board nevertheless recommended the adoption of the Myer system. To demonstrate that the difficulties could be overcome, Dr. Myer sought and eventually received permission to make extensive experiments under both day and night conditions.[6]

It was not until October, however, that Dr. Myer began his experiments and assigned to assist him was Lieutenant Alexander of the West Point faculty. Alexander's story of the exciting experiment is told in great detail in reports he made to Myer, reports still preserved in the National Archives in Washington. Alexander reported to Myer in New York City at 10:30 A.M. on October 5 and the training began with Dr. Myer lecturing for an hour on signal systems in general and his system in particular. "At 11:30 A.M., I commenced committing to memory the alphabet based upon the system & before 1 P.M. had completely mastered it," Alexander reported. For the next three hours they engaged in practice signaling across the room with the arms . . . "Although I worked rather slowly at first, I soon acquired much facility in the use of the signals . . ." wrote Alexander.[7]

Dr. Myer must have been pleased with the rapidity with which the young assistant caught on, for the next day, between 5 P.M. and 8 P.M., their first actual test was made between Fort Hamilton and Battery Hudson, about a mile and a quarter apart. "I have no accurate report of all the messages exchanged," stated Alexander, "but those sent out by myself amounted to over eighty words, exclusive of recognitions and assent. The time occupied in their transmission, was on an average, one word per minute." At his end, reception was good, Alexander reported, all of Myer's messages being "distinctly & clearly received (both day and night) to a great extent with my naked eye." Mistakes were few, and quickly corrected by repetition, "so that the communication was as perfect & complete as possible."[8]

On October 8, Myer and Alexander made their second test, this time between Bedloe Island and Fort Richmond, a distance of 5⅞ miles. Conducted between 2 P.M. and 9 P.M. under threatening and then rainy conditions, the experiment came off well, except when it was raining hard or when a vessel passed across the line of sight. At night, even a steady drizzle did not impair the transmission of messages. "The apparatus all worked admirably," Alexander told Myer. . . . "The experiment demonstrated to my entire satisfaction the possibility of communicating at this distance in all ordinary degrees of haze or darkness of sky, either by day or night, with perfect ease and certainty."[9]

Encouraged by the great progress after only two outdoor tests, Dr. Myer lengthened his sights and on October 11, he put a distance of 10¼ miles between him and Alexander, setting up their stations at Sandy Hook and Fort Hamilton. He must have been delighted when, during the final hour of work on that night, they exchanged forty-two words, excluding acknowledgments at the end of each message, "without the loss or repetition of a single one." Working mornings, afternoons and nights through October 14, under varying conditions of visibility, Myer and Alexander made amazing progress in communicating at a distance, especially in the repeating of passages not understood. "I was always able to stop you, or be stopped by you at once . . . with great ease and facility," reported Alexander.[10]

On October 20, at 9 A.M., Lieutenant Alexander again took his position on a sand hill at Sandy Hook and communications between Dr. Myer and him commenced:

DR. MYER: There is great excitement at Sandy Hook over Harpers Ferry. It is reported that the rioters are murdering the families in that vicinity. Wait a minute do you understand?

LT. ALEXANDER: Yes. Repeat one word before Ferry & one before 'are.'

DR. MYER: Harpers and rioters. Last night Colonel Lee started with eighty marines to visit the place. The rumor is probably exaggerated.

LT. ALEXANDER: Who are the rioters and what are their motives supposed to be? (*No reply seen.*)

DR. MYER: Send a message. Did you get my last?

LT. ALEXANDER: No, I didn't see it. Repeat.

DR. MYER: My answer to your question was "slaves and revolt." Do you understand?

LT. ALEXANDER: Yes. I am going to dinner now. Look for me at two.

DR. MYER: Good bye—at two.

LT. ALEXANDER: Good bye.

Thus did the young Georgian hear of John Brown's Raid on Harpers Ferry, an event that brought Robert E. Lee, T. J. Jackson, and Jeb Stuart under arms together for the first time, and which convinced many

Southerners of the inevitability of secession if a "Black Republican" won the election of 1860.

On October 28, Myer again increased the distance between himself and Alexander and, although 15¼ miles apart, between Highlands and Fort Hamilton, Alexander read the first message with ease. He signaled back, enthusiastically: "I believe we can send a message twenty miles if desirable. I know we can read signals much less clear than these." Equally enthusiastic, but with an economy of words, Dr. Myer replied: "We have succeeded."[11]

In his book, *Military Memoirs of a Confederate*, Porter Alexander states the signal experiments took three months, but in his lengthy report to Dr. Myer on November 2, 1859, he states after recording a message: "This completed these experiments."

In January 1860, Dr. Myer and Lieutenant Alexander went to Washington to present their report on the tests to the War Department and the impression they made was profound. Secretary of War John B. Floyd wrote, on February 9, 1860, to the chairman of the Senate Military Committee describing the "system of military signals" and the recently conducted tests:

"[. . .] They completely demonstrated the usefulness of these signals for Military operations under the many exigencies incident to the service. I consider the practicality of their use as established . . . I regard the general use of this system of signals by the regular army . . . as not only expedient but as of very great importance for the Military service of the United States."[12]

The man who received this letter was Senator Jefferson Davis of Mississippi. Exactly one year later to the day, he would be elected President of the Confederate States of America. And the signal system so highly recommended as of "very great importance to the Military service of the United States" would save his infant Confederacy from being crushed on the plains of Manassas in the first great battle of the Civil War.

III

From far-away Fort Steilacoom in Washington Territory, Porter Alexander wrote his sister, Clifford, on November 11, 1860:

"Of course, we are all much exercised now to know the result of the election which is all over, but which we can not hear of for three weeks yet. We suppose from the latest news we have that Lincoln is elected, and if so I *hope* and *expect* to be called in to help secede. If he is inaugurated, it will be too late to oppose him, as the purse and the sword will be in his hands and the Army and Navy are sworn to obey his commands. If he is elected I believe the interests of humanity, civilization, and self-preservation call on the South to secede, and I'll go my arm, leg, or death on it."[13]

Lieutenant Alexander had been at Fort Steilacoom not quite two months. Following a successful demonstration of the signal system before the Military Committees of both the Senate and the House of Representatives in Washington, he had returned to West Point, but on March 21, 1860, he had been granted three months' leave to marry Bettie Mason of King George County, Virginia. On his return to West Point from his honeymoon, he was ordered to Washington Territory. He and his wife sailed from New York on August 10 and on September 20, Lieutenant Alexander reported at Fort Steilacoom.

Following Lincoln's election there was considerable concern at the post among Southern officers whose native states, one by one, seceded from the Union. "There was generally little active interest taken by army officers in political questions," wrote Alexander in his *Military Memoirs of a Confederate*, "but, with few exceptions, the creed was held that, as a matter of course, in case war should result from secession, each officer would go with his state." In February, Alexander learned his native Georgia had seceded.

In March, Alexander's company was ordered back to West Point and on April 9, 1861, he and his wife sailed for San Francisco, where they arrived on April 20. They missed the Panama boat and had a ten-day layover in San Francisco. Waiting on the wharf for Alexander when he debarked was a messenger with a telegram, brought by Pony Express from Missouri, relieving him of duty with his company and ordering him to report to Lieutenant James B. McPherson in command on Alcatraz Island in the harbor.

This was upsetting to Alexander, who was determined to resign and follow his native Georgia out of the Union. The order compelled him to resign at once, and not after he had returned East, and this would deprive him of transportation for himself and wife, who were 6000 miles from home. He reported to Lieutenant McPherson, whom he quickly discovered to be "one of the most attractive and universally beloved and admired men" he had ever met.

Alexander explained his feelings, his intentions, his plight. He asked McPherson to forward his resignation and to give him a leave of absence which would enable him and his wife to return home, where he could await the acceptance of his resignation. Alexander pointed out that McPherson had the authority to do so, but unless it was granted, he would be detained in California for several months.

"If you must go," said McPherson, "I will give the leave of absence, and do all in my power to facilitate your going. But don't go. Those urgent orders to stop you here are meant to say that, if you are willing to keep out of the war on either side, you can do so. They mean that you will not be asked to go into the field against your own people . . . that is what these orders mean."

McPherson then outlined with prophetic foresight what was ahead for the South in the war which he declared would be a long and bitter one, regardless of what press and politicians were saying.

". . . For your cause, there can be but one result. It must be lost," declared McPherson. "Your whole population is only about eight millions, while the North has twenty millions. Of your eight millions, three millions are slaves, who may become an element of danger. You have no army, no navy, no treasury, and practically none of the manufactures and machine shops necessary for the support of armies, and for war on a large scale . . . You will be cut off from the rest of the world by blockade."

All this while, Lieutenant Alexander remained silent; he could not but admit the logic of McPherson's arguments. But as he listened, one thought kept uppermost in his mind: *I must go with my people!*

"Your cause must end in defeat," continued McPherson, "and the individual risks to you must be great. On the other hand, if you stay out here, you'll soon be the ranking engineer officer on the whole coast. Everyone of the older officers will soon be called East for active service, and there will be casualties and promotion . . . Meanwhile you will have every chance to make a reputation for yourself as an engineer."

McPherson stressed other opportunities—in ranching, in land investments which would be open to him as an adjunct to his Army duty.

"In four years you will be a rich man," he said. ". . . Here you have every opportunity for professional reputation, for promotion, and for wealth. Going home you have every personal risk to run, and in a cause foredoomed to failure."

McPherson's sincere appeal could not fail to impress Porter Alexander. It made him realize the gravity of the decision which he had to make. But the overruling factor was the question that every Southern officer in the United States service had to answer for himself: "Could he oppose his native state in a civil war?" However alluring was McPherson's picture of his personal future, Alexander knew that he had to go with the people of Georgia.

"What you say is probably all true," Alexander said, after a moment. "But my situation is just this. My people are going to war. They are in deadly earnest, believing it to be for their liberty. If I don't come and bear my part, they will believe me to be a coward. And I shall not know whether I am or not. I have just *got* to go and stand my chances."

"In your situation," replied McPherson, "I would probably feel the same way about it."

Alexander wrote his resignation, dated it May 1, 1861, and on the same day sailed for the East.[14]

Meanwhile, Alexander had written his brother, W. F. Alexander, to submit his name to the authorities at Montgomery for a commission in the Confederate Army. In so doing, Alexander's brother addressed himself to Secretary of War Walker: ". . . As to his qualifications and merits, I beg leave to refer to Col. Hardee of the Army. In addition to his military education received at West Point, where he graduated with high distinction, he is thoroughly acquainted with the Secret Signal service recently introduced into the U. S. Army by Major Meyer [Myer], having been detailed to assist that officer in his experiments . . ."

When Porter Alexander arrived in Richmond on June 1, a commission as Captain of Engineers in the Confederate Army was waiting for him.[15] Moreover, the three highest military men in the Confederacy all knew of his experience with the new signal system—Robert E. Lee, the President's military adviser, who had headed the board that approved them; Jefferson Davis who, as chairman of the Senate Military Committee, had witnessed a demonstration of the system and sparked the passage of the bill creating the United States Signal Corps; and, finally, Secretary of War Walker.

It was inevitable that Captain E. Porter Alexander would be drafted as a signal officer for the Confederate Army.

IV

"I . . . went to see President Davis. He expressed himself as glad to have my services & told me to prepare a set of signals at once . . ."

So wrote Captain Alexander to his wife on June 2, 1861. His subsequent letters reflected his impatience over not joining troops.

On June 6, he wrote: ". . . Really I ought to have been sent off somewhere before now . . . I think it most likely that I will be sent *everywhere*, that is, to start signal operations first at Norfolk, next at Yorktown, next at Aquia Creek, then between Manassas Gap and Harpers Ferry."

Alexander's old commandant of cadets during his first year at West Point, Brigadier General Robert Garnett, sent to oppose McClellan in Northwestern Virginia (the present West Virginia) invited Alexander to become a member of his staff. "I told him that I would like to go, & he applied to the President & Genl Cooper, both," Alexander told his wife on June 7, "but they told him that they wanted me to work the signals." His impatience for action showed through his next sentence: "If they will let me have my own way I can start the signals in operation everywhere from Norfolk to Harpers Ferry in a week or ten days &

then go on & catch up with Garnett in time for anything he wants . . ."

Four days later Alexander told his wife that "Gen. Beauregard applied for me & there is no telling where I will eventually go." But on June 21, still unassigned, Alexander fretted in Richmond: "I am very anxious to get to work, but Davis is evidently saving me for something for I've taken good care that he shan't *forget* or *overlook* me, & unless he had something special I think he would have sent me off if only to get rid of me before now . . ."

"No sign of orders for me yet," he wrote on June 25, "a delay which has effectually removed any conceit I may ever have that my services were worth anything." And on June 26, he wrote: "I *hate* this delay, for I'm afraid it is spoiling me & making me lazy."

Finally, however, Captain Alexander got a job. On June 29, he was ordered to take charge of five batteries of artillery, two in camp at Chimborazo, on the outskirts of Richmond, and nearly ready for the field, and three in barracks in the city, virtually untrained recruits without equipment. But before he could tackle the assignment, new orders came, directing him to report to General Beauregard at Manassas Junction with his system of signals.

Captain Alexander had sent for his wife, in the meantime, and he regretted that he would not be in Richmond when she arrived. But his assignment to Beauregard elated him. He wrote his wife on June 30:

". . . I am delighted that the orders are what they are. I will be serving with the largest army in the most important place, & that too our *best* General & one that we can all feel confident will lose nothing thro *mismanagement*. Then, too, besides my professional duties I will have charge of all the signals & *may* have an opportunity to render much service with them . . ."[16]

Captain Alexander reported to Beauregard on July 2, and immediately went to work to install the signal system and train men in its operation. He was kept busy day and night, for all details of the project fell upon his shoulders. He rode all over the countryside and selected sites for signal stations at Wilcoxen Hill, near the Junction, at Centreville and at Stone Bridge, where the Warrenton Pike crosses Bull Run. "They only gave me *privates* to work with, & I had everything to do," he wrote his wife, "even to feeding them at the different signal stations, & some of them are so stupid that I have to knock them down & jump on them & stamp & pound an idea into their heads."

Despite the slow arrival of the equipment he had gathered and ordered in Richmond, in a little more than a week Captain Alexander had the signal system in operation at Manassas, but he didn't anticipate any serious employment of it. "We are perfectly quiet & may remain so for a long time," he told his wife on July 10.

But in just eleven days, McDowell would make his bold movement around Beauregard's left flank and Captain Porter Alexander, with the morning sun at his back, high upon Wilcoxen Hill, would catch the glitter of distant cannon and musket barrels and bayonets and flash the news to Beauregard that the Federals were on his flank and rear.[17]

A few days after the battle, Alexander rode over the battlefield with General Johnston and General Beauregard. "The smell of the field was awful," he told his wife, "principally from the dead horses in some places in piles." He said that the Confederate army was too disorganized for offensive movements and blamed the "disgraceful mismanagement of the railroads" for shortages. The food crisis, he said, was critical and "our army is actually *almost* starving. They appointed Northrop Commissary General, a man who in the old Army had not seen his company or done a minute's work in seventeen years, & this is the result of it."[18]

Captain Alexander found himself busier than ever after Manassas. General Beauregard appointed him Chief of Ordnance and Artillery for his army—"a most complimentary appointment for so young an officer," he proudly told his wife—and among his other duties, he set up a printing press, tried out field telegraph wire, continued to supervise the signal system, and collected data from reports for the general.

General Albert Sidney Johnston, Confederate commander in the West, applied for Captain Alexander's services in his army, but Adjutant General Samuel Cooper promptly telegraphed back: CAPTAIN ALEXANDER CANNOT BE SPARED FROM MANASSAS. On September 29, Alexander was named Chief of Ordnance & Signal Officer for the Confederate Army of the Potomac, an early name for the Army of Northern Virginia.

In September, Alexander had gotten interested in rocket batteries and with Beauregard's permission had ordered the manufacture of rockets. But early in October, Beauregard instructed Alexander to "countermand all orders you may have given for the organization of a rocket battery."[19]

Early in November, Captain Alexander suggested to the War Department a program for expanding the use of the signal system which had proved so effective at Manassas. On November 10, 1861, Secretary of War Judah P. Benjamin wrote him:

"The President is much interested in your system of signals and attaches high value to it, and is disposed to adopt your suggestion in relation to the details of officers instructed by you for duty at other points . . ."

A Department of Signals was organized in Richmond and the charge of it, with the rank of colonel, was offered young Alexander, but he declined, being unwilling to leave the field for a desk job. The young captain developed a great fondness for General Beauregard and that the latter had a reciprocal feeling for his brilliant staff officer is indicated when, on January 30, 1862, Alexander sent a photograph of Beauregard to the general and asked for his autograph "as a souvenir for times to come." Beauregard signed the picture and returned it with a little note under Alexander's: "With much pleasure, since, I hope those times to come will be no worse than those that have gone by—but however they may be, I will always be happy to have you by my side."

When Beauregard was sent west to join Albert Sidney Johnston in Kentucky, in February 1862, he invited Alexander to accompany him as his Chief of Ordnance. Alexander turned down the offer. "I preferred staying here," he wrote his father, "to complete all the plans I now have & because I think it the most important and prominent place." He lamented Beauregard's departure, "on account of the moral effect of his presence both on the enemy & our own men: but I have fully as much confidence in Johnston's strategy & ability."

In this same letter, Captain Alexander showed a keen sense of appraisal, and intuitive grasp of the realities of the war. Discussing the re-enlistment campaign, and the lukewarm support of it by the troops, he said: "It is useless however to expect to carry on the war for any time by volunteering & I am very anxious to see drafting commenced . . ."[20]

When the Richmond authorities decided to pull back General Joe Johnston's army from the line of Bull Run, Captain Alexander mined Stone Bridge preparatory to blowing it up when Johnston moved out on March 9, 1862. For a week prior to departing he supervised the shipping, by rail, of the guns, ammunition, artillery equipment and other supplies to rear depots. During the withdrawal to the Rappahannock, Captain Alexander was shocked at the lack of discipline and excessive straggling of the Confederate troops. "Our soldiers are committing many shameful outrages which are a disgrace to the country & some ought to be & I hope will be, shot, as examples."

On March 18, as Johnston's army established itself near the Rappahannock, Alexander received from Secretary of War George W. Randolph an appointment to the temporary rank of Major of Artillery. On April 12, Alexander wrote Randolph asking for a permanent commission of Major of Artillery and that he be assigned to Ordnance duty. "I have been on Ordnance duty for many months & make this application with a view to a permanent assignment to Ordnance duty, & transfer from the Engineer Corps at the end of the war." On the same date Colonel Josiah Gorgas, Chief of Ordnance, wrote Randolph urging that Alexander's request be granted.[21]

V

During the early phases of McClellan's Peninsula Campaign against Richmond, Major Porter Alexander, as Joe Johnston's Chief of Ordnance, fulfilled various staff duties besides keeping the ammunition flowing.

At Williamsburg, on May 5, he was one of several staff officers to whom Major General James Longstreet reported himself indebted "for valuable assistance in conveying orders to different points of the field."

None of the battle reports for the two-day fight at Seven Pines, May 30–June 1, mentions Alexander, whose participation was doubtless confined to the routine duties of Chief of Ordnance. With the severe wounding of General Johnston at Seven Pines, Robert E. Lee became commander of the Army of Northern Virginia and it was under General Lee that young E. P. Alexander emerged as one of its most resourceful, energetic, and brilliant officers.

At Manassas, Porter Alexander was credited with one of the many "firsts" to emerge from the American Civil War, namely the battlefield transmission of messages by wigwag signals. In the Seven Days' Battles before Richmond, which Lee initiated late in June to dislodge McClellan from the gates of the Confederate capital, Major Alexander became the first Confederate to engage in aerial observation of a battlefield from a balloon.

Professor Thaddeus Sobieski Constantine Lowe, an experienced and enthusiastic balloonist, had convinced Abraham Lincoln in June of 1861 that aerial observation of the enemy was practicable. Accordingly, Lowe hoisted his gas bag over the Federal lines in Virginia and successfully observed the Confederate fortifications around Centreville during the "phony war" in the fall and winter of 1861–62. When McClellan started up the Peninsula in the spring of 1862, Lowe's air corps consisted of seven balloons and a Navy vessel on the Potomac, the first official aircraft carrier in history. His observations at Seven Pines and in the Seven Days' Battles have been rated by a student of the tools of war in 1861–65 as "of inestimable value to the Union Army."

Robert E. Lee must have thought well of the idea, for when Dr. Edward Cheves of Savannah sent him a balloon he had fabricated out of silk, Lee immediately put it to use to reconnoiter the Federal lines and troop movements. And the man chosen to do the observation was his young Chief of Ordnance. Alexander, in his *Military Memoirs of a Confederate*, states:

"My personal duties during the Seven Days' were the supervision and distribution of our ammunition supplies. Our organized division supply trains and brigade wagons worked smoothly, and no scarcity was felt anywhere.

"In addition to these duties, I was placed in charge of a balloon . . . made of silk of many patterns, varnished with gutta-percha car-springs dissolved in naphtha, and inflated at the Richmond Gas Works with ordinary city gas."[22]

Alexander devotes only ten lines more in his book to this exciting—

and profitable—operation, but, fortunately, he wrote a long letter to his father describing his experience in detail. "Two days before the com-- mencement of [the battles], Gen Lee ordered me to take charge of a balloon in addition to my other duties, & during the fighting to use it as far as practicable for discovering the movements of the enemy." After some trouble, the balloon was ready for use on Friday, June 27. It was too small to carry more than 800 feet of rope, besides Alexander's weight. "With that elevation," he explained, "the enemy in our front were concealed from a close observation by the dense timber, but the dust of every movement was visible & the farther slope of the Chickahominy valley where the fighting of that day occurred was in plain view."

He first went up about sunrise and before he came down at 11 A.M., "because the balloon had leaked so much," he observed the retreat of the Federals, "burning stores & blowing up ammon wagons." Alexander told his father that as he was easily made giddy, he undertook the work under orders and with no great zest—"with about as much alacrity as I would have undertaken any duty under a heavy fire," he said—but he was pleasantly surprised when he found the sensation aloft "a charming one." There was nothing disagreeable about it but a little seasickness when the wind blew. He explained the technique of indicating his findings from the balloon: "I took up with me some large black canvass balls & signalled to all the army in sight the movements of the enemy by suspending them under the balloon." Continuing, he wrote:

"That afternoon we refilled the balloon, & I went up again, staying up until dark, and having a fine view of the terrible fight about Gaines Mill, I could see the bursting of nearly every shell & the flash or smoke of every volley of musketry, making as grand and exciting a scene as the world ever shows.

"That night about one o'clock orders came from Gen. Lee for a large amount of ammon and the next day was occupied in sending out and distributing this, and I made no ascension. The weather being moreover too windy for it without much risk to the Balloon. On Sunday the enemy had commenced his retreat and I endeavored to get the Balloon down to Drury's Bluff on a steamer, but a thunder squall nearly wrecked it, & it was twelve at night before I was successful in getting up & finding their camp fires. We then returned and refilled, & I again went up at sunrise.

"Monday from Drury's Bluff & located the enemy. That afternoon I rode out to see Gen Lee, and almost before I knew it got into the fight of that day. I found the General under a hot fire & though I had nothing to do, I didn't like to leave him in it, & so stayed through the engagement, distributing my flask full of the Old Hurricane you sent me last year among the wounded."

Throughout Tuesday, July 1, Major Alexander was too busy bringing ammunition trains up to positions convenient to the troops and he didn't get into the furious fight at Malvern Hill, but the next day, General Lee sent him back for the balloon to discover the whereabouts of McClellan. At about 2 A.M. on July 3, Major Alexander and his balloon went down the James aboard the little gunboat *Teazer*. Continuing his balloon narrative, Alexander wrote his father:

"I made several ascensions from the deck of the boat & seeing the river clear of the enemy's gunboats in front went down many miles below the obstructions. About 9 a.m. the wind rose so that we had to exhaust and fold up the Balloon, & on the Captain's proposal I agreed to go with him down the river nearly to City Point where we could land & I could communicate with Gen Lee & the Army sooner than by returning to Richmond . . . The pilot ran us aground in a soft mud shoal, 100 yards from shore . . . The tide was commencing to ebb & every effort to get off proved unavailing so there was nothing left for it but to wait until late in the afternoon for flood tide & trust to luck that no gunboat would come up."

Major Alexander went ashore and found some Confederate cavalry pickets, through whom he sent a report to General Lee. After that he amused himself collecting arms scattered through the woods and fields and at 2 A.M. loaded them into his rowboat and started back to the *Teazer*. Just as he pushed away from shore, the Yankee gunboat *Maratanza* came into view around a bend, about half a mile off. Alexander continued:

"Two minutes later & our row boat would have been out in the stream of the mud shoal when our chances would have been slim, & as it was a 'skedaddle' to the cover of the woods was instinctively carried out as a sanitary measure by the whole boat crew and myself. . . . The *Maratanza* immediately opened on the *Teazer* & the latter replied once or twice, & then the officers having kindled a fire against the magazine & lashed down the safety valve abandoned her, & all escaped safely walking over the mud bank & taking cover in the woods. The steam pipe of the *Teazer* soon exploded, but did not injure the boat seriously, and the fire appears to have gone out for the Yankees came up and hauled her off. I got a horse from the pickets & joined Gen Lee, & that ended my ballooning."[23]

In his report on the Seven Days, Lee did not single out Major Alexander, but included him among those staff officers who gave "constant aid during the entire period." But what Lee thought of his energetic and enterprising young Chief of Ordnance may be deduced from the fact that within three weeks of his balloon adventure during the Seven Days, on July 17, 1862, Alexander was promoted to lieutenant colonel, with date of rank pushed all the way back to December 31, 1861. He had been a major only three months, when this promotion came through for the twenty-seven-year-old Georgian.

During the campaign of Second Manassas, late in August 1862, Lieutenant Colonel Alexander's function was to keep the troops supplied with ammunition. He took satisfaction in the workings of his organization and the way that it stood up during the severe campaign, conducted at a considerable distance from its depots.

When Lee, after the rout of Pope at Manassas, decided to invade Maryland, Alexander had replenished all expended ammunition and he and his wagon train followed close on Lee's headquarters. As the army advanced and consumed ammunition, Alexander shuttled wagons between each successive position and Staunton, where there was an ammunition depot.

On September 16, about noon, Lieutenant Colonel Alexander arrived at Shepherdstown with his ordnance train. When he rode across the Potomac and reported to General Lee, the latter ordered him to go to Harpers Ferry with all the empty wagons he could collect to take charge of the captured ordnance and ammunition. Alexander sent off 49 field pieces, 24 mountain howitzers, and a considerable artillery ammunition not suited to the caliber of the Confederate guns. However, he found much useful small arms ammunition and this he prepared to take with him. As he was collecting the ordnance from Bolivar Heights, where Stonewall Jackson had scored an impressive victory a few days earlier, Alexander saw the smoke of battle from Antietam. "I could not tell how the fighting was going," he wrote later, "but at the time no Confederate expected anything less than victory."

Until late at night on September 17, Alexander dispatched his wagons; the bulk to Winchester, the others to the ford near Sharpsburg. On the afternoon of September 18 he arrived at the ford, and there found orders to await Lee's army, which would recross the Potomac that night. Thus ended Lee's first invasion of the North.

On November 6, 1862, Colonel Stephen D. Lee, who had graduated from West Point three classes ahead of Porter Alexander, was promoted to brigadier general and sent to the West to command a brigade in the army of Lieutenant General John C. Pemberton. The next day, Lieutenant Colonel Alexander was ordered to assume command of Lee's artillery battalion.

From Vicksburg, on the last day of the month, Stephen D. Lee telegraphed his congratulations to his friend and successor:

WELL, ALICK, I AM GLAD YOU TOOK MY BATTALION—MANAGE THEM RIGHT & THEY WILL MAKE YOU A BRIG.[24]

VI

Although Lieutenant Colonel Alexander was made a battalion commander on November 7, 1862, almost a month elapsed before he was relieved of his duties as Chief of Ordnance of the Army of Northern Virginia. On December 4, Colonel B. G. Baldwin was named Alexander's successor, and the latter was able for the first time to devote all his effort to his battalion of six batteries—four from Virginia, and one each from Louisiana and South Carolina.

General Lee, on December 5, wrote Secretary of War Seddon urging the promotion of Alexander from lieutenant colonel to colonel "in order that he may possess sufficient rank to make his service most available." The next day Seddon replied: "Your recommendation of Lieutenant-Colonel Alexander for promotion shall be promptly submitted to the President, and, with his concurrences, shall be complied with." When the paper reached the President's desk, he wrote: "Application approved. J. D." Nevertheless, three months would go by before the third promotion sought for Porter Alexander between March 15 and December 5, 1862, would go through. Obviously, Robert E. Lee saw in the young Georgian one of the finest officers in the Confederacy.[25]

Before the guns started blazing at Fredericksburg, Lieutenant Colonel Alexander assisted Brigadier General William N. Pendleton, Chief of Artillery for the Army of Northern Virginia, in assigning positions for the various batteries on the high ground where Lee took up his position to await Burnside's tremendous assault.

An astute authority on Confederacy artillery, Jennings C. Wise, in *The Long Arm of Lee*, points out Alexander's considerable contribution to this "most judicious" disposition of the Confederate batteries: "In this work the services of Col. Alexander were of course invaluable. Both an engineer and an artilleryman of experience, he had constantly before him the necessities of communication, necessarily foremost in the mind of one so familiar with the duty of ammunition supply."

General Longstreet, while walking over the Confederate position on Marye's Heights with Alexander the day before the battle, pointed to an idle gun and suggested it be employed to help cover the field in front of the hill.

"General, we cover that ground now so well that we will comb it as with a fine-tooth-comb," replied Alexander. "A chicken could not live on that field when we open on it."[26]

After preliminaries on December 11 and 12—building pontoons and crossing the troops—the Federals mounted their massive attack at Fredericksburg on December 13. Alexander, whose guns were at the left center of the Confederate line, was busy from the Federal signal gun at 2 A.M. on the eleventh. Immediately, his batteries took up position and joined in when 145 Confederate guns blasted the town which Burnside was trying to occupy. "The firing was the heaviest I ever heard," Alexander wrote his father, "and the poor Burg is riddled and considerably burnt. The spectacle was a grand one as you may imagine."

Throughout December 12, Alexander opened a battery upon the streets at intervals and he elicited a warm response from the Federals, which suggested that his enfilading fire was more than just worrisome to the Yankees. For the second night, the artillerymen slept by their guns. Such was the situation on December 13, when the Federals launched a heavy attack on the Confederate right at Hamilton's Crossing and then followed with another at the other end of the Confederate line. Alexander described the battle, as he saw and fought it, in a letter to his father:

"On Saturday morning a heavy attack was made on the right of our line near the R.R., and very soon afterwards a similar one on a little bluff and range of hills on the outskirts of the town where we had a good many guns in pits and some infantry behind stonewalls in gullies, etc. The position is called in the papers 'impregnable,' but it is in reality of scarcely ordinary strength, and was but an outpost to our real 'line' which ran along a secondary range of hills, half a mile back of it. The Washington Artillery in these pits and our infantry repulsed this attack and several others, in which I assisted with two batteries coming behind them on the second range of hills and firing over their heads. I also searched for their pontoon bridges with some 'Napoleon' 12 Pr. guns and found, as I have since seen, the most important one. What damage I did I don't know, but I drew on me the fire of three batteries as hot as they could kindle it, and they kept it up on the position I had taken all day long—hours after I had gone elsewhere."

About 3:30 P.M., Alexander got word from the Washington Artillery that it was running short of ammunition and needed relief. Immediately, Alexander began moving his guns under, he told his father, "the heaviest fire I ever saw." Federal artillery raked the slope, he said, and "the houses and streets of the town were filled with infantry who kept the air so full of minié balls that their sound was as constant as the flow of water." He had one man and fourteen horses killed and a few wounded as he ran his guns into positions, but once there found comparative safety from the hail of lead. Continuing, he told his father:

"The enemy saw the Washington Artillery leaving and thought we had given it up and gave a loud hurrah and dashed at us again in immense columns, but my chests were full of canister and everything else, and the fire I kindled soon showed them their mistake. They pressed it, however, very hard and by dark, when they ceased their firing, my guns had averaged 100 rounds a piece at them. The infantry under us said that we killed more than the Washington Artillery had during the whole day."

About an hour after dark, Alexander and his men heard great cheering in the Union lines and shortly after General George Sykes's division of U. S. Regulars made a dash at the Confederate position. "We could see nothing but the flashes of their guns, and could scarcely aim at them," Alexander wrote his father, "but we poured out one second case shot and canister loose in the dark, and their prisoners call that repulse the bloodiest of the whole action. They certainly gave it up very soon and their flashes died out, after which I gave them a few farewell shots, and then we had a quiet night of it."

The next day, every one in the Confederate lines expected Burnside to make another assault, but the Union commander had had enough. He withdrew across the Rappahannock. "Their repulse on the right has been as complete as the one in front of the town," Alexander told his father, "and the ground everywhere is so strong that Burnside is afraid to face the music." And then this articulate young artillerist turned a neat sentence in describing the enemy's disposition across the Rappahannock: "His enormous force is now encamped where it was before, and for ten square miles, at least, the smoke hangs over his crowded camps like a city on fire."

Longstreet's report included Alexander among half a dozen officers who were "particular distinguished" in the battle and Lee hailed Alexander's "well-directed fire" as rendering "great assistance in repelling the assaults . "

Alexander had two narrow escapes during the battle, the first when his mare, Dixie, which he called his "*horse de combat*," was struck in the rump by a shell fragment and was badly lacerated, the other when a shell landed between her feet. "I thought for a moment that we were about to have another balloon ascension," Alexander wrote his father, "but it fortunately failed to explode."[27]

VII

While the Army of Northern Virginia was in winter quarters, following the Battle of Fredericksburg, General Pendleton, Chief of Artillery, called Colonel Stapleton Crutchfield and Lieutenant Colonel E. Porter Alexander into consultation concerning a reorganization of the artillery completely into battalions, which up to then had been only partially realized.

In his report, submitted to General Lee on February 11, 1863, General Pendleton's recommendations included:

"Alexander Battalion: Lieut.-Col. Alexander, of Georgia, is really entitled to the full rank of Colonel at the head of this battalion. We have no more accomplished officer. His commission should date from his original assignment to command."

General Lee, more than two months earlier, had recommended Alexander's promotion and the concurrence of both President Davis and Secretary of War Seddon had been immediate. Yet it was not until March 3, 1863, that Secretary Seddon made the appointment. In less than a year, Porter Alexander had advanced from a captain to colonel.

When the spring campaign opened in 1863, Union General Joseph Hooker, called "Fighting Joe" for reasons still obscure after a hundred years, had an army of more than 133,000 to Lee's 60,000. Hooker decided to make a wide movement to the right with the purpose of getting to Lee's left flank and rear in his fortified lines at Fredericksburg.

By the end of April, Hooker had 54,000 men at Chancellorsville and he was convinced that he had Lee in a bad way. Hooker declared in an order to his troops that "the enemy must either ingloriously fly, or come out from behind his defences, and give us battle on our own ground, where certain destruction awaits him." Alexander's comment, in his book, on Hooker's boast was this:

"And, indeed, if a general may ever be justified in enumerating his poultry while the process of incubation is incomplete, this might be an occasion. He was on the left flank and rear of Lee's only strong position with a force fully equal to Lee's, while another equal force threatened Lee's right. And somewhere in Lee's rear—between him and Richmond—was Stoneman with 10,000 sabres, opposed only by two regiments of cavalry, tearing up the railroads and waiting to fall upon Lee's flank when he essayed the retreat Hooker confidently expected to see."

On the night of April 29, Hooker was bubbling with confidence and to his staff he confided: "The Rebel army is now the legitimate property of the Army of the Potomac. They may as well pack up their haversacks and make for Richmond, and I shall be after them."[28]

When Lee learned on April 30 that Hooker had split his army in two, he was determined to strike one half or the other. He decided to attack at Chancellorsville. In this battle, generally considered Lee's greatest, Colonel Porter Alexander's battalion of artillery rolled along with Stonewall Jackson on the latter's famed flanking march early on May 2. In the afternoon, near Wilderness Church, there was an infantry attack by Jackson, but Alexander's guns were in reserve, inasmuch as there was no opportunity for artillery to engage the enemy. As the infantry rolled up the Federal line, the artillery followed in its wake and the battalion spent the night on the field.

During the late fighting Jackson's Chief of Artillery, Colonel Crutchfield, was wounded and he rode to the rear in the same ambulance with the fallen Stonewall. Command of all the field artillery now devolved upon Colonel Alexander. It was 10 P.M. when Alexander reported to Major General Jeb Stuart, who had succeeded General H. P. Hill in command of Jackson's corps.

Stuart ordered Alexander to reconnoiter the ground during the night and post the necessary guns before daybreak for an early attack. After examining the terrain, Alexander saw that the attack must be made through a dense woods between the Confederate and the Union lines. On the Federal edge of the woods, there were abatis and breastworks, heavily supported by artillery within canister range of the woods. Of the artillery problem, Alexander later reported:

"There were but two outlets through which our artillery could be moved—one on the Plank Road, touching within 400 yards of twenty-seven of the enemy's guns, protected by breastworks . . . as well as by two guns behind a breastwork thrown up across the road . . . The second outlet was a cleared vista or lane through the pines (a half mile to the south of the Plank Road), some 200 yards long by 25 wide. This opened upon a cleared ridge, held by the enemy's artillery, about 400 yards distant. This vista was reached . . . by two small roads."

At dawn, Alexander posted 17 guns to command the cleared area, known as Hazel Grove, and at daylight, when the attack commenced vigorously, Alexander began the job of clearing the enemy guns from this vantage spot. Within ninety minutes, he was successful and as the Federals guns retired from the ridge, the batteries of Pegram, Page, and Chamberlayne were rushed to occupy it.

From Hazel Grove, there was a fine field of fire into the Federal position, bringing both infantry and artillery under attack by the Confederate guns. As fast as orders could be dispatched, Alexander reinforced the batteries on Hazel Grove. He had almost 40 guns in action at one time, and the fire from the Confederate right was devastating. Alexander's report described the artillery action:

"About 9 a.m., the magnificent fire of our guns on the right, and the steady advance of our infantry, which had routed the enemy from the abatis lines, and was beginning to fire upon his entrenched artillery and forming for a charge, proved too much for the enemy's nerve, and with one accord his entire artillery limbered up and abandoned their breastworks, and retreated to the immediate vicinity of the Chancellorsville house, whence they again opened heavily."

As the Confederate infantry swept forward to occupy the abandoned Federal breastworks, Alexander's artillery on the right limbered up and galloped forward from Hazel Grove to take up a new position at the breastworks and in a field to the right. From there, joined by fire from the guns on the Plank Road, they opened up furiously on the positions at the Chancellor house and in a few moments drove the Federals from this, his third position. It was during this phase of the fighting that General Hooker was wounded when a brick, ripped by one of Alexander's shells from one of the columns, struck him on the head.

By 10 o'clock, the Federals had retreated to the Rappahannock and crossing operations were already under way. Colonel Alexander, filled with pride over the work of the artillery in routing Hooker, reported:

"This assault must ever be memorable for its fierceness, vigor and success, against superior numbers and a position that might well be deemed impregnable, and I consider the part borne by the artillery, in its prompt and thorough co-operation with the gallant assaults of the infantry, as the most brilliant page of its history."[29]

Oddly enough, as Douglas Southall Freeman noted, Colonel Alexander's superb handling of the corps artillery at Chancelorsville did not get the credit at the time that it deserved. He pointed out that Stuart mentioned Alexander only as to his assignment on the night of May 2–3; that A. P. Hill listed him fourth among artillery commanders deserving "special mention"; and that Lee included him among those "deserving especial commendation."

Freeman declared flatly that "Porter Alexander . . . first had seen the importance of Hazel Grove . . . and . . . had placed guns within easy distance of that eminence. At least as much credit belonged to Alexander as to Stuart, but the entry at the time was made on the account of the cavalryman . . . Nowhere at the time was the full value of the Georgian's service appreciated."

This position of Dr. Freeman is substantially the same as that taken earlier by the "biographer" of Lee's Artillery, Jennings C. Wise, who wrote: "Col. Alexander convinced Stuart that the Hazel Grove . . . was the key to the Federal line" and "Stuart was now to reap the benefit of Alexander's judicious disposition of the artillery," and "the superiority of fire attained by Alexander over the Federal artillery, alone made possible the success of Stuart's third infantry assault, for it was the withdrawal of their artillery that broke the backbone of the enemy's resistance."[30]

VIII

Lee's army, flushed by its victory at Chancellorsville and rested from a month of inactivity, was on the march, stretched out over a hundred miles. President Lincoln wrote General Hooker: "If the head of Lee's army is at Martinsburg, and the tail of it on the Plank road between Fredericksburg and Chancellorsville, the animal must be very slim somewhere. Could you not break him?"

Colonel Alexander, whose battalion had moved out from the Fredericksburg area on June 3, was camped at Culpeper on June 14. "We are once more abroad making history . . ." he wrote his father from there. "We made march (81 miles) in less than two days & a half . . . No one appears to have the faintest idea what we are going to do here . . . I only hope for us that we won't cross the Potomac for I don't believe we can ever successfully invade."

But Alexander soon found out that Lee was about to cross the Potomac and invade again. And so it was that on June 27, 1863, Longstreet's Corps, and Alexander's artillery with it, was in camp at Chambersburg, Pennsylvania, where it remained several days. On June 30, Alexander's battalion marched ten miles in the direction of Gettysburg, camping at the village of Greenwood.

The next day, when elements of the Confederate and Union armies collided northwest of Gettysburg, the great battle, sought by neither Lee nor Meade, began. But Colonel Alexander, in camp only a dozen miles off, knew nothing of the battle until dark when orders came to march at 2 A.M. on July 2 for Gettysburg. Alexander's 26 guns and the 10 guns of the Washington Artillery marched, under a bright moon, over an open road, uncluttered by infantry, and between 8 and 9 A.M. reached the field. Halting his battalion in a woods, Alexander promptly reported to General Lee and General Longstreet, who were together on a hill in the rear of the Confederate line. A dozen years after the war, Alexander wrote of his experience:

"I was told that we were to attack the enemy's left flank, and was directed to take command of my own battalion.—Cabell's battalion (with McLaws's division), 18 guns; Henry's battalion (with Hood's), 18 guns—leaving the Washington Artillery in reserve, and to reconnoitre the ground and cooperate with the infantry in the attack. I was especially cautioned in moving up the guns to avoid exposing them to the view of a signal station of the enemy's on Round Top mountain . . . I had just arrived, and knew nothing of the situation, and my instructions were to reconnoitre the flank to be attacked, and choose my own positions and means of reaching them."

Alexander spent a couple of hours reconnoitering the Federal position and the best route to get his guns up without observation. This called, at one fairly large exposed spot on the road, for a detour through some fields. A little later, while moving up the artillery attached to the divisions, Alexander saw a column of Hood's infantry halted at the open spot in the road. Instead of following the covered path Alexander had used with his battalion, the infantry sent back to Longstreet for orders. Alexander wrote:

"My general recollection is that nearly three hours were lost in that delay and countermarch, and that it was about 4 p.m. when Hood became engaged heavily on our extreme right, with Henry's battalion aiding him, while, with 18 guns of my own battalion and Cabell's 18, I attacked Hooker's Corps at the Peach Orchard."

Alexander's guns were supported by McLaws' division in the woods to the rear. From the fringe of the woods, Alexander's battalion blazed away from about 500 yards from the Federals, while Cabell's guns fired from about 700 yards. For more than an hour, Alexander's guns were engaged and then McLaws charged and carried the Peach Orchard. In his first published account of this fight, in the *Southern Historical Society Papers* in September 1877, all Alexander said of his participation in the charge was this:

"When McLaws charged . . . my batteries followed him closely and going into action in and around the Orchard, and the firing was kept up thence till after dark."

In a piece written for *Century Magazine* and republished in 1885 in *Battles and Leaders of the Civil War*, Alexander was more descriptive:

"Every battery was limbered to the front, and the two batteries from the rear coming up, all six charged in line across the plain and went into action again at the position the enemy had deserted. I can recall no more splendid sight, on a small scale—and certainly no more inspiriting moment during the war—than that of the charge of these six batteries. An artillerist's heaven is to follow the routed enemy, after a tough resistance, and throw shells and canister into his disorganized and fleeing masses. Then the explosions of the guns sound louder and more powerful, and the very shouts of the gunners, ordering 'Fire!' in rapid succession, thrill one's very soul . . . Everything was in a rush. The ground was generally good, and pieces and caissons went at a gallop, some cannoneers mounted, and some running by the sides—not regular line, but a general race and scramble to get there first."

In his *Military Memoirs of a Confederate*, Alexander is at his most reticent regarding his performance at the Peach Orchard:

"While the infantry was passing, my four batteries, which had been engaged in the cannonade, were gotten ready and the whole six followed the charge of the infantry, and came into action in and about Peach Orchard . . . The enemy was driven back with severe loss . . ."[31]

It remained, however, for a modern authority on the employment of artillery, Jennings C. Wise, to put a proper evaluation on Alexander's artillery charge on the second day at Gettysburg. "Perhaps no more superb feat of artillery drill on the battlefield," he wrote, "was ever witnessed than this rapid change of position of Alexander's Battalion."

Colonel Alexander did not have much time for rest that night. His sound horses had to be fed and watered and the dead and disabled animals had to be replaced from the wagon teams. Ammunition had to be replenished, the ground examined and batteries adjusted. And the wounded, both Confederate and Federal, who lay around the batteries, had to be cared for. About 1 A.M., Alexander made a bed of fence rails and got two hours of sleep before he was up again at 3 A.M. to put the batteries into position. The Washington Artillery, in reserve the previous day, joined Alexander before dawn.

With the first light of dawn, Alexander perceived that he had placed about twenty of his guns so that Federal artillery on Cemetery Hill enfiladed the line. "I had a panic, almost," he wrote, "for fear the enemy would discover my blunder and open before I could rectify it." Fortunately, the enemy's line of vision was not so good, and Alexander rapidly made the necessary adjustments.

However, a little later in the morning Lee came up and stated that the attack would be directed at Cemetery Hill, and this necessitated a considerable number of changes in the positions of the guns. As Alexander supervised the move, "as inoffensively as possible," the Yankee guns began to harass. "But we stood it all meekly," wrote Alexander, "and by 10 o'clock . . . we had seventy-five guns in what was virtually one battery, so disposed as to fire on Cemetery Hill and the batteries south of it, which would have a fire on our advancing infantry."

Alexander, whom Longstreet had put in command of the guns for the action because Colonel J. B. Walton, Chief of Artillery for the Corps, was daily becoming less active physically, secured nine extra howitzers from General Pendleton, commander of all of Lee's artillery. He intended to take them into the charge with Pickett's infantry, and he placed them in a hollow in a thicket, with no orders other than to wait until they were sent for.

About 11 A.M., skirmishing broke out on A. P. Hill's front, where sixty-three guns of his corps were placed to the left of Alexander's seventy-five. Hill's artillery and then the enemy's got into the affair and soon a hundred guns were blasting away. But it gradually died down and, said Alexander, "the whole field became silent as a churchyard until 1 o'clock."

The signal for the attack was to be two guns fired by the Washington Artillery, posted in the middle of Longstreet's artillery. Colonel Alexander was to observe the fire and give the word to Pickett at the propitious moment to attack. Shortly after noon, while Alexander was standing at a favorable lookout point to the left of his guns, a courier of General Pickett at his side, a messenger galloped up with a note from Longstreet.

Colonel: If the artillery fire does not have the effect to drive off the enemy or greatly demoralize him, so as to make our efforts pretty certain, I would prefer that you should not advise Pickett to make the charge. I shall rely a great deal on your judgment to determine the matter, and shall expect you to let General Pickett know when the moment offers.

Alexander was startled by this note, which more than suggested that there was an alternative to the attack and placed upon him the responsibility of making the choice. "If that assault was to be made on General Lee's judgment it was all right, but I did not want it made on mine," Alexander wrote in 1884. He elaborated on his reaction to Longstreet's note in his book. "Until that moment, though I fully recognized the strength of the enemy's position, I had not doubted that we would carry it, in my confidence that Lee was ordering it," he wrote in 1907. "But here was a proposition that *I* should decide the question. Overwhelming reasons against the assault at once seemed to stare me in the face."[32]

Alexander handed Longstreet's note to General A. R. Wright, who was standing with him, expressing his views on the position into which Longstreet had placed him. General Wright advised him to set them down on paper and send them to General Longstreet. Accordingly, Alexander dispatched the following note to his corps commander:

General: I will only be able to judge of the effect of our fire on the enemy by his return fire, for his infantry is but little exposed to you and the smoke will obscure the whole field. If, as I infer from your note, there is an alternative to this attack, it should be carefully considered before opening our fire, for it will take all the artillery ammunition we have left to test this one thoroughly, and, if the result is unfavorable, we will have none for another effort. And even if this is entirely successful, it can only be so at a very bloody cost.[33]

General Longstreet soon replied to Colonel Alexander's answer to his first message:

Colonel: The intention is to advance the infantry if the artillery has the decided effect of driving the enemy off, or having other effect such as to warrant us in making the attack. When the moment arrives advise General Pickett, and of course advance such artillery as you can use in aiding the attack.

Alexander read the note and showed it to General Wright, who had, on July 2, charged successfully over the same ground with his brigade to carry the Union line. Receiving no support, Wright had been compelled to withdraw.

"What do you think of it? Is it as hard to get there as it looks?" asked Alexander.

"The trouble is not in getting there," replied Wright. "I went there with my brigade yesterday . . . The trouble is to stay there after you get there, for the whole Yankee army is there in a bunch."

Colonel Alexander realized now that the cannonade would begin as planned and it was up to him to decide whether or not Pickett would charge. "I determined to see Pickett and get an idea of his feelings," he wrote. "I did so, and finding him both cheerful and sanguine, I felt that if the artillery fire opened, Pickett must make the charge." He then dispatched another message to Longstreet:

General: When our fire is at its best, I will advise Gen. Pickett to advance. (In his *Battles and Leaders* piece, Alexander quoted his note thus: "When our artillery fire is at its best, I shall order Pickett to charge.")[34]

The signal guns went off. Alexander looked at his watch. It was 1 P.M. and the cannonade opened. Soon almost all the guns of both armies set up a terrific roar. "Before the cannonade opened I had made up my mind to give Pickett the order to advance within fifteen or twenty minutes after it began," wrote Alexander. But when he saw the enemy's entrenched position and the terrific fire the Federals were delivering, he didn't have the heart to send infantry against it. He let the minutes tick by, hoping for something to develop. Then at 1:25 P.M. he hurried off a note to Pickett:

If you are coming at all you must come at once, or I cannot give you proper support; but the enemy's fire has not slackened at all; at least eighteen guns are still firing from the cemetery itself.

Five minutes later, the fire from the Federal line slackened and the guns in the cemetery limbered up and left the position. "If he does not run fresh batteries in there in five minutes," said Alexander to another officer, "this is our fight." He kept his glass anxiously focused on the vacated sector of the Federal line. After five minutes, he sent a note to Pickett:

For God's sake, come quick. The eighteen guns are gone; come quick, or my ammunition won't let me support you properly.

When Pickett got Alexander's note, he took it to Longstreet. The latter read, but made no reply.

"General, shall I advance?" asked Pickett.

Longstreet, reluctant to give the order, turned away. Pickett saluted.

"I am going to move forward, sir," he said, and wheeling his horse, he rode off to launch Pickett's Charge.

About 1:40 P.M., Longstreet rode up to Colonel Alexander, who explained the artillery situation, showing confidence in the charge, but expressing concern that the ammunition might not hold out for as long as he wanted.

"Stop Pickett immediately," ordered Longstreet, "and replenish your ammunition."

"That would take too long, General, and the enemy would recover from the effect our fire is now having and, moreover, we have very little with which to replenish it."[35]

"I don't want to make this attack," declared Longstreet. "I would stop it now but that General Lee ordered it and expects it to go on. I don't see how it can succeed."

Even as Longstreet spoke, Pickett's division swept out of the woods, soon to be joined on its left by Pettigrew. Alexander rode forward a bit with General Dick Garnett, a warm personal friend, and they parted for the last time, for Garnett was killed in the attack. Alexander then rode up and down his lines, selecting guns with sufficient ammunition to follow the charging Pickett.

In a moment the Federal line was ablaze with fire, the artillery concentrating on the advancing gray line, with the Yankee riflemen also unleashing a terrific fire upon the charging Confederates. Alexander rushed his guns in support of Pickett, opening fire on the Federal batteries. "No one could have looked at that advance without feeling proud of it," wrote Alexander. ". . . Pickett's men never halted, but opened fire at close range, swarmed over the fences and among the enemy's guns— were swallowed up in smoke, and that was the last of them . . . As soon as it appeared that the assault had failed, we ceased firing in order to save ammunition in case the enemy should advance. But we held our ground as boldly as possible, though we were entirely without support, and very low in ammunition."

Pickett's Charge had been in vain—the Battle of Gettysburg was over. In writing his father after the battle, Porter Alexander reiterated what he had said in a previous letter about invasion:

"I do not think we can ever successfully invade, the ammunition question alone being enough to prevent it. Moreover, our army is not large enough to stand the casualties even of a victory in the enemy's country."[36]

IX

Much had been said about the South's advantage in the Civil War because of its interior lines of communications. But it was not until nearly two months after Gettysburg that the Confederacy made use of its interior lines to shuttle troops from Virginia to the Western theater.

Two divisions of Longstreet's corps, with Alexander's artillery, were sent west to help General Braxton Bragg effect a significant victory over Federal General William S. Rosecrans and regain Tennessee and its foodstuffs for the South.

Because the Federals had occupied Knoxville, it was necessary for the troop movement by rail to be a circuitous one of about 925 miles via Petersburg, Wilmington, Augusta, Atlanta, and Ringgold. On September 9, the first trainload, carrying infantrymen of Hood's and McLaws' divisions, headed west.

The Battle of Chickamauga was fought on September 19–20, 1863. Only five of Longstreet's brigades arrived in time for the fight but they

played an important part in the Confederate breakthrough that routed
the Federals and sent Rosecrans scurrying back to Chattanooga. At the
time of the battle, Alexander's artillery was en route from Wilmington
to Augusta. His guns finally were unloaded at Ringgold, Georgia, on
September 25. Although he was not on hand to see General Bragg muff
the opportunity to crush Rosecrans, he apparently heard a lot about it.
On September 30 he wrote his father that as soon as he had arrived,
Longstreet had him prepare to bombard the enemy's fortified line at
Chattanooga. He arranged 30 howitzers as mortars and 30 rifled guns
on Lookout Mountain to enfilade their lines and encampment. He continued:

"I have no doubt but that we could have made them leave the town,
but last night Gen. Bragg countermanded the order, & we are today in
statu quo, no prospect of Bragg making up his mind what to do at all.
Everybody—Lieut Genls even seem to feel disgusted at his incapacity
which let Rosecrantz's [sic] Army take its own time to retreat behind
his works at Chattanooga, & allowed the fruits of a bloody but *decisive*
& *complete* victory slip through his hands. Gen. Longstreet says the rout
at Bull Run was no worse than that of the Yankees here & from it all we
have gained but some 40 pieces of Arty & a few thousand prisoners—
altogether not worth Hood's leg. This Army is far inferior to the Army
of Va. in organization & equipment & spirit, & I regret very much I ever
left the latter tho of course I could not help it. We have no horse yet for
my Battn & there seems little or no prospect of getting any so that my
Battn can't fight very soon. I however will always have a chance & command all of Longstreet's Arty in any engagement."[37]

On November 3, Bragg ordered Longstreet, with General Joe Wheeler's cavalry, to attack Burnside who held Knoxville with 12,000 troops.
Delays in transportation prevented all of Longstreet's attack force from
assembling at Loudon, about thirty miles from Knoxville. The train of
flatcars carrying Alexander's men and guns—the horses he had acquired
were driven by road—took twelve hours to go sixty miles. "The cannoneers were required to pump water for the engine and to cut up fence
rails for fuel along the route," Alexander said.

Longstreet made contact with Burnside on November 15 and skirmishing followed daily as the Federals fell back into Knoxville on November
17. In preparation for the assault on the Federals' fortifications, Alexander had placed his thirty guns well, posting them to fire on the works
and to enfilade the adjacent lines. A few of the howitzers, however, he
improvised into mortars, by preparing skids at a 45-degree angle and
running the axle of the howitzer up on the skids, leaving the wheels in
the air on each side of the skids, and leaving the trail on the ground. The
piece was then regulated until it had an elevation of 60 degrees. Alexander had experimented with this in Virginia and had actually prepared

howitzer-mortars at Chattanooga for the bombardment Bragg called off.

The attack, scheduled for November 25, would be directed at Fort Sanders and this was the plan: First the mortars would open to get the range. Then the direct-fire guns would do the same, both firing slowly and deliberately. Then a strong line of sharpshooters would rush the enemy's rifle pits. When these were occupied, the sharpshooters would concentrate upon the parapet and embrasures of the fort. Then all the guns would pour a rapid fire into the fort for about half an hour. Under cover of this fire, the sharpshooters and a storming column would charge the fort.

It was a well-planned attack, but when word came that reinforcements under Generals Archibald Gracie and Bushrod Johnson, two brigades with about 2600 men, were coming, the attack was postponed until November 27. When they arrived, General Danville Leadbetter, Bragg's Chief Engineer, who was familiar with the Knoxville fortifications, induced Longstreet to postpone the attack again and make it above the town at Mabry Hill.

Colonel Alexander accompanied Longstreet and Leadbetter and others on a careful reconnaissance and all agreed that the proposed point of attack was much too strong a position. "The hill was strongly fortified," wrote Alexander, "and there was no cover within a mile for the formation and advance of an assaulting column. So it was unanimously decided to go back to the plan of assaulting Fort Sanders and I was ordered to get the guns back upon the hills across the river."

This he did early on November 28, but rain and fog so obscured the enemy lines that the attack was postponed again, to Sunday, November 29.

Meanwhile rumors had reached Longstreet's force that Bragg had suffered a crushing defeat at Chattanooga and had fallen back into Georgia. With no definite confirmation, plans went ahead for the execution the next morning of the previously prepared plan.

Then, late Saturday afternoon, more vacillation and indecision seized Longstreet. Alexander related it:

"Gen. Longstreet suddenly changed the plan of attack I believe under advice of Gen. Leadbetter, and ordered that instead of beginning at sunrise and being preceded by a crushing fire of artillery concentrated on the fort and covered by an enveloping swarm of sharpshooters, a surprise should be attempted just before dawn by the infantry alone.

"This was a great disappointment to the artillery. We had been working incessantly day and night to get fixed right, and now after several days all our work was to go for naught, and we were to have no place in the picture except to fire the signal guns and throw a few shells in front of a column and at the lines to right and left of the fort."

The assault came and, though valiantly made, was repulsed. A second assault was planned, this time with artillery and sharpshooters, partially as originally planned, but before it could be launched a courier arrived with telegraphic orders from Richmond to Longstreet to break off the Knoxville campaign and rejoin the beaten Bragg at Dalton, Georgia. However, a message from Bragg said that Sherman was out to intercept Longstreet and that the latter should retreat northeast into East Tennessee and eventually rejoin Lee in Virginia. On April 22, 1864, after several months in winter quarters in East Tennessee, Longstreet's corps and Alexander's battalion of artillery were back in the Army of Northern Virginia.[38]

X

As early as March 1863, when Porter Alexander was still waiting to receive his promotion to colonel of artillery, considerable talk reached his ear that he had been recommended to become a brigadier general and command an infantry brigade.

He wrote his father on March 11:

"Gen. Jackson applied for me, a short while since as a Brig. Gen. & I heard today—somewhat confidentially, that us was to command *Lawton's Brigade*. I suppose therefore that Gen. Lawton is to [be] promoted . . . I have very little idea however that I will receive the promotion as it has already been before the President more than long enough to be made, if no objection existed, & except for the increased pay & pride in the compliment, I very much prefer to command of my Battn. wh. is as independent & as conspicuous as a Division of Infantry."

On August 14, after the return of the army from Gettysburg, General Pendleton recommended Alexander for promotion to brigadier general and Robert E. Lee discussed it with Longstreet in a letter six days later. Longstreet, on August 21, 1863, replied to Lee: "Yours of the 20th upon promotion of Arty Officers is rec. & if Alexander is made Brigadier what can we do with Col. Walton? Col Walton is anxious to be assigned to duty at Mobile and if this can be done it will be well."

There was more correspondence between Lee and Longstreet in this matter, for on September 3, 1863, the latter again replied to a message from the commander of the Army of Northern Virginia, expressing a preference for Colonel Alexander as Chief of Artillery of the corps, "provided a position, away from this army, can be given Col. Walton." Longstreet pointed out that Colonel J. B. Walton, originally commander of the Washington Artillery, and then Chief of Artillery of Longstreet's corps, was "a meritorious officer" and felt there would be great injustice in "placing an officer, now under his command, over him." This, he told

Lee, would "counterbalance the good to be effected by the promotion of Col. Alexander to his position."[39]

More than two months later, on November 20, 1863, General Pendleton again urged the promotion of Colonel Alexander, but nothing came of it at the time. Meanwhile the abortive Knoxville Campaign had ended and Longstreet had gone into winter quarters in East Tennessee. On December 28, Alexander got a leave of thirty days with authority to ask for an extension of thirty more, and he returned to Richmond to see his wife.

Meanwhile, General Joe Johnston, now in command of the Army of Tennessee, applied for Colonel Alexander to be his Chief of Artillery, but Lee had turned down the request. Johnston had written General Bragg, now virtually President Davis's Chief of Staff, on December 27, complaining:

"I have applied for Col. Alexander, but Gen. Lee objects that he is too valuable in his present position to be taken from it. His value to the country would be more than doubled, I think, by the promotion and assignment I recommend."[40]

Such was the reputation of the young Georgian that practically every commanding or high-ranking general at some time wanted his services . . . Beauregard, Stonewall Jackson, Joe Johnston, Longstreet, and above all, Lee himself.

While Alexander was on leave in Richmond, he heard of General Johnston's bid for his services, and the promotion that would go with it. He wrote his wife on February 21, 1864:

"Gen. Johnston has applied two or three times, & Gen Bragg, who is now here as counsellor to the President, has recommended it also. Gen. Lee has also applied for me—Gen Cooper thinks as Chf of Arty of his whole Army but I think he is mistaken in it & that Gen Lee has only applied for me to be promoted & sent to Longstreet, who is still accounted part of Lee's Army . . . Gen Cooper says that there is little or no doubt of my being promoted as soon as the President has time to look at the matter but it is doubtful to which I will be sent . . ."

Six days later, Alexander, still in Richmond, wrote his wife again, and there was bitterness in the tone his letter took in discussing the ramifications of his proposed promotion:

"Gen Lee objected to my being transferred from Longstreet's Corps, which he still considers as part of his army & so the President refused Johnston's application & keeps me with Longstreet though he promises to promote. It is a little unfair on me as neither Lee or Longstreet ever secured my promotion when I was not wanted elsewhere and now they retain me in an inferior position to the one I am asked to take elsewhere. Moreover there is no prospect of Longstreet ever rejoining Lee but every prospect of his own going to Johnston & then I will be in a sub-ordinate position to the very office for which I was recommended."

But Colonel Alexander's fears were groundless. The long-talked-about promotion came on March 1, 1864, dating from February 26, and when the winter was over in East Tennessee, Longstreet's Corps marched into Virginia and rejoined Lee.[41]

In the fighting on the North Anna and Grant's blood bath at Cold Harbor early in June, Alexander's batteries were actively engaged in mowing down the charging bluecoats. "Naturally, as the attack had been on the largest possible scale," wrote Alexander of Cold Harbor, "the re-pulse was unusually severe and bloody; and the roar of the battle, while it lasted, probably exceeded even that of the combats in the Wilderness . . . The sound of the battle reached Richmond, and men came out on the streets to listen to it."

Grant spent a week of indecision after his frightful losses at Cold Harbor and then he made up his mind to cross the James and move upon Petersburg with his whole force. Of Grant's move, Alexander wrote: "It involved the performance of a feat in transportation which has never been equalled, and might well be considered impossible, without days of delay." Alexander said that Grant had crossed the James so efficiently that "Lee refused for three days to believe it."

However, when Lee realized the situation, he crossed the James and took up his position in a strong Petersburg defense line which had been built the year previous. The Confederate works at Petersburg, Alexander wrote, "were of the best character, with some guns of position mounted and all the forest in front cleared away to give range to the artillery."[42]

Then began, on June 17, 1864, the 10-months siege of Petersburg which would be only the long-drawn-out prelude to Appomattox.

Alexander's first days in the Petersburg trenches were busy, and he noted for almost a week "severe sharpshooting and artillery practice with-out intermission day or night." On June 29, on a reconnaissance, Alex-ander was struck by a sharpshooter's bullet at a range of about 600 yards, the ball striking his left arm on the inside, just below the armpit and lodging under the bone in the armpit, fortunately missing the artery. "It benumbed my arm and staggered me a little bit," he wrote his wife, "but I walked straight on to keep the rascal from knowing that he had hit me." The ball compressed the nerve and gave Alexander great pain, but it was removed and he was given leave to return to Washington, Georgia, where his wife was staying with Alexander's family.

Alexander's friend, General Moxley Sorrel, gives a different version of his wounding. He wrote that Alexander loved to shoot quail with an old-fashioned horse pistol when he was off duty, and that after firing, he would go out looking for lead from which he cut the tiny cubes to fire in his pistol. Sorrel wrote:

"At Petersburg his only want for his private gunning was lead to melt into small shot, and gathering some . . . he received an unexpected contribution—a bullet in his shoulder, hot from the enemy . . ."[43]

Before leaving Petersburg to recuperate from his wound, General Alexander became convinced that the Federals were digging a mine under the Elliott Salient in the line, not very far from the outskirts of Petersburg. Alexander wrote:

"At that point, incessant fire was kept up by their sharpshooters, while a few hundred yards to the right and left the fire had been gradually allowed to diminish, and men might show themselves without being fired at. That indicated that some operation was going on, and for several days I had expected to see zigzag approaches started on the surface of the ground. When several days had passed and nothing appeared, I became satisfied that their activity was underground . . . On my way to the cars next day, I was driven by Lee's headquarters, where I reported my belief about the mine."

On July 30, when the mine exploded and Billy Mahone's division marched over from the right to turn chaos into victory in the bloody battle of the Crater, General Alexander was in Washington, Georgia, recuperating from his wound. He did not return to the army until about August 12, for two days after that date, he reported to his wife that he was "in as good condition as ever" and would return to active duty the next day.[44]

XI

During nearly four years of fighting, Porter Alexander had come into frequent contact with General Lee, and his respect for and confidence in "Marse Robert" was limitless. But he had always approached Lee as if he were someone on a pedestal, commanding awe as well as affection.

Yet in his camp, about five miles below Richmond, General Alexander had almost daily contact with Lee and he was amazed at the ease with which he could approach the commander and speak with him. He wrote his wife on October 25, 1864:

"I see a great deal of the General & he is always very kind to me & I feel as much at home in his presence as in yours & less embarrassment in any official intercourse—even to making suggestions that I ever felt with any Comdg Offr—wh is what I *once* believed could never be."[45]

From the fortifications, Alexander kept up a steady correspondence with his wife in Georgia, telling her all the small talk of relatives in Richmond and including some brief comments on the military situation.

On November 1, he wrote that "the question of arming the Darkeys is now discussed a great deal & . . . many officers are strongly in favor of it, I . . . am much opposed to it as inhuman & unChristian and bad policy."

"All is quiet on our lines," Alexander penned on November 18, "but we feel great anxiety about Georgia. I think that if Hood goes towards Nashville he will accomplish nothing . . ."

On December 4, Alexander told his wife that Lee had ordered him to place torpedoes in the James River and on December 14 he reported a continued quiet front.

He wrote touchingly to his wife on Christmas Day: "We have never had but one Christmas together in our lives, but I hope that the next one will be a happier occasion."

He wrote on January 3 about "the great New Year's dinner to the Army," which, he said, "proved a complete fizzle." For the part of his command, north of the James, about 1500 men, there came "182 pounds of meat, a little bread & four or five bushels of turnips & potatoes . . ."

Late in January 1865, General Alexander left for three weeks at home on leave and on his return to the lines he wrote on February 21 of conditions in Richmond: "I find people here feeling pretty blue at our prospects," he said, "but with abundance of pluck, & considerable hope of foreign intervention & of a change in tide of war. The sentiment about putting Negroes in the army is also undergoing a great change & very little doubt is now felt but that Congress will very soon do it." In this same letter, General Alexander told his wife that he had invested $2000 in blockade-running stock and hoped for dividends in gold.

On March 2, Alexander reported that the men were living on corn-meal and that liquor—applejack—was not being issued to the men and officers.

After-the-war happiness for his wife, children, and himself was the theme of a letter on March 10 and, on March 15, he told his wife of a rumor that had come to his ears that he was to be made a major general, but put no stock in it.

"I believe there is now *no prospect* of any fighting in my command, & if there is any at all it can only be from behind our breastworks," he reassured his worrying spouse on March 16. On March 23, he wrote, he was ordered to add all the artillery in Richmond's intermediate and inner defense lines to his command. He reassured his wife again on March 24: "I don't see how the Yankees can fight us on this side of the river, for it would only be fun for us & murder to them."

"Unless Grant intends leaving everything for Sherman to do he will probably be 'pegging away' pretty soon," General Alexander told his wife on March 26. "This army appears to be in good spirit & its numbers are sufficiently respectable to make me feel very hopeful of the result."[46]

On April 1, 1865, Alexander wrote: "Mrs. Davis has left & the Arsenal & Laboratory are being removed so that everybody is convinced now that Richmond is going to be evacuated. I don't begin to believe it myself, however, for our Army is able to give some hard blows in its defence."

When he wrote that letter, General Alexander did not know of the debacle that very day at Five Forks on the extreme right of Lee's line, which made the evacuation of Richmond and Petersburg necessary to protect the existence of the army.

At midnight on April 1, General Alexander pulled his guns out of the lines he had been so confident of holding and his command took the road to Appomattox with Lee's army.[47]

On April 7, the bulk of Lee's rapidly thinning force crossed the Appomattox at Farmville and Lee instructed General Alexander to set up artillery to cover the passage of the remainder of the army and then personally to see that both the railroad and highway bridges at Farmville were destroyed after the Confederates cleared them. As the Federals came into sight, Alexander fulfilled his mission and the pressure of the pursuing enemy was relieved for the time being.

The next day, the first quiet day of the retreat, found Alexander riding beside General Pendleton, who told him that some of the leading generals had conferred and felt that they should tell Lee that the cause was now hopeless. They agreed Longstreet should approach Lee but the latter indignantly replied that now was the time to hold up Lee's hands, not beat them down. Pendleton then made the suggestion himself, only to meet a rebuff from Lee: "There are too many men here to talk of laying down their arms without fighting."

Late on April 8, Lee learned that, by another road, the Federals had got to Appomattox Courthouse before him, thus cutting off his retreat through that point. He, too, began to sense the hopelessness of his situation. Shortly after sunrise on April 9, Lee called General Alexander to him. Seated on a log, Lee spread out a map before them.

"Well, we have come to the Junction, and they seem to be here ahead of us," he said. "What have we got to do today?"

Alexander said that his command, being north of the James, had done no fighting at Petersburg, and very little during the retreat. He told Lee what his men, having heard surrender talk, had called to him from the ranks:

"We don't want to surrender any ammunition. We've been saving ammunition all the war. Hope we were not saving it for a surrender."

"General, if you see fit to try and cut our way out," Alexander told Lee, "my command will do as well as they have ever done."

"I have only two divisions, Field's and Mahone's, sufficiently organized to be relied upon," Lee replied. "All the rest have been broken and routed and can do no good. Those divisions are now scarcely 4000 apiece, and that is far too little to meet the force now in front of us."

"Then we have only two courses," declared Alexander. "Either to surrender, or to take to the woods and bushes, with orders, either to rally on Johnston, or perhaps better, on the Governors of their respective states. If we surrender this army it is the end of the Confederacy. I think our best course would be to order each man to go to the Governor of his own State with his arms."

"What would you hope to accomplish by that?" asked Lee.

". . . If we surrender this army, every other army will have to follow suit," said Alexander. ". . . Let the Governor of each State make some sort of a show of force and then surrender on terms which may save us from trials for treason and confiscations."

Lee listened in silence. "As I talked," Alexander later wrote, "it all looked so reasonable that I hoped he was convinced." The young artillerist continued, earnestly:

"But, General, apart from all that—if all fails and there is *no hope*— the men who have fought under you for four years have got the right this morning to ask *one* favor of you," pleaded Alexander. "We know that you do not care for military glory. But we are proud of the record of this army. We want to leave it untarnished to our children. . . . We have the right to ask you to spare us the mortification of having to ask Grant for terms and have him answer that he has no terms to offer . . ."

As Lee still remained silent, Alexander felt he had scored his point. Then Lee spoke:

"If I should take your advice, how many men do you suppose would get away?"

"Two thirds of us," answered Alexander. "We would be like rabbits and partridges in the bushes, and they could not scatter to follow us."

"I have not over 15,000 muskets left," said Lee. "Two thirds of them divided among the States, even if all could be collected, would be too small a force to accomplish anything. All could not be collected. Their homes have been overrun, and many would go back to look after their families.

"Then, General, you and I as Christian men have no right to consider only how this would effect us. We must consider its effect on the country as a whole. Already it is demoralized by the four years of war. If I took your advice, the men would be . . . compelled to rob and steal in order to live . . . We would bring on a state of affairs it would take the country years to recover from.

". . . You young fellows might go to bushwhacking, but the only dignified course for me would be to go to Gen. Grant and surrender myself and take the consequences of my acts."

Lee paused for a moment.

"But I can tell you one thing for your comfort," he said, "Grant will not demand unconditional surrender. He will give us as good terms as this army has the right to demand, and I am going to meet him in the rear at 10 A.M. and surrender . . ."

Years later, in his *Military Memoirs of a Confederate*, Alexander wrote:

"I had not a single word to say in reply. He had answered my suggestion from a plane so far above it, that I was ashamed of having made it. With several friends, I had planned to make an escape on seeing a flag of truce, but the idea was at once abandoned by all of them on hearing my report."[48]

When the end came at Appomattox, E. Porter Alexander was still six weeks away from his thirtieth birthday. From Captain of Engineers to General of Artillery he had managed to play important roles in most of the dramatic scenes of the Great American Tragedy.

XII

The versatility and rare gifts of mind and personality which made E. Porter Alexander one of the most outstanding soldiers in the Confederacy marked him for civilian leadership in the postwar South.

In January 1866, General Alexander became professor of Mathematics and Civil and Military Engineering at the University of South Carolina and remained an educator until October 1869. In that year, he became president of the Columbia Oil Company in Columbia, South Carolina, then in 1871 he became superintendent of the Charlotte & Augusta Railroad.

For many years he continued as a railroad executive, serving at various times as president of the Savannah & Memphis Railroad and also of the Central of Georgia Railroad and for two years as vice-president of the Louisville & Nashville Railroad.

He was appointed by President Cleveland to the United States Commission of Railroads and Canals and was for the two years 1885–87 a government director of the Union Pacific Railroad.

In 1901, General Alexander was engineer-arbitrator of the boundary dispute between Costa Rica and Nicaragua.[49]

About this time, he began to write his remarkable critique on the Army of Northern Virginia, *Military Memoirs of a Confederate*, published in 1907.

This was no "quickie" to justify conduct or salvage a reputation as were so many of the books by Confederate combatants. Rather, it was the expert examination under a microscope by a skilled soldier of the military campaigns which encompassed the four-year life span of the Confederate States of America.

At the beginning of his prefatory comments, General Alexander stated:

"The *raison d'être* of the following pages is not at all to set forth the valor of Confederate arms nor the skill of Confederate generals. These are as they may be, and must here take their chances in an unpartisan narrative, written with an entirely different object. That object is the criticism of each campaign as one would criticize a game of chess, only to point out the good and bad plays on each side, and the moves which have influenced the result."[50]

How well he succeeded Civil War scholars have known for years. Douglas Southall Freeman has called it the "best critique" and "the most valuable single commentary" on Lee's Army. At the time of its publication, said Dr. Freeman, "the book caused mutterings because General Alexander was thought by some veterans to have been unduly critical of General Lee. With the years, Alexander's study has grown in the esteem of military historians until now it is one of the most frequently quoted of Confederate authorities."[51]

Alexander did not write merely from memory. He had access, naturally, to the vast number of wartime letters which he wrote his wife, his father and other members of the family and to his articles published both in the *Southern Historical Society Papers* and *Century Magazine* a quarter of a century and more before he wrote his book. Moreover, he had access to the Official Records, with the reports of Federal and Confederate leaders on all the campaigns in which he fought from First Manassas to Appomattox.

The concluding passage of E. Porter Alexander's preface contains brave, noble words, written three years before his death on April 28, 1910, at Savannah, Georgia, and nearly half a century after he stood on Wilcoxen Hill in Virginia and saved the Confederates from envelopment by his vigilance:

"The world has not stood still in the years since we took up arms for what we deemed our most invaluable right—that of self-government. We now enjoy the rare privilege of seeing what we fought for in the retrospect. It no longer seems so desirable. It would now prove only a curse. We have good cause to thank God for our escape from it, not alone for our sake, but for that of the whole country and even of the world.

"Had our cause succeeded, divergent interests must soon have further separated the States into groups, and this continent would have been given credit. . . . It is surely not necessary to contrast what would have been our prospects as citizens of such States with our conditions now as citizens of the strongest, richest and—strange for us to say who once called ourselves 'conquered' and our cause 'lost'—the freest nation on earth.

". . . Our Union is not built to perish. Its bonds were not formed by peaceable agreements in conventions, but were forged in the white heat of battles, in a war fought out to the bitter end, and are for eternity."[52]

It is evident from these lines from the pen of one of the South's most brilliant soldiers that E. Porter Alexander was not only a great Confederate but a great American as well.

NOTES

1. The President's Brother-in-Law: GENERAL DICK TAYLOR

[1] Richard Taylor, *Destruction and Reconstruction* (New York, 1879), 49. Hereafter cited as *Destruction and Reconstruction*.

[2] Kenneth Trist Urquhart, *General Richard Taylor and the War in Virginia, 1861–1862*. (Unpublished thesis, Tulane University, 1958), 2. Hereafter cited as Urquhart, *Taylor*.

[3] *Destruction and Reconstruction*, 49–50.

[4] Ibid., 40.

[5] General D. H. Maury, "Sketch of Richard Taylor," in *Southern Historical Society Papers*, Vol. VII, No. 7 (July 1879), 345. Hereafter cited as Maury, *Taylor*.

[6] Douglas Southall Freeman, *The South to Posterity* (New York, 1939), 85–86. Hereafter cited as Freeman, *The South to Posterity*.

[7] *Destruction and Reconstruction*, 262; Maury, *Taylor*, 345.

[8] Jackson Beauregard Davis, "The Life of Richard Taylor," in *The Louisiana Historical Quarterly*, Vol. XXIV, No. 1 (January 1941), 54–55. Hereafter cited as Davis, *Taylor*.

[9] *Destruction and Reconstruction*, 12–13, 15–16; Lane C. Kendall, "The Interregnum in Louisiana in 1861," in *The Louisiana Historical Quarterly*, Vol. 16, No. 4 (October 1933), 645.

[10] Davis, *Taylor;* 61; *Destruction and Reconstruction*, 16; *War of Rebellion: A Compilation of Official Records of the Union and Confederate Armies*, Series IV, Vol. I, 750. Hereafter cited as *O.R.* and all references will be to Series I, unless otherwise indicated.

[11] *Destruction and Reconstruction*, 16–18; *O.R.* II, 559, 496, 498, 537, 465.

[12] *O.R.* II, 1000; *Destruction and Reconstruction*, 22–23.

[13] Davis, *Taylor*, 42; *O.R.* V, 914; Urquhart, *Taylor*, 29–30; *Destruction and Reconstruction*, 23–24.

[14] *O.R.* V, 936.

[15] Charles L. Dufour, *Gentle Tiger* (Baton Rouge, 1957), 3. Hereafter cited as Dufour, *Gentle Tiger; Destruction and Reconstruction*, 24; Mary Boykin Chesnut, *A Diary from Dixie* (edited by Ben Ames Williams, Boston, 1949), 159. Hereafter cited as Chesnut, *Diary*.

[16] *Destruction and Reconstruction*, 47.

[17] Ibid., 24–26; Dufour, *Gentle Tiger*, 199, 5.

[18] Ibid., 161, 163; *Destruction and Reconstruction*, 25.

[19] Ibid., 26, 44.

[20] Urquhart, *Taylor*, 35–36; *O.R.* V, 939, 961, 1030; *Destruction and Reconstruction*, 35–36.

[21] Douglas Southall Freeman, *Lee's Lieutenants* (New York, 1943) I, 349. Here-

after cited as Freeman, *Lee's Lieutenants:* Freeman, *The South to Posterity*, 86; *Destruction and Reconstruction*, 37–39.

22 Ibid., 50, 79–80.

23 Ibid., 50.

24 Ibid., 51–52.

25 Ibid., 52–53.

26 Ibid., 54–55.

27 Ibid., 56.

28 Ibid., 57; Henry Kyd Douglas, *I Rode With Stonewall* (Chapel Hill, 1940) 58. Hereafter cited as Douglas, *I Rode With Stonewall*.

29 *Destruction and Reconstruction*, 57–58.

30 J. H. Worsham, *One of Jackson's Foot Cavalry* (New York, 1912), 87.

31 *Destruction and Reconstruction*, 58–59; Douglas, *I Rode With Stonewall*, 59.

32 *Destruction and Reconstruction*, 59, 61.

33 Col. G. F. R. Henderson, *Stonewall Jackson and the American Civil War* (One Volume Edition, New York, no date), 269. Hereafter cited as Henderson, *Jackson*.

34 *Destruction and Reconstruction*, 74; George M. Neese, *Three Years In the Confederate Horse Artillery* (New York, 1911), 74–75.

35 Col. Henry B. Kelly, *The Battle of Port Republic* (Philadelphia, 1886), 15–19; Captain Samuel D. Buck, *With the Old Confeds, Actual Experiences of a Captain in the Line* (Baltimore, 1925), 38.

36 *Destruction and Reconstruction*, 77–78; Jackson to Cooper, June 10, 1862, in *Richard Taylor File*, in National Archives.

37 *Destruction and Reconstruction*, 79–81, 83–85, 90, 86–87, 93.

38 Urquhart, *Taylor*, 72, 74.

39 *O.R.* XV, 791; Taylor to Pettus, August 25, 1862, in Chicago Historical Society.

40 *O.R.* XV, 820.

41 Moore to Davis, December 26, 1863, in *Richard Taylor File*, in National Archives.

42 *Destruction and Reconstruction*, 112; Davis, *Taylor*, 72, 76.

43 *O.R.* XXVI, Part 2, 71, 394–95.

44 *O.R.* XXXIV, Part 2, 891, 869, 901.

45 Ibid., 1002.

46 *O.R.* XXXIV, Part 1, 505–6, 512–13, 517, 519.

47 Joseph H. Parks, *General Kirby Smith, CSA* (Baton Rouge, 1954) 382.

48 *O.R.* XXXIV, Part 1, 526; *Destruction and Reconstruction*, 162; Ludwell H. Johnson, *Red River Campaign, Politics and Cotton in the Civil War* (Baltimore, 1958), 132. Hereafter cited as Johnson, *Red River Campaign*.

49 *O.R.* XXXIV, Part 1, 526; *Destruction and Reconstruction* 160–61; Johnson, *Red River Campaign*, 134; *O.R.* XXXIV, Part 1, 564–65; Napier Bartlett, *Military Record of Louisiana* (New Orleans, 1875), 13.

50 *O.R.* XXXIV, Part 1, 527; Sarah A. Dorsey, *Recollection of Henry Watkins Allen* (New York, 1866), 263; Maury, *Taylor*, 344; *O.R.* XXIV, Part 1, 565–68; *Destruction and Reconstruction*, 169–71.

51 *O.R.* XXXIV, Part 1, 549, 584.

52 Ibid., 549, 541–43, 594, 595, 545–46, 538–40, 546–49, 597, 540–41.

53 *Destruction and Reconstruction*, 44.

54 Ibid., 196; Davis, *Taylor*, 100–1; *O.R.* XLI, Part 2, 993, 990–91; Chesnut, *Diary*, 424, 432.

55 Moore to Davis, December 26, 1863, op. cit.; Dupré to Davis, February 2, 1864, in *Richard Taylor File*, in National Archives; Allen to Davis, April 16, 1864, in ibid., in National Archives; Kirby Smith to Davis, April 16, 1864, in ibid., in National Archives.

56 *O.R.* XLI, Part 1, 117, 90, 92–94, 99–100, 103–4, 111–12, 816, 818.

57 *Destruction and Reconstruction*, 197, 201; *Confederate Veteran*, Vol. 13, No. 5 (May 1905), 200.

58 *Destruction and Reconstruction*, 204, 206; Davis, *Taylor*, 106.

59 *Destruction and Reconstruction*, 217, 226, 229.

60 Ibid., 239.
61 Ibid., 240–47.
62 Ibid., 248; Davis, *Taylor*, 115, 117–18; Maury, *Taylor*, 345.

2. *Beau Sabreur of the Valley:* GENERAL TURNER ASHBY

1 John Esten Cooke, *Life of Stonewall Jackson* (New York, 1863), 167; Douglas, *I Rode With Stonewall*, 79; *Destruction and Reconstruction*, 26; Rev. James B. Avirett, *The Memoirs of General Turner Ashby and His Compeers* (Baltimore, 1867), 226. Hereafter cited as Avirett, *Ashby;* John D. Imboden, "Stonewall Jackson in the Shenandoah," in *Battles and Leaders of the Civil War* (New York, 1887), Vol. II, 291–92. This four-volume work, edited by Robert Underwood Johnson and Clarence Clough Buel, will hereafter be cited as *Battles and Leaders.*
2 Avirett, *Ashby*, 226–27, 232–33.
3 Douglas to Helen Boteler, July 24, 1862, in *Henry Kyd Douglas Manuscripts* at Duke University; *O.R.* XII, Part 1, 712.
4 Thomas A. Ashby, *Life of Turner Ashby*, 14–31. Hereafter cited as Ashby, *Ashby;* John Esten Cooke, *Wearing of the Gray* (Bloomington, Indiana, 1959), 70. Hereafter cited as Cooke, *Wearing of the Gray.*
5 Avirett, *Ashby*, 21; Ashby, *Ashby*, 35, 36–38, 39, 42–43, 50–58.
6 Ibid., 45–49.
7 Ibid., 56–57; Stefan Lorant, *The Presidency* (New York, 1951), 244.
8 Ashby, *Ashby*, 56–57, 63; E. A. Pollard, *Southern History of the War, The Second Year of The War*, (New York, 1864), 52–53.
9 John D. Imboden, "Jackson at Harper's Ferry," in *Battles and Leaders*, Vol. I, 124; *O.R.* II, 787, 861, 881.
10 Avirett, *Ashby*, 395–98; *O.R.* II, 904, 952.
11 *O.R.* II, 954; Avirett, *Ashby*, 399.
12 Ibid., 107–16; Ashby, *Ashby*, 80–88; Clarence Thomas, *General Turner Ashby, The Centaur of the South* (Winchester, 1907), 29–31. Hereafter cited as Thomas, *Ashby.*
13 Dufour, *Gentle Tiger*, 130–33; Avirett, *Ashby*, 117.
14 Ibid., 120–22; *O.R.* V, 858–59.
15 *O.R.* V, 247–48, 241; Ashby to Cooper, November 7, 1861, in Chicago Historical Society.
16 *O.R.* V, 913, 937; Frank Cunningham, *Knight of the Confederacy, General Turner Ashby* (San Antonio, 1960), 87–88. Hereafter cited as Cunningham, *Knight of the Confederacy.*
17 Thomas, *Ashby*, 191–93.
18 William Thomas Poague, *Gunner With Stonewall, Reminiscences of William Thomas Poague* (Monroe F. Cockrell, editor; Jackson, Tennessee, 1957), 12–14; *O.R.* V, 390.
19 Boteler to "Dear Phil," September 8, 1861, in *Turner Ashby File*, in National Archives; *O.R.* V, 889, 891, 919–20.
20 R. L. Dabney, *Life and Campaigns of Lieutenant General Thomas J. Jackson* (New York, 1866), 261. Hereafter cited as Dabney, *Jackson. O.R.* V, 395.
21 *O.R.* XII, Part 3, 880; Jackson to Ashby, March 14, 1862, in *Thomas Lee Settle Papers* at Duke University: Jackson to Boteler, May 6, 1862, in *Alexander Robinson Boteler Papers* at Duke University.
22 Ashby, to Benjamin, March 17, 1862, at Chicago Historical Society; *O.R.* V, 1053, 1059–60, 1063.
23 Cooke, *Wearing of the Gray*, 64; Avirett, *Ashby*, 155–56.
24 *O.R.* XII, Part 1, 380–83; Thomas, *Ashby*, 60.
25 *O.R.* XII, Part 1, 385, 383–84; Avirett, *Ashby*, 272.
26 Thomas, *Ashby*, 74–75, 193–94, 70; Avirett, *Ashby*, 172.
27 Avirett, *Ashby*, 173–74; McHenry Howard, *Recollections of a Maryland Confed-*

erate Soldier and Staff Officer Under Johnston, Jackson and Lee (Baltimore, 1914), 84–85. Hereafter cited as Howard, *Recollections.*

[28] *O.R.* XII, Part 3, 880; Howard, *Recollections,* 90; *Destruction and Reconstruction,* 72; Cooke, *Wearing of the Gray,* 69; Dabney, *Jackson,* 327.

[29] A. R. Boteler, "Jackson in 1862," in *Southern Historical Society Papers,* Vol. 40, 171. Hereafter cited as Boteler, *Jackson.* Douglas, *I Rode With Stonewall,* 82–83.

[30] Hotchkiss to wife, April 20, 1862, in *Jed Hotchkiss Papers,* in Library of Congress; Avirett, *Ashby,* 176; Thomas, *Ashby,* 209–10; Howard, *Recollections,* 90.

[31] Thomas, *Ashby,* 195; Avirett, *Ashby,* 177; *O.R.* XII, Part 3, 880; Jackson to Boteler, May 6, 1862, in *Alexander R. Boteler Papers* at Duke University.

[32] Avirett, *Ashby,* 180; *O.R.* XII, Part 3, 880.

[33] *O.R.* XII, Part 3, 893, 892–93, 898; Thomas, *Ashby,* 91.

[34] Avirett, *Ashby,* 187–88; *O.R.* XII, Part 1, 703; Dufour, *Gentle Tiger,* 176–77; Thomas, *Ashby,* 197; Dabney, *Jackson,* 371.

[35] *O.R.* XII, Part 1, 703; Dabney, *Jackson,* 373; Poague, *Gunner With Stonewall,* 23.

[36] *O.R.* XII, Part 1, 704; *O.R.* XII, Part 3, 902; *O.R.* XII, Part 1, 706; *Destruction and Reconstruction,* 59.

[37] Dabney, *Jackson,* 382; Avirett, *Ashby,* 271; *O.R.* XII, Part 1, 706–7.

[38] Boteler, *Jackson,* 171; Jackson to Boteler, May 6, 1862 in *Alexander R. Boteler Papers* at Duke; Avirett, *Ashby,* 206.

[39] *O.R.* XII, Part 1, 711–12.

[40] Avirett, *Ashby,* 218–19; Thomas T. Munford, *Narrative of the History of the 2nd Va. Cav. Regiment* (Manuscript), in *Munford-Ellis Family Papers (Thomas T. Munford Division)* at Duke University. Hereafter cited as Munford, *Narrative.*

[41] *Confederate Veteran,* Vol. 23, No. 2 (February 1915), 72; Avirett, *Ashby,* 222.

[42] Munford, *Narrative.*

[43] Ibid.

[44] Dabney, *Jackson,* 400.

3. *Stonewall of the West:* GENERAL PAT CLEBURNE

[1] Colonel I. W. Avery, 4th Georgia Cavalry, quoted in Thomas Robson Hay, *Pat Cleburne, Stonewall Jackson of the West,* introductory essay to reprint of Captain Irving Buck, *Cleburne and His Command* (New York, 1908 and Jackson, Tennessee, 1959), 63–64. Hereafter cited as Buck, *Cleburne and His Command.* Hay's essay hereafter cited as Hay, *Pat Cleburne.*

[2] W. J. Hardee, in the New Orleans *Picayune,* July 12 and 19, 1867, reprinted in *Southern Historical Society Papers,* XXXI, 151–63; Buck, *Cleburne and His Command,* 64.

[3] Judge L. H. Magnum, quoted in Buck, *Cleburne and His Command,* 74, 77–78; *Musters of 41st Regiment (W. O. 12/5443-6)* in Public Records Office, London; Lieut. Col. Arthur J. L. Fremantle, *Three Months in the Southern States, April-June, 1863* (New York, 1864), 153. Hereafter cited as Fremantle, *Three Months in the Southern States;* Dr. Charles E. Nash, *Biographical Sketches of Gen. Pat Cleburne* (Little Rock, 1898), 10–11, 15, 25, 38.

[4] Buck, *Cleburne and His Command,* 78–79, 83; Basil W. Duke, *Reminiscences of Gen. Basil W. Duke* (New York, 1911), 69–70.

[5] Buck, *Cleburne and His Command,* 87; *Cleburne File,* in National Archives.

[6] Sherman to Grant, April 5, 1862, in *O.R.,* X, Part 2, 94; Grant to Halleck, April 5, 1862, in *O.R.,* X, Part 1, 89.

[7] Cleburne's Report, in *O.R.,* X, Part 1, 580–684. Brief passages have been placed in direct quotes; Hardee's report, in *Ibid.,* 570.

[8] Buck, *Cleburne and His Command,* 104–7, 109; Hardee, in *Southern Historical Society Papers,* XXXI, 153.

[9] Buck, *Cleburne and His Command,* 110–13; *Confederate Veteran,* XVII, 449.

10 Buck, *Cleburne and His Command*, 116–17; Hardee, in *Southern Historical Society Papers*, XXXI, 154.

11 *O.R.*, XX, Part 2, 508–9; Buck, *Cleburne and His Command*, 118; Cleburne File, in National Archives shows promotion came on December 20, 1862, to rank from December 13.

12 Cleburne's Report, *O.R.*, XX, Part 1, 843–52; Hardee, in *Southern Historical Society Papers*, XXXI, 154; Bragg's Report, *O.R.*, XX, Part 1, 664.

13 Stanley F. Horn, *The Army of Tennessee* (Indianapolis, 1941), xi–xii, 210. Hereafter cited as Horn, *The Army of Tennessee*.

14 *O.R.*, XX, Part 1, 699, 684, 683, 682; Horn, *The Army of Tennessee*, 222–25.

15 Buck, *Cleburne and His Command*, 128–29.

16 *Confederate Veteran*, XII, No. 4 (April 1904), 176; ibid., XIV, No. 1 (January 1906), 14; Buck, *Cleburne and His Command*, 129; *Confederate Veteran*, XII, No. 8 (August 1904), 391.

17 Buck, *Cleburne and His Command*, 129; Fremantle, *Three Months in the Southern States*, 153.

18 Buck, *Cleburne and His Command*, 130.

19 Horn, *The Army of Tennessee*, 247.

20 D. H. Hill, "Chickamauga—The Great Battle of the West", in *Battles and Leaders*, III, 641. Hereafter cited, Hill, *Chickamauga*.

21 Cleburne's Report, *O.R.*, XXX, Part 2, 153–58.

22 Hill, *Chickamauga*, 662; *O.R.*, XXX, Part 1, 192.

23 Buck, *Cleburne and His Command*, 158–59.

24 Ibid., 162; Cleburne's Report, *O.R.*, XXXI, Part 2, 745–53; Horn, *The Army of Tennessee*, 301.

25 Buck, *Cleburne and His Command*, 175–77. Cleburne's reply to Bragg's staff officer has been put into direct quotes.

26 Buck, *Cleburne and His Command*, 179–85; Cleburne's Report, *O.R.*, XXXI, Part 2, 753–58; *Confederate Veteran*, XII, No. 11 (Nov. 1904), 526–27; Sam Watkins, *Co. 'Aytch' etc.* (Nashville, 1882), 110.

27 P. D. Stephenson, "Reminiscences of the Late Campaign of the Army of Tennessee, etc.", in *Southern Historical Society Papers*, XII, (1884), 38; Cleburne's Report, op. cit.

28 Buck, *Cleburne and His Command*, 188–91. The conversation has been put into direct quotes, with several slight but immaterial changes.

29 Wirt Armistead Cate, ed., *Two Soldiers. The Campaign Diaries of Thomas F. Key, C.S.A. . . . and Robert F. Campbell, U.S.A. . . .* (Chapel Hill, N.C., 1938). Hereafter cited as Cate, *Two Soldiers*, 16–18.

30 Buck, *Cleburne and His Command*, 191–200.

31 Hay, *Pat Cleburne* in Buck, *Cleburne and His Command*, 45–50; Ibid., 189–90, 360–61; Patton Anderson to Leonidas Polk in Bromfield L. Ridley, *Battles and Sketches of the Army of Tennessee*, (Mexico, Mo., 1906), 291; Gist to Bragg, March 9, 1864, in *Braxton Bragg Papers*, Western Reserve Historical Society.

32 Buck, *Cleburne and His Command*, 53 and *note*.

33 John B. Hood, *Advance and Retreat* (New Orleans, 1880), 296. Hereafter cited as Hood, *Advance and Retreat*.

34 Hay, *Pat Cleburne*, in Buck, *Cleburne and His Command*, 50–51.

35 Cate, *Two Soldiers*, 32; Buck, *Cleburne and His Command*, 361; E. I. Drake, ed., *Annals of the Army of Tennessee* (Nashville, 1878) 339–45.

36 Buck, *Cleburne and His Command*, 187, 201; Hardee, in *Southern Historical Society Papers*, XXXI, 157.

37 *Confederate Veteran*, II, No. 7 (July 1894), 204.

38 James D. Richardson, *A Compilation of the Messages and Papers of the Confederacy* (2 Vols., Nashville, 1906) I, 425.

39 Buck, *Cleburne and His Command*, 202, 205–7; Horn, *The Army of Tennessee*, 331.

40 Cleburne's Report, *O.R.*, XXXVIII, Part 3, 720–26.

41 Buck, *Cleburne and His Command*, 223–25; *Confederate Veteran*, XIV, No. 7 (July 1906), 328.

[42] Buck, *Cleburne and His Command*, 227, 229–30; Horn, *The Army of Tennessee*, 350–53.

[43] Hood, *Advance and Retreat*, 185–86.

[44] Buck, *Cleburne and His Command*, 242–44; *Confederate Veteran*, XI, No. 5 (May 1903), 221; Hardee in *Southern Historical Society Papers*, XXXI, 162.

[45] Buck, *Cleburne and His Command*, 247–57; Horn, *The Army of Tennessee*, 359–68.

[46] Buck, *Cleburne and His Command*, 260–65; Horn, *The Army of Tennessee*, 383–85.

[47] Ibid., 386–93; Col. Henry Stone, "Repelling Hood's Invasion of Tennessee", in *Battles and Leaders*, IV, 446.

[48] Horn, *The Army of Tennessee*, 387–88; Hood, *Advance and Retreat*, 286; Gen. B. F. Cheatham, "The Lost Opportunity at Spring Hill, Tennessee", in *Southern Historical Society Papers*, IX, 530.

[49] Horn, *The Army of Tennessee*, 388, 392.

[50] Hood, *Advance and Retreat*, 287; Horn, *The Army of Tennessee*, 390–92.

[51] Ibid., 394; Gen. J. C. Brown to Cheatham, October 24, 1881, in *Southern Historical Society Papers*, IX, 538–39.

[52] Buck, *Cleburne and His Command*, 280; Horn, *The Army of Tennessee*, 395–97.

[53] Ibid., 397–98; Buck, *Cleburne and His Command*, 280–81; Hood, *Advance and Retreat*, 293–94, 297.

[54] Buck, *Cleburne and His Command*, 290.

[55] Horn, *The Army of Tennessee*, 399–401.

[56] Buck, *Cleburne and His Command*, 292–93.

[57] Buck, *Cleburne and His Command*, 294–95, 297; *Confederate Veteran*, XIII, No. 8 (August 1905), 356; Ibid., V, No. 10 (October 1897) 513; *Jefferson Davis, The Rise and Fall of the Confederate Goverment* (2 Vols., New York, 1881), II, 577; Hardee, *Southern Historical Society Papers*, XXXI, 163.

4. *Confederate Corsair:* LIEUTENANT "SAVEZ" READ, C.S.N.

[1] Charles W. Read's report in *O.R.*, XLVIII, Part 1, 206.

[2] Allan Pinkerton's report in ibid., 204–5.

[3] Clarence Jeffries, "Running the Blockade on the Mississippi", in *Confederate Veteran*, Vol. 22, No. 1 (January 1914), 23. Hereafter cited as Jeffries, *Running the Blockade*.

[4] James M. Morgan and John P. Marquand, eds., *Prince and Boatswain*, (Greenfield, Mass., 1915), 31. Hereafter cited as Morgan, *Prince and Boatswain*.

[5] Ibid.

[6] Admiral W. S. Schley to Winfield M. Thompson, no date but about 1904, copy in possession of Read's grandson, Mallory J. Read; *Dictionary of American Biography* (New York 1929) XV, 420.

[7] Morgan, *Prince and Boatswain*, 33; Pinkerton's report, in *O.R.*, XLVIII, Part 1, 205.

[8] Schley to Thompson, op. cit.

[9] Charles W. Read, "Reminiscences of the Confederate States Navy" in *Southern Historical Society Papers*, Vol. 1, No. 5 (May 1876), 331. Hereafter cited as Read, *Reminiscences*.

[10] Ibid.

[11] Morgan, *Prince and Boatswain*, 33 note.

[12] Read, *Reminiscences*, 332; Morgan, *Prince and Boatswain*, 33–34.

[13] Ibid., 34.

[14] Ibid., 36.

[15] Ibid.

[16] Ibid., 36–39.

[17] Ibid., 40–43.
[18] Read, *Reminiscences*, 341.
[19] Ibid., 342–43; Read to Whittle, May 1, 1862, in *Official Records of the Union and Confederate Navies in the War of the Rebellion* (Washington, 1894–1922), Vol. 18, 332–33. Hereafter cited as *O.R.N.*, and unless otherwise noted all references are to Series I; Morgan, *Prince and Boatswain*, 43–44.
[20] Read, *Reminiscences*, 344.
[21] *O.R.N.*, 18, 332–33.
[22] Read to J. K. Mitchell, April 26, 1862 (two letters, same date), in *J. K. Mitchell Papers*, Virginia Historical Society. Hereafter cited as *Mitchell Papers*. Read, *Reminiscences*, 344.
[23] *O.R.N.*, 18, 333–34, 331.
[24] Ibid., 311.
[25] *Fire and Alarm Telegraph Message Book*, in New Orleans Public Library.
[26] *O.R.N.*, Series II, 2, 241.
[27] Read, *Reminiscences*, 349–51; Isaac N. Brown, "The Confederate Gunboat 'Arkansas,'" in *Battles and Leaders*, III, 573. Hereafter cited as Brown, *Arkansas*.
[28] Read, *Reminiscences*, 351–54.
[29] George W. Gift, "The Story of the Arkansas," in *Southern Historical Society Papers*, XII, 50. Hereafter cited as Gift, *Arkansas*.
[30] Brown, *Arkansas*, 574–76; Gift, *Arkansas*, 116, 119; Read, *Reminiscences*, 354.
[31] Davis to Welles, July 16, 1862, in *O.R.N.*, 19, 6; Welles to Davis, August 2, 1862, in ibid., 7.
[32] Farragut to Davis, July 15, 1862, in ibid., 7; Farragut to Davis, July 16, 1862, in ibid., 8.
[33] Brown, *Arkansas*, 577.
[34] Read, *Reminiscences*, 357.
[35] Brown, *Arkansas*, 577.
[36] Ibid., 577–78.
[37] Ibid., 578.
[38] Read, *Reminiscences*, 358–59; Brown, *Arkansas*, 579.
[39] John N. Maffitt, *Journal*, in *J. N. Maffitt Papers*, in Southern Historical Collection, University of North Carolina. Read states in manuscript narrative (in possession of Mallory J. Read) that he reported to Maffitt in September 1862. Hereafter cited as Maffitt, *Journal*.
[40] Read, *Reminiscences*, 362, Edward Boykin, *Sea Devil of the Confederacy* (New York, 1959), 84. Hereafter cited as Boykin, *Sea Devil*.
[41] Charles W. Read, *Manuscript Narrative* in possession of Mallory J. Read. Hereafter cited as Read, *Manuscript*.
[42] Maffitt, *Journal*.
[43] Read, *Manuscript*.
[44] Ibid.
[45] Boykin, *Sea Devil*, 147.
[46] Read, *Manuscript*. Conversation is partially reconstructed into direct quotes.
[47] *O.R.N.*, 2, 644–45, 679; Read, *Manuscript;* George Dewey, *Autobiography of George Dewey, Admiral of the Navy* (New York, 1913), 75.
[48] Read, *Manuscript*.
[49] *O.R.N.*, 2, 655–57.
[50] *O.R.N.*, 2, 273–78; Gideon Welles, *Diary of Gideon Welles, Secretary of the Navy Under Lincoln and Johnson* (3 vols. Boston and New York, 1911), I, 327. Hereafter cited as Welles, *Diary:* New York *Tribune*, June 15, 16, 17, 1863.
[51] *Southern Historical Society Papers*, XXIII (1895), 276–77; *O.R.N.*, 2, 304–6, 340; New York *Tribune*, June 27, 1863; *O.R.N.*, 2, 655–57, 321–22; Welles, *Diary*, I, 347.
[52] Read, *Manuscript*.
[53] Ibid.; *O.R.N.*, 2, 322–23, 657; A. A. Hoehling, in Portland *Telegram*, May 18, 1958.
[54] Morgan, *Prince and Boatswain*, 53, 56; Read, *Manuscript; O.R.N.*, 2, 327, 655.
[55] Morgan, *Prince and Boatswain*, 57–60; Walter Scott Meriwether in Charleston,

Mississippi, *Mississippi Sun*, June 24, 1921. Hereafter cited as Meriwether, *Mississippi Sun*. *Dictionary of American Biography*, XV, 420.

⁵⁶ Morgan, *Prince and Boatswain*, 60; Meriwether, *Mississippi Sun*, June 24, 1921; *O.R.N.*, 11, 747, 797, 803; Read, *Manuscript*.

⁵⁷ George S. Bernard, compiler and editor, *War Talks of Confederate Veterans* (Petersburg, Va., 1892), 231–36. Hereafter cited as Bernard, *War Talks;* W. F. Shippey, "A Leaf From My Log Book," in *Southern Historical Society Papers*, XII (1884), 416–21.

⁵⁸ Mallory to Bulloch, February 17, 1865, in *O.R.N.*, II, 2, 798; W. H. Wall in New Orleans *Times-Democrat*, May 25, 1903.

⁵⁹ Ibid.; *Confederate Veteran*, XXII, No. 1 (January 1914), 22; H. Allen Gosnell, *Guns on the Western Waters* (Baton Rouge, La., 1949), 193; Read's report in *O.R.N.*, 22, 168.

⁶⁰ Ibid.

⁶¹ New Orleans *Times-Democrat*, May 23, 1903.

⁶² *Confederate Veteran*, XXI, No. 1, 22.

⁶³ New Orleans *Times-Democrat*, May 23, 1903.

⁶⁴ *Confederate Veteran*, op. cit.

⁶⁵ *O.R.N.*, 22, 148–49; *O.R.*, XLVIII, Part 1, 204; *Confederate Veteran*, op. cit.

⁶⁶ New Orleans *Times-Democrat*, May 23, 1903.

⁶⁷ *Confederate Veteran*, op. cit.; *O.R.N.*, 22, 167.

⁶⁸ Morgan, *Prince and Boatswain*, 68–72.

5. *The Cannoneer Wore Specs:* COLONEL WILLIE PEGRAM

¹ Jennings C. Wise, "The Boy Gunners of Lee," in *Southern Historical Society Papers*, XLII (October 1917), 156; *O.R.*, XXI, 648; *General Harry Heth Manuscript*, University of Virginia. Hereafter cited as *Heth Manuscript*. Robert Stiles, *Four Years Under Marse Robert* (New York & Washington, 1910), 109. Hereafter cited as Stiles, *Four Years Under Marse Robert*.

² John Haskell, *The Haskell Memoirs*, edited by Gilbert E. Govan and James W. Livingood (New York, 1960), 83. Hereafter cited as Haskell, *Memoirs*. William Gordon McCabe in "The University Memorial," 714–16, quoted in Armistead Churchill Gordon, *Memories and Memorials of William Gordon McCabe* (2 vols., Richmond, 1925), 158–160. Hereafter cited as Gordon, *Memories and Memorials*.

³ J. C. Goolsby, *Confederate Veteran*, Vol. VI, No. 6 (June 1898) 271; Stiles, *Four Years Under Marse Robert*, 109; Gordon, *Memories and Memorials*, 170; *O.R.*, XI, Part 2, 837; *O.R.*, XLII, Part 1, 858; *O.R.*, XIX, Part 1, 981; *O.R.*, XI, Part 2, 843; *Heth Manuscript*.

⁴ Gordon McCabe, in *Pegram-Johnson-McIntosh Papers* at Virginia Historical Society, Richmond. Hereafter cited as *Pegram-Johnson-McIntosh Papers*. Gordon, *Memories and Memorials*, 175.

⁵ *Pegram Family Papers*, in Southern Historical Collection, University of North Carolina. Hereafter cited as *Pegram Family Papers*.

⁶ Gordon, *Memories and Memorials*, 159; Pegram to Sister Jennie, November 10, 1860, in *Pegram-Johnson-McIntosh Papers*.

⁷ Pegram to Charles Ellis Munford, April 18, 1861, in *Munford-Ellis Family Papers* at Duke University. Hereafter cited as *Munford-Ellis Family Papers*. Pegram to Sister Mary, May 3, 1861, in *Pegram-Johnson-McIntosh Papers;* W. Gordon McCabe, in *Southern Historical Society Papers*, Vol. XIV, 11.

⁸ *O.R.*, II, 476; Gordon, *Memories and Memorials*, 159.

⁹ *O.R.*, V, 114–15.

¹⁰ Gordon, *Memories and Memorials*, 160; Pegram to Sister Jennie, April 3, 1862, in *Pegram-Johnson-McIntosh Papers*.

¹¹ *O.R.*, XII, Part 1, 433–36; E. P. Alexander, *Military Memoirs of a Confederate*

(New York, 1908 and Bloomington, Ind., 1962), 90. Hereafter cited as Alexander, *Military Memoirs*.

12 *Confederate Veteran*, Vol. 38, No. 3 (March 1930), 113, 125; *Southern Historical Society Papers*, Vol. XIV, 12; *O.R.*, XI, Part 2, 837.

13 *O.R.*, XI, Part 2, 839, 813, 843; *Southern Historical Society Papers*, Vol. XIV, 12.

14 *Southern Historical Society Papers*, Vol. XIV, 12; Alexander, *Military Memoirs*, 176, 180; Pegram to Sister Mary, August 8, 1862, in *Pegram-Johnson-McIntosh Papers*.

15 Alexander, *Military Memoirs*, 181; Pegram to Sister Jennie, August 14, 1862, in *Pegram-Johnson-McIntosh Papers*.

16 *O.R.*, XII, Part 2, 226, 184, 218; Pegram to Sister Jennie, August 14, 1862, in *Pegram-Johnson-McIntosh Papers*.

17 Alexander, *Military Memoirs*, 188–190; Pegram to Mother, September 7, 1862, in *Pegram-Johnson-McIntosh Papers*.

18 Henderson, *Jackson*, 432; Pegram to Mother, September 7, 1862, in *Pegram-Johnson-McIntosh Papers*; Alexander, *Military Memoirs*, 194; *O.R.*, XII, Part 2, 67?.

19 Alexander, *Military Memoirs*, 220; Clifford Dowdey and Louis H. Manarin, *The Wartime Papers of R. E. Lee* (Boston and Toronto, 1961), 292–93. Hereafter cited as *Wartime Papers of Lee;* Pegram to Mother, September 7, 1862, in *Pegram-Johnson-McIntosh Papers*.

20 *O.R.*, XIX, Part 1, 980–81.

21 Ibid., 981, 984; C. G. Chamberlayne, *Ham Chamberlayne-Virginian, etc.* (Richmond, 1932), 112. Hereafter cited as Chamberlayne, *Ham Chamberlayne; Southern Historical Society Papers*, Vol. XIV, 13; Pegram to Sister Jennie, October 7, 1862, in *Pegram-Johnson-McIntosh Papers*.

22 *O.R.*, LI, Part 2, 639; *O.R.*, XIX, Part 2, 623, 649, 653.

23 Pegram to Sister Jennie, October 7, 1862, in *Pegram-Johnson-McIntosh Papers;* Pegram to Sister Jennie, October 24, 1862, in *Pegram-Johnson-McIntosh Papers*.

24 Alexander, *Military Memoirs*, 288; *O.R.*, XXI, 636, 645–48, 649–50; Thomas L. Livermore, *Numbers and Losses in the Civil War* (Reprint edition, Bloomington, Indiana, 1957) 96; *O.R.*, XXI, 648.

25 Jennings Cropper Wise, *The Long Arm of Lee* (2 vols., Lynchburg, Va., 1915), 425. Hereafter cited as Wise, *The Long Arm of Lee; O.R.*, XXV, Part 2, 635.

26 Pegram to Sister Jennie, January 8, 1863, in *Pegram-Johnson-McIntosh Papers; Southern Historical Society Papers*, XIV, 15.

27 Wise, *The Long Arm of Lee*, 413–14, 416, 419–20.

28 Ibid., 443–44; *O.R.*, XXV, Part 1, 796–98; Alexander, *Military Memoirs*, 321–24.

29 Ibid., XXV, Part 1, 937–39; *Confederate Veteran*, Vol. V, No. 6 (June, 1897), 288.

30 *O.R.*, XXV, Part 1, 938–39, 804, 824, 886; Chamberlayne, *Ham Chamberlayne*, 176; John Munford to Cousin Sallie Munford, May 14, 1863, in *Munford-Ellis Papers; Southern Historical Society Papers*, XIV, 15.

31 Pegram to Sister Mary, May 11, 1863, in *Pegram-Johnson-McIntosh Papers;* Freeman, *Lee's Lieutenants*, II, 696; Douglas Southall Freeman and Grady McWhiney, *Lee's Dispatches* (New York, 1957), 91.

32 John Munford to Cousin Sallie Munford, June 12, 1863, in *Munford-Ellis Papers; O.R.*, XXVII, Part 2, 610; Chamberlayne, *Ham Chamberlayne*, 187–88.

33 Sallie Munford to John Munford, June 29, 1863, in *Munford-Ellis Papers;* Fairfax Downey, *The Guns at Gettysburg* (New York, 1958), 18. Hereafter cited as Downey, *The Guns at Gettysburg; Southern Historical Society Papers*, XIV, 16.

34 *O.R.*, XXVII, Part 2, 637–39, 609–11, 677–79, 678, 612.

35 *O.R.*, XXIX, Part 1, 896; Pegram to Sister Mary, September 10, 1863, in *Pegram-Johnson-McIntosh Papers; O.R.*, XXXVI, Part 1, 1039; Pegram to Sister Mary, December 16, 1863, in *Pegram-Johnson-McIntosh Papers*.

36 Pegram to Sister Mary, February 11, 1864, in *Pegram-Johnson-McIntosh Papers*.

37 *William J. Pegram Carded Records* in National Archives; Wise, *The Long Arm of Lee*, 833.

38 *O.R.*, XXXVI, Part 1, 1040–52.

39 Pegram to Sister Mary, July 21, 1864, in *Pegram-Johnson-McIntosh Papers; Heth Manuscript;* Freeman, *Lee's Lieutenants,* II, 672; Gordon, *Memories and Memorials,* 175.
40 *O.R.,* XLII, Part 1, 858; *Heth Manuscript;* Chamberlayne, *Ham Chamberlayne,* 264.
41 *Southern Historical Society Papers,* XIV, 17.
42 Chamberlayne, *Ham Chamberlayne,* 290; Pegram to Mother, October 28, 1864, in *Pegram-Johnson-McIntosh Papers.*
43 John Pegram to Mother, February 3, 1865, in *Pegram-Johnson-McIntosh Papers;* Pegram to Sister Mary, March 14, 1865, in *Pegram-Johnson-McIntosh Papers;* Pegram to Sister Jennie, March 10, 1865, in *Pegram-Johnson-McIntosh Papers.*
44 W. Gordon McCabe to Mary Pegram, April 4, 1865, quoted in Chamberlayne, *Ham Chamberlayne,* 317–19; Gordon, *Memories and Memorials,* 163–66, 168–75.

6. *The Peevish Commissary:* COLONEL L. B. NORTHROP

1 Chesnut, *A Diary From Dixie,* 99.
2 Henry Stuart Foote, *The War of the Rebellion, etc.* (New York, 1866), 358–59. Hereafter cited as Foote, *The War of the Rebellion.*
3 Douglas Southall Freeman, *R. E. Lee* (4 vols. New York, 1934–35), II, 494–95. Hereafter cited as Freeman, *R. E. Lee.*
4 Jefferson Davis, *The Rise and Fall of the Confederate Government* (2 vols., New York, 1881), I, 303, 315.
5 Jeremy P. Felt, "Lucius B. Northrop and the Confederacy's Subsistence Department," in *The Virginia Magazine,* Vol. 69, No. 2 (April 1961), 182.
6 Chesnut, *Diary,* 205; Ellsworth Eliot, Jr., *West Point in the Confederacy* (New York, 1941), XX; Warner, *General in Gray,* 225; Foote, *The War of the Rebellion,* 358.
7 Special Report, Adjutant General's Office, November 24, 1847, in *Record Group 94,* National Archives; Northrop to General R. Jones, December 6, 1843; in ibid.; *Dictionary of American Biography,* Vol. 13, 567.
8 Special Report, Adjutant General's Office, November 24, 1847, op. cit; Davis to Adjutant General, January 19, 1848, in *Record Group No. 94,* National Archives; Davis to Marcy, May 5, 1848, in *Ibid.;* Davis to Polk, June 23, 1848, in ibid.; Calhoun and A. P. Battle to Polk, July 6, 1848, in ibid.
9 Francis Bernard Heitman, *Historical Register and Dictionary of the United States Army* (2 vols., Washington, 1903) I, 751; Willard E. Wright, ed. "Some Letters of Lucius Bellinger Northrop," in *The Virginia Magazine,* Vol. 68, No. 4 (October 1960) 457. Hereafter cited as Wright, *Northrop Letters.* Joseph T. Durkin's *Stephan R. Mallory, Confederate Navy Chief* (Chapel Hill, North Carolina, 1954), 293.
10 Northrop to William E. Woodruff, January 2, 1861, in Wright, *Northrop Letters,* 460–62; *O.R.,* IV, I, 191, 1176; Davis to Northrop, February 1, 1881, in Dunbar Rowland, *Jefferson Davis, Constitutionalist, etc.* (10 vols., Jackson, Mississippi, 1923), VIII, 587. Hereafter cited as Rowland, *Davis.* Walker to Maynadier, April 9, 1861, in Walker, *Letter Book,* Library of Congress; Maynadier to Walker, April 15, 1861, in *O.R.,* IV, I, 221; Northrop to Bishop Lynch, May 17, 1861, in Wright, *Northrop Letters,* 464.
11 *O.R.,* IV, I, 338–39; Northrop to Bishop Lynch, May 17, 1861, in Wright, *Northrop Letters,* 463; Northrop to Bishop Lynch, January 30, 1862, in ibid., 465.
12 Chesnut, *Diary,* 99; Davis to Beauregard, August 4, 1861 in *O.R.,* II, 507–8; Gilbert E. Govan and James W. Livingood, *A Different Valor, The Story of Gen. Joseph E. Johnston, CSA.* (Indianapolis, 1956), 64–65.
13 John D. Imboden, "Incidents of the First Bull Run," in *Battles and Leaders,* I, 239.
14 R. B. Lee to Northrop and Northrop to Lee, September 7, 1861, *No. 4170 in Office of Sec. of War, Box No. 9, Record Group 109,* in National Archives; Lee to Cooper, September 12, 1861, *No. 5508,* ibid.

15 Rowland, *Davis*, IV, 126–28; Davis to Johnston, September 18, 1861, in *O.R.*, V, 857; Benjamin to Johnston, September 19, 1861, ibid., 857–58; Benjamin to Myers, September 20, 1861, ibid., 867; Myers to Benjamin, September 21, 1861, ibid., 871; Johnston to Benjamin, September 22, 1861, ibid., 872–73; Benjamin to Johnston, September 24, 1861, ibid., 877; Northrop to Davis, March 31, 1878, in Rowland, *Davis*, VIII, 146.

16 Walker to Northrop, August 26, 1861, in *Walker Letter Book*, Library of Congress; Fontaine W. Mahood, *History of the Commissary Department of the Confederate States of America.* Typescript in Virginia Historical Society, 2–6. Hereafter cited as Mahood, *History of the Commissary.* Captain Mahood, who served under Northrop, died in 1875. His manuscript was typed about 1905 and annotated by an unidentified person from the *Official Records.* Ibid., 13; Northrop to Davis, August 21, 1861, in Rowland, *Davis*, IV, 125; ibid., Vol. VIII, 590, 499, 377; ibid., Vol. IX, 311, 352, 391; *O.R.*, IV, I, 886.

17 Alfred Hoyt Bill, *The Beleaugered City* (New York, 1946), 144; Wilfred Buck Yearns, *The Confederate Congress* (Athens, Ga., 1960), 114; *O.R.*, IV, 574.

18 Ibid., IV, I, 1101; Northrop to Walker, August 24, 1861, *Office of Secretary of War, Box No. 7 in Record Group 109*, in National Archives; *O.R.*, IV, I, 1049–50.

19 Johnston to Davis, February 25, 1862, in *O.R.*, V, 1081; Davis to Johnston, February 28, 1862, in ibid., 1084; Northrop to Davis, January 14, 1885, in Rowland, *Davis*, IX, 326; Northrop to Davis, March 9, 1885, ibid., 352; Noland to Northrop, March 27, 1862, in *O.R.*, IV, I, 1038–39.

20 Beauregard to Cooper, April 16, 1862, in *O.R.*, X, Part 2, 422–23.

21 General Orders No. 30, Corinth, April 30, 1862, in ibid., 478; Northrop to Randolph, May 31, 1862, in ibid., 571–72.

22 Northrop to Benjamin, January 18, 1862, in *O.R.*, IV, I, 870.

23 Ruffin to Northrop, October 18, 1862, in *Papers Relating to Subsistence Dept., CSA*, at Virginia Historical Society; R. M. Davis to Northrop, October 30, 1862 (two letters same date), in ibid.; Northrop to Jefferson Davis, May 23, 1880, in Rowland, *Davis*, VIII, 457; J. B. Jones, *A Rebel War Clerk's Diary* (New York, 1958), 113–14. This is the one-volume edition, edited by Earl Schenck Miers, of a work originally published in 1866. Hereafter cited as Jones, *Rebel War Clerk.*

24 Ruffin to Randolph, November 8, 1862, *Papers Relating to the Subsistence Dept., CSA*, at Virginia Historical Society; Davis to Randolph, November 13, 1862, in ibid.; Ruffin's Report to Joint Committee of Congress, January 1864 in ibid.; Northrop's Report in ibid.

25 Northrop to Davis, April 23, 1878, in Rowland, *Davis*, Vol. VIII, 183.

26 Northrop to Davis, May 23, 1880, in ibid.

27 Mahood, *History of the Commissary*, 46; Edward Younger, ed., *Inside the Confederate Government, The Diary of Robert Garlick Hill Kean* (New York, 1957), 47. Hereafter cited as Younger, *Kean Diary.*

28 *Journal of the Confederate Congress* (7 Vols., Washington, 1904), VI, 9; Freeman, *R. E. Lee*, IV, 181; Northrop to Davis, March 31, 1878, in Rowland, *Davis*, VIII, 147; Lee to Seddon, January 12, 1863, in *O.R.*, LI, Part 2, 669; Crenshaw to Northrop, January 12, 1863, in *O.R.*, XXI, 1088–91.

29 Lee to Seddon, January 20, 1863, in *O.R.*, XXI, 1100–1101.

30 Northrop endorsement on above, January 28, 1863, in *O.R.*, LI, Part 2, 674–75.

31 *Journal of the Confederate Congress*, VI, 25, 525; ibid., IV, II, 574–75; Younger, *Kean Diary*, 38–39.

32 *O.R.*, IV, II, 405.

33 These telegrams are in the Confederate Museum, Richmond.

34 Mahood, *History of the Commissary*, 21–23; Northrop to Seddon, June 4, 1863, in *O.R.*, IV, II, 574–75.

35 Younger, *Kean Diary*, 86; Mahood, *History of the Commissary*, 25–26; *O.R.*, XXX, Part IV, 547–50, 673.

36 Mahood, *History of the Commissary*, 28.

37 Chesnut, *Diary*, 285; Yearns, *The Confederate Congress*, 233, 121; Jones, *Rebel War Clerk*, 256.

38 E. Merton Coulter, *The Confederate States of America 1861–1865* (Baton Rouge, Louisiana, 1950), 252.

39 Jones, *Rebel War Clerk*, 291, 292.

40 Mahood, *History of the Commissary*, 29; Northrop to Davis, May 14, 1879, in Rowland, *Davis*, 390.

41 *O.R.*, XXIX, Part 2, 843–44, 862.

42 Jones, *Rebel War Clerk*, 319; Mahood, *History of the Commissary*, 33.

43 Jones, *Rebel War Clerk*, 323; *Journal of the Confederate Congress*, VI, 681; Younger, *Kean Diary*, 136.

44 Jones, *Rebel War Clerk*, 342–43, 349; Mahood, *History of the Commissary*, 36, 38, 41, 47.

45 Mahood, *History of the Commissary*, 45–46; Northrop to Seddon, July 26, 1864, in *Record Group 109*, National Archives.

46 French to Northrop, September 15, 1864, in *Papers Relating to the Commissary Dept., CSA*, at Virginia Historical Society.

47 *Estimate of Stocks of Meat on Hand . . . to October 15, 1864*, in ibid.; Mahood, *History of the Commissary*, 52; Warner, *Generals in Gray*, 225. The *Northrop File*, in National Archives gives December 23, 1864, as the date of his temporary rank as a brigadier general; *O.R.*, IV, III, 930–32; Frank Vandiver, ed., *The Civil War Diary of Josiah Gorgas* (Tuscaloosa, Alabama, 1947), 157.

48 *O.R.*, XLVI, Part 2, 1034, 1039–40, 1209–10; Younger, *Kean Diary*, 200.

49 Mahood, *History of the Commissary*, 61; *O.R.*, XLVI, Part 2, 1246; Jones, *Rebel War Clerk*, 508.

50 Davis to Northrop, April 7, 1865, in Rowland, *Davis*, VI, 536–37; Northrop to Bishop Lynch, July 26, and September 11, 1865, in Wright, *Northrop Letters*, 476–77; *Northrop File*, in National Archives.

51 Northrop to Davis, April 29, 1879, in Rowland, *Davis*, VIII, 388; ibid., June 22, 1879, in ibid., 401; ibid., December 15, 1879, in ibid., 434.

52 Northrop to Davis, April 21, 1878, in ibid., 181; ibid., July 25, 1881, IX, 5; ibid., March 31, 1878, VIII, 147; ibid., April 21, 1878, VIII, 181; ibid., February 2, 1880, VIII, 440–41.

53 Northrop to Davis, September 8, 1886, in Rowland, *Davis*, IX, 469; ibid., July [no date] 1882, ibid., IX, 179; ibid., February 25, 1885, ibid., IX, 346; Davis to Northrop, March 3, 1885, in ibid., IX, 349.

54 Northrop to Davis, April 21, 1878, in ibid., VIII, 180, 184.

55 Northrop to Davis, September 15, 1889, in ibid., X, 138.

56 *Dictionary of American Biography*, Vol. 13, 567.

57 Northrop to Davis, February 6, 1881, in Rowland, *Davis*, VIII, 591.

7. *Every Inch a Soldier:* GENERAL BILLY MAHONE

1 *Confederate Veteran*, Vol. 34, No. 8 (August 1926), 299; ibid., Vol. 30, No. 10 (October 1922), 367; Nelson M. Blake, *William Mahone of Virginia, Soldier and Political Insurgent* (Richmond, 1935) 151. Hereafter cited as Blake, *Mahone*.

2 G. Moxley Sorrel, *Recollections of a Confederate Staff Officer* (Reprint, Jackson, Tennessee, 1958), 264–65. Hereafter cited as Sorrel, *Recollections;* John S. Wise, *The End of an Era* (Boston and New York, 1899), 325. Hereafter cited as Wise, *The End of an Era; Confederate Veteran*, XIV, No. 11 (November 1906), 500.

3 Wise, *The End of an Era*, 325–26; Sorrel, *Recollections*, 264; Freeman, *Lee's Lieutenants*, III, xxxviii.

4 Undated clipping from unidentified Roanoke, Virginia, newspaper in *William Mahone File* at Virginia Military Institute (VMI); Mahone to General Thomas T. Munford, July 22, 1882, in *Munford-Ellis Papers* at Duke University.

5 Wise, *The End of an Era*, 320–21; Blake, *Mahone*, 10–11; *Mahone File* at VMI.

6 Blake, *Mahone*, 13, 11–37; Wise, *The End of an Era*, 321.

7 Blake, *Mahone*, 38–40.

8 Ibid., 40–41; *O.R.*, LI, Part 2, 52; Mahone to "My Dear Sir," May 8 1861, in *Mahone File* at VMI; *O.R.*, LI, Part 2, 165.

9 *Confederate Military History*, Vol. III, 634; *O.R.*, IX, 38, *O.R.*, XI, Part 3, 485.

10 *O.R.*, XI, Part 3, 502, 514–15, 519; *O.R.*, XI, Part I, 636.

11 *O.R.*, XI, Part 3, 518; *O.R.N.*, VII, 800–1.

12 *O.R.*, XI, Part 3, 544–45, 548.

13 *O.R.*, XI, Part 1, 945, 983–84; Walter Clark, ed., *Histories of the Several Regiments and Battalions from North Carolina in the Great War 1861–1865* (5 vols., Raleigh, 1901) Vol. I, 693; *Major J. W. Ratchford Manuscript* in Daniel H. Hill, Jr., Papers, 20, 22, in Department of Archives and History, Raleigh, North Carolina.

14 *O.R.*, XI, Part 2, 796–801, 981, 672.

15 *O.R.*, XI, Part 3, 651; *O.R.*, XIX, Part 1, 841–42.

16 *O.R.*, XXI, 614–15, 609; Virginia Legislators to President Davis, January 13, 1863, both in *Mahone File* in National Archives.

17 Longstreet to French, February 9, 1863, and Anderson to French, March 30, 1863, both in *Mahone File* in National Archives.

18 Anderson to Cooper, March 30, 1863, with endorsements of Longstreet (April 4, 1863) and Lee (April 8, 1863), in *Mahone File* in National Archives.

19 *O.R.*, XXV, Part 1, 862–64, 853; Blake, *Mahone*, 46 note, 48.

20 *O.R.*, XXVII, Part 2, 621.

21 *O.R.*, XXIX, Part 1, 428–29, 843.

22 Virginia State Senators to President Davis, March 8, 1864, in *Mahone File* in National Archives.

23 *O.R.*, XXXVI, Part 1, 1090–91; Sorrel, *Recollections*, 285–86, 231–32.

24 *O.R.*, XXXVI, Part 2, 967; *O.R.*, XXXVI, Part 1, 329, 1030–31; *O.R.*, LI, Part 2, 930, 977.

25 Freeman, *Lee's Lieutenants*, Vol. III, 552–53; *O.R.*, XXXVI, Part 3, 873; Mahone to Henry Storm, June 17, 1878, in *Mahone Papers* at Duke University.

26 Clifford Dowdey, *Lee's Last Campaign* (Boston and Toronto, 1960), 296; Alexander, *Military Memoirs*, 549; *O.R.*, XXXVI, Part 1, 1032, 1033–35.

27 *The Wartime Papers of Lee*, 792.

28 Wise, *The End of an Era*, 319–20; W. Gordon McCabe, "Defence of Petersburg," in *Southern Historical Society Papers*, Vol. II, No. 6 (December 1876), 273–74. Hereafter cited as McCabe, *Petersburg*.

29 *O.R.*, LI, Part 2, 1026; *O.R.*, XL, Part 2, 685.

30 *O.R.*, LI, Part 2, 1028; *O.R.*, XL, Part 2, 575; *Wartime Papers of Lee*, 813.

31 *O.R.*, XL, Part 3, 179, 775.

32 McCabe, *Petersburg*, 283–84; Wise, *The End of an Era*, 351–58; Henry L. Pleasants, Jr., and George H. Straley, *Inferno at Petersburg* (Philadelphia & New York, 1961), 47–48, 77.

33 McCabe, *Petersburg*, 279, 285; Alexander, *Military Memoirs*, 568; Blake, *Mahone*, 55.

34 George S. Bernard, "The Battle of the Crater," in *Southern Historical Society Papers*, Vol. XVIII (1890), 4–5. Hereafter cited as Bernard, *Battle of the Crater;* McCabe, *Petersburg*, 290.

35 Bernard, *Battle of the Crater*, 5; Mahone in Bernard, *War Talks*, 213–14.

36 Bernard, *Battle of the Crater*, 8, 36; Bernard, *War Talks*, 214; McCabe, *Petersburg*, 290.

37 Bernard, *Battle of the Crater*, 37.

38 McCabe, *Petersburg*, 290–91; Bernard, *War Talks*, 214.

39 Wise, *The End of an Era*, 364; McCabe, *Petersburg*, 293.

40 Wise, *The End of an Era*, 365–66; *Confederate Veteran*, Vol. XIV, No. 4 (April 1906), 178; ibid., Vol. XV, No. 11 (November, 1907), 490. *Southern Historical Society Papers*, Vol. XXV, 85; McCabe, *Petersburg*, 293.

41 *Confederate Veteran*, Vol. III, No. 1 (January, 1899), 13; Mahone to Charles S. Venable, August 7, 1876, in *Charles S. Venable Papers* in Virginia Historical Society; *O.R.*, XLII, Part 2, 1156.

42 Alexander, *Military Memoirs*, 574; O.R., XLII, Part 2, 628, 940; McCabe, *Petersburg*, 6, 296.

43 O.R., XLII, Part 2, 683–84; *Wartime Papers of Lee*, 844; O.R., XLII, Part 1, 853, 854; ibid., XLII, Part 3, 613.

44 O.R., XLVI, Part 2, 1210; Freeman, *R. E. Lee*, IV, 63; O.R., XLVI, Part 3, 1379.

45 O.R., XLVI, Part 3, 1385; James Longstreet, *From Manassas to Appomattox* (Philadelphia, 1896), 614–15. Hereafter cited as Longstreet *From Manassas to Appomattox*; O.R., XLVI, Part 1, 1125.

46 Longstreet, *From Manassas to Appomattox*, 615; Freeman, *Lee's* Lieutenants, III, 714.

47 Poague, *Gunner With Stonewall*, 118; O.R., XLVI, Part 3, 619; Longstreet, *From Manassas to Appomattox*, 624–25, placed in direct quotes.

48 O.R., XLVI, Part 1, 1266–67; Wise, *The End of an Era*, 428; *Confederate Veteran*, Vol. 22, No. 7 (July, 1914), 312–13.

49 Benjamin F. Butler, *Butler's Book* (Boston, 1892), 880, 886–87.

50 The resume of Billy Mahone's postwar career is drawn from Nelson M. Blake, *William Mahone of Virginia*, 70–274, passim.

51 *Confederate Veteran*, Vol. 30. No. 10 (October 1922), 367; ibid., Vol. 29, No. 6 (June 1921), 213; ibid., Vol. 39, No. 7 (July 1931) 262; Dunbar Rowland, *Jefferson Davis, Constitutionalist* (10 vols., Jackson, Mississippi, 1923), X, 137.

52 Blake, *Mahone*, 265–66, 274.

8. *Rebel Propagandist:* HENRY HOTZE

1 Jones, *Rebel War Clerk*, 310.

2 Frank Lawrence Owsley, *King Cotton Diplomacy* (second edition, Chicago, 1959), 155. Hereafter cited as Owsley, *King Cotton Diplomacy*.

3 Burton, J. Hendrick, *Statesmen of the Lost Cause* (New York, 1939), 392. Hereafter cited as Hendrick, *Statesmen of the Lost Cause*.

4 Freeman, *The South to Posterity*, 24–25.

5 *Mobile Daily Register*, May 11, 1887; U. S. Census, 1850.

6 *Mobile Daily Register*, May 2, 1858; ibid., May 11, 1887.

7 O.R. LII, Part 2, 42–43.

8 Henry Hotze, "Three Months in the Confederacy Army," in *The Index*, May 1—October 29, 1862 (Printed in facsimile, with introduction and notes by Richard Barksdale Harwell, University of Alabama, 1952), 13–33.

9 O.R. IV, I, 596, 611–12; O.R.N., II, III, 280; *Confederate States, Special Orders of the Adjutant and Inspector General's Office* (no place, no date), 163.

10 O.R.N., II, III, 117; Henry Hotze, *Dispatch Book* in Library of Congress. Hereafter cited as Hotze, *Dispatch Book*.

11 O.R.N., II, III, 293–94; Owsley, *King Cotton Diplomacy*, 156.

12 Quoted in Owsley, *King Cotton Diplomacy*, 11; William H. Russell, *My Diary North and South* (New York, 1863), 43; Owsley, *King Cotton Diplomacy*, 20–1; Varina Howell Davis, *Jefferson Davis: A Memoir by His Wife* (New York, 1890), II, 160.

13 Owsley, *King Cotton Diplomacy*, 56; O.R.N., II, III, 315; Hotze, *Dispatch Book*, 6–8.

14 O.R.N., II, III, 325; Hotze, *Dispatch Book*, 11–13.

15 O.R.N., II, III, 346–47; Hotze, *Dispatch Book*, 15–20; London *Morning Post*, Feb. 22, 1862, quoted in Yeuell Y. Harris, *Henry Hotze, Confederate Propagandist Abroad* (Unpublished Thesis Duke University, 1945), 29–30.

16 O.R.N., II, III, 346–47; Hotze, *Dispatch Book*, 21.

17 O.R.N., II, III, 352–54; Hotze, *Dispatch Book*, 24–28.

18 O.R.N., II, III, 347; Hotze, *Dispatch Book*, 29–31.

19 *O.R.N.*, II, III, 360–63, 399–400; Charles L. Dufour, *The Night the War Was Lost* (New York, 1960), 295.

20 *O.R.N.*, II, III, 400–1.

21 *The Index*, May 1, 1862.

22 *O.R.N.*, II, III, 424; *The Index*, May 15, 1862.

23 *O.R.N.*, II, III, 535, 537, 567; Henry Hotze, *Letter Book* in Library of Congress. Hereafter cited as Hotze, *Letter Book*.

24 *O.R.N.*, II, III, 659–60; *The Index*, for dates cited.

25 DeLeon to Hotze, October 1, 1862, in *Henry Hotze Papers* in Library of Congress.

26 Hotze, *Letter Book; O.R.N.*, II, III, 633, 565; Paul DuBellet, *The Diplomacy of the Confederate Cabinet*, 27, quoted in Harris, *Henry Hotze*, 92; *Papers of Clement C. Clay*, quoted in Harris, *Henry Hotze*, 96.

27 Hotze, *Letter Book, O.R.N.*, II, III, 661, 902.

28 *The Index*, August 28, October 2, October 9, October 16, November 27, December 11, 1862.

29 Ibid., March 26, May 28, July 23, October 8, December 10, 1863.

30 Ibid., March 31, April 21, May 19, June 23, November 24, December 29, 1864.

31 *O.R.N.*, II, III, 661.

32 Ibid., 401; *American Historical Review*, Vol. XXXV (July 1930), 814, 816; *O.R.N.*, II, III, 850, *The Index*, November 5, 1863.

33 *O.R.N.*, II, III, 768, 785; *American Historical Review*, XXXV, 816.

34 *O.R.N.*, II, III, 1024–25.

35 Ibid., 1013.

36 Ibid., 1061.

37 Ibid., 1078; *O.R.* IV, II, 24; *O.R.N.*, II, III, 1090, 1091.

38 *O.R.N.*, II, III, 1115–16, 1143–44, 1209–10.

39 Ibid., 785; Hotze, *Letter Book*.

40 *O.R.N.*, II, III, 1179, 1207; Hotze, *Dispatch Book*, 395–97.

41 McRae to Hotze, September 11, 1863, in *Henry Hotze Papers; The Index*, September 10, 1863; McRae to Hotze, September 17, 1863, in *Henry Hotze Papers*.

42 *O.R.N.*, II, III, 915; *The Index*, dates cited.

43 Mann to Hotze, January 26, 1865, in *Henry Hotze Papers; The Index* dates cited.

44 Bulloch to Hotze, April 25, 1865, in *Henry Hotze Papers;* Hotze, *Letter Book*.

45 *The Index*, August 12, 1865.

46 The file of *The Index* used in this sketch are at the Howard-Tilton Library, Tulane University.

47 Charles P. Cullop, *Henry Hotze, Confederate Propagandist* (Unpublished master's thesis, University of Virginia, 1959), 147; Mobile *Daily Register*, May 11, 1887.

9. *The Articulate Artillerist:* GENERAL E. P. ALEXANDER

1 Alexander's Narrative (Draft No. 2), in *E. P. Alexander Papers*, in Southern Historical Collection, University of North Carolina. Hereafter cited as *Alexander Papers*.

2 Alexander to Wife, no date in ibid; Alexander, *Military Memoirs*, 30–33.

3 Sorrel, *Recollections*, 70, 119, 260.

4 Freeman, *Lee's Lieutenants*, II, xliii; Dowdey, *Lee's Last Campaign*, 141; Clifford Dowdey, *Death of a Nation* (New York, 1958), 284; Downey *The Guns at Gettysburg*, 64.

5 Ellsworth Eliot, Jr., *West Point in the Confederacy* (New York, 1941), xxiii, xxiv; *Alexander Papers;* Alexander, *Military Memoirs*, 1–3.

6 *Report of Board of Officers, March 12, 1859, No. 53 L of 1859*, War Department, Adjutant General's Office, Letters received, in *Record Group 94*, National Archives.

[7] Alexander to Myer, October 17, 1859, Letter No. 1, *Record Group 94*, National Archives.

[8] Alexander to Myer, October 17, 1859, Letter No. 2, *Record Group, 94*, National Archives.

[9] Alexander to Myer, October 17, 1859, Letter No. 3, *Record Group 94*, National Archives.

[10] Alexander to Myer, October 18, 1859, *Record Group 94*, National Archives.

[11] Alexander to Myer, November 2, 1859, *Record Group 94*, National Archives.

[12] Ibid., Alexander, *Military Memoirs*, 3; Floyd to Davis, Feb. 9, 1860, *War Department Reports to Congress, Vol. 9*, in National Archives.

[13] Marion Alexander Boggs, compiler, *The Alexander Letters, 1787–1900* (Savannah, 1910), 219–20. Hereafter cited as Boggs, *The Alexander Letters.*

[14] *Alexander Papers*, Special Orders No. 56, March 21, 1860; Alexander, *Military Memoirs*, 4, 5–7.

[15] W. Felix Alexander to Walker, March 2, 1861, in *Alexander File* in National Archives; Alexander, *Military Memoirs*, 13.

[16] These letters are in *Alexander Papers.*

[17] Alexander to Wife, July 10, in *Alexander Papers.*

[18] Alexander to Wife, July 27, July 31, August 1, 1861, in *Alexander Papers.*

[19] Alexander to Wife, August 16, 1861, in ibid.; *O.R.* IV, 426; General Orders No. 34, September 29, 1861, in *Alexander Papers.* Alexander to father, August 31, 1861, in *Alexander-Hillhouse Papers* in Southern Historical Collection, University of North Carolina. Hereafter cited as *Alexander-Hillhouse Papers.* Beauregard to Alexander to father, February 10, 1862, in *Alexander-Hillhouse Papers.*

[20] Benjamin to Alexander, November 10, 1861, in *Alexander Papers;* Alexander, *Military Memoirs*, 52; Beauregard to Alexander, Jan. 30, 1862 *Alexander Papers;* Alexander to father, February 10, 1862, in *Alexander-Hillhouse Papers.*

[21] Alexander to father, March 20, 1862, in *Alexander-Hillhouse Papers;* Alexander to Wife, March 18, 1862, in *Alexander Papers;* Randolph to Alexander, March 18, 1862, in *Alexander Papers;* Alexander to Randolph, April 12, 1862, in *Alexander File*, National Archives.

[22] *O.R.*, XI, Part 1, 568; Robert V. Bruce, *Lincoln and the Tools of War* (Indianapolis & New York, 1958), 85–87; Alexander, *Military Memoirs*, 172.

[23] Alexander to father, July 24, 1862, in *Alexander-Hillhouse Papers.*

[24] *O.R.* XI, Part 2, 498; Randolph to Alexander, July 17, 1862, in *Alexander Papers;* Alexander, *Military Memoirs*, 219, 242, 272; Special Order No. 235, November 7, 1862, in *Alexander Papers;* S. D. Lee to Alexander, November 30, 1862, in *Alexander Papers.*

[25] General Orders No. 130, December 4, 1862, in *Alexander Papers; O.R.*, XXI, 1046; Wise, *The Long Arm of Lee*, 358; Lee to Secretary of War, December 5, 1862, in *Alexander File* in National Archives; *O.R.*, XXI, 1051.

[26] *O.R.*, XXI, 564; Wise, *The Long Arm of Lee*, 372–73; James Longstreet, "The Battle of Fredericksburg," in *Battles and Leaders*, III, 79.

[27] Boggs, *Alexander Letters*, 243–47; *O.R.*, XXI, 571, 555.

[28] Wise, *The Long Arm of Lee*, 416; Seddon to Alexander, March 3, 1863, in *Alexander Papers;* Alexander, *Military Memoirs*, 321–24.

[29] *O.R.*, XXV, Part 1, 822–24; Alexander, *Military Memoirs*, 348.

[30] Freeman, *Lee's Lieutenants*, II, 652; Wise, *The Long Arm of Lee*, 507, 554.

[31] Alexander, *Military Memoirs*, 373; Alexander to father, June 14, 1863, in *Alexander-Hillhouse Papers;* Alexander, Letter in *Southern Historical Papers*, IV, 3 (September 1877), 100–2; Alexander, "The Great Charge and Artillery Fighting at Gettysburg," in *Battles and Leaders*, III, 360. Hereafter cited as Alexander, *The Great Charge, B. & L.* Alexander, *Military Memoirs*, 399.

[32] Wise, *The Long Arm of Lee*, 647; Alexander, *The Great Charge, B. & L.*, III, 361–62; Alexander, *Military Memoirs*, 421.

[33] Ibid., 421; Alexander, *The Great Charge, B. & L.*, 363.

[34] Alexander, *Military Memoirs*, 421–22; Alexander, *The Great Charge, B. & L.*, 363.

[35] Ibid., 364. Alexander's words have been put into direct quotes.

[36] Ibid., 364–66; Alexander to father, no date, but shortly after Gettysburg, in Boggs, *Alexander Letters*, 251.

[37] Alexander, *Military Memoirs*, 448–49; Alexander to father, September 30, 1863, in *Alexander-Hillhouse Papers*.

[38] Alexander, *Military Memoirs*, 480–81; E. Porter Alexander, *Personal Recollections of the Knoxville Campaign* (Typescript), in Library of Congress.

[39] Alexander to father, March 11, 1863, in *Alexander-Hillhouse Papers; O.R.,* XXIX, Part 2, 841; Longstreet to Lee, August 21, 1863, and Longstreet to Lee, September 3, 1863, in *Alexander File* in National Archives.

[40] *O.R.,* XXIX, Part 2, 841; Special Order No. 38, Hdqrs. in East Tennessee, December 28, 1863, in *Alexander File* in National Archives; Joseph E. Johnston, *Narrative of Military Operations, etc.* (New York, 1874), 288.

[41] Alexander to Wife, February 21 and February 27, 1864, in *Alexander Papers.*

[42] Alexander, *Military Memoirs*, 540, 546–547.

[43] Alexander to Wife, July 1, 1864, in *Alexander Papers;* Sorrel, *Recollections,* 260–61.

[44] Alexander, *Military Memoirs*, 563–64; Alexander to Wife, August 14, 1864, in *Alexander Papers.*

[45] Alexander to Wife, October 25, 1864, in *Alexander Papers.*

[46] Alexander to Wife, dates cited, in *Alexander Papers.*

[47] Alexander to Wife, April 1 and April 3, 1865, in *Alexander Papers.*

[48] Alexander, *Military Memoirs*, 603–6. Some of Alexander's words have been put into direct quotes.

[49] Wise, *The Long Arm of Lee*, 759; Eliot, *West Point*, 288.

[50] Alexander, *Military Memoirs*, vii.

[51] Freeman, *Lee's Lieutenants*, III, 809; Freeman, *R. E. Lee*, IV, 566; Freeman, *The South to Posterity*, 177–78.

[52] Alexander, *Military Memoirs*, viii–ix.

SOURCES AND BIBLIOGRAPHY

Only those items which were drawn upon directly or were perused for background information are included in the following list of sources and bibliography:

MANUSCRIPTS

Library of Congress:
Jed Hotchkiss Papers
Henry Hotze Papers
Henry Hotze Dispatch Book
Henry Hotze Letter Book
James M. Mason Papers
Leroy Pope Walker Letter Book

National Archives:
Confederate Army Records, Record Groups 94 and 109.
Richard Taylor File
Turner Ashby File
Patrick Ronayne Cleburne File
William J. Pegram Carded Records
Lucius B. Northrop File
William Mahone File
E. P. Alexander File

Tulane University Archives:
Jefferson Davis Papers in Louisiana Historical Association Collection.

Virginia Historical Society:
J. K. Mitchell Papers
Pegram-Johnson-McIntosh Papers
Papers Relating to Subsistence Department, C.S.A.
Charles S. Venable Papers

Southern Historical Collection, University of North Carolina:
E. P. Alexander Papers
Alexander-Hillhouse Papers
J. N. Maffitt Papers
Pegram Family Papers

Duke University Division of Manuscripts:
Alexander Robinson Boteler Papers
Henry Kyd Douglas Manuscripts

William Mahone Papers
Munford-Ellis Family Papers
Thomas Lee Settle Papers

North Carolina Department of Archives and History, Raleigh:
J. W. Ratchford Manuscript in Daniel H. Hill, Jr., Papers

Western Reserve Historical Society, Cleveland:
Braxton Bragg Papers, in William Palmer Collection

New Orleans Public Library:
*Fire and Alarm Telegraph of the City of New Orleans,
Record of Messages Received and Sent, 1860–1863*

Chicago Historical Society:
Richard Taylor Letter
Turner Ashby Letters (2)

Virginia Military Institute:
William Mahone File

University of Virginia:
Henry Heth Manuscript

Public Record Office, London, England:
Musters of 41st British Regiment (P. R. Cleburne entries)

Individual:
Charles W. Read Manuscript and Papers in possession
of Mallory J. Read, Arlington, Virginia

OFFICIAL RECORDS (Published)

War of the Rebellion: A Compilation of the Official Records of the Union and Confederate Armies. 130 Vols., Washington, 1880–1891.
Official Records of the Union and Confederate Navies in the War of the Rebellion. 30 Vols., Washington, 1894–1922.
Journal of the Confederate Congress. 7 Vols., Washington, 1904.
Confederate States, Special Orders of the Adjutant and Inspector General's Office, no place, no date.

UNPUBLISHED THESES

Coop, Leander Morrow. *Henry Hotze, Confederate Propagandist Abroad,* University of Alabama, 1943.
Cullop, Charles P. *Henry Hotze, Confederate Propagandist.* University of Virginia, 1959.
Durden, Robert F. *"The Index": Confederate Newspaper in London, 1862–1865.* Emory University, 1948.
Harris, Yeuell Y. *Henry Hotze, Confederate Propagandist in England.* Duke University, 1945.
Urquhart, Kenneth Trist. *General Richard Taylor and the War in Virginia, 1861–1862.* Tulane University, 1958.

NEWSPAPERS

New Orleans:
The Picayune
The Times-Democrat

Mobile:
  The Daily Register

London, England:
  The Index

Charleston, Mississippi
  The Mississippi Sun

New York:
  Tribune

Portland, Maine:
  Telegram

PERIODICALS

American Historical Review
Civil War History
Confederate Veteran
Louisiana Historical Quarterly
Louisiana History
Southern Historical Society Papers
Tennessee Historical Quarterly

GENERAL REFERENCE WORKS

Boatner, Mark M., III. *The Civil War Dictionary*, New York, 1959.
Dictionary of American Biography. New York, 1929. 20 Vols., and supplement.
Eliot, Ellsworth, Jr., *West Point in the Confederacy*. New York, 1941.
Freeman, Douglas Southall, *R. E. Lee*. 4 Vols., New York, 1934–1935.
———, *Lee's Lieutenants—A Study in Command*. 3 Vols., New York, 1942–1946.
Warner, Ezra, *Generals in Gray*. Baton Rouge, Louisiana, 1959.

BOOKS AND ARTICLES

Alexander, E. P., *Military Memoirs of a Confederate*. New York, 1907 and Bloomington, Indiana, 1962 (with introduction and note by T. Harry Williams).
———, *Personal Recollections of the Knoxville Campaign*. Typescript in Library of Congress.
———, "The Great Charge and Artillery Fighting at Gettysburg," in Vol. III, Robert U. Johnson and Clarence C. Buell, *Battles and Leaders of the Civil War*. 4 Vols., New York, 1887.
Ashby, Thomas A., *Life of Turner Ashby*. New York, 1914.
Avirett, Rev. James B., *The Memoirs of General Turner Ashby and His Compeers*. Baltimore, 1867.
Bartlett, Napier, *Military Record of Louisiana*. New Orleans 1875.
Bernard, George S., "The Battle of the Crater," in *Southern Historical Society Papers*, XVIII (1890).
———, Compiler-editor, *War Talks of Confederates*, Petersburg, 1892.
Bill, Alfred Hoyt, *The Beleaguered City*. New York, 1946.
Blake, Nelson M., *William Mahone of Virginia*. Richmond, 1935.
Boggs, Marion Alexander, compiler, *The Alexander Letters*, 1787–1900. Savannah, 1910.
Boteler, A. R., "Jackson in 1862," in *Southern Historical Society Papers*. XL.
Boykin, Edward, *Sea Devil of the Confederacy*. New York, 1959.
Brown, Isaac N., "The Confederate Gunboat 'Arkansas,'" in *Battles and Leaders of the Civil War*, Vol. II.

Buck, Irving, *Cleburne and His Command*. New York, 1908 and Jackson, Tennessee, 1959 (with introductory essay and notes by Thomas Robson Hay).

Buck, Samuel D., *With the Old Confeds. Actual Experiences of a Captain in the Line*, Baltimore, 1925.

Butler, Benjamin F., *Butler's Book: Autobiography and Personal Reminiscences. . . .* Boston, 1892.

Chamberlayne, C. G., *Ham Chamberlayne—Virginian, etc.*, Richmond, 1932.

Cheatham, Gen. B. F., "The Lost Opportunity at Spring Hill," in *Southern Historical Society Papers*. IX.

Chesnut, Mary Boykin, *A Diary from Dixie* (edited by Ben Ames Williams), Boston, 1949.

Clark, Walter, ed., *Histories of the Several Regiments and Battalions from North Carolina in the Great War 1861–1865.* 5 Vols. Raleigh, 1901.

Cockrell, Monroe F., ed., *Gunner With Stonewall, Reminiscences of William Thomas Poague.* Jackson, Tennessee, 1957.

Cooke, John Esten, *Life of Stonewall Jackson*, New York, 1863.

——*Wearing of the Gray.* New York, 1867, and Bloomington, Indiana, 1959 (with introduction and notes by Philip Van Doren Stern).

Coulter, E. Merton, *The Confederate States of America 1861–1865.* Baton Rouge, Louisiana, 1950.

Cunningham, Frank, *Knight of the Confederacy, General Turner Ashby.* San Antonio, 1960.

Dabney, R. L., *Life and Campaigns of Lieutenant General Thomas J. Jackson.* New York, 1866.

Davis, Jefferson, *The Rise and Fall of the Confederate Government.* 2 Vols. New York, 1881.

Davis, Varina Howell, *Jefferson Davis: A Memoir by His Wife.* 2 Vols. New York, 1890.

Davis, Jackson Beauregard, "The Life of Richard Taylor," in *Louisiana Historical Quarterly*, XXIV, No. 1 (January 1941).

Dewey, George, *Autobiography of George Dewey, Admiral of the Navy.* New York, 1913.

Dorsey, Sarah A., *Recollections of Henry Watkins Allen.* New York, 1866.

Dowdey, Clifford, *Lee's Last Campaign.* Boston and Toronto, 1960.

——and Louis H. Manarin, *The Wartime Papers of R. E. Lee*, Boston and Toronto, 1961.

Downey, Fairfax, *The Guns at Gettysburg.* New York, 1958.

Douglas, Henry Kyd, *I Rode With Stonewall.* Chapel Hill, N.C., 1940.

Dufour, Charles L., *Gentle Tiger: The Gallant Life of Roberdeau Wheat.* Baton Rouge, La., 1957.

——*The Night the War Was Lost.* New York, 1960.

Duke, Basil W., *Reminiscences of General Basil W. Duke*, New York, 1911.

Durkin, Joseph T., *Stephen R. Mallory, Confederate Navy Chief.* Chapel Hill, N.C., 1954.

Eliot, Ellsworth, Jr., *West Point in the Confederacy.* New York, 1941.

Evans, Clement Anselm, *Confederate Military History.* 12 Vols. Atlanta, 1899.

Felt, Jeremy P., "Lucius B. Northrop and the Confederacy's Subsistence Department," in *The Virginia Magazine*, Vol. 69, No. 2. April 1961.

Foote, Henry Stuart, *The War of the Rebellion, etc.* New York, 1866.

Freeman, Douglas Southall, *The South to Posterity: An Introduction to the Writing of Confederate History.* New York, 1939.

——and Grady McWhinney. *Lee's Dispatches.* New York, 1957.

Fremantle, Arthur J. L., *Three Months in the Southern States, April–June, 1863,* New York, 1864.

Gift, George W., "The Story of the Arkansas," in *Southern Historical Society Papers*, XII (1884).

Gist, Rev. W. W., "The Battle of Franklin," in *Tenn. Hist. Magazine*. Vol. 6, No. 3.

Gordon, Armistead Churchill. *Memories and Memorials of William Gordon McCabe.* 2 Vols. Richmond, 1925.

Gosnell, H. Allen, *Guns on the Western Waters: The Story of River Gunboats in the Civil War.* Baton Rouge, 1949.

Govan, Gilbert E. and James W. Livingood, *A Different Valor. The Story of Gen. Joseph E. Johnston, C.S.A.* Indianapolis, 1956.

Haskell, John, *The Haskell Memoirs.* Edited by Gilbert E. Govan and James W. Livingood. New York, 1960.

Hay, Thomas Robson, *Pat Cleburne, Stonewall of the West.* (Introductory essay in reprint edition of Buck's *Cleburne and His Command*). Jackson, Tennessee, 1959.

Heitman, Francis Bernard, *Historical Register and Dictionary of the United States Army.* 2 Vols., Washington, 1903.

Hendrick, Burton J., *Statesmen of the Lost Cause.* New York, 1939.

Henderson, Col. G. F. R., *Stonewall Jackson and the American Civil War* (one volume edition). New York, undated.

Hill, D. H., "Chickamauga—The Great Battle of the West," in *Battles and Leaders.* III.

Hood, John B., *Advance and Retreat.* New Orleans, 1880.

Horn, Stanley F., *The Army of Tennessee.* Indianapolis, 1941.

Hotze, Henry, *Three Months in the Confederate Army.* (Facsimile from *The Index*, May 1—October 29, 1862, edited with notes by Richard B. Harwell). Tuscaloosa, Alabama, 1952.

Howard, McHenry, *Recollections of a Maryland Confederate Soldier and Staff Officer Under Johnston, Jackson and Lee.* Baltimore, 1914.

Imboden, John D., "Stonewall Jackson in the Shenandoah," in *Battles and Leaders*, II.

———, "Jackson at Harpers Ferry," in *Battles and Leaders*, I.

———, "Incidents of the First Bull Run," in *Battles and Leaders*, I.

Jefferies, Clarence, "Running the Blockade on the Mississippi," in *Confederate Veteran*, Vol. 22, No. 1 (January 1914).

Jones, J. B., *A Rebel War Clerk's Diary.* 2 Vols. New York, 1866 and 1958 (one volume edited by Earl Schenck Miers).

Johnson, Ludwell H., *Red River Campaign, Politics and Cotton in the Civil War.* Baltimore, 1958.

Kelly, Col. Henry B., *The Battle of Port Republic.* Philadelphia, 1886.

Kendall, Lane C., "The Interregnum in Louisiana in 1861," in *The Louisiana Historical Quarterly*, Vol. XVI, Nos. 2, 3, 4; Vol. XVII, Nos. 1, 2, 3, 4, (1933–34).

Livermore, Thomas L., *Numbers and Losses in the Civil War in America, 1861–1865.* Boston, 1900 and Bloomington, Indiana, 1957 (with introduction by Edward E. Barthell, Jr.).

Longstreet, James, *From Manassas to Appomattox.* Philadelphia, 1896.

———, "The Battle of Fredericksburg," in *Battles and Leaders*, III.

Mahood, Fontaine W., *History of the Commissary of the Confederate States of America.* Typescript in Virginia Historical Society.

Maury, Dabney H., "Sketch of Richard Taylor," in *Southern Historical Society Papers*, Vol. VII, No. 7 (July 1879).

Morgan, James Morris, " 'Savez' Read" in Morgan and John P. Marquand, *Prince and Boatswain.* Greenfield, Massachusetts, 1915.

McCabe, William Gordon, "Defence of Petersburg," in *Southern Historical Society Papers*, II, No. 6 (December 1876).

Nash, Dr. Charles E., *Biographical Sketches of Gen. Pat Cleburne.* Little Rock, 1898.

Neese, George M., *Three Years in the Confederate Horse Artillery.* New York, 1911.

Owsley, Frank Lawrence, *King Cotton Diplomacy.* 2nd edition, Chicago, 1959.

Parks, Joseph H., *General Kirby Smith, C.S.A.*, Baton Rouge, 1954.

Pleasants, Henry L., Jr. and George H. Straley, *Inferno at Petersburg.* Philadelphia and New York, 1961.

Pollard, E. A., *Southern History of the War: The Second Year of the War.* New York, 1864.

Read, Charles W., "Reminiscences of the Confederate Navy," in *Southern Historical Society Papers*, Vol. I, No. 5 (May 1876).

Richardson, James D., *A Compilation of the Messages and Papers of the Confederacy.* 2 Vols. Nashville, 1906.

Ridley, Bromfield L., *Battles and Sketches of the Army of Tennessee.* Mexico, Mo., 1906.

Rowland, Dunbar, *Jefferson Davis, Constitutionalist, etc.* 10 Vols. Jackson, Miss., 1923.

Russell, William Howard, *My Diary North and South.* New York, 1863.

Shippey, W. F., "A Leaf From My Log Book," in *Southern Historical Society Papers,* XII (1884).

Sims, Crownover, "The Battle of Franklin," in *Tennessee Historical Quarterly,* Vol. 14.

Sorrel, G. Moxley, *Recollections of a Confederate Staff Officer.* New York, 1905 and Jackson, Tennessee, 1958 (with introduction by Bell I. Wiley).

Stephenson, P. D., "Reminiscences of the Late Campaign of the Army of Tennessee, etc.," in *Southern Historical Society Papers,* XII (1884).

Stiles, Robert, *Four Years Under Marse Robert.* New York, 1903.

Stone, Col. Henry, "Repelling Hood's Invasion of Tennessee," in *Battles and Leaders,* IV.

Taylor, Richard, *Destruction and Reconstruction.* New York, 1879.

Thomas, Clarence, *General Turner Ashby, The Centaur of the South.* Winchester, 1907.

Tucker, Glenn, *Chickamauga, Bloody Battle in the West.* Indianapolis and New York, 1961.

Vandiver, Frank, ed., *The Civil War Diary of Josiah Gorgas.* Tuscaloosa, 1947.

Watkins, Sam, *Co. 'Aytch' etc.* Nashville, 1882.

Welles, Gideon, *Diary of Gideon Welles, Secretary of the Navy Under Lincoln and Johnson.* 3 Vols. Boston and New York, 1911.

Wise, Jennings Cropper, *The Long Arm of Lee.* 2 Vols. Lynchburg, Virginia, 1915.

——, "The Boy Gunners of Lee," in *Southern Historical Society Papers,* XLIII (October 1915).

Wise, John S., *The End of an Era.* Boston and New York, 1899.

Worsham, J. H., *One of Jackson's Foot Cavalry.* New York, 1912.

Wright, Willard E., ed., "Some Letters of Lucius Bellinger Northrop," in *The Virginia Magazine,* Vol. 68, No. 4 (October 1960).

Yearns, Wilfred Buck, *The Confederate Congress.* Athens, Georgia, 1960.

Younger, Edward, ed., *Inside the Confederate Government, The Diary of Robert Garlick Hill Kean.* New York, 1957.